CORPORATE POWER IN A GLOBALIZING WORLD

A Study in Elite Social Organization

WILLIAM K. CARROLL

UNIVERSITY PRESS

1904 ❦ 2004

100 YEARS OF
CANADIAN PUBLISHING

OXFORD
UNIVERSITY PRESS

70 Wynford Drive, Don Mills, Ontario M3C 1J9
www.oup.com/ca

Oxford University Press is a department of the University of Oxford.
It furthers the University's objective of excellence in research, scholarship,
and education by publishing worldwide in

Oxford New York

Auckland Bangkok Buenos Aires Cape Town Chennai
Dar es Salaam Delhi Hong Kong Istanbul Karachi Kolkata
Kuala Lumpur Madrid Melbourne Mexico City Mumbai Nairobi
São Paulo Shanghai Taipei Tokyo Toronto

Oxford is a trade mark of Oxford University Press
in the UK and in certain other countries

Published in Canada
by Oxford University Press

Copyright © Oxford University Press Canada 2004

The moral rights of the author have been asserted

Database right Oxford University Press (maker)

First published 2004

All rights reserved. No part of this publication may be reproduced,
stored in a retrieval system, or transmitted, in any form or by any means,
without the prior permission in writing of Oxford University Press,
or as expressly permitted by law, or under terms agreed with the appropriate
reprographics rights organization. Enquiries concerning reproduction
outside the scope of the above should be sent to the Rights Department,
Oxford University Press, at the address above.

You must not circulate this book in any other binding or cover
and you must impose this same condition on any acquirer.

National Library of Canada Cataloguing in Publication

Carroll, William K.
Corporate power in a globalizing world : a study in elite social
organization / William K. Carroll.

Includes bibliographical references and index.
ISBN 0-19-541759-3

1. Corporate power–Canada. 2. Corporations–Political aspects–
Canada. 3. Corporations–Canada–Sociological aspects. 4. Elite
(Social sciences)–Canada. I. Title.

HD2809.C384 2003   338.7'4'0971   C2003-904585-4

1 2 3 4 - 07 06 05 04

This book is printed on permanent (acid-free) paper ∞.
Printed in Canada

Contents

	Acknowledgments *v*
Chapter 1	Surveying the Terrains of Corporate Power 1
I	**The Organizational Terrain** *13*
Chapter 2	From Oligarchy to Corporate Governance: The End of the Old Boys' Network? *14*
Chapter 3	Strategic Control and Intercorporate Enterprises *41*
Chapter 4	Disorganized Capitalism and Transnational Finance Capital *66*
II	**The Spatial Terrain** *87*
Chapter 5	Westward Drift: The Shifting Geography of Corporate Power *88*
Chapter 6	Continental Connections: Toward a North American Corporate Elite? *106*
Chapter 7	The Canadian Corporate Elite in the Global Power Structure *127*
III	**The Hegemonic Terrain** *153*
Chapter 8	Consolidating a Neoliberal Policy Bloc *with Murray Shaw* *154*
Chapter 9	Integrating Corporate and University Governance for a Globalizing World *with James B. Beaton* *180*

IV   Conclusion *199*

Chapter 10   Corporate Power and Neoliberal Democracy *200*

Appendix 1: Internet Resources *219*

Appendix 2: A Note on Method *222*

Appendix 3: Corporate Names and Abbreviations *226*

Notes *231*

References *260*

Index *275*

Acknowledgments

This book had its origins in a long conversation I had with Meindert Fennema on a train from Amsterdam to Bielefeld to attend the 1994 World Congress of Sociology. In the course of discussing the globalizing and neoliberal shifts that were transfiguring capitalism, our longstanding interest in mapping structures of corporate power was renewed, and we decided to try to organize an international collaborative effort to follow up on the ten nations study that had traced corporate networks as of the mid-1970s (Stokman et al., 1985). A standard research grant from the Social Sciences and Humanities Research Council of Canada, awarded in 1995, enabled me to collect the extensive data on corporations based in Canada, the United States, and other countries on which this study draws. In this I was ably assisted by James Beaton, Colin Carson, Conor Douglas, Jean Hansen, Melissa Moroz, Mark Reed, Theona Russow, and Murray Shaw.

Although I began disseminating findings at conferences in 1998, it was really during my sabbatical leave of 2000–1 that the research began to bear fruit. In that year Meindert and I joined Malcolm Alexander and Rob Mokken as fellows-in-residence at the Netherlands Institute for Advanced Study in the Humanities and Social Sciences, constituting part of a theme group on globalization and social organization. I benefited enormously from our close collegial interaction, and managed to complete half of the manuscript by the end of my stay at NIAS—a facility unrivalled for its combination of scholarly rigour and *gezellig feestjes*. Early versions of four of those chapters have already appeared in scholarly journals: Chapter 4 in the *Canadian Journal of Sociology* (vol. 27 [2002], 339-71), Chapter 5 in the *Journal of Canadian Studies* (vol. 36 [2002], 118-42), Chapter 8 in *Canadian Public Policy* (vol. 27 [2001], 1-23, with Murray Shaw as co-author), and Chapter 9 in *Studies in Political Economy* (no. 62 [2000], 71-98, with James Beaton as co-author).

In the spring of 2001, on Bob Brym's advice, I approached Oxford Acquisitions Editor Megan Mueller with my prospectus. She responded with an enthusiasm that has carried us through the past two years of writing, rewriting and editing. The constructive criticisms of two anonymous reviewers were indispensable in advancing the manuscript from prospectus to first draft and then to the penultimate version. Sally Livingston's meticulous copy-editing contributed a final finish to the text.

Through it all, my wife Anne Preyde and sons Myles and Wesley endured my long retreats into the study with only occasional protests. Without their support the project would have been abandoned long ago. Having already dedicated an earlier volume on corporate power to Anne, I dedicate this one to Myles and Wesley.

Chapter 1

Surveying the Terrains of Corporate Power

At the centre of what Immanuel Wallerstein (2000) calls the capitalist world-system are the post-industrial democracies. Citizens of these democracies have had an ambivalent relationship with the large corporations that power, and dominate, their local economies. The idea that we should acquiesce to business leadership is clear in clichés from the 1950s, like 'What's good for General Motors is good for America' (and, by implication, the world). More recent pronouncements, often by commentators in the financial pages, have glorified the success of globalizing businesses such as Bombardier and SNC-Lavalin as 'a rising tide [that] lifts all boats' (Mander, 1996). But social protests from the mid-1990s onward have challenged the project of corporate globalization (Carroll, 2002; McNally, 2002). There has been a growing skepticism about the fit between democracy, as a way of life organized around self-governance, and corporate capitalism, as a way of life organized around large profit-seeking firms governed by constellations of wealthy shareholders, institutional investors, and high-paid executives (Korten, 1995; Scott, 1997; Clarke, 1997; Dobbin, 1998; Laxer, 1998; Klein, 2000).

In exploring the social organization of corporate business in late-twentieth century Canada, this book takes the skeptical perspective. The tradition of studies of Canada's corporate elite is well established. From Gustavus Myers (1972) through Libbie and Frank Park (1973) and more recently Linda McQuaig (1995), we can trace a line of muckraking radical scholarship. In the work of Peter C. Newman (1975; 1998), Diane Francis (1986) and others, we find a line of business journalism that has been by turns critical of and awestruck by the concentration of power at the top of the corporate economy. Finally, beginning with John Porter's *Vertical Mosaic*, a third stream of literature has placed the corporate elite under social-scientific scrutiny. Surprisingly, however, there has been no comprehensive scholarly study of the corporate elite since the 1980s (Ornstein, 1998). My own work in this field has continued since the publication of *Corporate Power and Canadian Capitalism* (Carroll, 1986), but in the form of articles on particular topics. This book takes a more integrative approach to the subject. The first step is to delineate precisely what we mean by 'corporate power'.

CORPORATE POWER IN MODERN CAPITALISM

Shortly before his death in 1920, Max Weber offered an action-theory definition of power as 'the probability that one actor within a social relationship will be in a position to carry out his own will despite resistance' (Weber, 1947). Since then, social science has evolved a complex vocabulary for conceptualizing power in social life (Bridge, 1997). In his influential synthesis of perspectives, Steven Lukes (1974: 57) called for a 'deeper analysis of power relations'—deeper than the behavioural studies of decision-making that Robert Dahl (1961) and others published in the 1960s. Underpinning the visible exercise of power are systemic inequities in the control of resources that enable the dominant groups to frame agendas, make decisions, and secure compliance. These systemic inequities create a *unilateral dependence* that for Peter Blau (1964:117–18) is at the heart of power. The dependence of subordinates obliges them to comply with the requests of the powerful, lest the latter cease to provide for their needs.

Corporate power is the power that accrues to enormous concentrations of capital—in the modern world, large corporations. Workers, communities, and states are unilaterally dependent on large corporations that may or may not choose to invest in a given place at a given time (Bowles and Gintis, 1986), and in this fundamental sense the concentration of corporate capital is a concentration of corporate power. Corporations had already emerged in Europe and North America by the middle decades of the nineteenth century, when Karl Marx (1967) drafted his prescient remarks on 'the modern joint-stock company' (published posthumously in the third volume of *Capital*). But it was not until the twentieth century that corporate power was fully consolidated in all the advanced capitalist nation states. Increasingly, this power has been projected beyond national states in the form of transnational corporations (TNCs) and banks (Barnet and Cavanagh, 1994), a global capital market (Held et al., 1999:220), and a complex of quasi-state institutions such as the World Bank, the International Monetary Fund, and, since 1994, the World Trade Organization (Robinson and Harris, 2000).

Marx, of course, is the social theorist of capitalism *par excellence*, not because his ideas are very useful in predicting prices, output, and the like (they are not), but because of his acute sociological and historical analysis of capitalism as a distinctive way of life that in the twenty-first century is now more 'universal' than ever before (Micklethwait and Wooldridge, 2000). What Marx gives us is a starting point for empirical analysis of corporate capitalism as a system of *class power*. Marx holds that control over the economic surplus is a decisive form of power. In any class society, the dominant class's control of economic resources—the means of production—enables it to appropriate the economic surplus that is produced by the subordinate class.[1] Control of the surplus does more than fund an exorbitant standard of living for the dominant class. It also places the economic future largely at that class's disposal, and relegates others to positions of unilateral dependence.

As a social system organized around class inequality, capitalism is distinctive in the way it redeploys a considerable portion of the economic surplus into ever more sophisticated technologies, which raise labour productivity enough to generate even greater surpluses. But it is also distinctive in the market-mediated character of its social relations.² Capital never exists as a unified entity but only as many units—the most important of which are large corporations. Capitalists compete with each other in the quest to claim a sufficient share of the economic surplus to keep them 'in the game': that is, an above-average profit. Moreover, in corporate capitalism the vast scale of production requires an elaborate apparatus for financing new production, getting commodities to final consumers, and so on. As a result, the economic surplus is competitively subdivided not only among industrial corporations but among all lines of investment, from finance and real estate to industry and retail commerce, as investors of whatever stripe strive for above-average rates of return. For their part, in a capitalist system workers resist their own exploitation (e.g., through union activism), but they also compete with each other for jobs and income. As corporations gain the structural power to play one national workforce off against another, the prospect of a 'race to the bottom', with workers underbidding each other to the benefit of transnational capital, worries trade unionists and social-justice activists alike. Capitalism's subordinate class, however, is no more homogeneous than its dominant class. What worries some is welcomed by others, in particular those wage and salary earners whose relatively secure employment and private pensions have, in an era of deteriorating social programs, catapulted them into an 'investor aristocracy' (Harmes, 1998).

Perhaps the most vivid example of the role played by markets in mediating social relations is the sale and purchase of body parts. But in fact such mediation can be observed everywhere, and that ubiquity encourages the notion that, in contemporary capitalism, classes and other socially structured phenomena have been supplanted by possessive individuals making rational choices in an ever-changing panoply of markets (Rupert, 2000). 'There is no such thing as society,' declared Margaret Thatcher in the 1980s. In contrast, the present study proceeds from the assumption that class continues to tell, and that an analysis of the social organization of big business can tell quite a lot about the structure of corporate power in society.

But how might we conceptualize this power, and the corporate elite that wields it? The most obvious place to begin is with the corporate directorate. Vested with final authority over the affairs of the corporation, the board of directors is at the apex of a hierarchy that reaches down to the shop floor. Just as directorates are sites of authority within corporate power structures, individual directors are agents of corporate power. Moreover, through cross-appointment of directors, the boards of major corporations overlap with each other. Such interlocks draw directorates into an intercorporate network, just as they draw directors into a socially integrated corporate elite.

The thesis advanced here is that the corporate elite constitutes the *leading edge* of a ruling class that, though a small minority of the Canadian population, actually extends far beyond the population of leading corporate directors.³ In narrow economic terms, this class includes some fabulously wealthy rentier capitalists who do not participate in the direction of large corporations, as well as many middle-range capitalists, whose investments, executive positions, or business networks do not lead them onto the major corporate boards. More broadly, the ruling class encompasses

TABLE 1.1
Forms, Agents, and Sites of Corporate Power

	Economic domain	Extra-economic domain
Forms	Power exercised as capital *accumulation*: operational, strategic, and allocative power	Power exercised as *hegemony*: elite integration (cohesion), business leadership in politics and culture (reach)
Agents	Top executives, major shareholders (individual and institutional), bankers, with assistance of technical experts	Organic intellectuals, including capitalists involved in business leadership
Sites	Internal management structures; corporate directorates; directorates of financial institutions, pension funds	Corporate directorates, private clubs, policy-planning groups, university governance boards, etc.

what Antonio Gramsci (1971) called 'organic intellectuals' whose positions in the social division of labour align them closely with the needs and interests of capitalists.[4] Lawyers, consultants, academics, and other professionals who are active in the higher echelons of management provide expertise that is indispensable to corporate business today. In the structure of economic power, such advisors are always subordinate to the capitalists themselves; yet in the political and cultural fields, they are often the ones who lead the way. The corporate elite includes both capitalists and organic intellectuals, as does the wider ruling class. Yet it is important to make a clear distinction between the economic and extra-economic domains of corporate power and to consider the forms, agents, and sites of power specific to each domain. Table 1.1 presents a typology of corporate power that summarizes these points. The table elaborates on Marx's early distinction between a 'class in itself', whose members share a common position vis-à-vis the means of production, and a 'class for itself', whose social organization enables it to define and pursue common interests, to articulate a more or less comprehensive social vision, and so on. In contemporary capitalism, the corporate elite is crucially engaged in both these 'economic' and 'extra-economic' aspects of class formation.

Capital Accumulation as Corporate Power

Within the economic domain, the exercise of corporate power plays an integral part in the accumulation of capital (see Table 1.1). Power in this domain resides in the people and organizations that *control capital*. Given that enormous concentrations of capital have been assembled into large corporations, a key question is how the control of capital is attained and maintained in and through these corporations. Here we must distinguish three forms of economic power, each entailing the control of capital (cf. Mintz and Schwartz, 1985; Scott, 1997):

- *Operational* power is the power to control the labour processes within each firm that actually produce the economic surplus. It is the power of management, visible in a chain of command in which agency is increasingly circumscribed as one moves down the line from top management through middle management, etc. As Wright (1978) notes, only top business management belongs to the capitalist class. Middle and lower levels actually occupy 'contradictory class locations', sandwiched between capital and labour.
- *Strategic* power involves control of the corporation itself, often through ownership of the largest bloc of shares. This is the power to set business strategies for the company or set of companies assembled under common control into an enterprise. It has long been recognized that the dispersal of corporate shares across many small investors leads not to 'people's capitalism' but to a stronger concentration of strategic power in the hands of major shareholders (Perlo, 1958), whose ownership of a small proportion of voting shares can be sufficient to give them control of the board of directors (Scott, 1986).
- *Allocative* power stems from control of credit, of the money-capital on which large corporations (and, incidentally, states) depend, particularly when expanding or retooling operations, launching takeover bids, or coping with reduced revenue as a result of economic contraction. This form of power entails a unilateral dependence of various agents—industrial capitalists but also governmental and non-governmental organizations—on the suppliers of financing.

Each of these forms of economic power has its characteristic agents and sites in the accumulation process. As we have seen, operational power is wielded by managers within internal corporate management structures. Strategic power can involve complex alignments of major shareholders, whether individual or institutional: although it is centred in the board of directors, where major strategic decisions are made, it often cuts across individual companies through interlocking directorates and intercorporate ownership (Berkowitz and Fitzgerald, 1995). The situation is similar for allocative power, which accrues to agents and organizations controlling the financial assets that fund new investment. As Beth Mintz and Michael Schwartz point out, the fact that financial institutions control vast pools of money-capital gives them, and the bankers who manage them, an allocative power over corporations in need of financing, whether short- or long-term. 'The choices made by financials to support one firm or industry—or even a country—over another, or to enter or depart from one area of investment, often represent the crucial, determining reality within which nonfinancial corporations operate' (1985:96). Allocative power may be centred in the institutions that control money-capital, but it entails complex relations between creditors and debtors, and these relations are often visible in the structure of interlocking directorates between financial institutions and corporations.

The key point is that corporate boards of directors show traces of all three kinds of power. In thinking about how operational, strategic, and allocative power might be traced at the level of corporate boards, Scott's (1997) concept of 'constellations of interests' is particularly apt. Boards include among their members the firm's top management (at a minimum, the CEO), thus ensuring links into the structure of operational power. Their mandate of general oversight locates them at the centre of corporate power, and means that their members may include major shareholders, institutional investors, and creditors. The precise constellation of top managers, shareholders, creditors, and the like will vary from firm to firm—a company tightly controlled by a single family may have predominantly family members and senior management on the board, for example, while a company heavily in debt to financial institutions may have mostly bankers. Moreover, with changes in patterns of share-ownership, corporate finance, and corporate governance norms, the overall balance of power between senior management, major shareholders, and creditors may shift as well, leading to changes in the composition of corporate boards. The reforms of corporate governance practices implemented by the Toronto Stock Exchange in the mid-1990s are an important instance, whose structural impact is explored in Chapters 2 and 4.

Most important, the strategic and allocative forms of corporate power often entail institutional *relations between* corporations, and interlocks between corporate directorates. The literature on interlocking directorates as links in a network of economic power is vast (Fennema and Schijf, 1979; Schwartz, 1987; Mizruchi, 1996; Scott, 1997).[5] The research literature shows that there is a definite social organization of corporate business, in which the boards of leading companies are connected on the basis of business strategies and the prevailing relations of allocative and strategic power. At a minimum, interlocks enhance the 'business scan' of the overlapping boards (Useem, 1984), enabling directors 'to observe how other firms confront and resolve problems and policy making decisions that are common to all firms' (Glasberg, 1987: 22).[6]

This social organization serves to *integrate the different forms of corporate capital*—industrial, financial, commercial—into what has been termed *finance capital* (Thompson, 1977; Steven, 1994). As defined by Henk Overbeek, 'finance capital' refers to 'the integration of the circuits of money capital, productive capital and commodity capital under the conditions of monopolization and internationalization of capital by means of a series of links and relationships between individual capitals' (1980:102). This integration of capital occurs at the levels of both individuals and corporations. At the corporate level, financial and industrial forms of capital are closely integrated through interlocks between bank boards and industrial directorates, through intercorporate ownership relations (often centred on investment companies whose assets are simply accumulations of corporate shares), and so on. The specific structures of capital integration vary from country to country, because of legal and cultural differences (Scott, 1997), but the basic pattern of financial-industrial coalescence has been evident in all advanced capitalist formations (Fennema and Schijf, 1979). At the level of individuals, this integration manifests itself in the financial-industrial elite that sits atop the capitalist class—a set of well-connected corporate directors whose affiliations with both corporations and financial institutions empower them as agents of strategic and allocative power: in other words, as *finance capitalists* (Zeitlin, 1989).

However, this social organization extends beyond the corporate capitalists whose ownership of capital (or salaried positions atop managerial hierarchies) gives them control of corporate capital. Other board positions are filled by the organic intellectuals who serve as their advisors—the lawyers, accountants, academics, and retired politicians who provide crucial technical expertise and experience, sometimes to several large firms (Niosi, 1978). Such advisors make up an important stratum of the corporate elite, one that exercises not only economic power, but also the second characteristic form of corporate power: hegemony.

BUSINESS LEADERSHIP AS CORPORATE POWER

As several scholars have noted (Sonquist and Koenig, 1975; Useem, 1984; Domhoff, 1998), corporate elites are not organized solely through the practices of accumulation—according to the interests that particular firms or capitalists have in linking up with others in some sort of strategic alignment. As the leading edge of a ruling class, the corporate elite expresses more than an aggregation of economic interests pursuing profit. To be sure, members of the elite, and of the capitalist class, relate to each other in instrumental terms, as means towards the particular end of profit. But they are also bound together as fellow members of a dominant class. By the same token, the elite's material source of power—its control over concentrations of capital and thus economic surplus—is not its only power resource. The corporate elite is also a condensation of cultural and political power. The elite's hegemony consists in its capacity to exercise leadership beyond the world of corporate business, in civil society and vis-à-vis the state. It is this form of power that renders the capitalist class a class for itself. The corporate elite is arguably the most important element in the exercise of such power. Here again, social organization is of great importance. Were the corporate elite to be fragmented into warring groups, there would be no structural basis for class hegemony. By contrast—and notwithstanding the divisions that may stem from the cut-and-thrust of competitive accumulation—a socially integrated corporate elite can reach a consensus on long-term goals and vision. On that basis it can speak politically with a single voice, and lead.

The schematic depiction of corporate power in Table 1.1 identifies two distinct forms of class hegemony. The internal structure of the corporate elite—its *cohesion* as a well-integrated network, inclusive of various capitalist interests—nurtures a solidaristic 'business community'. Frequent interaction builds up a fund of common experiences, a collective consciousness, and a shared vision of the world. Interlocking directorships, particularly those involving advisors to multiple corporations, are important vehicles of elite integration, even if social cohesion is no more than an unintended consequence of interlocking (Scott and Hughes, 1980:36). So, according to Porter (1965) and Clement (1975), are elite private clubs, residential segregation within elite neighbourhoods, and other devices of social closure and elite solidarity.

The second form of class hegemony identified in Table 1.1 is *reach*. Some modicum of solidarity and consensus is necessary to ensure the corporate elite's *reach* into the public sphere. There are many ways in which corporate power is extended into the public sphere, and the traffic is by no means one-way. The flow of corporate capitalists into government is complemented by the migration of retiring politicians into the corporate elite.[7] This two-way traffic is important in itself. Hegemony is not about the brute dominance of capitalists over other interests in society. Indeed, naked dominance is, as Gramsci (1971) insisted, the opposite of hegemony. The class hegemony in which the corporate elite participates is an ongoing accomplishment of *business leadership*, which includes the absorption of leaders and ideas from other spheres into the world of corporate business and which relies not on coercion but on persuasion. Hegemony is rule with the consent of the governed—but consent does not necessarily mean democracy. As was mentioned at the outset of this book, there is a deep-seated contradiction between the democratic practices of self-governance and the rule of corporate capital, however effective the latter might be in organizing the consent of subordinate groups. Bourgeois hegemony is about muting that contradiction and constructing common-sense verities to fill the gap between democratic aspiration and the lived reality of class inequality.

The corporate elite's reach into civil society is only one aspect of this hegemony,[8] but it is an important one. In this instance, the role of organic intellectuals is particularly crucial. It is not unusual for capitalists themselves to exercise cultural and political leadership, wielding economic power and at the same time contributing as intellectuals to the construction of hegemony.[9] Nevertheless, capital's hegemony still relies heavily on the agency of organic intellectuals who are not themselves capitalists. Such individuals take up ancillary roles in the world of business—often as advisors or consultants—yet are organizers of culture and politics. Although 'capitalists involved in business leadership' are included among the 'agents' of hegemony in Table 1.1, the corporate elite's hegemonic reach depends on 'outside' corporate directors who exercise leadership in extra-economic fields such as policy-planning and university governance.

GLOBALIZATION AND NEOLIBERALISM: CORPORATE POWER IN TRANSITION

With the exception of my earlier investigation of the Canadian corporate network (Carroll, 1986), which spanned three decades, 1946–76, most major studies of the social organization of corporate power in Canada have fixed on a single point in time, whether the mid-1950s (Porter, 1965; Park and Park, 1973), the early 1970s (Clement, 1975), or the late 1970s (Niosi, 1981). The present book, however, is about *corporate power in transition*. Its task is to chart the changing structure of corporate power in the last quarter of the twentieth century. This period has been associated with various 'isms'—neoliberalism, post-industrialism, post-fordism, post-modernism, etc.—but in every case it has come to be known as an era of wide-ranging political, economic, and cultural transformation. Although, for brevity's sake, I have worked the image of a 'globalizing world' into this book's title, this is not to endorse the view that any single process of 'globalization' can account for all developments in corporate-elite organization. Nor does it imply that globalization is a recent phenomenon.

The world has been 'globalizing' at least since the formation of the modern capitalist world-system more than five centuries ago (Wallerstein, 2000). By the turn of the twentieth century—the time when the classic theorists of imperialism made their observations—the major European powers had subdivided the globe into competing colonial empires (Bukharin, 1973; Hobson, 1965). In the context of classic imperialism, finance capital—the integration of industrial and financial capital under conditions of monopolization and internationalization—characteristically took a nationally centred form, compartmentalized within the economic spaces defined by the major powers and prone to intense rivalry with other nationally delimited blocs of capital (Hardt and Negri, 2000).

As Hirst and Thompson (1996) point out, much of the twentieth century brought a reinforcement of national capitalisms, punctuated by two world wars—hardly a globalizing move towards a borderless world. The years following the Second World War did see some important globalizing developments, including the Bretton Woods institutions of global capitalist governance and the tremendous expansion of American-based transnational corporations into Canada, Western Europe, Latin America, and elsewhere through an 'open door' for US exports and investments that broke up the old colonial empires and re-centred world capitalism around the American superpower. Yet these were also years in which nationally organized labour movements and social-democratic parties took advantage of the long post-war boom and pressed successfully for expansive social programs and full-employment economic policies, which became crystallized in the so-called Keynesian welfare state. Such a state form presumes and reinforces a bounded 'national economy' that can be effectively managed by macroeconomic policies (Atkins, 1986).

In the last quarter of the twentieth century, however, a new dynamic took hold in the advanced economies. After the American retreat from the dollar standard, in 1971, effectively deregulated international currencies, and as billions of OPEC-inflated petro-dollars flooded into offshore currency markets, money gradually became de-linked from national states. The global credit system became progressively privatized, while global electronic trading made money more fluid (Kurtzman, 1993). This led to an increase in 'the structural power of finance' (Germain, 1997:106). Meanwhile, foreign trade and foreign direct investment grew spectacularly. Much of the latter was redirected toward developing countries, whose share of world foreign investment flows jumped from one-quarter to two-fifths between 1970 and 1996 (Burbach, 1999:18). By the 1990s, international flows of money-capital and direct investment gave enhanced allocative and strategic powers to the financial institutions and transnational corporations that respectively controlled them. International agreements—whether GATT/WTO-sponsored or regional (e.g., NAFTA, EU)—enlarged the scope within which those powers could be exercised. Corporate capital had assumed truly global proportions.

Perhaps most significant in what Dick Bryan calls 'recent globalization' is that the rapid growth in cross-national trade, credit, and investment has subverted the very distinction between cross-border and domestic flows. 'The global integration of accumulation means that economic calculations of all kinds—from purchases in the supermarket to the determination of the prime interest rate—are subject, quite explicitly, to international calculation' (Bryan, 1995:13). In a globalizing world all kinds of agents and organizations are drawn into transnational economic processes, even if they do not participate in foreign trade and foreign investment themselves. The fact that competitors function in a globalized field is enough to lead even exclusively 'local' businesses to adopt the standpoint of global capital (Ross and Trachte, 1990:7–9).

It is this structurally rooted shift in the general horizons of economic calculation—for various agents at various sites within the world system—that marks our present era. To adopt the standpoint of global capital is to make 'international competitiveness' one's watchword and to recognize that failure to make the grade will mean the withdrawal or withholding of investment. This sanction applies not only to businesses but to states whose policies stray too far from the political preferences of the corporate capitalists and institutional investors who make up the so-called international investment community. Their control of internationalized money capital—in particular, their willingness to buy or hold bonds and currency issued by one state, in preference to other options—gives them substantial allocative power over national states. As Tony Clarke has put it, 'currency speculators already play a major role in determining a broad spectrum of national government policies ranging from credit systems, money supply and interest rates to debt management, investment policies and taxation' (Clarke, 1997:60).

Recent globalization, then, is not only an economic process, but a political one. It is no accident that the globalization of capital and the consolidation of a neoliberal policy paradigm have gone hand in hand (Teeple, 2000). What the latter prescribes is a 'globalization of the state', not only through such supra-national bodies as the WTO but through a 'redefinition of the role and purpose of government in the emerging world order' (Gill, 1995:85–6). The state's role in international competition now consists not of promoting 'its' *capitalists*, nor of managing an integrated national economy, as in the days of the Keynesian welfare state, but of promoting its *territory* as an attractive site for investment (Burbach, 1999).[10]

In this market-driven approach to governance the state becomes somewhat of an accessory to accumulation in maintaining a 'level playing field' for investors, whether local or foreign-based.[11] As Colin Leys points out, 'It is not just that governments can no longer "manage" their national economies; to survive in office they must increasingly "manage" national politics in such a way as to adapt *them* to the pressures of transnational market forces' (2001:1). The constituent elements of neoliberalism—the priority given to 'sound money' and low inflation, the attacks on the collective power of unions, the policies of fiscal retrenchment, of downsizing social services, of privatization, of 'flexible labour markets', of deregulation and free trade—are all directed toward enhancing international competitiveness by imposing the discipline of the market. But in magnifying the impact of global market forces on working people and communities they also shift the balance of power toward capital, whose criterion of profitability is given priority over other possible goals such as a decent standard of living for all citizens, a flourishing of the arts, or a healthy environment.

In short, since the mid-1970s the globalization of capital and the consolidation of neoliberalism have operated in tandem, the one feeding on and facilitating the other. By the close of the twentieth century the provisional result was an enhancement of corporate power across a wide range of domains. The impact of all this on the structure of corporate power in Canada, and the role of the Canadian corporate elite in promoting and consolidating the regime of neoliberal globalization in Canada, are complex issues, which will be taken up in the nine chapters that follow.

TERRAINS OF CORPORATE POWER: ORGANIZATIONAL, SPATIAL, HEGEMONIC

Focusing on the Top 250 Canadian corporations, this study employs *network analysis* to map three distinct terrains of corporate power.[12] Whether we emphasize the power that resides in the accumulation of capital or the power that resides in business leadership, corporate power assumes distinctive organizational forms. The next three chapters map this *organizational terrain*, focusing on the issues of elite integration, closure, and culture (Chapter 2), the strategic control of large corporations (Chapter 3), and the intricacies of allocative power and transnational investment in the changing form of finance capital (Chapter 4).

Corporate power is always exercised from specific sites, and some analysts (Sassen, 1991; Alderson and Beckfield, 2002) argue that it is increasingly concentrated in a few global cities housing the command centres of TNCs and financial markets. An earlier literature emphasized the regional and international unevenness of capitalist development, and examined the place of Canadian capitalism and of Canada's regions, within the larger world-system (Resnick 1989; Brym, 1985). The middle chapters of this book map the spatial terrain of corporate power. Within Canada, this terrain consists of a regionalized network in which the larger Canadian cities, particularly Toronto and Montreal, serve as corporate command centres (Chapter 5). But the spatial terrain also extends continentally, in a network of interlocks between the largest firms based in Canada and the United States (Chapter 6). Beyond the continental domain is the global network of the capitalist world-system within which Canada's corporate power structure is embedded (Chapter 7).

Finally, there is the *terrain of class hegemony*, which can also be charted through network analysis. One aspect of hegemony—the corporate elite's social organization as a more or less integrated business community—is explored in Chapter 2. Now, the final section will map some of the ways in which the elite's reach, in the form of cultural and political power, extends into key areas of civil society. In its exercise of business leadership the corporate elite has articulated and championed neoliberalism as a hegemonic project ostensibly 'in step' with globalizing times. Chapter 8, co-authored with Murray Shaw, traces the development of a neoliberal policy bloc in which leading corporate directors participate in the governance of influential policy-planning groups, and collaterally explores the changing alignment of corporate capital and political parties as revealed by the former's donations to the latter. Chapter 9, co-authored with James Beaton, examines the governance-level relations that link large corporations with universities in a confluence of interest that has been termed the 'corporatization of higher education' (Newson, 1994).

Conclusion

Beyond highlighting the most significant insights from the body of the book, the final chapter applies those insights to the problem raised at the outset: the deeply rooted tension between corporate power and democracy. How do the forms of corporate power analyzed here delimit and define 'the real world of democracy' in these times? The phrase is from C.B. MacPherson, that formidable theorist of liberal democracy in an earlier era (MacPherson, 1962; 1977). In a globalizing world organized substantially around the interests of corporate capital, has the rather pallid liberal democracy that MacPherson knew four decades ago become hollowed out? Do the transnational social movements that have railed against corporate globalization since the mid-1990s offer possibilities for more democratic 'globalization from below' (Wilson and Whitmore, 1998)? These issues are briefly addressed in Chapter 10.

I

The Organizational Terrain

Chapter 2

From Oligarchy to Corporate Governance: The End of the Old Boys' Network?

Canada's elite has long had a reputation for closure and cohesiveness, reaching back to colonial times when 'the ruling classes of Upper and Lower Canada formed a tight set of family relations and were firmly based on a union of interlocking interests' (Clement, 1975: 50). The corporate form of capitalist organization took hold late in the nineteenth century, and as early as 1908–13—a period of extensive mergers—a tightly integrated network of interlocking directorates among the largest corporations gave a few dozen major capitalists sway over much of the economy (Piedalue, 1976; De Grass, 1977). In his 1975 bestseller, *The Canadian Establishment*, Volume 1, Peter C. Newman wrote that

> Without being a social compact, the confederacy of Canadian Establishments—loosely knit yet interlocking—forms a psychological entity. Its members share habits of thought and action, common sets of values, beliefs, and enemies. They consider themselves an untitled aristocracy whose virtue has been certified by elevation to one of the dominant elites (1975:446).

There is a long tradition of sociological analysis emphasizing the social closure of the 'higher circles' (Mills, 1956; Domhoff, 1998)—the restricted access to elite positions that enforces a kind of monoculture within the business community. Vivid images of the Protestant Establishment (Baltzell, 1964), the Vertical Mosaic (Porter, 1965), and an 'old boys' network' manned by a few dozen corporate capitalists easily come to mind. Such a network can provide a basis for business leadership. A socially integrated elite is capable of reaching consensus on common issues and strategies.

The fate of the old boys' network—and more broadly of corporate capital's largely oligarchic social organization—is the focal point of this chapter. By way of entry, let us first deal with some matters of terminology. What exactly is meant by 'social closure' and 'elite cohesiveness'—the defining attributes of old boys' networks? In the neo-Weberian tradition best exemplified by Frank Parkin, social closure is 'the process by which social collectivities seek to maximize rewards by restricting access to resources and opportunities to a limited circle of eligibles' (Parkin, 1979:44). An elite secures such privilege, at the expense of other groups, through *exclusionary practices* that give rise to a social category of 'ineligibles or outsiders' (1979:45). Parkin helpfully contrasts aristocratic and bourgeois forms of exclusion. The former is built around an ascriptive lineage system, the latter around universal criteria that are indifferent to ascriptive attributes. However, since the bourgeoisie is a ruling class whose social power is founded on its control of heritable private property, 'there is . . . a permanent tension within this class resulting from the need to legitimate itself by preserving *openness of access*, and the desire to reproduce itself socially by resort to *closure on the basis of descent*' (Parkin, 1979:47; emphasis added). The rise of credentialism—the inflated use of educational credentials as a way of restricting access to key positions—needs to be assessed in light of this tension. In aristocratic or caste systems, families of the dominant group pass on their privileges directly to their own descendents. In capitalism, 'succession along kinship lines must be accomplished in conformity with the application of criteria that are ostensibly indifferent to the claims of blood' (1979:63). Viewed in this light, the professionalization of corporate management not only mobilizes talent in the larger population and opens channels into the corporate elite. It also enables established families to pass on privilege as 'cultural capital' signifying fitness for participating in the life-world of the elite.

Closure is analytically distinct from *cohesiveness*, by which we mean the social organization that is an integral aspect of elite hegemony. The mechanisms of closure certainly provide for cohesion and thus help members of the corporate elite to reach consensus and exercise political-cultural direction. With closure, as Weber (1947:428–9) emphasized, comes social prestige—a crucial element in a ruling group's hegemony. However, elite closure can also pose legitimation problems. With the advance of bourgeois society, aristocratic forms of closure become culturally archaic. They conflict both with established cultural elements, such as the liberal commitment to equal opportunity, and with emerging cultural elements, such as the late-twentieth-century pluralist commitment to multiculturalism.

As business journalists have suggested (Newman, 1998; Partridge, 1998), there is reason to doubt that such closure remained entirely intact at the close of the twentieth century, in Canada or elsewhere (Zweigenhaft and Domhoff, 1998). The socio-cultural sources of change are several:

- the multiculturalism and feminism championed by new social movements and implemented to some extent in various equity policies (Fraser, 1997; Day, 2000),
- neoliberalism's own emphasis on competitive individualism, which—in rejecting an ethics of solidarity—recommends meritocracy over plutocracy (Chossudovsky, 1975; Beauchemin, 1997), and
- a rising 'global' consciousness within corporate business—a notion that world-class business should shed traditional corporate paternalism and establish the climate for 'total organizational creativity', unlocking 'the creative potential of workers, suppliers, and customers' (Dauphinais and Price, 1998:20–2).

Considering all this, it is reasonable to ask whether in recent years ossified and oligarchic forms of elite closure have given way to greater diversity and openness.

This is the central issue probed here. How have the social structure and culture of the elite changed? To what extent has the elite become less exclusive and more representative of the broad population? Have credentialized advisors, technical experts, and professionals gained ground in elite circles, compared to major shareholding capitalists? These matters are explored in the first section below, on the *changing composition* of the corporate elite. The second section applies a network analysis to the issues of *structural cohesiveness and closure*. Has the elite become less focused on a tightly knit old boys' network, a 'confraternity of power' cemented by common memberships in private clubs? Finally, the third section explores the significance of an emerging *discourse of corporate governance*—evident in the business press and in interventions by business leaders in the mid-to-late 1990s. Can this discourse be read as a project of moral and intellectual reform within the corporate elite? If so, what are the implications for elite social organization and corporate hegemony?

WHITHER THE VERTICAL MOSAIC?

In 1965, Porter described a system of stratification in Canada that placed the British charter group at the top. The French charter group held a decidedly secondary position, and other ethnic groups were positioned according to the often disadvantaged status accorded to them on their entry as immigrants. The economic elite itself—the 985 Canadian-resident directors of the 170 dominant corporations of the 1950s—was entirely male and overwhelmingly of British ancestry (Anglo-Scottish-Irish), reflecting the fact that economic development had been in the hands of British Canadian males (Porter, 1965:264, 286).[1] Only 6.7 per cent of the elite could be classified as French-Canadian, even though French Canadians made up about a third of the 1951 population. Very few non-charter groups were represented at all. Porter depicted the elite as a homogeneous group, whose members interacted not only in the boardrooms but in elite clubs reserved for those with the money and cultural credentials to gain admission. The overwhelming dominance of 'the Brits' extended well beyond the corporate economy: 'given the hegemony of British language, culture, and social and political institutions, English Canada before the 1960s was, for most purposes, a monocultural, monolingual, single-nation state, and made no apologies for being so' (Day, 2000:178). Wallace Clement's (1975) follow-up investigation replicated Porter's basic findings but with a slightly lower level of British predominance in the economic elite of 1972 (86.2 per cent) and a slight increase in the representation of French and other ethnic backgrounds. Later research also detected a weakening in British predominance (Niosi, 1981; Ornstein and Stevenson, 1984; Ogmundson and McLaughlin, 1992). Apparently, the trend since the 1950s has been towards a modicum of multiculturalism within Canada's corporate elite.

Feminists have pointed to the gender-blindness of Porter's conception of the 'vertical mosaic'. In highlighting the stark ethnic inequities around which Canadian society was structured, Porter gave scant attention to women's exclusion from social power. He 'did not consider how the vertical mosaic was gendered in all of its manifestations' (Hamilton, 1996:3). The 'confraternity of power' that Porter described (1965:540–1) was, as Bonnie Fox (1989:138) has written, a *brotherhood*. Indeed, the most striking aspect of elite homogeneity has been the exclusion of women. Much of the elite's social solidarity has been founded on a masculinist ideology of male bonding, underwritten by the exclusion of women from corporate boardrooms, elite private clubs, and the like. Yet women *have* been active in the life of the elite, not only in socializing the next generation, instilling the proper class sensibilities and capacities, but in extending the reach of elite influence into civil society. As Fox notes, 'upper-class women's involvement in service organizations, philanthropic groups, social and educational reform bodies, and other community organizations typically protects class interests' (1989:139). Although the scope of the present study does not extend to these issues, it is possible to present some indications of the changing gender composition of Canada's corporate elite, and of the positioning of women within it.

Porter and Clement included as members of the economic elite all the directors of the very largest corporations. However, in structural terms this designation is over-inclusive. Most members of this group—more than three-quarters of directors—hold only single directorships in large corporations. As I have argued elsewhere (Carroll, 1984:248), it is the holders of multiple directorships—the intercorporate linkers—who are the appropriate population to analyze in mapping the corporate elite as a social network (cf. Ashley, 1957; McKie, 1976). Michael Useem (1981) refers to these individuals as corporate capital's *dominant stratum*: those directors who sit on two or more major corporate boards. Typically numbering fewer than 500, this group generates the entire network of interlocking directorates, and, along with the 250 or so largest Canadian corporations, is the object of this study. Indeed, *hereafter the term 'corporate elite' will be synonymous with what Useem calls the dominant stratum*. In this sense, the net cast here is relatively small. Clearly, if an old boys' network has persisted it should be found within the dominant stratum of corporate directors. Alternatively, changes in the structure and composition of the group of corporate interlockers might signal the decline of the old business oligarchy. We need to interrogate our data as to how tightly knit or diffuse the elite's network is, and how social categories like gender and ethnicity are represented and positioned within it. The key questions thus revolve around the network's cohesiveness, its centralization, and its closure. Our starting point in this section is simply the overall composition of the elite.

The profile of the corporate elite in Table 2.1, based on 489 individuals in 1976 and 426 in 1996, furnishes a longitudinal comparison. The trend is unmistakably toward a *reduction in closure*:[2]

- By 1996 nearly one in ten of the leading corporate interlockers was female, up from a base of zero in the 1950s and less than one per cent in 1976. While the 1996 proportion can hardly be considered a bourgeois-feminist triumph, it does represent an erosion of patriarchal closure.
- There was a definite erosion in the predominance of the British charter group, although even in 1996 nearly two-thirds of the elite appeared to trace their origins to the British Isles. The ethnic groups gaining representation in the corporate elite were diverse but nearly entirely European: the trajectory of develop-

ment was toward a *Eurocentric multiculturalism*. Whereas in 1976, 90.6 per cent of the elite were British or French in background, twenty years later, in 1996, 82.3 per cent were members of the two European charter groups; yet less than one per cent (all of them ethnically Japanese or Chinese) came from ethnic backgrounds outside of Europe. Compared to the population overall, this newfound multiculturalism looks rather tepid. The overall demographic trend in Canada from 1971 to 1991 was towards erosion of European ethnic predominance. In the higher echelons of corporate capital, however, this sea-change registered merely as a modest increase in elite members of Asian background.[3] In effect, the dominance of the British charter group was reduced, but the elite as a whole remained Eurocentric in its ethnic composition.[4]

- There was a striking *decrease* in the proportion of members belonging to one or more elite social clubs. In the 1950s the common pattern was for members of the elite to belong to three or four clubs in their city of residence (Porter, 1965:304). In 1976, clubs were still a basic aspect of the elite's life-world, and half of all members belonged to *four or more*. Yet by 1996, consistent with trends in the US (Barnes and Ward, 2002), nearly half of the elite reported no club memberships, and only 22 per cent belonged to four or more.[5]
- Finally, the table shows an interesting combination of a *greying of the elite* and an *accumulation of educational credentials*, particularly the MBA/MComm, and other post-baccalaureate degrees. The middle of the age distribution (ages 51–65) accounted for about three-fifths of the elite in both years (61.3 per cent and 58.2 per cent respectively), but the post-retirement age proportion increased substantially.

It is difficult to say much about the three women who were members of the elite in 1976, except to note that, consistent with the tradition of patriarchal closure,

TABLE 2.1
A Social Profile of the Canadian Corporate Elite, 1976 and 1996

Percentage of elite who were . . .	1976	1996
Women	0.6	9.2
British background	77.9	63.8
French background	12.7	18.3
German background	3.5	4.7
Jewish background	2.0	4.0
Scandinavian background	1.8	3.1
Other European background	1.8	4.9
Asian background	0.2	0.9
Members of one or more elite club(s)	89.9	54.3
Over 65 years old	21.9	30.5
Without a bachelor's degree	27.3	15.4
With MBAs or MComms	4.8	13.7
With other post-baccalaureate or professional degrees	38.5	50.7

none of them belonged to any exclusive social club. The two for whom we could determine birth year were both 50 years old—nine years younger than the mean age for the 1976 elite. By 1996, few of the 39 women in the elite participated in the private world of elite social clubs. Of the 37 women whose biographical information we could trace, 30 did not belong to any elite clubs. Only four of the seven who were members of one or more clubs belonged to any of the key clubs mentioned in Porter's and Clement's studies,[6] and only one, Helen Sinclair, an executive with Bankworks Trading Inc., belonged to two of the key clubs. Men in the elite, on the other hand, belonged to as many as ten clubs in 1996, and some, like Allan Taylor, retired chair of the Royal Bank, were members of five of the seven key clubs. Overall, half of the men belonged to two or more clubs, and nearly a quarter of them belonged to four or more. At the close of the twentieth century the network of club memberships was still largely a male preserve.

Since the leading lights of the corporate elite accumulate club memberships as they age,[7] this finding may have to do with persistent age differences among men and women in the elite. In 1996 the women had a mean age of 53, compared with a mean of 61 for the men. In 1996 there was also a difference between the genders in educational background, but here the contrast cannot be neatly quantified. Women were over-represented in the categories of advanced academic training— 25 per cent of elite members holding master's degrees were women, and 15.2 per cent of Ph.D.s were women. Yet women also accounted for a disproportionate share of those with the least education: 16.7 per cent of those without any post-secondary education were women (three of these seven being members of wealthy shareholding families).[8] In contrast, men were over-represented among those with the most standard professional passports in the world of corporate business—law degrees (95.7 per cent) and MBAs (94.7 per cent)—as well as among those with bachelor's degrees (96.4 per cent).

THE CLASS STRUCTURE OF THE CORPORATE ELITE

With this preliminary analysis pointing to a weakening in closure along ethnic and gender lines, we now consider the elite's class composition. In the 1970s a raft of neo-Marxist studies led to some major advances in the analysis of class (Poulantzas, 1975; Carchedi, 1977; Wright, 1978), which were subsequently applied in empirical studies of the Canadian class structure (Johnston and Ornstein, 1982; Clement and Myles, 1994). While it is clear that directors of large corporations participate in what Carchedi (1983) calls the global *function of capital*—controlling the work of executives who are responsible for the whole of the enterprise—not all corporate directors are active, functioning capitalists. A certain proportion of corporate directors are advisors to corporate capitalists. They are *organic intellectuals* of the capitalist class, entrusted with 'organising the general system of relationships external to . . . business itself' (Gramsci, 1971:6).[9] Such intellectuals are 'organic' in a double sense: they are 'organizers' of an advanced capitalist way of life and their intellectual work is functionally—organically—predicated on the dominance of capital in human affairs.[10]

Jorge Niosi's (1978; 1981) investigations of corporate business from the 1970s have relevance here. In criticizing the notion of a homogeneous corporate elite, Niosi sorted the directors of 136 large Canadian-controlled corporations into four groups: (1) legal advisors, (2) financial advisors, accountants, and technicians, (3) managers, and (4) large stockholders (1978:133–45; 1981:15). The first two groups are corporate capital's organic intellectuals. The latter two are the actual corporate capitalists who wield strategic and/or operational control in the world of corporate business, and whose own income derives principally from the economic surplus that capital appropriates from labour. In effect, Niosi's class categorization distinguishes between those directors whose ownership of capital or incumbency in top executive positions enables them to wield capitalist *authority* and those who participate as advisors. Niosi found that the latter had only nominal holdings of company shares and received modest compensation for their board service. Corporate officers, however, received generous salaries and frequently accumulated shares in the company, all of which aligned them with the major shareholders who in Niosi's view constitute the dominant section of the bourgeoisie, controlling actual corporations through the voting rights that accrue to owners of large blocks of shares (1981:16).

The present analysis follows Niosi's, but makes some additional distinctions. The complexity of corporate organization and business strategies draws a wide spectrum of organic intellectuals into the corporate elite as their advice is sought by multiple large corporations. Based on the biographical descriptions of members of the elite in standard reference publications, we can classify corporate advisors into six categories:

- legal advisors (lawyers actively practising law as their main pursuit, typically in one of the large legal firms identified by Clement (1975) and Niosi (1978:135–40),
- consultants (management consultants, financial consultants, engineers, geologists, other scientists not employed within academe),
- academic advisors (professors, university presidents, professional policy researchers employed by organizations such as the C.D. Howe Institute),
- state officials (members of the Senate of Canada, public servants, ambassadors, lieutenant-governors),
- other advisors (outside corporate directors with or without other occupations, including retired politicians and administrators, deputy chairs of major corporate boards, medical doctors, trade unionists, and freelance editors),
- *éminences grises* (retired business executives serving as outside directors of several large corporations).

Among *corporate executives* we may distinguish between (1) presidents or CEOs in Top 250 corporations, (2) lower-level executives in the Top 250, and (3) executives or proprietors of corporations outside the Top 250. In terms of corporate power, the first of these groups is clearly dominant and constitutes a nexus of strategic and operational control. Those in the second category may exercise more operational control (internal to a given firm) than strategic control over investment. The third category encompasses a wide range of situations, but generally involves operational and often strategic control over middle-sized businesses.

What Niosi's research tells us is that the corporate elite has its own class structure, which needs to be charted if we are to reach a sociological understanding beyond the superficial image of 'powerful people'. Following Niosi, and using his own findings to classify some individuals in 1976, we consider the most powerful class position within the elite to be that of *major shareholders*: people who own enough voting stock to claim a position on a corporation's board. Here the ownership of capital—the ultimate basis for economic power in a bourgeois society—is decisive, and the status one occupies in a managerial hierarchy is irrelevant. These very rich individuals and families personify the dominance of the capitalist class; yet they make up only a segment of the corporate elite.[11]

Table 2.2 shows that the elite consists mostly of capitalists, some actively functioning and others retired. Within the actively functioning category major shareholders make up a slightly increasing proportion—running against the notion that corporate capital is becoming increasingly 'depersonalized'—that is, owned institutionally rather than by persons (Scott, 1997). By 1996 slightly more than one-tenth of the elite were major shareholders. On the other hand, non-presidential executives decreased as a proportion of the elite.[12] The tabulation also reveals growth in certain strata of the corporate advisors. Lawyers make up a fairly constant one-tenth of the elite, and in neoliberal times there has been no increase in the tiny complement of state officials. However, the proportions of retired capitalists, consultants, and academics increased, from 7.0 to 15.2 per cent overall.

As for the intersections of gender and class, in 1976 two of the three elite women held high-status positions in the public sphere but were marginal to the world of corporate business.[13] This gendered marginality continued into the late 1990s, as

TABLE 2.2
Class Positions in the Corporate Elite (%)

Class Position	1976	1996
Major shareholder in a Top 250 firm	9.2	10.6
President/CEO of a Top 250 firm	21.9	17.9
Other executive in a Top 250 firm	12.1	7.5
Chair of a Top 250 firm	5.3	6.6
Executive or proprietor in a smaller firm	31.1	30.1
Éminence grise	2.9	6.8
Legal advisor	10.8	9.9
Consultant	3.1	4.9
Academic advisor	1.0	3.5
State official	1.4	0.9
Other advisor	1.2	1.2
Total	**100.0**	**100.0**

women tended to hold advisory positions; 38.4 per cent of women (compared with only 6.7 per cent of men) were consultants, academic advisors, or other advisors. Most of the male advisors were corporate lawyers—in fact, 10.4 per cent of all the men in the elite were legal advisors, but only 5.1 per cent of the women. Finally, among the advisors, women were entirely absent from the categories of *éminences grises* and state officials. Beyond these advisory positions the pattern of male dominance in positions of capitalist authority continued into the late twentieth century. More than a quarter of men were either CEOs (19.4 per cent) or chairs of top corporate boards (7.3 per cent); only one woman was a CEO and none chaired a board. More than half of all women in the elite held positions of capitalist authority, but most of them were executives in smaller firms (35.9 per cent of women, compared with 29.5 per cent of men). The other authority positions showed no discernible gender differentiation in the sheer numbers; however, it is worth noting that all four of the women who were major shareholders of Top 250 companies had achieved that status by virtue of a family connection with a male corporate owner.[14] Not only do women remain under-represented in the elite, but they tend to inhabit its lower strata as advisors or lower-level executives. A glass ceiling continues to restrict entry into all but a few top-level positions in the class structure of the corporate elite (Fleming, 1991:163; Hughes, 2000).

Bearing in mind that surnames can provide only crude and gender biased indications of ethnicity, we can nevertheless venture some analysis of the intersection between ethnicity and class within the corporate elite. Given the overwhelming predominance of the British charter group in 1976, comparisons of class positioning across ethnic groups at that time are not terribly meaningful. Still, the very few corporate interlockers with non-British surnames were in some respects positioned distinctively in the class structure of the elite, and these ethnic distinctions offer further clues to the elite's trajectory.

Considering as three contrasting groups the French, Jewish, and 'other' non-charter members of the elite, there was a definite movement 'upward' by French-Canadian corporate directors. In 1976 the French group was over-represented in the lower echelons of the elite: more than a quarter (25.8 per cent) of all French-Canadian elite members were corporate advisors, but not a single one was an *éminence grise*. The French-Canadian directors who wielded capitalist authority tended to be executives in smaller firms or lower-level executives in dominant ones. In fact, 51.6 per cent of the entire French-Canadian segment occupied one of these positions (compared with 43.2 per cent in the elite overall). Only 4.8 per cent of French-Canadians were major shareholders in a Top 250 firm, and 17.7 per cent were presidents, CEOs, or board chairs. Twenty years later, in 1996, French Canadians not only made up a larger proportion of the elite, they occupied more powerful positions. Although still under-represented among the *éminences grises* (only 2.6 per cent of French-Canadian members fitted this designation), they had gained status at the higher reaches of capitalist authority—as major shareholders (19.5 per cent) and as presidents and CEOs (16.9 per cent) of dominant firms.

As in the US (Zweigenhaft and Domhoff, 1998:23–7), Jews make up a small but increasing proportion of the corporate elite, and our cross-tabulation shows a distinctive class positioning. In 1976, six of the ten Jewish members of the corporate elite were major shareholders in Top corporations, suggesting that for them—in contrast to the charter groups—personal control of corporate capital was the main basis for membership in the corporate elite. This pattern was evident, to a lesser extent, among members of other non-charter groups, one-quarter of whom were major shareholders in Top corporations and none of whom was an *éminence grise* in 1976. By 1996, Jewish members of the elite continued to be over-represented among major shareholders.[15] However, the distribution of other non-charter ethnic minorities now resembled the overall class distribution except that they were nearly completely excluded from the *éminence grise* category. The latter, of course, is a particularly 'sedimented' category, in the sense that the stratum of retired corporate capitalists who remain active in corporate governance at any given time will reflect past stratification patterns. The legacy of the Vertical Mosaic was plain in 1996, when 25 of the 29 *éminences grises* had British backgrounds.

OLD BOYS NO MORE?

This chapter is the place where we introduce the rudiments of network analysis as a means of depicting the social structure of the corporate elite. In the sociology of elites, Stephen Berkowitz (1980) has argued that classic studies such as C. Wright Mills's (1956) and John Porter's (1965) ignored important *relational* aspects of corporate power, relying instead on a simple 'aggregative' approach which 'can tell us little about the *systemic* relationships among elements' of the elite (Berkowitz, 1980:15). As a structure, a social network consists in a collection of *points*, representing social units or actors of some kind, and *lines*, representing social relations of some kind. When we apply this idea to the leading corporations and their directors, we notice that the set of interlocking directorates constitutes a *dual* network: a structure of interlocking corporate boards (sharing common directors) and of interlocking corporate directors (sitting on common boards). This *duality* of corporate networks is itself an important property, which obliges us to consider the individual director and the corporate board as interdependent units of analysis (Brieger, 1974; Carroll, 1984).

Here, our concern is with how the multiple board affiliations of individual directors knit them into a more or less cohesive bloc at the centre of corporate power. Structurally speaking, this is what we mean by an integrated elite. A first step is to map the interpersonal network that is generated by common board memberships among directors of the largest corporations. Corporate directors have contact with other directors simply by serving with them on a single board. A simple measure of elite cohesion is the mean number of interpersonal contacts among corporate directors—that is, the average number of fellow directors with whom a corporate director serves. For directors of single companies this is strictly a function of the size of corporate boards, which on average *fell* from 13.27 in 1976 to 11.30 in 1996. For directors of multiple dominant firms—our corporate elite—it is a function both of the size of boards and of the number of directorships held. We will examine the reasons for the decrease in board size later on, but for now we can note its impact in *thinning* the network of interpersonal contacts. The mean number of interpersonal contacts among members of the elite dropped from 34.0 to 20.8.[16]

What impact did the thinning of the interpersonal network have on the elite? Is it evidence that the old boys' network has been weakening? One way of getting a grip on this issue is to examine some basic features of network integration. In the first place, we can ask whether the members of the corporate elite constitute what network analysts call a connected component (all of whose members are directly or indirectly inter-connected), or are fragmented into several disjointed components. A simple way of assessing this is to consider the size of the elite's dominant component, the largest set in which all points are ultimately reachable by all other points. We find that nearly the entire elite remained configured as a connected set of points across the decades. In 1976, 485 of the 489 corporate-elite members belonged to the dominant component; in 1996, 424 of the 426 were mutually reachable. Nevertheless, with the thinning of ties, the *density* of the lines—the relative incidence of direct ties among individuals—dropped from 0.065 to 0.044. By 1996 only 4.4 per cent of all the pairs of corporate-elite members served together on one or more Top 250 board.

This decrease in density meant an increasing *distance* between persons in the network (see Figure 2.1). In 1976, the corporate elite was a very small world indeed. Most members of the connected component could reach each other either directly (i.e., they served on the same board) or at one remove (i.e., they served on different boards that each included a common third member of the elite). Although the distance between persons did not increase dramatically, the shift was enough that by 1996 only two-fifths of pairs could reach each other at distance 2 or less. In the 1970s the elite's board affiliations generated an interpersonal network in which most directors were either corporate colleagues (on a common board) or colleagues of colleagues, forming a tightly knit community. By 1996 the elite's life-world was less densely integrated.

If we look more closely within the network, it is possible to distinguish the centrally positioned members from the marginal ones. The most immediate measure of centrality is simply the number of Top boards on which a director sits. In both years there was considerable variation in the numbers of directorships held by individuals, but the tendency was towards a reduction in those numbers by 1996, from a mean of 3.06 to 2.83. The number of so-called big linkers (Stokman, Ziegler, and Scott, 1985)—those holding four or more directorships and thus having direct contact with all the other elite members who served on those boards—fell from 128 to 82. At the top end of the 1976 distribution, John H. Moore, chair and president of the investment company Brascan Ltd, was a director of 10 Top firms and thus had the greatest number of direct ties to other members of the corporate elite. In total, Moore served on one board or another with 109 other members of the elite. Ian Sinclair, chair and president of Canadian Pacific, had nine major directorships in 1976 and placed second in interpersonal contacts, with direct ties to 103 other members of the elite. By 1996, the top end of the distribution of directorships was again claimed by the chair of Brascan, Senator Trevor Eyton. However, his ten directorships created contacts with only 49 other elite members. Former Alberta

FIGURE 2.1
Distances in the Interpersonal Network, 1976 and 1996

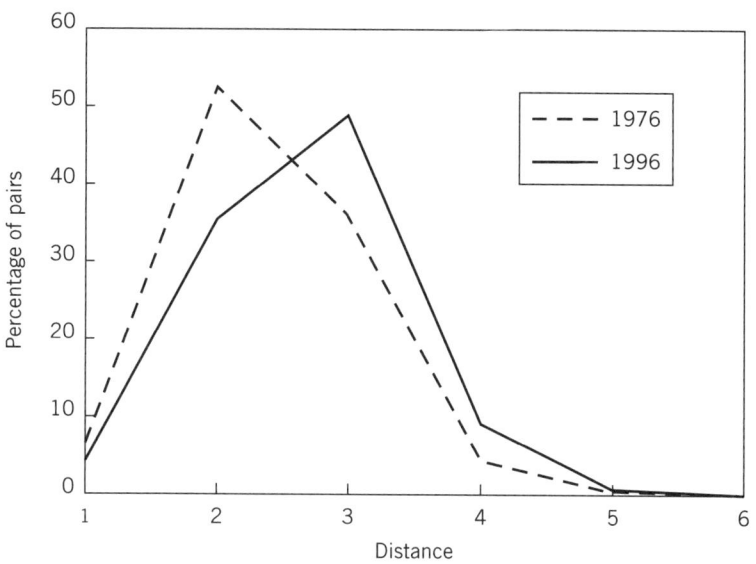

Premier Peter Lougheed, with eight directorships, had the most interpersonal contacts (66).

We can see how, particularly for the big linkers, a reduction in the number of directorships held, combined with the decrease in directorate size, meant a considerable decline in interpersonal contacts. The result was a decrease in elite integration. As directors trimmed corporate affiliations and as boards shrank, the capacity of well-connected directors to serve as the interpersonal network's central 'hubs' diminished. In 1976 the direct ties that men like Moore and Sinclair had to a substantial proportion of the entire elite meant that most of the elite were linked either directly or at one remove (e.g., through common ties to Moore or Sinclair). By 1996 this was no longer the case. If we consider the centre of the network to consist of directors with at least 50 direct contacts in the elite, that centre shrank from 101 members to only nine. By 1996 the corporate elite had a looser—though by no means fragmented—social organization.

Historically, bank boards have been central nodes in the Canadian corporate network (Piedalue, 1976; Porter, 1965; Clement, 1975). Part of the reason for the emptying-out of the centre has to do with the decreased prominence of the five big chartered banks as meeting points for great numbers of the corporate elite. In 1976, as Table 2.3 shows, the boards of each bank brought together dozens of elite members—the Canadian Imperial Bank of Commerce (CIBC) alone had 41 on its board. Banks are prohibited from interlocking with each other, so the number of elite members directing one or another bank can be added to determine the pro-

TABLE 2.3
Number of Elite Directors Serving on a Board of One of the Big Five Banks

	1976	1996
Bank of Montreal	39	17
Bank of Nova Scotia	26	17
CIBC	41	21
Royal Bank of Canada	36	22
Toronto-Dominion	30	20
Total	172	97

portion of the entire elite that sits on bank boards. We can see from the tabulation that a total of 172 members of the elite, 35 per cent of its total membership, sat on a major bank board in 1976. For many of these people, service on two or three other boards would easily provide direct contact with a sizable fraction of the elite. Twenty years later, the banks played a less integrative role, although their boards continued to have more elite members than did other boards. The total of 97 members on the big five bank boards represented 23 per cent of the elite.

The decline in the integrative capacity of the most central individuals, and the most central boards, suggests that the old boys' network became more diffuse. Perhaps the most revealing way of probing for 'old boys' is to search for a core group of directors who are heavily interlocked with *each other*. Using Seidman's 'k-core' criterion, Figure 2.2 compares the size and structural integration of core groups nested within the interpersonal network. The 'k' in k-core is the criterion for establishing the membership of a core group. Each member of the identified core group must be directly tied to at least k other members of the group. In 1976 the centre of the network consisted of a '36-core' of 80 directors: each of the 80 sat on one or more boards with at least 36 of the other 79. These 80 directors made up a very tight inner circle nested within a 30-core of 116 directors, which in turn was nested within a 27-core of 147 directors. By 1996 the centre of the network was more diffuse. The most integrated group was a 20-core of 43 directors, nested within a 17-core of 63 directors, which in turn was nested within a 16-core of 115 directors. To express the difference in terms of density, in 1976 the central group of 116 heavily interlocked directors had a density of 0.38: nearly two-fifths of the most central directors sat together on one or more boards! In 1996 the central group of 115 heavily interlocked directors was only half as dense (0.19).[17]

Let us consider these groups as reasonable approximations of an old boys' network, with the difference in density revealing a loosening in the network. We can also distinguish as more peripheral regions the inner and outer margins, as shown in Figure 2.2, with the outer margin extending to the least central members of the elite in each year. For 1976, we designated as the inner margin 153 individuals (31 per cent of the elite) who although not in the central group of 116 did belong to the 27-core; for 1996 we designated the 126 individuals (30 per cent of the elite) who were not in the central group of 115 but did belong to the 11-core.

FIGURE 2.2
Core Groups Within the Interpersonal Network

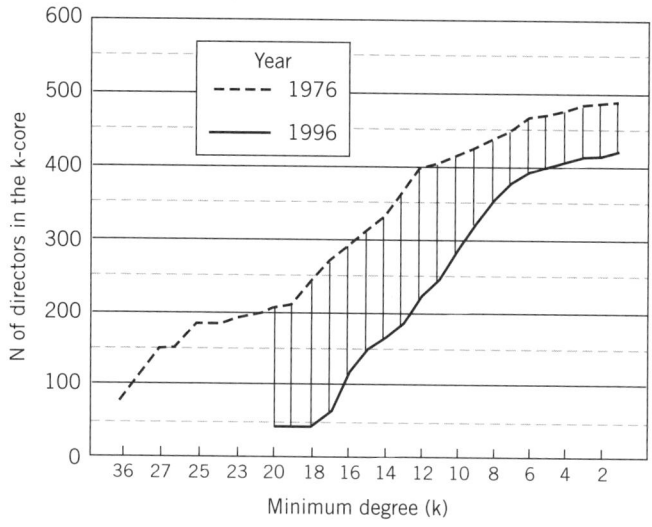

Lines indicate the number of directors included in the k-core at a given step.

Distinguishing these regions enables us to assess whether the central group constitutes an old boys' network. Rytina and Morgan's 'arithmetic of social relations' (1982:103–6) gives us an ideal-typical scenario for such a network. An old boys' network implies that within a larger population there is a group whose members, drawn from a common elite background, interact extensively with each other and only sporadically with the majority group, whose cohesion is negligible. If the old boys 'collectively combine the size of a minority, modest self-selection, and an abundance of contacts, the result is a connected core and a disconnected collection of hangers on' (1982:106). In such a situation, 'the old boys are in a far better position to make arrangements with each other on the basis of mutual trust' and 'to facilitate the formation of larger, more effective coalitions' involving the larger population (104).Table 2.4 shows the extent of contact within and across the network's core (i.e., central group) and margins.[18] In 1976 the network resembled the Rytina and Morgan scenario in that the inner and outer margins were much less integrated than the core. But instead of 'hanging on' to core members, directors in the inner margin tended to have contacts with each other. The same pattern was sustained in 1996, but the mean degrees were generally halved. The interpersonal network has been centralized around a core, but not in the highly hierarchical manner of a full-fledged old boy's network.

Of course, the interpersonal contacts summarized in Table 2.4 arise out of directorships with corporations that occupy varying positions in the intercorporate network. Banks, as we have seen, have been among the most central firms in the network. Hence the directors of banks will tend to be central in the interpersonal network, as they meet with many other members of the elite who also

TABLE 2.4
Mean Degree Within and Between Core and Margin, 1976 and 1996

1976 Mean sectoral degrees			
	Outer margin	Inner margin	Core
Outer margin	7.9	7.6	6.0
Inner margin	3.9	23.3	8.9
Core	2.8	8.2	43.7

1996 Mean sectoral degrees			
	Outer margin	Inner margin	Core
Outer margin	4.9	3.4	3.1
Inner margin	2.3	12.2	5.9
Core	1.9	5.4	22.2

serve on bank boards. In fact, the banks have supplied the interpersonal network's core with the lion's share of its members. In 1976 *all of the 116 'core' directors held bank directorships*, and 56 of the inner-margin members were bank directors. In 1996 *every one of the 97 members of the corporate elite who held a bank directorship was in the core*. Clearly, and despite the declining numbers of corporate interlockers on bank boards, the banks continued to be at the heart of the network, and serving on a bank board continued to be a passport into a central position in the corporate elite. Corporate directors without such a passport were largely excluded from the most concentrated meeting-points in the network. They tended to occupy more marginal positions, and by implication their contacts also tended to be on the margins. In this way, the interpersonal network continued to be structured in two tiers, around the hegemonic position of the banks as key allocators of financial capital (Mintz and Schwartz, 1985; cf. Marx, 1967:368, 402).

With the core-periphery distinction we can also compare the positions of social categories—ethnicity, class, and gender—in the elite. Does the elite's social organization amplify or reduce the disparities in representation we noticed earlier? Considering first the positioning of ethnic groups, in 1976 'Brits' not only predominated numerically; they were also slightly over-represented in the network's core, where 83 per cent had British backgrounds while 10 per cent was French Canadian and 1 per cent was Jewish. By 1996, despite a declining presence overall (to 64 per cent), Brits were still over-represented at the core (74 per cent), while those of French background accounted for only 11 per cent. Among the non-charter ethnic groups, corporate directors of Jewish background made definite inroads into the elite's core. In 1976 seven of ten Jewish members of the elite were positioned on the outer margin and only one was in the core. By 1996 four of the 17 Jewish members were in the core and seven were in the inner margin.

Class position had some bearing on centrality in the interpersonal network. The centrality of retired executives increased over the two decades, as their numbers more than doubled. By 1996, 41.4 per cent of the *éminences grises* were in the core, compared to 28.6 per cent two decades earlier. There was also a tendency toward greater differentiation in centrality for certain categories of corporate capitalists. In 1976 chairs of Top corporations were slightly less likely to be positioned in the core than were lower-level executives. By 1996 chairs were especially central (46.4 per cent in the core) and lower-level executives peripheral (15.6 per cent in the core).

As for gender, in neither year does it appear that women's marginal position in the world of corporate business was exacerbated by marginality in the network. The patriarchal character of the corporate elite has mainly to do with the exclusion of women from major corporate boards and from positions of capitalist authority. Although relatively few women directed multiple major corporations, they were less likely than men to be on the margins of the network. In 1976, two of three elite women were actually in the core group while the third was positioned on the inner margin. In 1996, ten of the 39 women were in the core and 14 were on the inner margin. It may be that the few women who direct large corporations gain visibility in elite interpersonal networks and, with greater visibility, attract more invitations onto corporate directorates. They become, in the words of one recruiter, members of '"a cast of usual suspects" who are in high demand but rarely in the position to take on any additional roles' (Hughes, 2000:9).

If gender in itself had little bearing on one's position in the interpersonal network, membership in exclusive clubs was another matter. Table 2.5 shows the average number of memberships in seven key clubs, for directors positioned at the centre and on the margins of the interpersonal network. The clubs include the six organizations that Porter and Clement distinguished (based in Montreal, Toronto, or Ottawa), plus the Vancouver Club. In both years we find that the more centrally positioned directors belong to more clubs. But as the 'eta^2' statistic shows, the relationship is not a strong one.[19] Although in these aligned networks economic and cultural forms of elite power intermingle—people at the core of the corporate-interlock network tend to meet each other in the same exclusive clubs—there are many instances in which directors on the margins of the corporate-interlock network are central in the club co-membership network, and vice versa.[20] In this way, the network of elite clubs provides an additional field for the formation of solidarity, away from the narrow economic horizons of the boardroom, and involving a cross-section of corporate directors, some more central in the world of economic power than others. This is part of the stitching-together of leading capitalists and their

TABLE 2.5
Number of Club Memberships for Directors in the Network Core and Margins

Network position	Mean number of memberships in seven key clubs	
	1976	1996
Core	1.541	0.827
Inner margin	1.377	0.793
Outer margin	0.875	0.350
Grand mean	1.188	0.606
Eta^2	0.061	0.056

advisors, but with the extensive decline in club membership, the fraying of the fabric that elite clubs provides is undeniable.

Notwithstanding the falling rates of participation, elite clubs comprise a parallel network worthy of some further investigation. In 1976 a substantial 29 per cent of the elite belonged to *two or more* of the seven key clubs, and these heavy participants were heavily interconnected. The probability of any pair of them belonging to *two or more* common clubs was 0.40. Viewed inter-organizationally, the corporate elite carried many ties across the seven clubs, as Figure 2.3 shows. Elite membership among four clubs located in Montreal (Mt Royal and St James) and Toronto (Toronto and York) was heavily intertwined. For instance, 88 members of the elite belonged to the Toronto Club and 77 to the York, the latter setting a lower limit on the number of overlapping memberships between the two. Fully 60 of those 77 actually belonged to both clubs. Indeed, in 1976 five members of the corporate elite each belonged to five of the seven clubs, and another 15 belonged to four. In the network of club memberships, this group of 20 formed a tightly interwoven core. For example, Royal Bank Chair W. Earle McLaughlin's memberships in five clubs meant that he shared four memberships with 15 others in the group of 20, and three with the other four in the group.

By 1996 only 15 per cent of the corporate elite belonged to two or more of the seven clubs. The likelihood of any pair of them belonging to two or more common elite clubs was 0.46. Defection from the St James Club was especially dramatic, and consistent with Newman's (1998:90) claim that it has recently 'found new life catering to a lower rank of entrepreneurs'. Elite memberships in the Toronto, York, and Mt Royal Clubs still showed substantial overlaps, but with lower rates of participation: only two directors belonged to five of the seven clubs and only six belonged to four clubs. The three most prominent club members were Allan R. Taylor and William I. Turner, Jr (each of whom belonged to the same five clubs) and Cedric E. Ritchie (whose four club memberships overlapped exactly with Taylor and Turner's).[21] The overlapping club memberships of Taylor, Ritchie, and Turner suggest a remnant of the old boys' network. But this clique did not extend any further into corporate-elite ranks. Even more dramatically than the network of corporate directorships, the network of club memberships had thinned in the intervening two decades, supporting Newman's claim that

> the classic men's dining clubs have become relics of another age. Like the Old Establishment's adherents whom they fed, housed and cosseted, these institutions depended on exclusivity for their justification. Now that the Establishment is open to anybody, regardless of their pedigree or school tie, the clubs that perpetuated those notions have lost their reason for existence. To be clubbable means precisely nothing (1998:95–6).

With the decline of elite clubs as informal venues for business community formation *came a further softening of stratification* within the elite, even though, as Table 2.6 shows, the patterns of differential club participation persisted in attenuated form. By 1996 men participated in the world of clubs far more than women—but

FIGURE 2.3

Overlapping Memberships Among Seven Elite Clubs, 1976 and 1996

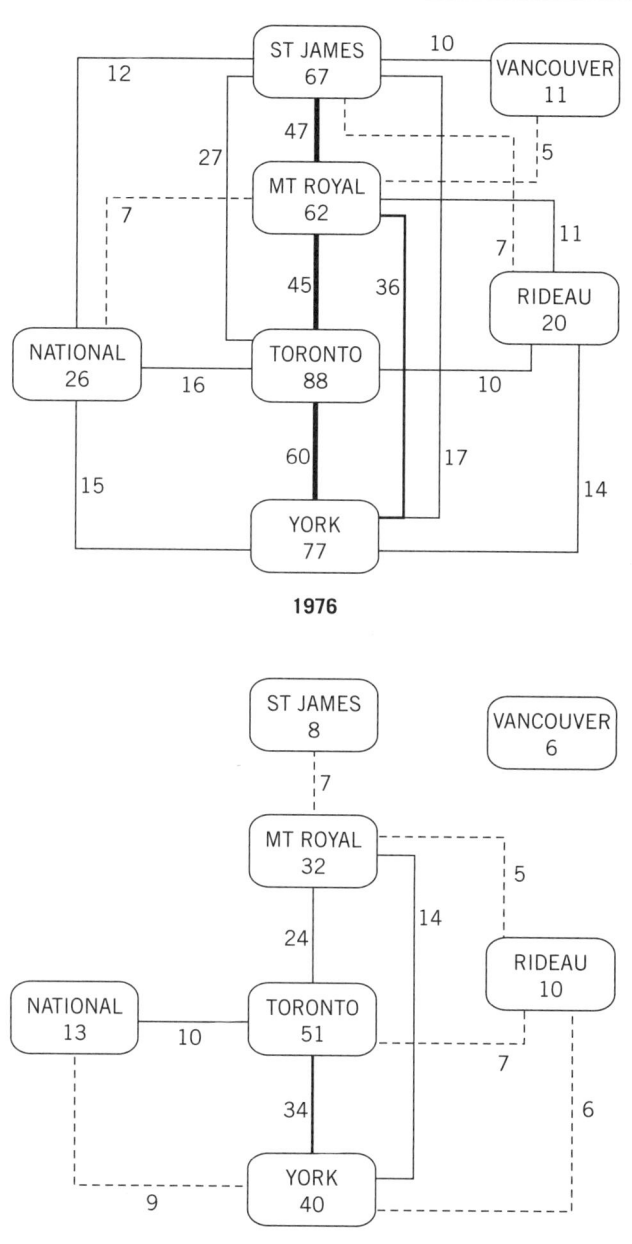

Values on lines and line thicknesses (broken to heavy) indicate the number of corporate-elite members belonging to both clubs; values within boxes indicate the number of corporate-elite members belonging to a given club.

TABLE 2.6

Mean Number of Memberships in Seven Elite Clubs

	1976	1996
Men	1.19	0.65
Women	0.00	0.14
British	1.31	0.72
French	0.74	0.45
Jewish	0.44	0.41
Other ethnic backgrounds	0.84	0.40
Major shareholder	1.21	0.67
CEO or president	1.52	0.51
Lower exec in Top firm	1.28	0.42
Chair in Top firm	1.84	0.88
Exec in other firm	1.00	0.56
Éminence grise	1.71	1.12
Legal advisor	0.73	0.62
Other advisor	0.55	0.48
Grand mean	1.19	0.61

some women were club members, whereas none were in 1976. And while the 'Brits' continued to predominate, differences had narrowed among the ethnic groups.[22] Even more striking was the attenuation of differences among class segments. In 1976 the clubs were key meeting points for presidents, CEOs, and chairs of top companies as well as *éminences grises*. By 1996 top executives were no longer much involved. Even among board chairs and *éminences grises*—the elite segments with more discretionary time and a stock of status accruing to their seniority—extensive club membership was a minority practice. The clubs had lost their centrality within the corporate elite and with it much of their exclusionary clout as enforcers of invidious distinction.

To summarize these trends in social organization, after the mid-1970s there was a definite loosening and opening-out of the interpersonal network. These transitions were the result of decreasing corporate board size and falling rates of participation on multiple corporate boards and in elite clubs, which gave a lower profile to the institutions that had been central to the corporate elite—the bank boards and private clubs. At the same time, the elite manifested a growing Eurocentric cosmopolitanism, some chinks in its patriarchal armour, and an (unsurprising) increase in educational and professional credentials. Yet there were also continuities. Among the long-established patterns that persisted was the predominance of active, functioning capitalists, including major shareholders, within the elite; of 'Brits' among the elite's *éminences grises*; and of men among club members. In these patterns we can find traces of the strategic, operational, and allocative power discussed in Chapter 1, but no clear sense of its structuring. This will be the focus of the next two chapters. First, however, the structural transitions described above need to be placed within the context of cultural transitions that partly account for the weakening of old boys' ties.

Corporate Governance and Moral Reform

The field of corporate culture is, of course, vast. Under that rubric we could well investigate the rise in the 1980s and 1990s of several influential discourses—for example, 'integrated risk management', 'strategic flexibility', or 'dynamic efficiency' (Nottingham, 1996; Bettis and Hitt, 1995)—each with implications for the business strategies, social identities, and moral fibre of the corporate elite. Some discourses will have no more than an 'arbitrary' and ephemeral character; failing to gain an institutional basis in business practice, these are soon forgotten. But others function more along the lines of what Gramsci called 'organic' ideologies. These are cultural emergents—new cognitive, motivational, and moral frameworks for corporate business—that help to shape and define corporate capital's organizational terrain.

Such is the case with the discourse of good 'corporate governance', which gained currency in the 1990s, both in academe and in corporate business. Academics from business schools were heavily involved, often as consultants, in 'promoting' good governance practices (*Corporate Decision-Making in Canada*, 1995). Academics and corporate capitalists came together in groups like the Institute of Corporate Directors (ICD) 'to ensure that directors [were] well-prepared to deal effectively with the responsibilities of their positions, and ... informed about the ever-changing demands of corporate governance'.[23]

To the extent that this discourse of corporate governance now informs the practices of corporate power, it offers a relatively open window on the self-understanding of the top tier of the capitalist class with regard to the direction of large corporations. Looking through that window, we can see a good deal. But to understand what is going on under the rubric of 'corporate governance', we need to read the discourse symptomatically, to situate corporate governance in a structural context of globalization, heightened competition, financial instability, and neoliberal policy. The corporate-governance initiative can be viewed as a practical response to challenges that big business has faced in an era of globalization. The consequences of governance reform for the structure of finance capital will be taken up in Chapter 4. Here let us consider the initiative's implications for overall elite organization.

In Canada the movement for corporate governance was, until 1993, limited to marginal campaigns by individual shareholders contesting the entrenched power of senior management. Then, in the wake of a series of financial scandals that culminated in the collapse of Confederation Life, the Toronto Stock Exchange (TSE) initiated a task force on corporate governance. Chaired by Peter Dey, an investment banker and former chair of the Ontario Securities Commission, the task force brought together a diverse collection of capitalists and intellectuals, in an extensive process of outreach and consultation (Thain, 1995:76–86).

The task force's main recommendations, adopted by the TSE in 1995, comprise 14 guidelines, enumerated in paragraph 825–774 of the *Toronto Stock Exchange*

Company Manual. Companies listed on the TSE are supposed to follow these guidelines, and are required annually to disclose their compliance, justifying any departures. For our purposes, the most relevant guidelines may be summarized as follows (numbers in parentheses correspond to the enumerated points in the TSE *Company Manual*):

1. That boards become *more active in stewardship of the corporation*, including strategic planning, risk assessment, succession planning and communications (#1).
2. That boards be *constituted with a majority of 'unrelated directors'*: independent of management and of any interest or relationship which could interfere with directors' ability to pursue the best interests of the corporation, 'other than interests and relationships arising from shareholding' (#2).
3. That boards appoint *a nominating committee made up of outside directors*, a majority of whom are unrelated directors. This committee or another appropriate one should assess the effectiveness of the board and the contributions of individual directors. Boards should also adopt measures to orient and train new directors. In general, with the exception of the executive committee, board committees should be made up of outside directors, a majority of whom are unrelated directors (#4, 5, 6, 9).
4. That every board examine its size and where appropriate, *reduce the number of directors to facilitate 'more effective decision-making'* (#7).
5. That boards have in place structures and procedures to function independently of management. Structurally, this means either *appointing a non-executive chair or a 'lead director'* or a committee charged with ensuring board autonomy. Procedurally, it may mean convening regular board meetings without management present (#12).

These reforms, which resembled contemporaneous initiatives in the US and UK, aimed to make the boards of publicly listed firms *more active and effective centres of governance*—independent of management, relatively uninfluenced by interests other than shareholders, small enough to function efficiently, and composed of well-oriented, high-performance directors.

The concern for improved corporate governance expresses a bundle of interests, both instrumental and normative. Good governance means efficiency, reliability, shareholder value, and profitability, but it also signals an upgrading of corporate ethics—a concern for the democratic rights of shareholders, for sincerity and transparency in accounting practices, for open recruitment and diversity on corporate boards, for effective, rational decision-making. These emergent norms can be seen as a project of moral and intellectual reform within the corporate elite, an attempt by business leaders to build consensus around a new paradigm. As Robert Brown, a member of the TSE's Committee on Corporate Governance, declared:

> It is important, both to the corporate community and to society in general, that business achieve a higher degree of credibility. To do this, business must put its

own house in order, starting with fundamental ethics and corporate governance issues and flowing on to responding more actively and publicly to the concerns of our society (Brown, 1994:41).

It is the emphasis on 'credibility' and 'ethics' that signifies a concern beyond the instrumental value of profit—a program of moral reform. In any bourgeois hegemonic project, ethical reach must not contradict accumulation needs, 'for though hegemony is ethical-political, it must also be economic, must necessarily be based on the decisive function exercised by the leading group in the decisive nucleus of economic activity' (Gramsci, 1971:161). Thus corporate governance reforms are closely attuned to the *heightened competition* that has accompanied recent globalization. The reforms do double-duty as ethical-political initiatives and as means to improve competitiveness while lowering both the risk of failure and the cost of capital.

It was, of course, heightened competition alongside diminishing profit rates on productive capital that led institutions like Confederation Life to make the speculative investments that eventually collapsed when the bubble burst in the early 1990s. In this sense, the corporate governance movement is rooted in the problem of capitalist crisis, which from capital's own viewpoint appears not as a systemic tendency but as a micro-economic problem of 'risk management'.[24] It is worthwhile to probe the content of this new morality, as a window on the changing culture of corporate capital and as a partial interpretation of the changes we have observed in elite social organization. Its core values validate (1) a meritocratic professionalism that also promotes a cosmopolitan ethos; (2) an emphasis on effective, democratic decision-making; and, underwriting both of these, (3) the priority of shareholder value.

Meritocracy
Consistent with the findings from our network analysis, new governance norms are intended to *open up recruitment* so that the selection of corporate board members is based on merit. Since the mid-1990s the business press has often discussed the elimination of cronyism and the old boys' network.[25] The turn from cronyism to merit and professionalism has implied a reconstitution of corporate boards. By the mid-1990s, the 'Rio Algom model'—according to which a board consists of all outside directors plus the CEO—had become the standard and boards were 'beginning to pride themselves on their independence' from management (Noakes, 1997:20). In its July 2000 follow-up report, the Dey committee noted that recruitment of directors must emphasize the universalist criterion of demonstrated competence over particularist attributes such as contacts in the 'old boys' network'. The report strongly favoured 'diversity' in the composition of boards, and suggested looking among former senior public servants and 'qualified women in management' for new directors with the potential to 'broaden the pool'. Through merit-based selection processes conducted with an eye to diversity, Canadian corporations can position themselves 'to participate in a globalized business environment' (*The State of Governance in Canada*, 2000:3). In this way, the 'merit' norm incorporates a cos-

mopolitan commitment to 'world standards' and implicitly denigrates localist practices. On this issue as on others, the moral commitment to improved corporate governance blends with the emerging demands of accumulation. Behind this embrace of globalism is the push towards heightened international competition, and the fear of 'not making the grade'.[26]

Effective, democratic decision-making

New governance norms also emphasize improvements in performance as a result of democratic decision-making. In this instance, governance reforms are intended to *open up free and full discussion*—to stimulate the mutual learning that occurs under conditions of social symmetry rather than hierarchy.[27] Within the new governance framework, regular meetings of outside directors only, without management, make it possible to pursue 'problems' that would not be revealed if the CEO were in attendance. Autonomy from management enables board members to undertake the *reasoned discussion* necessary to meet the competition from other cognitively well-resourced boards.[28]

Effective board-level decision-making is also facilitated by the downsizing of corporate boards. Matthew Barrett, CEO of the Bank of Montreal and a leader in corporate governance reforms since 1991, has pondered the significance of shrinking the Bank's board from 54 to 17 and removing most insiders. At its peak the Bank's board was larger than some provincial legislatures. 'One doesn't have to be an expert in group dynamics to know it is virtually impossible to hold an in-depth discussion with 54 people in the room' (Barrett, 1999:D5). The new 'leaner, meaner' board (Barrett's description) includes only two insiders, and thus in his estimation promotes more effective, rational communication. Since insiders are unlikely to disagree with the CEO in front of outside directors, it is best to 'avoid wasting scarce board seats on insiders' (1999:D5). Again, reform is seen as eliminating distortions in the communicative practices of corporate directorates. To promote effectiveness, outside board members are favoured over internal management for their broader perspectives, which ultimately improve competitiveness.

Relatedly, corporate governance committees now enjoy increased power within directorates, while executive committees have been on the wane. The latter, inventions of the post-war era of incrementally increasing board size, created two classes of directors, with major decisions reserved for the executive committee. As the *Financial Post* explained in its series on the 'newly empowered individual director' ('Under the gun…', 1996:6): 'with the new focus on corporate governance, everyone is more equal.' Part of moral reform, then, is a move toward *democratization*. Decision-making within the board is to be inclusive—rather than centralized within a small committee of insiders—and decisions are to be determined by the quality of the argument.

Shareholder value

Underwriting the entire project of moral reform is a concern for '*shareholder value*'. On one level this term is ideological code for capital's unquenchable thirst for surplus value, and in particular for the self-expansion of financial capital in the form of corporate share prices and dividends—a process of dubious sustainability (Lazonick and O'Sullivan, 2000). On another level, however—more relevant to the bourgeoisie—'shareholder value' carries a heavy moral connotation of fairness and collective welfare. Within the discourse of corporate governance, shareholders *deserve* to have their investments properly valorized; furthermore, with the sharpening of international competition, the vitality of the national economy *depends* on this happening. As Jog and Hofstatter observe,

> the shareholder revolution seems to be gathering momentum. These days, it is rare to read an annual report that doesn't, at least rhetorically, refer to the importance of creating shareholder value. Some institutional investors are claiming that they are increasingly attracted to companies that indicate their focus is creating shareholder value (1998:24).

Matthew Barrett argues similarly that the most powerful force driving reform has been the rise of activist institutional investors pursuing maximal shareholder value. 'In effect, institutional investors have become the gear mechanism that transmits the demands of the marketplace to the boardroom' (1999:D5). Barrett states the key ethical norm clearly: 'No management has the right to take decisions that could materially affect shareholder value without the board's approval' (1999:D5). What he describes is a scenario in which the board's stewardship of shareholder value grants it control over management. Boards must therefore be *more active, leaner* (thus effective decision-making units) and *independent*.

In a similar vein, the 2000 follow-up to the Dey report concluded that 'the quality of corporate governance in the marketplace is a key factor in establishing efficient capital markets.' (*The State of Governance in Canada*, 2000:4). Efficient capital markets in turn are an important competitive factor in today's global capitalism. Noting that 'the Canadian marketplace has sustained some notorious scandals since the publication of the [Dey] report,' the follow-up suggested that 'these scandals have negatively impacted the international market's perception of Canadian companies and have caused a general increase in the cost of capital for Canadian companies accessing capital outside Canada' (2000:4). Here again, moral reform is carefully aligned with accumulation needs.[29]

Viewed as a project of moral and intellectual reform, the new norms of corporate governance fit closely with a neoliberalized political environment in which state regulation has given way to business self-regulation in a context of intensified competition. Quite apart from the project's *success* in transforming the actualities of corporate power, the new norms of merit, diversity, transparency, democracy, and the like signal a transition in the culture of the corporate elite. Open recruitment of board members eliminates the dead weight of plutocratic cronyism, mobilizes talent, and rewards merit, so that corporations are directed by dynamic, capable individuals. Moves to enhance the board's autonomy from management and to equalize the roles of directors help to create the conditions for free and full discussion, and, it is hoped, optimal decisions. Smaller, leaner boards facilitate the same rational choices. The pursuit of 'world standards' means that the best practices in governance are adopted in Canada, improving the country's competitive edge. The emphasis on value creation for shareholders furnishes a quantitative norm that gives capital owners their just deserts while revitalizing the national economy. In the new narrative—which is not to be mistaken for reality—as Canadian firms maximize shareholder value they improve their reputation in the international investment community, decreasing the cost of borrowing abroad in a virtuous circle of capital self-expansion.

As we have seen, one of the factors driving these reforms has been the intensified competition that recent globalization has unleashed. Corporate governance is *rooted in new pressures for directors to perform well*. According to Gillies, what lies behind the heightened interest in corporate governance is business's dismal performance throughout the 1990s, combined with high-profile corporate failures and the almost universal adoption of free trade. 'If a firm is not managed as effectively as the world's best firms in its industry, it will not survive' (Gillies, 1997:P8). Cronyism and recruitment via the old boys' network become liabilities. 'Companies must have, and are seeking and getting, the highest quality of directors . . . with experience, independence and time to devote to monitoring the activities of the organization and to assist in setting strategies for the future' (1997:P8).

If heightened competition and the associated risk of financial collapse have been salient structural factors, the most immediate causal agent driving the reform movement has been the rise of active institutional shareholders with an interest in corporate strategy. In 1996 institutional investors held 40 per cent of the equity of publicly traded Canadian companies. According to one account, they were 'no longer willing to wait for others to act' ('Shareholder values', 1996).[30] Traditionally, institutional investors exercised allocative power through their *exit* option, rather than strategic power in the form of *voice*. If unsatisfied with a firm's performance, an institutional investor would simply redeploy its capital elsewhere (Glasberg, 1989). But as share capital has become concentrated under the control of a few major institutional investors, the exit option has become less viable. Selling large blocks of equity onto the open market pushes the price down before the sale is complete. As major institutional investors become locked in to their equity stakes, they turn to the exercise of voice as a profit-maximization strategy, exerting 'steadily increasing pressure' on corporate managers to improve performance and 'working to improve the governance of firms in which they invest' (Morck and Nakamura, 1995:497).[31]

IMPLICATIONS FOR ELITE SOCIAL ORGANIZATION

The new corporate governance regime has important implications for the Canadian corporate network, the most obvious of which has been a reduction in the size of corporate directorates. A progress report on adoption of TSE guidelines, after five years, based on responses from 635 CEOs, found that although only one-fifth of boards met 'occasionally' without management present, two-thirds had either a chair independent of management or an independent lead director, and 77 per cent had a majority of directors unrelated to management. Significantly, the report praised companies for cutting board size down to a more manageable level, leading TSE senior vice-president John Carson to exclaim that the new guidelines 'have helped change the landscape of corporate governance' (McQueen and Kuitenbrouwer, 1999:C5).

The trends toward decreased board size and increased complements of outside, 'unrelated' directors help account for the sparser interpersonal network we have found in the late 1990s, the decreased presence of non-presidential insiders, and the increased presence of retired corporate capitalists serving as well-connected outside directors. And if extensive cross-directorships render a board 'unable to do more than rubber stamp CEO decisions' (Noakes, 1997:20), the renewed emphasis on active stewardship has deterred members of the elite from 'collecting' directorships. One report from 1996 observes that the number of outside directorships considered appropriate for a CEO has come down dramatically, to a maximum of only three or four ('Hard target . . .', 1996). Moreover, the overriding concern for shareholder value has led companies like the Royal Bank to require that directors buy a substantial number of shares 'to more closely align the interest of the directors with the company'.[32] No longer trophies, directorships now represent heavy commitments in terms of work and even investment. These pressures have contributed to the decrease in the number of multiple directorships held by members of the elite, weakening the old boys' network.

The reforms have particularly reduced the capacity of big banks to serve as central meeting points for core members of the elite. As they implemented the TSE guidelines in the post-1994 environment, bank boards shrank.[33] Facing the same performance pressures as industrial corporations, banks responded by adopting the leaner-meaner governance framework championed by Matthew Barrett. Banks remain relatively central to the network, but reduced board size and sparser interlocking by leading directors have decreased the size and density of the corporate elite's core, and de-centralized the network as a whole.

Finally, the meritocratic aspect of governance reform helps account for the enhanced presence of women and non-British ethnic groups at the upper levels of corporate power and the diminished importance of clubs in the life of the elite. The elite has become less monocultural and less petrified, less a fixture of socially exclusive corporate boards and private clubs, and more diverse in composition, even if its ethnic and gender profile still contrasts sharply with that of the Canadian population in general.

Conclusions

The changes we have traced in elite social organization and corporate culture have developed in a dialectical relationship of structure and agency. Changes in structure—in the composition of the elite and the density of its social relations—have been guided by a conscious program of moral reform, undertaken in a context of increasing competition, financial deregulation, and growing power on the part of institutional investors. The impetus behind this restructuring is elite agency responding to broad politico-economic developments. The desire to create the conditions for effective capital accumulation has interacted with concerns about legitimation arising from financial scandals and panics (which, incidentally, have shown no sign of abating in the new century). Indeed, corporate governance movements in Canada, the US, and elsewhere have failed to stabilize the juggernaut of corporate capitalism—whose American variant has careened from scandal to financial panic and back again. But if in the heartland of 'shareholder value' the fruits of a capitalism driven by corporate share prices have been massive fraud and the bankruptcy of major corporations like Enron and Worldcom,[34] in Canada the corporate governance movement was nevertheless a significant factor in bringing certain organizational changes to the corporate elite. By the late 1990s we find changes in two important areas:

- A corporate elite whose composition no longer reflected the exclusivity, in terms of ethnicity and gender, typical of the traditional oligarchy. The new corporate elite, though still Eurocentric, was more multicultural and less patriarchal. Educational credentials were more significant than exclusive club memberships, and there was a greater complement of advisors from academic and other fields of expert knowledge.
- A weakening of the interpersonal network that knits leading corporate directors into a business community. Reflecting the slimming-down of directorates (especially bank boards) and the reduction in directorships per director, this weakening made the network's core less of a densely-woven old boys' network. A looser, less centralized network, less representative of corporate insiders, may support new cultural practices of open communication among directors in the pursuit of maximum shareholder value.

In short, a shift has taken place *within the corporate elite*, from oligarchy to democracy. But this shift should not be mistaken for a democratization of economic relations. As we have seen, the reform project has not opened corporate governance to popular-democratic participation. In the representative democracy of corporate capital, one share gets one vote, and non-shareholders are excluded from the electorate. Corporate-governance discourse makes only symbolic concessions to vaguely defined 'stakeholders' such as workers and communities. Yet beyond their impact in tilting priorities in the direction of 'shareholder value', the reforms may have contributed to a new structure of corporate hegemony—a more porous elite social organization, admitting of greater possibilities not only for the ruling class's reach into civil society, but for civil society's reach into the ruling class, and thus for more effective business leadership.

Chapter 3

Strategic Control and Intercorporate Enterprises

In tracing the fate of the old boys' network and the emergence of a governance reform initiative, the preceding chapter shed some light on recent structural and cultural transformations in the Canadian corporate elite. But crucial elements of the elite's class power remain unprobed. The power of corporate directors is ultimately grounded not in their networks and social closure but in their control of capital (Sweezy, 1972; Niosi, 1978). The *hegemonic* power that accrues to a cohesive corporate elite—even one stocked with professionalized directors, executives, and advisors, and suggestive of a meritocratic and multicultural symbolic order—is rooted in economic power. As I emphasized in Chapter 1, that power takes three specific forms: operational, strategic, and allocative. This chapter and the next will focus successively on the structuring of strategic and allocative power within the corporate elite.

John Scott (1997)—to whom I am indebted for the distinction between strategic, operational, and allocative forms of economic power in advanced capitalism—has provided an incisive and comprehensive analysis of the literature on corporate ownership and control that has accumulated since Berle and Means's path-breaking study of 1932, which argued that in large corporations there is a trend, over time, towards dispersal of shares and a 'separation of ownership and control'. This thesis has never had much relevance beyond the US and perhaps Britain (La Porta, Lopez-De-Silanes and Shleifer Andrei, 1999; Morck, Strangeland and Yeung, 2000), since they are the only countries with substantial numbers of large corporations whose voting shares are sufficiently dispersed that no one shareholding interest is able to control the legally mandated election of directors at the firm's annual general meeting. Nevertheless, Berle and Means can be credited with stimulating a longstanding research program into the forms of strategic control over large corporations. The distinctions between various kinds of companies—those under the absolute (or semi-absolute) control of a single owner, those controlled by a major shareholder owning a majority of shares, those controlled by a shareholder owning a minority of shares sufficiently large to enable strategic control, and those with no identifiable controlling owner—have guided many empirical studies into matters as varied as society-wide class structure and micro-economic business performance.

What is clear, seven decades on, is that the corporate form of organization has turned out to be a structure of economic power in which most owners of corporate shares are passive investors, wielding no influence whatsoever over corporate strategy. The strategic power to direct the corporations that dominate advanced capitalism is highly centralized in three identifiable kinds of agents: major shareholders, top-level salaried managers, and financiers. But as Scott notes,

> shareholders, financiers, and executive managers are ... analytical categories, and they do not necessarily refer to separate and distinct individuals. The financiers who provide loan capital, for example, may also be large shareholders, and major shareholders may be members of the executive hierarchy (1997:40).

Far from the 'decomposition of class' that sociologists like Bell (1961) and Dahrendorf (1959) predicted would be a consequence of the dispersal of corporate shares, 'the corporate form ... creates the conditions under which various groups may struggle for the social power of command' (Scott, 1997:41). The provisional results of these ongoing struggles over the control of capital are discernible on the boards of major corporations. A firm dominated by a single shareholding family will typically have a small board populated by family members and their lieutenants. A company lacking any one dominant shareholder will typically have a more complex *constellation of interests* represented on the board, which may include various financial institutions and institutional investors whose combined share ownership would be large enough to give them minority control, but who lack the required unity. Scott makes a persuasive case that, at least in the US and Britain, the trend in the largest corporations has been towards control by constellations of interests woven together through networks of intercorporate shareholding, financial dependence, and loosely structured directorate interlocks (1997:47–50, 123). He describes this pattern as a transition from *personal* to *impersonal* forms of ownership and control, resulting in 'an impersonal system of finance capital' in which 'the principal owners of company shares are other companies and financial intermediaries' (1997:15, 16).

The situation is different in Canada, however, and indeed in the rest of the world. Canada—unlike the US—is well known to have had high levels of concentrated shareholding, as have the Japanese and continental European economies (Carroll and Lewis, 1991; Buckley, 1997). Porter's tabulation in *The Vertical Mosaic* (1965:591–5) shows, as of 1960, a dearth of large Canadian corporations lacking clear proprietary controlling interest. Various studies since Porter (Niosi, 1978; Dhinga, 1983; Antoniou and Rowley, 1989; Morck, Strangeland and Yeung, 1998) have repeatedly found that 'the Canadian corporate network is characterized by the large degree of majority or strong minority control, and by the incorporation of many firms within larger corporate groups' (Burgess, 2002:249), whether the controlling interest be a family or another corporation. Other studies have traced the corporate empires through which capitalists such as E.P. Taylor, Paul Desmarais, and Edward and Peter Bronfman have wielded strategic power over multiple companies through pyramided intercorporate ownership (Park and Park, 1973; Newman, 1975; Francis,

1986). Each corporate empire can be analyzed as an *enterprise group*—a set of firms under common strategic control, whose members are typically linked via interlocking directorates and intercorporate ownership. One of the central questions for this chapter is whether enterprise groups, which dominated the Canadian economy from the 1950s and well into the 1980s, were still dominant as the twentieth century drew to a close.

THE CHANGING ACCUMULATION BASE

Corporate groups need to be placed within the broader context of the corporate elite's *accumulation base*. As the leading segment of the capitalist class, any corporate elite depends on the practices of capital accumulation that sustain its members' claims to economic power. In each case, the specific accumulation base is itself the cumulative product of a succession of political-economic practices and relations (Carroll, 1982; Carroll and Alexander, 1999). In Canadian studies, the nature of the corporate elite's accumulation base has been the subject of considerable debate, reflecting differing conceptions both of Canadian capitalism and of the Canadian capitalist class. A pivotal issue has been the role of foreign-based centres of strategic control in structuring corporate power within Canada. With Robert Brym (1989), we can trace out two opposed positions: those of the 'nationalists' and the 'internationalists'. Inspired by Kari Levitt's *Silent Surrender* (1970), Tom Naylor's (1972) influential left-nationalist narrative cast Canada as a 'rich dependency' whose economy has been marked by *dependent relations* between domestic and foreign-controlled capital. According to Naylor, the dominance of commercial interests has led to underdevelopment and compradorization. The reluctance of the dominant elite of commercial capitalists to fund local industry resulted in a pattern of weak 'industrialisation from without', as leading Canadian business interests aligned themselves in a dependent manner with American corporations and their Canadian branch plants. Wallace Clement's (1975; 1977) studies of corporate elites and corporate interlocking in the 1970s attempted to establish a systematic empirical basis for these claims.

The alternative, 'internationalist' viewpoint has emphasized the similarities between Canada and other advanced capitalist economies of comparable size. These similarities include Canada's sustained domestic control of most large-scale corporate assets throughout the era of American global hegemony, the nationally focused character of its corporate network, and the growth in recent decades of Canadian-controlled foreign investment flowing into a wide range of countries (Moore and Wells, 1975; Carroll, 1986; Burgess, 2002).

In this chapter and the following one, one of our concerns will be to assess these contrasting scenarios against evidence from the last quarter of the twentieth century. Our starting point is the relation between corporate ownership and control. In the next chapter we will explore the inter-relations of industrial sector, corporate 'nationality', and transnational reach—issues that bear directly on the corporate elite's position in global capitalism.

Corporate Ownership and Control

A rudimentary issue in the analysis of corporate ownership and control is the extent to which the shares of large corporations are either dispersed among many shareholders or concentrated under the control of one agent. Reports in the Canadian business press note a recent dispersal of shareholding, which McQueen has described as a 'democratizing trend [that] offers shareholders a greater chance to cause change' in corporate strategy and management (1999:D4). Among our Top 250s we find some corroborative evidence (see Table 3.1). But even in 1996 fewer than one-fifth of Top 250 firms were without an identifiable controlling shareholder. After nearly a century of purported 'managerial revolution', the number of Canadian companies in which such a revolution could actually be identified was minuscule, particularly if we recall (1) the tenacity of personal and family control in the mid-sized and smaller firms that make up most of the private sector and (2) the tendency for large corporations whose shares are widely held to be controlled by a constellation of interests (Scott, 1997).

What Table 3.1 does not show, for the majority of companies controlled by one or another identifiable interest, is the *type of owner* in control of a given firm. This issue is complicated by the extensive practice in Canada of intercorporate ownership. Any firm owned by another company is *ultimately* controlled by the major shareholder—if any—at the top end of a chain of intercorporate ownership. For instance, in 1976 the Weston family directly controlled George Weston Ltd but they *ultimately* controlled British Columbia Packers through George Weston Ltd's 83 per cent interest in the latter. Since both direct and ultimate control are relevant features of the corporate power structure, Table 3.2 includes both. In 1996 as in 1976, most companies were still directly under the control of another corporation, although this form of ownership did decrease somewhat.

In 1976, half of all companies that were *not* directly controlled by another corporation were personally controlled in 1976; by 1996 this figure had fallen to a third. However, the number of firms under *direct* corporate control but under ultimate *personal* control doubled. Overall, then, ultimate personal control actually increased to 30.7 per cent. Thus capital was *not* in fact depersonalized: wealthy capitalist families and individuals simply made greater use of intercorporate ownership as a means of wielding strategic control. Most strikingly, by 1996 the group of com-

TABLE 3.1
Dispersion and Concentration of Share Ownership in the Top 250 (%)

Share ownership	1976	1996
Dispersed	12.8	19.0
Minority control (10–49%)	25.3	27.1
Majority control (50–79%)	23.7	17.8
Semi-absolute control (80%+)	38.1	36.0
Total	100.0	100.0

TABLE 3.2
Direct and Ultimate Owners of Top 250 Corporations (%)

Type of owner	1976			1996		
	No corporate owner	Owned by another corporation	All firms: ultimate control	No corporate owner	Owned by another corporation	All firms: ultimate control
Personal	50.5	12.5	27.8	32.3	29.2	30.7
State	14.6	1.3	6.7	14.7	2.3	8.6
Constellation of interests	27.2	7.2	16.1	23.6	6.2	21.8
Institutional investors	1.9			14.2		
Non-proprietary	5.8	0.7	2.7	15.0	3.8	9.3
Foreign corporate		78.3	46.7	—	58.5	29.6
Total	100.0	100.0	100.0	100.0	100.0	100.0
N	103	152	255	127	130	257

panies controlled by Edward and Peter Bronfman and their associates, through the investment companies Edper and Brascan, constituted a substantial block of corporate capital, accounting for 10 of the 38 firms controlled directly by corporations but ultimately by persons.

Also of interest is the increasing importance of state control suggested by Table 3.2. As McBride (2001) has shown, one of the priorities of neoliberal policy in the 1980s and 1990s was the privatization of state assets. McBride (2001:86–7) lists ten federal and nine provincial Crown corporations that were privatized between 1986 and 1996. It is curious, therefore, that the proportion of Top 250 companies ultimately controlled by one or another state actually increased modestly, pointing up the continuing active role of the state in various aspects of capital accumulation. Of course, several companies under state control in 1976 were privatized (e.g., Canadian Cellulose, Air Canada, the CNR, and Alberta Government Telephones), but other state-owned enterprises effectively took their places among the largest companies, as governments turned to gambling as a fund-raising activity (Loto-Quebec); commercialized activities that had previously been carried out within government departments (Canada Post); or, in case of Saskatchewan's purchase of control of Crown Life and removal of its head office to Regina, continued to pursue development strategies premised on state control of capital.

Of course, any categorization scheme provides only a glimpse of the deeper reality of corporate power. For instance, the Bank of Canada is still formally owned by the government of Canada, but the shift to monetarist policy in the 1980s and 1990s meant that the central bank became less an instrument of state policy and more a creature of the international investment community.[1] Similarly, the fact that by the late 1990s the post office had become one of the country's dominant corporations hardly marks an aggrandizement of the state's economic power. Instead it signals the neoliberalization of public services, as state bodies internalize commercial principles focusing on market flexibility and global competitiveness (Shields and Evans, 1998:81). What these examples do show is that the transition to neoliberalism has not meant a simple withdrawal of the state from the world of corporate business. Later in this chapter we explore, as one aspect of that engagement, the set of board-level relations between state-owned corporations and corporations directly controlled by the capitalist class.

Table 3.2 also registers a dramatic increase in large companies controlled ultimately by neither capitalists nor states but by 'non-proprietary' interests, such as workers and members (as in cooperatives and credit unions) and policy holders (as in life-insurance mutuals). Because in these organizations voting rights are democratically shared out among members (or policy-holders) such companies are legally immune to strategic control by a dominant owning interest. Over the two decades, there was not only a net increase in this category, but a shift in its composition. In 1976 six of the seven firms were life-insurance mutuals,[2] and although their ownership structures precluded strategic control by a dominant shareholder, these companies were well-ensconced in the corporate power structure.[3] By 1996 only five life insurers numbered among the 24 companies that were ultimately controlled in non-proprietary ways.[4] Most of the others were credit unions and similar financial institutions (numbering eight), agricultural cooperatives (eight), and firms in which employees collectively held the largest blocks of shares (three).[5]

Perhaps the two most significant tendencies in Table 3.2 have to do with ultimate control by foreign-based corporations,[6] which declined dramatically, and ultimate control by constellations of interest, which increased moderately. The decline in foreign-controlled companies is what lies behind the overall shift away from intercorporate ownership as a predominant form of direct control. Among domestically controlled companies there was actually an *increase* in direct corporate control (from 33 to 54 firms).[7] What accounts for the increase in ultimate control by constellations of interests is the expansion of institutional investment as a distinct form of direct control.[8]

In 1976, with one exception—the Caisse de Dépôt et Placement du Québec ('the Caisse'), which held minority positions in M. Loeb (26 per cent), Norcen (14 per cent), and Provigo (25 per cent) but was not represented on any of those boards—the shareholdings of institutional investors were not effectively concentrated but spread across wide portfolios.[9] By 1996 institutional investors had amassed minority holdings in 18 Top firms that otherwise had no major shareholders. These we have classified as directly controlled by institutional investors. However, since institutional investors have not generally exerted active strategic control over the firms in which they take positions, we have classified the same 18 as ultimately controlled by constellations of interests (which obviously include the institutional investors). It is this expansion of concentrated institutional holdings that accounts for the overall increase in the proportion of companies ultimately controlled by constellations of interest. In effect, the increased concentration of capital in the hands of

TABLE 3.3
Ultimate Strategic Control of Top Corporations, Percentage by Industry

Ultimate strategic control	resources	manufacturing	utilities	Sector financial	investment	trade	other	Total
1976								
Personal	14.3	23.3		36.0	57.1	44.1	60.0	27.8
Constellation of interests	14.3	12.5	38.9	26.0		8.8		16.1
Foreign corporate	66.7	61.7	27.8	14.0	14.3	47.1	40.0	46.7
State	4.8	2.5	33.3	10.0	28.6			6.7
Non-proprietary				14.0				2.7
Total	100.0	100.0	100.0	100.0	100.0	100.0	100.0	100.0
1996								
Personal	30.8	36.9	18.8	16.0	62.5	33.3	50.0	30.7
Constellation of interests	30.8	19.4	50.0	14.0	12.5	10.0	12.5	21.8
Foreign corporate	11.5	38.8	3.1	32.0	12.5	46.7	12.5	29.6
State	7.7		28.1	12.0	12.5	6.7	25.0	8.6
Non-proprietary	19.2	4.9		26.0		3.3		9.3
Total	100.0	100.0	100.0	100.0	100.0	100.0	100.0	100.0

institutional investors has transformed the controlling constellations of some of Canadian's largest corporations. Firms like BCE, Inco, Stelco, and Domtext, whose shares in 1976 were widely held, had major and sometimes multiple institutional shareholders by 1997.[10] As we noted in Chapter 2, the rise of institutional investors has intensified pressure for shareholder value—a key norm in the emerging corporate-governance framework.

These shifts in strategic control were to some extent industry-specific (Table 3.3). In 1976, large resource-based firms were predominantly controlled by foreign-based corporations exerting majority or semi-absolute control. In resources, the massive shift away from concentrated share ownership reflected increased domestic control by persons and constellations of interest. Similar, though less pronounced, shifts took place in the other industrial sectors, so that by 1996 major shareholders—all but two of them resident in Canada[11]—controlled 32.3 per cent of all large industrial corporations (up from 19.5 per cent in 1976), while control by foreign-based corporations had been halved.

Yet among financial institutions the opposite pattern prevailed as foreign corporate control became more prevalent. Remarkably, by 1996 only seven financial institutions (six of them chartered banks, legally prevented from having major shareholders) had widely dispersed shares—although, as we have seen, another five life insurers continued to be structured as mutuals. The latter would become ordinary joint-stock companies by the early 2000s, but the increased presence of credit unions seemed an enduring reality. As for investment companies, the Caisse continued as a vehicle for both managing money and strengthening the Quebec economy—a dual mandate unique in North America.[12] The other state-controlled investment company, Canada Development Corporation, met its demise in 1987 as federal economic strategy traded industrial policy for neoliberalism (McBride, 2001).

Strategic Control and Network Centrality

The shifting patterns of strategic control in the corporate elite's accumulation base tell us something about transitions in the structure of corporate power. The rise of institutional investors meant an increase in control through complex constellations of interests, while foreign corporate control expanded in the financial sector and contracted in the industrial sector. These shifts in the accumulation base may have implications for the shape and form of the corporate network. In an earlier study of Australia and Canada, Malcolm Alexander and I (1999) found that forms of strategic control can influence the extent to which corporate boards interlock. In both countries, state-controlled and foreign-controlled corporations tended to interlock less with other large corporations than did corporations controlled by persons or constellations of interests, and companies under private control were particularly detached from the corporate network. There are good reasons why these kinds of firms might be structurally marginal. State-controlled firms have been identified more with public mandates than with private accumulation (at least until the recent era of commercialization). Hence their boards may be detached from the business community. Subsidiaries of foreign corporations have often tended to operate simply as local branches of TNCs, with management integrated into the larger transnational organization. Privately owned companies have no public 'float' of shares and thus no institutional investors or other corporate investors with equity interest. The greater presence of state control, foreign control, and private corporate ownership in Australia lent an 'introverted' character to many Australian boards. As a result, Australia's network was much sparser than Canada's (Carroll and Alexander, 1999).

A simple measure of network centrality for corporations is the number of other corporations with which a given firm shares one or more director—the *degree* of interlocking. This indicates a company's participation in the network, but it does not tell us much about the nature of that participation. To provide more detail, degree can be calculated for different types of directorate interlocking, including 'thick' ties carried by multiple directors (see Figure 3.1). Over the two decades the mean degree of all kinds of interlocks fell, but the greatest proportionate drop was for *primary interlocks*—ties involving the sharing of a director who is also an officer of one or both of the interlocked firms. The reasons for this particularly steep decline in primary interlocking, which have much to do with the governance reforms we examined in Chapter 2, will be explored in Chapter 4. What Figure 3.1 provides is a baseline against which to judge the trends in degree of interlocking for each category of ultimate control, shown in Figure 3.2.

Here we find substantial differences in the extent to which corporations under different forms of ultimate strategic control participate in the network, and also

FIGURE 3.1
Degree of Interlocking by Type of Tie

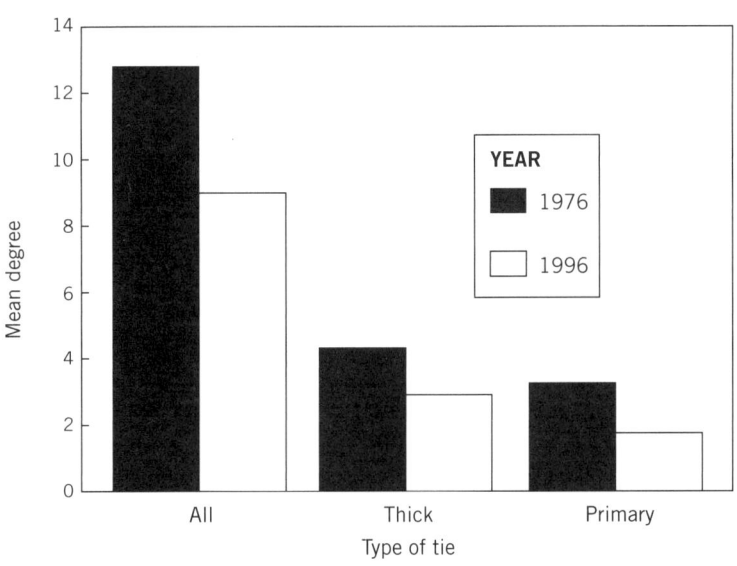

FIGURE 3.2
Degree of 'Primary' and 'All' Interlocking, Firms Grouped by Ultimate Strategic Control

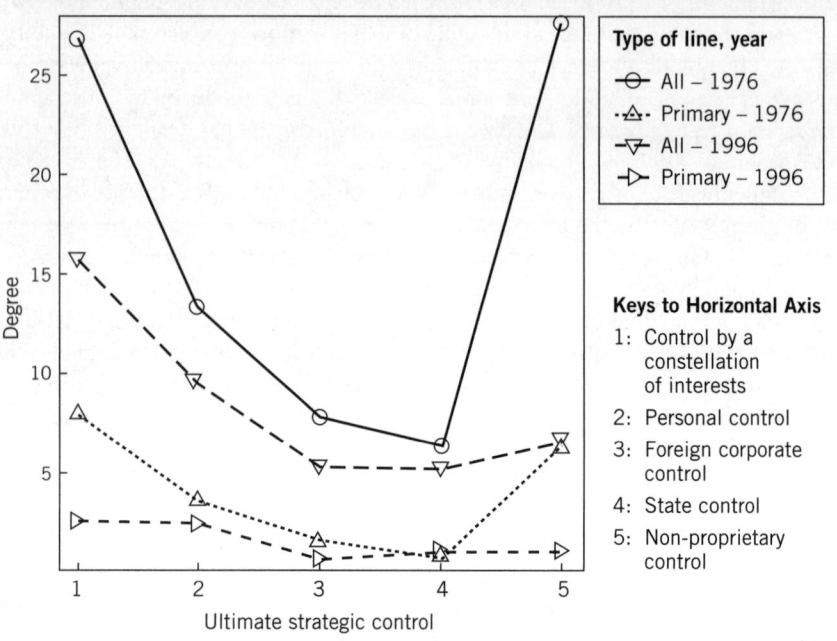

Lines show means.

some shifting over time within the categories. Consistent with other research (Scott, 1997), we find that companies ultimately controlled by constellations of interest were most central. But by 1996 their relative centrality had been greatly reduced, particularly in the case of primary interlocks. Companies ultimately controlled by persons were not particularly central in the network. However, relative to other firms they became more involved in primary interlocking as wealthy families and individuals made greater use of intercorporate control, which is often accompanied by the exchange of inside directors. Corporations under state or foreign corporate control participated decidedly less in the network, although for the former there was the same sort of temporal shift. In 1976, state-controlled firms were marginal in the network of primary interlocks. Their (relatively few) directorate-level ties to other Top 250 companies were carried by outside directors. By 1996, state-controlled firms showed an increase in primary interlocking, even if their mean degree of primary interlocks was barely two-thirds the value of the overall mean. Finally, firms ultimately controlled by non-proprietary interests showed the greatest shift of all, as overall participation in the network plummeted—whether we consider all directors or only interlocked officers.

These trends are based on mean differences, allowing us to calculate, through analysis of variance, the proportion of total variance in degree of interlocking that is accounted for by the group differences charted in Figure 3.2 ('eta-squared').

We find that for all interlocks the proportion of variance explained fell from .317 to .205, while for officer interlocks variance explained dropped from .256 to .163. Network centrality now had less to do with distinct types of ultimate controlling interests.[13]

Mean differences in ultimate control, however, give us only a first cut at the analysis. For three of the categories of control, the distribution of degree of interlocking in 1996 was highly skewed: a relative handful of corporations elevated the mean for the entire category. Among companies under non-proprietary control, closer inspection revealed a vast difference in centrality between the five life-insurance mutuals and other firms. In 1996, the five life insurers were interlocked on average with 20 Top 250 firms. Two industrial corporations in which employees owned the largest blocks of share capital were also relatively central in the corporate network,[14] yet the other 17 companies—16 of them credit unions and agricultural cooperatives—were decidedly on the margins of the corporate network, averaging only 0.65 interlocks. The reduced centrality of non-proprietary firms is explained by the shifting composition of this category. By 1996 what had been a small group of leading financial institutions, heavily linked into the corporate network, was a broader category in which a few highly interlocked life insurers coexisted with firms whose more democratic organization and accountability to members rendered them entirely marginal to the corporate elite.

THE NETWORK OF 'STATE CAPITAL'

Companies under state control also showed great diversity in centrality. Of 22 firms in our 1996 Top 250 under ultimate state control, six shared no directors with any Top company; two were interlocked with only one board; and four were interlocked with only two boards. However, the ten most interlocked state-controlled companies, listed in Table 3.4, were each linked to four or more Top corporations, and the most central of them, Petro-Canada, shared directors with 23 dominant corporations.

TABLE 3.4
Degree of Interlocking for 22 State-Controlled Corporations, 1996

Name	Degree	Name	Degree
Petro-Canada	23	Manitoba Hydro	2
Provigo Inc.	19	EPCOR Utilities	2
Ontario Hydro	17	British Columbia Hydro	2
Bank of Canada	10	Canadian Commercial Corp.	1
Gaz Metropolitain	9	Canada Post Corp.	1
Crown Life Insurance	7	Loto-Quebec	0
Export Development Corp.	7	Liquor Control Board of Ontario	0
New Brunswick Power	5	Canada Mortgage and Housing Corp.	0
Caisse de dépôt et placement	5	Canadian Wheat Board	0
Hydro-Québec	4	Farm Credit Corp.	0
Business Development Bank	2	Saskatchewan Power Corp.	0

To the extent that 'state capital' has a presence in the structure of the Canadian capitalist class today, Table 3.4 provides clues to its character. Looking at this list, we can see traces of the role that provincial governments have played in developing and delivering electrical power to industry and households; we can also see traces of the concerns that regional states (particularly Quebec) have had with fostering local accumulation (preferably under local control); the federal industrial strategy of the 1970s, which included the creation of Petro-Canada; and the continuing activity of the federal state in promoting Canadian exports and managing the national currency.

The network of interlocks around these 10 firms, the core of which is shown in Figure 3.3, takes in 71 corporations ultimately controlled by capitalist interests. However, all but 16 of the latter were interlocked with only one of the ten relatively central state-controlled companies. The firms whose boards interlocked with two or more of the central 10 state-controlled companies are shown in the figure. Within this relatively small subset, the prominence of Petro-Canada, Provigo, the Bank of Canada, and Gaz Metropolitain is striking. In contrast, only four of Ontario Hydro's 17 total interlocks link it to the companies that make up this core network of state-controlled and capitalist-controlled corporations—suggesting that in 1996 Ontario Hydro's board was more integrated into the wider business community than were other state-controlled companies. Much the same could be said of Petro-Canada, whose status as state-controlled in 1996 was equivocal.[15] Among the capitalist-controlled companies, the Manulife board appears as most closely interwoven with the boards of state-controlled companies.

Overall, corporations controlled by the state had weak ties in the Canadian corporate elite, carried by single outside directors. Only three of 26 ties linking state-controlled firms with capitalist-controlled firms were 'thick', compared with roughly one in three ties among the Top 250 as a whole. The notable exception to this pattern appears to be Quebec, which also had the most elaborate state–capitalist assemblage in 1996, organized around the Caisse, whose vice-president sat on the boards of three corporations in which the investment company held a sizeable interest.[16] In Quebec the continued state commitment to economic nation-building has furnished the political basis for an exceptional configuration of state–corporate relations. Certain state-controlled firms are well connected in the larger network, and these tend to be companies in which the state is the largest minority shareholder. PetroCanada, Provigo, and Gaz Metropolitain are effectively public-private partnerships arising out of industrial policies promoting local control of corporate capital. As such, they have substantial share floats and potentially extensive institutional shareholders. The evidence suggests that as the neoliberal policy paradigm has been consolidated such corporations have been especially good candidates for privatization, given convivial circumstances and political will. In the mid-1970s private-sector capitalists formed a majority on the boards of Air Canada and the CNR (Niosi, 1981:115). By the late 1990s both companies had been effectively privatized. Much the same can be said of Ontario Hydro, which was well ensconced in the larger corporate network in 1996, the year before the move began towards privatization. In each of these cases, board-level ties into the corporate elite may have facilitated privatization.

FIGURE 3.3
Interlocks Involving the Leading State-Controlled Corporations, 1996

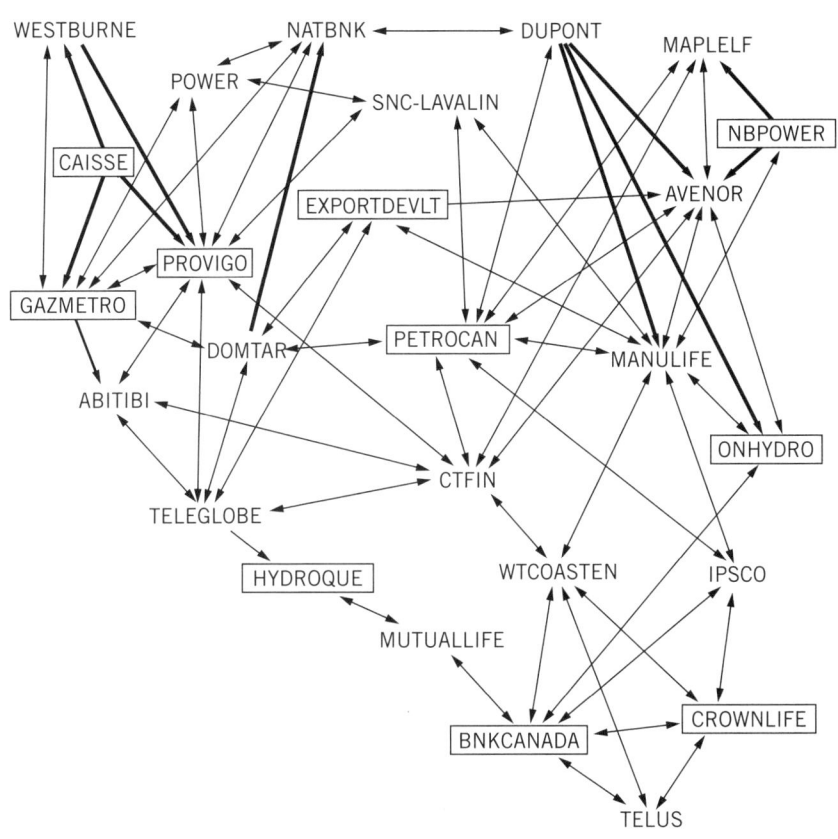

State-controlled firms are shown in boxes; primary interlocks are shown in bold, with arrows emanating from the executive's main firm.

PRIVATE OWNERSHIP AND NETWORK MARGINALITY

A final connection between accumulation base and levels of interlocking lies in the extent to which a firm's share capital has been either entirely concentrated in the hands of a single owning interest, or dispersed among many owners. As I discovered in my comparative research with Malcolm Alexander, when a corporation is privately owned by a single (personal or corporate) interest, its board tends to be introverted: composed of that interest and its representatives, including internal management. This situation is at the opposite pole from control by a constellation of interests, each of which might be represented on the board, with a resulting tendency towards extensive interlocking with other corporate boards. In Canada, most large privately owned firms have been subsidiaries of foreign corporations, mainly

American. In 1976, of 75 privately owned companies in our Top 250, 60 were foreign-controlled; in 1996, the fraction was 58 of 82. In both years, these companies were particularly detached from the corporate network, as Table 3.5 shows, but so were privately held companies under ultimate personal or state control. Conversely, companies with some public float of share capital tended to participate in the corporate network, regardless of the locus of ultimate control. The relative success of domestic capitalists in reclaiming control of the large-scale corporate sector is evident in the table's second row. In 1976, 59 of the Top 257 companies were ultimately controlled by foreign-based corporations, yet not wholly owned by their parents. Unlike their wholly owned counterparts, these firms participated heavily in the Canadian network. In 1996, foreign-controlled companies with a substantial Canadian share float continued to be tightly woven into the corporate network, but the number of firms in this category had dropped dramatically. The marginality of the foreign-controlled firms stems mainly from private ownership. In the classic transnational organizational design discussed by Hill (2000), wholly owned subsidiaries are mere operational divisions of their parents. Their boards of directors are not centres of strategic power: corporate strategy is devised at the head office. In its implications for a firm's network centrality, such a situation is as far removed as one can get from control by a constellation of interests.

To summarize the changes to the elite's accumulation base, four points merit emphasis:

1. Wealthy families and individuals have not receded as important agents in the exercise of strategic power. There has not been a pervasive 'depersonalization' of capital, although there was by 1996 a tendency for personal control to be exerted indirectly, through intercorporate ownership.
2. Despite the transition to a neoliberal policy paradigm, the state has continued to play an active role in corporate business, through large state-controlled corporations that actually became more numerous across the two decades, although they were less implicated in industrial strategy, except in Quebec.

TABLE 3.5

Degree of Interlocking: Privately Held Versus Publicly Traded Corporations

Ultimate control	Concentration of shares	1976			1996		
		All interlocks	Primary interlocks	N	All interlocks	Primary interlocks	N
Foreign corporate	Privately held	3.77	0.57	60	3.07	0.50	58
	Publicly traded	11.92	2.61	59	12.67	1.49	18
Personal	Privately held	5.00	0.00	1	3.50	2.17	6
	Publicly traded	13.29	3.60	70	9.84	2.49	73
State	Privately held	6.57	0.86	14	3.22	1.00	18
	Publicly traded	5.33	0.00	3	14.50	1.75	4

3. As the number of large corporations controlled by foreign interests fell, the numbers controlled by constellations of interests or members and employees rose, indicating a certain shift in the agencies of strategic control within the corporate elite. This shift casts doubt on notions that the elite's accumulation base is being transferred into the hands of foreign capitalists, but it also points to transitions in strategic control, particularly as share capital has accumulated in the hands of institutional investors.
4. Companies controlled by constellations of interests have been the heaviest participants in corporate interlocking; firms that are closely held by singular interests tend to have introverted boards and marginal network positions. To a large degree, the marginality of foreign-controlled corporations stems from a trend for the diminishing complement of large foreign-controlled firms to be wholly owned by their transnational parents.

INTERCORPORATE OWNERSHIP AND ENTERPRISE GROUPS

The marginality of wholly owned foreign subsidiaries is only one structural implication of intercorporate ownership. A good number of domestically controlled firms—33 in 1976 and 57 in 1996—have also been controlled by other corporations. Foreign corporate ownership is typically a straightforward relation between parent and subsidiary, but the ownership linkages among domestically controlled companies form a more complex network.

To map the intercorporate ownership network in both years of this study, we relied on the systematic data collected since the 1960s under the Corporations and Labour Unions Returns Act, which have been published on an irregular basis in Statistics Canada's *Intercorporate Ownership*.[17] If we consider as a (directed) tie any situation in which a Top 250 firm owned 5 per cent or more of the shares of another Top 250 firm, the intercorporate ownership network included 54 firms in 1976 and 71 in 1996. However, in both years a great many intercorporate ownership ties occurred as simple dyads: parent-affiliate relations that did not extend to any other major corporations.[18] Dyads accounted for 14 companies in 1976 and 22 companies in 1996, and for certain dyads the chain of ownership extended ultimately to foreign corporations.[19] However, most companies participating in intercorporate ownership were controlled domestically, supporting Burgess's (2002) claim that intercorporate ownership among the largest corporations has helped to maintain an accumulation base for Canadian capitalist interests.

Although in each year there were a few intercorporate triads,[20] we are interested in the larger groupings of corporations connected into complexes of potentially unified strategic control. Figures 3.4 and 3.5 show these groupings, with arrows indicating the direction of the investment and line thickness indicating the proportion of a company's shares held by a given corporate owner. In 1976 the intercorporate ownership network was clearly segmented into five groupings, which took in 34 companies. Although three companies had multiple corporate owners, the predominant pattern was for intercorporate ownership to be hierarchically configured in unified

FIGURE 3.4
Intercorporate Ownership Among Top Canadian Corporations, 1976

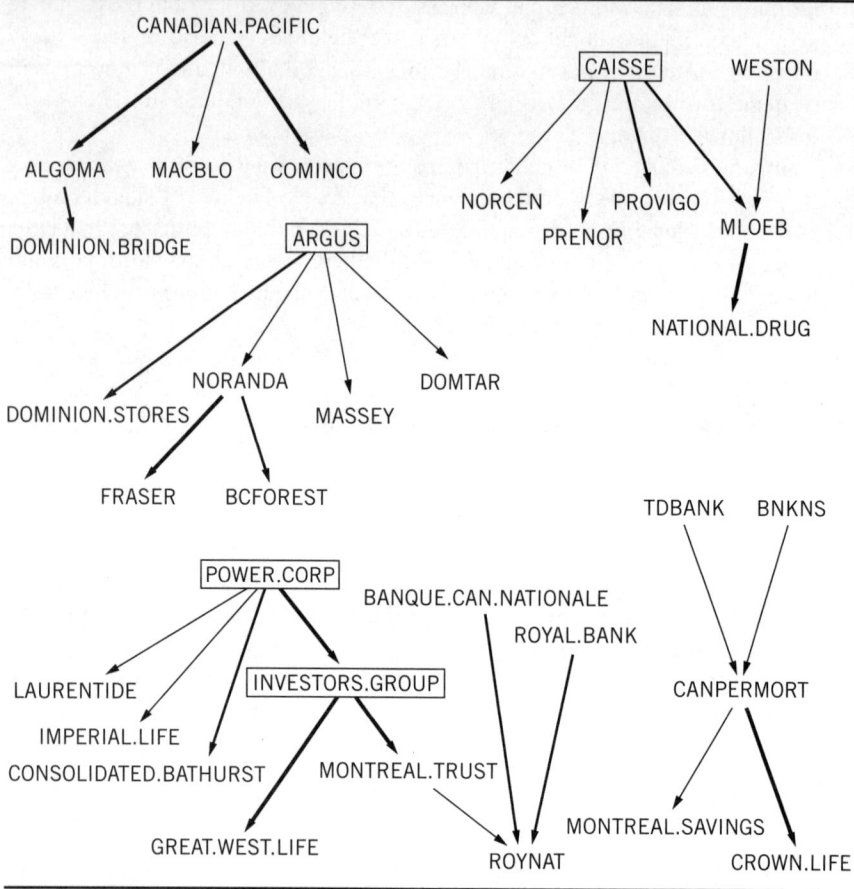

Lines show holdings of more than five per cent. Line thickness indicates proportion of shares held. Investment companies are in boxes.

structures of strategic command. In three groups, the vehicle for strategic control was an investment company whose entire asset base consisted of the shares of other corporations. Two investment companies, Argus Corp. and Power Corp., were under personal control. The third, the Caisse, was owned by the government of Quebec. The other major centre of strategic control was Canadian Pacific, then at the apex of the diversification strategy from which it would retreat in the 1980s and 1990s. Four chartered banks were minority owners of other leading financial institutions in 1976, indicating a certain interweaving of capital across the 'pillars' of the financial system.

By 1996 intercorporate ownership ties pulled 37 dominant firms into one connected component of the network. Although the network had become less segmented, it was still clustered around several companies whose assets consisted of blocks of share capital. When we compare the networks, several changes stand out.

FIGURE 3.5
Intercorporate Ownership Among Top Canadian Corporations, 1996

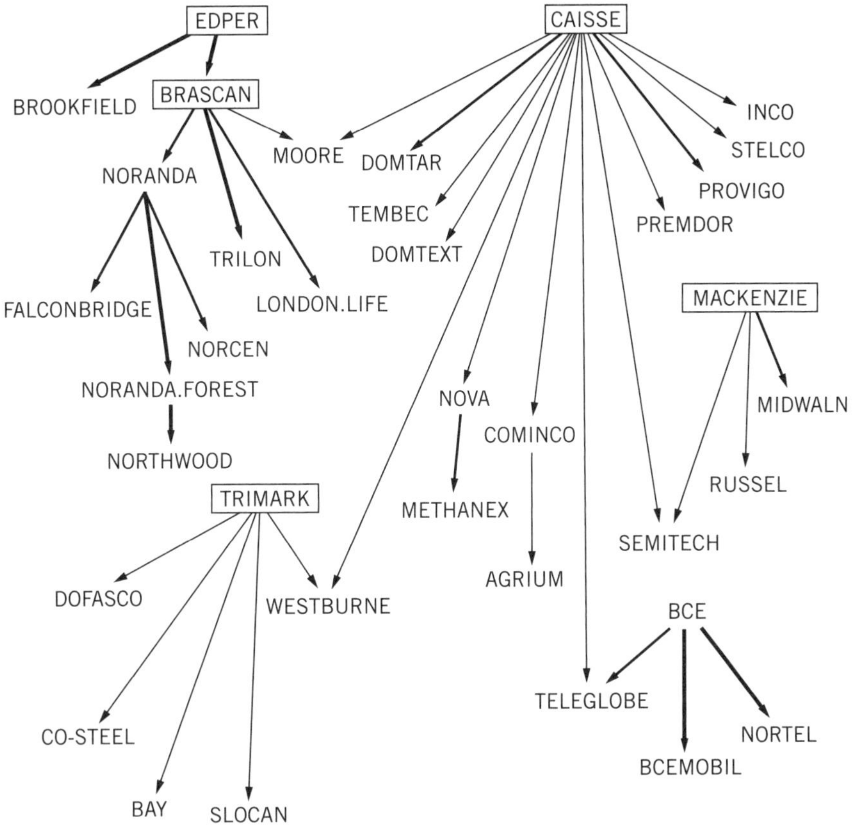

Lines show holdings of more than five per cent. Line thickness indicates proportion of shares held. Investment companies are in boxes.

In 1976 Brascan had just recently been reconfigured as a full-fledged investment company. By the mid-1990s, under the control of Peter and Edward Bronfman, it had become the major personally controlled centre of strategic corporate power. The Caisse had also expanded its portfolio of major corporate investments. Two mutual funds—Trimark Investment Management and Mackenzie Financial—had emerged as key loci of share capital.

The line thicknesses make it clear that the groups headed by Edper/Brascan and BCE were bona fide *enterprise groups*. Their affiliates were under at least significant minority and typically majority control, and intercorporate ownership was reinforced by extensive directorate interlocking, creating a structure of unified strategic command (see Berkowitz and Fitzgerald, 1995). For instance, The Edper Group Ltd, owners of 47 per cent of Brascan's voting shares, shared four directors with

Brascan, and Brascan in turn shared five directors with Noranda and London Life, four with Trilon Financial and Norcen Energy, three with Noranda Forest, two with Falconbridge and Brookfield Properties, and one with Northwood—all firms controlled within the group. However, Brascan's 10 per cent interest in Moore Corp., a passive investment, was not matched by any interlocks. Similarly, BCE shared three directors with its majority-owned affiliates Norcen and BCE Mobility, although it had only a single outside director in common with Teleglobe, in which BCE held a non-controlling 22 per cent interest.

In contrast, most of the ownership ties stemming from the three institutional investors either were secondary to the principal shareholder's stake or amounted to less than 10 per cent of the affiliate's share capital. Seven of the Caisse's 13 strategic blocks made up less than 10 per cent of the affiliate's share capital. Only in the cases of Provigo (the Caisse had a hefty 37 per cent stake and two shared directors) and Westburne Inc. (the Caisse held 13 per cent of shares and had one interlock) was there any relation between the Caisse's investments and its directorate interlocks. Between Trimark and Mackenzie, only the latter appeared to exercise active strategic control over one of its affiliates, the investment bank Midland Walran. Mackenzie owned one fifth of Midland Walran's shares and shared with it two directors (including Alexander Christ, Mackenzie's president). Most strikingly, Trimark—which had substantial stakes in five major Canadian corporations—was entirely detached from the network of interlocks. These institutional investors generally refrained from exerting actual strategic control; however, their weak ownership ties drew the configuration into a single component.

Comparing the two sociograms, we may note the decline of some of the enterprise groups that dominated the Canadian economy in the 1960s and 1970s. The Power Corp. group shrank to three financial firms (Power Corporation of Canada, Power Financial Corp. and Great-West Lifeco). The Canadian Pacific group, once at the very centre of corporate power (Carroll, 1986), was reduced by 1996 to the parent and two affiliates, Pan Canadian Petroleum and Laidlaw.[21] The Argus group disappeared completely in the wake of Conrad Black's 1978 *coup d'état* (Newman, 1982:101–44).[22] The imperious and impetuous Black, after gaining control of most of Canada's newspaper market but failing in his attempt to establish *The National Post* as a hard-line neoliberal alternative to the soft-line neoliberal *Globe and Mail*, cashed in his chips in 2001 and joined the British peerage. With this, Black breathed new life into a Canadian tradition that goes back to Max Aitken (Lord Beaverbrook) and Roy Thomson (Lord Thomson of Fleet). He also demonstrated that not all members of Canada's corporate elite have followed the modernizing route that leads away from ancient oligarchic institutions.

The Network of Thick Interpersonal Ties

These metamorphoses of leading enterprise groups have had ramifications on the structure of the corporate elite. In enterprise groups corporate power is wielded not only at the *organizational* level, through intercorporate ownership, but at the *interpersonal* level, as small groups of associated capitalists and their advisors collaborate in directing strategically aligned firms. It is the latter that interests us at this point. What associated capitalists create is a network of *thick interpersonal ties*—'thick' in that two (or more) persons direct two, three, four, or more of the same corporations, and thus meet each other on a whole set of boards.

Thick ties tend to follow lines of intercorporate strategic control (Carroll, 1984; Carroll and Lewis, 1991; Berkowitz and Fitzgerald, 1995), and for good reason. Often, the interest controlling a company has several representatives on the board. If intercorporate ownership figures in the control relation, there will likely be a 'thick' interlock between the parent and the affiliate. In this aspect of network structure we again find a loosening of relations. In 1976, 304 of the 489 members of the elite had one or more thick interpersonal ties to another member of the elite, and the mean number of thick ties per director was 2.33. By 1996 the number of elite directors with one or more thick interpersonal ties had dropped to 238; the mean was 1.85. In both years, the distribution of thick interpersonal ties was quite skewed: a considerable share of all thick ties in the interpersonal network was claimed by relatively few directors—an elite within the elite. In 1976, 28 individuals each sat on multiple boards with nine or more members of the corporate elite. Although they made up only 5.7 per cent of the elite, they accounted for 28.4 per cent of all thick interpersonal ties. Two decades later, 27 individuals (6.3 per cent of the entire elite) each had seven or more thick interpersonal ties, accounting for 31.0 per cent of all such ties. Figures 3.6 and 3.7 show the corporate affiliations of these most central directors in the network of thick ties.[23] In these two-mode sociograms, both corporations and directors appear as points (with the firms enclosed in ovals). Each person's directorship with a corporation is a directed line, leading from person to firm. Where a person serves as an executive or chair of the board, the line connecting that person to the corporation is bolded. This extended mode of presentation is useful in discerning groups of corporations and directors that may cluster around the strategic control of capital, whether through personal share ownership or intercorporate ownership.

In 1976 the key participants in thick ties carried a larger and more integrated formation. The 28 persons and 43 companies were linked via 145 directorships into a single component. The 1996 network included only 25 firms, with which 27 directors had 99 directorships. Moreover, it was segmented into two distinct components, a dominant component of 23 firms and 19 directors and a smaller component of two communications firms controlled by Edward Rogers and his associates. Indeed, without the multifarious corporate affiliations of Peter Lougheed the dominant component would break apart. Beyond these general architectural comparisons, it is clear that the elite members who participate extensively in thick interpersonal ties are the key players in enterprise groups built around intercorporate ownership. In 1976, the Argus and Power groups are visible in the sociogram's top left and right corners, even without the boundaries we have sketched to delineate each group. These groups display a relatively introverted pattern of interlocking, with executive responsibilities clearly assigned among the associated capitalists. In the Power group, Paul Desmarais, controlling shareholder of Power Corp., has executive responsibilities with Power and with Imperial Life. Desmarais's lieu-

FIGURE 3.6

Individuals and Corporations in the Network of Thick Interpersonal Ties, 1976

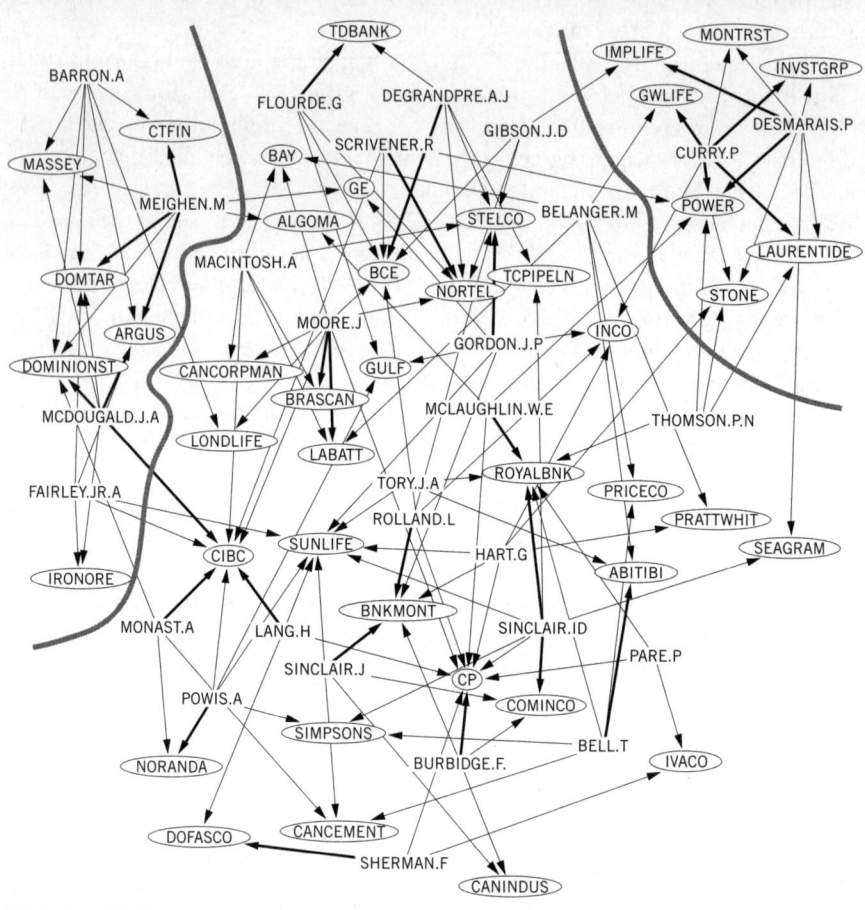

Thick lines indicate that the person held an executive position in the firm. Corporations are in ovals.

tenant, Peter Curry, is the salaried president of Power Corp. but also fulfils executive functions in Laurentide Financial, Investor's Group, and Great-West Life. Investment banker Peter N. Thomson, the major shareholder of Power prior to Desmarais's ascension, continues to sit as an outside director of three companies in the group. The same scenario describes the Argus group, two of whose principals (John A. McDougald and Max Meighen) hold inside positions in Argus and one other group firm.[24]

It is striking how completely separated from each other the two main enterprise groups were in 1976. However, each was linked into a vast *middle ground*, where the pattern of group-affiliations did not show the same tendency towards introversion. For the Argus group, the most important portal to the larger network was the group's bank, the Canadian Imperial Bank of Commerce. Two Argus directors

FIGURE 3.7
Individuals and Corporations in the Network of Thick Interpersonal Ties, 1996

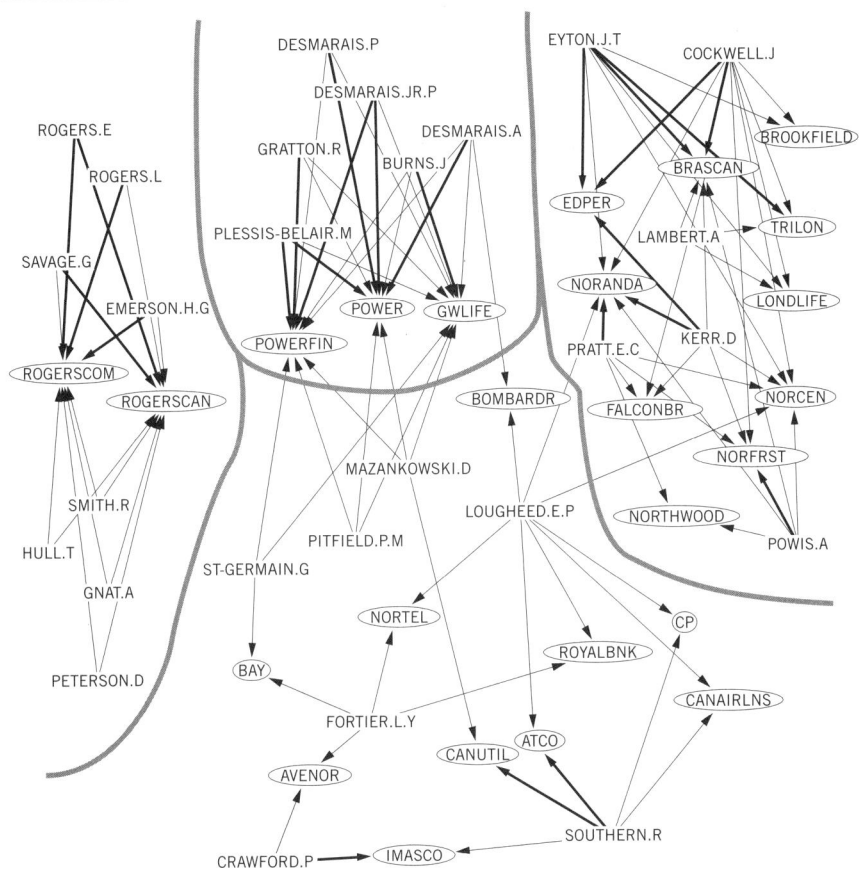

Thick lines indicate that the person held an executive position in the firm. Corporations are in ovals.

shown in Figure 3.6 sat on the CIBC board, and McDougald was a CIBC vice-president. For the Power group, the Royal Bank of Canada was the key portal. Not only did Peter Thomson sit on the Royal's board, but Royal Chair W. Earle McLaughlin was a Power Corp. director.

What is it, however, that makes the centre hold? In both years, certain intercorporate financial relationships play a role. In 1976 the ownership relation between Canadian Pacific (CP) and Cominco was functionally managed by having CP Chair and CEO Ian Sinclair also sit on the Cominco board as a vice-president, while CP president Frederick Burbidge also sat on the Cominco board. A similar arrangement can be seen between Jean de Grandpré and Robert Scrivener in the management of Bell Canada and its subsidiary, Northern Telecom. John H. Moore, who in 1976 had a somewhat tenuous claim to strategic control of Brascan and thus to

Brascan's affiliate, Hudson's Bay Company, also was the principal shareholder in John Labatt, and these relations of strategic control are evident in Moore's inside directorships with Brascan and Labatt and his outside directorship with the Bay. Moore's associate Alexander MacIntosh helped cement these relations as an outside director of all three firms; he also sat with Moore on the board of Brascan's banker, the CIBC. Although these small clusters of intercorporate strategic control lacked the scope of the two major groups, they nevertheless seemed to be organized along the same lines, and in each case strong ties to one or more of the chartered banks were part of the package. Ian Sinclair was not only the lead capitalist in the Canadian Pacific group; he was also a Royal Bank vice-president. Bell Chair Jean de Grandpré was a Toronto-Dominion Bank director, and TD vice-president Gérard Plourde directed both Bell and Northern Telecom. We thus find a confluence of directorships reinforcing both strategic control in industrially centred enterprise groups and credit relations between the groups and the banks. This sort of capital integration is precisely what is meant by 'finance capital'.

But capital relations such as these do not entirely explain the integrated character of the 1976 network. At that time the middle ground included a number of companies whose shares were so dispersed that we consider them to have been controlled by constellations of interests. In fact, the most well-connected companies—the ones that really integrated the middle ground by furnishing meeting points for five or more of the 28 central directors—were companies controlled by constellations of interests: three banks, a life-insurance mutual (Sun), and such industrial corporations as Canadian Pacific, Stelco, and Bell. It was this form of strategic control that generated a plethora of integrative ties. As the controlling constellations overlapped, so did the social circles of leading corporations. A final integrative aspect of the 1976 network is found in the several corporate advisors who served as outside directors to numerous firms, thereby pulling otherwise separate capitalist interests together, however weakly. For instance, Marcel Bélanger, a chartered accountant who served on several royal commissions and the like in the 1970s, directed companies in the Power and Brascan groups.[25]

By 1996 (Figure 3.7) organic intellectuals were if anything playing an even more salient mediating role. The network's core was leaner, sparser, and structured more exclusively on the basis of strategic control, with organic intellectuals playing the main mediating role. Much of the middle ground had collapsed with the disappearance of bankers as central participants, the weakened presence of industrial and financial companies controlled by constellations of interest, and the reassertion of concentrated share ownership as the preeminent criterion of corporate power. Indeed, were it not for the outside directorships of such retired politicians as Peter Lougheed and Donald Mazankowski, the network would be even more fractured.[26]

The configuration in Figure 3.7 is almost entirely organized around three groups—the familiar Brascan and Power cliques plus a corporate dyad detached from the rest of the network and involving the major shareholders of Rogers Communications and its majority-owned subsidiary Rogers Cantel (namely, Edward and Loretta Rogers), their salaried executives G. Savage and H.G. Emerson, and four outside directors of the two firms, including former Ontario premier David Peterson. Detached from other capitalist interests, the Rogers group manifests an intense introversion. Its eight members all have thick ties to each other by virtue of serving on both boards, but their thin ties to other members of the elite are few and far between.

Across the two decades, as corporate directors trimmed their multiple affiliations they eliminated many of the outside directorships that had stitched the interpersonal network into a densely connected core. In 1976, centrality in the network of thick interpersonal ties implied centrality in the overall interpersonal network. In fact, 23 of the 28 directors charted in Figure 3.6 were among the 50 corporate directors with the most interpersonal contacts, and 19 of them were positioned in the core of the interpersonal network that we analyzed in Chapter 2. By 1996 only 11 of the 27 directors in Figure 3.7 numbered among the 50 most central individuals in terms of all interpersonal contacts, and only six of them belonged to the interpersonal network's core. With a few exceptions such as Peter Lougheed, Purdy Crawford, and Yves Fortier, those at the centre of the old boys' network—or its remnants—and those at the centre of the network of thick interpersonal ties (the country's key associated capitalists) were different people. There was, by 1996, rather less of a structural basis within the elite for integration across the competing interests embedded, as enterprise groups, in the network of strategic control.

GLOBALIZATION AND CANADIAN ENTERPRISE GROUPS: BRASCAN AND POWER CORP.

The Brascan group actually has a storied history in Canadian investment imperialism (Park and Park, 1973:135–49); however, Brascan lost its dominant position in the Brazilian utilities sector in 1978, with the nationalization of its main subsidiary. Brascan thus became a cash-rich takeover target. In 1979 Peter and Edward Bronfman gained control and began to restructure the group into an extensive financial-industrial empire (Carroll and Lewis, 1991:501), which in 1996 retained minor interests in Brazil but mainly controlled Canada-based corporations (see Figure 3.5). In 1996, while in transition from family control under Peter Bronfman (who died in December 1996) to collective control under 'Partners Inc.' (a consortium of 25 Brascan insiders including Jack Cockwell and David Kerr), the group included the six people and 10 companies shown in Figure 3.7, plus other partners like Robert Harding and Timothy Price (both executives of Edper). All of the companies were under unified strategic control, thanks to a complex hierarchical pattern of share-ownership that centred on Brascan and included financial institutions like Trilon and London Life and industrial corporations like Norcen, Noranda, and Falconbridge, leading ultimately back to Peter Bronfman and his partners. The fact that Noranda and Falconbridge were leading Canada-based transnational corporations underlines the international reach of the Brascan group. Although most group companies were domestically oriented in 1996, these capital relations involved the group in a circuitry of transnational investment. From a focus on Brazil the group had grown to become a centre of transnational finance capital, radiating from Toronto but connecting ultimately to locations as disparate as Mexico, Germany,

Australia, Japan (all sites of Noranda subsidiaries), the Caribbean, Chile, Argentina, Britain, France, Belgium, and South Africa (all sites of Falconbridge subsidiaries). Trevor Eyton, who in 1996 continued as chair, expressed the global orientation of Brascan's top management: 'Within our group of companies, the rule is that if we are not within the top 25 percent in the industry on a world basis, measured in world currencies, then we shouldn't be in the business, and we get out of it' (Newman, 1998:140).

Power Corporation also shows a transnational trajectory, although its initial accumulation base was in the Canadian hydroelectric sector. In the 1970s and 1980s, under Paul Desmarais's control, the group was restructured to include a diversified financial holding company—Power Financial—as well as industrial corporations with primarily domestic operations. By 1996 the Power group was still controlled by Paul Desmarais, with the active participation of sons Paul Jr and André. As depicted in Figure 3.7, the group was composed of nine persons and just three companies, all three of them holding purely financial assets. One of the striking changes from the mid-seventies, for both Brascan and Power Corp., was the appearance of major financial institutions as core group companies. The previous pattern, as with the Argus empire of 1976, was for the holding company to own strategic blocs of shares in several operating companies. By the late 1990s, however, the two leading corporate empires were structured in good part around emergent financial conglomerates that had become vehicles both for strategic control of firms and for financial intermediation—with a commensurate weakening of ties between corporate empires and the chartered banks.

Indeed, in 1996, there seemed little left in Canada of the Power group beyond its control of paper assets. Viewed as a Canadian fixture, the group appeared to be in an advanced state of atrophy, having been whittled down organizationally to a clump of financial assets with little connection to the world of production and having lost many of its thin ties to the Canadian corporate elite. But behind the lower Canadian profile of the Power group, and of Paul Desmarais Sr, lies a successful campaign of transnational expansion. As early as the 1970s Desmarais made a foray into Europe to invest $20 million in the French investment banking group Paribas. When the Mitterand government announced plans to nationalize Paribas in 1981, Desmarais joined other wealthy investors in a capital strike that transferred their shares to Pargessa, a Swiss-based holding company. In 1989 Desmarais, in partnership with Belgian capitalist Albert Frère, gained majority control of Pargessa. With Frère, Desmarais next launched the Groupe Bruxelles Lambert, which he has described as 'kind of the Power Corp. of Belgium' (quoted in Newman, 1998:175). Desmarais's block in Pargessa is held through Power Financial, and catapults the Power group into a major transnational empire:

> Desmarais and Frère are now in on most of the big deals in Europe and strategically control premier industrial and media holdings. They also have minority partnerships and personal and business relationships with some of the continent's key financial players. In the past year alone, Desmarais and Frère forged a partnership with Germany's family-controlled Bertelsmann media conglomerate to form the

largest multimedia company in Europe ... and bought the biggest single equity stake in a new French utilities player with the second largest market capitalization in France. That's on top of already controlling Banque Bruxelles Lambert, one of Belgium's largest banks with $155 billion in assets, and Petrofina, the Belgian-based giant oil and gas and petrochemicals group that had sales of $25 billion in 1996 (Leger, 1997:6).

Paul Desmarais's lower profile in the Canadian corporate power structure mainly reflects his status as a full-fledged *transnational finance capitalist* with extensive ties into the European corporate elite. These ties give the Desmarais family a share in the control of some of Europe's largest industrial and financial companies. The examples of Brascan and the Desmarais empire demonstrate that major investment companies, each controlling diversified financial institutions, have functioned as vehicles of transnationalization for finance capitalists based in Canada. But with the Desmarais group, full-fledged transnationalization raises other questions as well. By shifting the group's centre of gravity, does such transnationalization weaken the 'national identity' that might have been ascribed to the capital under Paul Desmarais's control? In what sense is the Desmarais group 'Canadian' and in what sense is it European, or perhaps global? And what are the implications of such transnationalization for the structural integrity of the Canadian corporate elite? Does a global shift in investments mean a weakening of the domestic network, as corporate capitalists take to a transnational playing field? We will begin to explore these and related questions in the next chapter.

Chapter 4

Disorganized Capitalism and Transnational Finance Capital

In their study of the transformations that marked the closing decades of the twentieth century, Scott Lash and John Urry (1987) depict 'the end of organized capitalism'—the uneven transition in the world system's centre from a capitalism structured around national corporate economies regulated by national states to a more globalized capitalism less subject to effective national regulation. Of course, the end of *nationally* organized capitalism is only one side of a *reorganization* of capital into a more globalized field of accumulation, within which the policies of particular states are disciplined both by the threat of capital strikes and by neoliberal norms enforced by institutions such as the World Trade Organization (Teeple, 2000; Robinson and Harris, 2000). Lash and Urry (1987:5–6) describe an array of structural and cultural changes under the rubric of this transition,[1] some of which, in Scott's (1997) view, furnish a basis for linking recent globalization to the 'loosening' of national corporate networks.

This chapter explores the implications of capitalist disorganization for a Canadian corporate network whose centre of gravity has been eminently 'national': What happens to such a network as capital becomes transnationalized and national capitalism becomes 'disorganized'? On the other hand, the fate of Canada's corporate network might hold implications for the thesis of disorganized capitalism: To what extent, we might ask, could the persistence within the Canadian network of features of organized capitalism place qualifications on 'capitalist disorganization' as a supposedly general process?

FINANCE CAPITAL AND CAPITALIST DISORGANIZATION

As a first step toward answering these questions, we should sketch the structure of corporate capital in the era of organized capitalism. Rudolph Hilferding (1981 [1910]) originally offered the concept of organized capitalism as part of his theory of monopoly capital. For Hilferding, writing in early-twentieth century Europe,

> modern capitalism at the national level had succeeded—as a result of the economic dominance of the large corporations and the banks and the changed relation of the

bourgeoisie to the state, which had led to extensive state intervention in the economy—in introducing a degree of planning into economic life (Bottomore, 1981:14).

Although state regulation was integral to organized capitalism, so was the organization of national economies around structures of *finance capital*—which Hilferding defined as the fusion of concentrated industrial and bank capital. Hilferding saw the advent of finance capital as allowing a greater degree of planning by both capitalists and states, but he has often been misinterpreted as postulating a theory of bank control of industry (e.g., Niosi, 1978). Actually, 'finance capital' posits a double-sided integration of capital, within which the *issue of finance* becomes critical. With the concentration and centralization of capital in large corporations whose financing needs were often extensive, industrialists were obliged to enter into the monetary sphere themselves, just as financial institutions came into closer contact with client manufacturers and traders. Increasingly, large businesses were likely to be involved in both 'financial' and 'non-financial' activities, and to enter into 'various forms of organization, alignment and co-operation' (Scott, 1997:104). Financial–industrial alignments came to structure much of the field of corporate power within each capitalist nation-state (Fennema and Schijf, 1979). The same alignments provided economic platforms for international expansion, particularly in the form of foreign investment (Bukharin, 1973).

Certainly there have been adequate grounds for applying this thesis to Canada. A raft of research has documented the formation of a corporate network in Canada, organized around dense ties between financial institutions and industrial corporations, beginning in the early twentieth century (Piedalue, 1976; Richardson, 1982) and continuing into the 1980s (Carroll, Fox, and Ornstein, 1982; Carroll, 1986; Carroll, 1991). This financial-industrial bloc was shaped both by practices and institutions of organized capitalism—including the interventionist state—and by Canada's specific location in the world economy. Banks and other major financial institutions were centrally positioned, not only because of their strategic importance as allocators of credit to industry, but because the state mandated a *pillarization* of financial services, with chartered banks, investment dealers, life insurers, and trust companies each authorized to engage in a specified kind of financial intermediation (Neufeld, 1972; Babad and Mulroney, 1993). Although companies *within* each pillar were generally prohibited from interlocking, an extremely dense network of directorate interlocking grew up *across pillars*, resulting in a highly integrated financial sector (Richardson, 1988). In the years following the Second World War a dramatic increase in American control fuelled concerns that a comprador element was displacing indigenous entrepreneurship (Levitt, 1970) and that Canada's financial sector was aligned more with expansionist American industry than with domestic industrial capital (Clement, 1975; Clement, 1977). Subsequent research, however, showed that subsidiaries of foreign TNCs have marginal positions in the corporate network (a finding replicated in the preceding chapter), and that Canadian network was integrated primarily along a financial-industrial axis of domestically controlled firms (Carroll, Fox, and Ornstein, 1982; Carroll, 1986).

Yet if by 1980 the corporate network in Canada could be fairly described as one of the most integrated of all the advanced capitalist formations (Ornstein, 1989), later developments might tell a different story. In our analysis of changes to the Canadian corporate network between the mid-1970s and mid-1980s, Scott Lewis and I provided some evidence of a decline in the centrality of banks and bankers and noted that the banks were busy expanding internationally (Carroll and Lewis, 1991). This seemed to support Andreff's thesis of the rise of 'transnational finance capital', according to which capital relations cross national borders under the aegis of transnational corporations and banks in a way that renders industrial and financial capital *organically linked in their internationalization*' (Andreff, 1984:66). Among the possible scenarios as to how *transnational* finance capital might appear in the Canadian corporate network, two stand out:

1. Industrial and financial capital emanating from Canada might be organically linked in its internationalization. This would imply that, as in Switzerland (Rusterholz, 1985), the corporate network becomes re-centred around an expanding sector of Canadian-based TNCs, both industrial and financial, with minimal 'disorganization' of the network.
2. The 'national' financial–industrial axis might become *disarticulated*, as Lash and Urry (Lash and Urry, 1987:5) themselves suggest. Global expansion of TNCs has meant a growing disarticulation of national economies, first evident on the periphery (Amin, 1974). As economies of the centre also become disarticulated 'the networks of capital, commercial and personal relations become less dense and more fragmented, and the various fragments become tied into close capital, commercial and personal relations with global enterprises based outside their boundaries' (Scott, 1997:152; Davis and Mizruchi, 1999). On this account, we would expect the Canadian network to become less integrated—'disorganized'. In particular, the transnationalized segment would become *relatively detached from national capital*.[2]

In appraising these scenarios, the impact of transnational investment on the shape and form of the corporate network is key. However, the supposed 'end of organized capitalism' would also mean a weakening of national economic regulation, which might have its own implications for the network. The same can be said of a third development, which (as we saw earlier) has been intimately linked to neoliberal globalization: reforms to corporate governance altering the practices and composition of corporate boards. This chapter therefore proceeds in three stages:

1. First, in a contextual analysis I describe how these three eventualities brought economic transitions that might be expected to have reshaped the Canadian corporate network.
2. I next consider the impact of these developments on the network, in shifting the *composition* of Top corporations and (in the case of corporate governance reforms) altering the business practices that actually *produce* interlocking directorates.
3. Finally, I bring the first two steps into a network analysis that compares the 1976 and 1996 configurations, highlighting the structural impact of all three developments.

1. Disorganized Capitalism and the Changing Context of Corporate Power

a. Transnationalization

As Dicken (1992:86) points out, 'the transnational corporation is the single most important force in the accelerated development of a global economic system,' transforming both the countries that are home to TNC head offices and the countries that host TNC subsidiaries. Table 4.1 shows the overall composition of foreign direct investment *in and from* Canada between 1970 and 1996, with direct investment referring to capital tied up in actual foreign-controlled enterprises. Foreign direct investment *from* Canada grew at a much faster rate. By 1996 its stock nearly equalled the stock of foreign investment in Canada. The US became a relatively less important *source* of foreign direct investment after 1970 while direct investment controlled beyond the USA and Britain increased. In 1970, Britain and the US—the historical metropoles for Canadian capitalism—accounted for 92 per cent of foreign direct investment. By 1996 they accounted for 76 per cent.

As for Canadian direct investment abroad, the proportion placed in the US expanded in the 1980s but later contracted. In the same period the proportion of all direct investment abroad placed in continental western Europe and Japan grew rapidly. In the 1970s and 1980s, growth of direct investment in non-OECD countries did not keep pace; however, subsequent growth saw nearly one-fifth of all Canadian direct investment abroad located outside the OECD as of 1996. Despite the continuing importance of US–Canada capital relations, the tendency was toward *a more cosmopolitan profile* in sources and destinations of direct investment, matching the general tendency among developed capitalist countries (Dicken, 1992).

TABLE 4.1
Trends in Foreign Investment in and from Canada (Total Stock)

	US	UK	Other EU	Japan	Other OECD	Other	Total %	Total $C	As a % of GDP*
A. Foreign direct investment in Canada									
1970	81	10	6	0	2	1	100	27 B	37.2
1980	78	9	8	1	2	2	100	65 B	24.6
1988	67	14	8	3	4	3	100	114 B	22.7
1996	68	8	13	4	4	4	100	180 B	27.0
B. Canadian direct investment abroad									
1970	54	10	5	1	2	29	100	7 B	9.6
1980	63	11	5	0	5	16	100	28 B	10.6
1988	64	11	7	1	4	14	100	80 B	15.9
1996	54	10	11	2	4	19	100	171 B	25.6

* calculated at basic prices; currency is in constant (1996) dollars.

SOURCE: Statistics Canada, *Canada's International Investment Position, 1926 to 1996*. Catalogue no. 67-202. Ottawa: May 1997, 38, 48; Statistics Canada, *Canadian Economic Observer Historical Statistical Supplement*. Catalogue no. 11-210-XIB. Ottawa: July 2001, Table 1.

As for the *weight* of transnational investment in the national economy, by 1996 transnational direct investment—whether terminating or originating in Canada—exceeded one quarter of GDP.[3] For foreign direct investment in Canada this represented a *net decrease* since the high tide of American penetration in 1970, but for Canadian direct investment abroad it meant *a dramatic increase*, as Canadian capitalists shifted their attention to an expanding field of transnational accumulation (Burgess, 2002).

b. Financial deregulation

If transnational investment constitutes a key economic facet of national capitalist disorganization, deregulation—which often amounts to the privatization of regulatory functions (Sassen, 1999)—has been its political correlate. It is not difficult to see why. Once internationalized, capital 'requires "freedom" from national controls or intervention' (Teeple, 2000:51), and state managers keen to attract new investment adjust their policy frameworks accordingly.[4] Further, as national economies become porous, state intervention becomes less effective, enhancing the appeal for state managers of deregulatory moves, which in turn amplify the disorganizing thrust of the world market.[5] When Canadian state managers adopted a neoliberal framework in the 1980s, they claimed that deregulation would bring market discipline into various economic contexts, ostensibly promoting profitability and international competitiveness. Deregulation was introduced on two broad fronts. To facilitate Canada's insertion in the world economy, the federal government renounced the nationalist industrial strategy of the 1970s—a last attempt to revive the paradigm of organized capitalism—by abolishing controls on foreign direct investment and then adopting the Free Trade agreements of 1989 and 1994 (McBride, 2001). On a sectoral basis, it launched major initiatives to deregulate capital, the most momentous of which targeted the financial sector. With these reforms, the regulated segmentation of financial capital into 'four pillars' was abolished, intensifying competition among financial institutions and permitting Canada's major banks to become universal banks, but also allowing foreign banks greater access to the Canadian market (Bodkin, 1990).

c. Corporate governance reforms

The *corporate governance reforms* discussed in Chapter 2 were the stepchildren of deregulation, and are thus implicated in national capitalist disorganization. In the 1990s, partly in response to financial crises and scandals that developed in the wake of deregulation, corporate business around the world began to embrace a movement for sound corporate governance (Sklair, 2001:152–9). By 1999 the OECD had adopted a set of non-binding corporate governance guidelines, after consultation with its member countries as well as with the World Bank, IMF, and non-member countries. The close connections between good corporate governance and neoliberal globalization are evident in the OECD trend report on this issue:

> Improving corporate governance has emerged as a priority in all OECD Member countries during the past few years. The enhanced accountability, transparency, and

integrity flowing from improved corporate governance practices create value for shareholders and other stakeholders, reduce the cost of capital, and increase a company's competitiveness in the global marketplace.⁶

Consistent with Sassen's (1999) notion of the privatization of regulatory functions, 'the central plank of the corporate governance movement's position was that corporations deserved the right to police themselves' (Sklair, 2001:154).

Our account in Chapter 2 established that in Canada deregulation and heightened competition led financial institutions to pursue more speculative investment strategies, which unravelled during the deep recession of the early 1990s. The adoption by the Toronto Stock Exchange of the Dey task force's recommendations as guidelines for listed companies in 1995 signalled a new regime of responsible corporate governance. The key reforms, summarized on p. 34 above, aimed to make the boards of publicly traded firms more active and effective centres of governance—independent of management, relatively uninfluenced by interests other than shareholders, small enough to function efficiently, and composed of well-oriented, high-performance directors. In encouraging smaller, more effective boards, discouraging the holding of extensive multiple directorships, and shifting the emphasis towards 'unrelated' directors, the reforms fostered a looser network carried more by outside directors than executives.

Moreover, in recomposing boards according to shareholder power the new norms discouraged a longstanding practice of Canadian finance capital: the representation of bankers on the boards of their industrial clients. The new insistence that corporations should maximize shareholder value followed the market-oriented logic of capitalist disorganization and expressed the emerging activism of institutional investors whose control over large proportions of corporate shares now limits their 'exit' options, obliging them to become more proactive vis-à-vis management.⁷

To summarize this contextual analysis, in the increased extent of cosmopolitan transnationalization of direct investment, in the deregulation of the financial sector, and in the emergence of new corporate governance norms we find sources of possible network disorganization that may have operated in step with a globalizing dynamic 'disorganizing' the national economies of world capitalism's centre. The question is whether and how these developments have actually registered within the corporate network.

2. Transnationalization, Deregulation, and Governance Reforms: Network Implications

a. Transnationalization

As we saw in Chapter 3, the kinds of firms that number among the largest concentrations of capital in a given country have a formative relevance to a corporate network. Like the types of strategic control analyzed there, our first two sources of network disorganization operate at one remove from network structure, changing the overall composition of the set of large corporations, and through that, the structure of the network. The key issue is whether transnationalization of investment

TABLE 4.2

Largest Canadian Corporations Cross-Classified by Country of Control and Industrial Sector (%)

1976	Country of control						
Industrial sector	Canada	US	UK	Other European	Asian-Pacific	Other	Total % (N)
Resources	19.0	66.7		9.5		4.8	100.0 (21)
Manufacturing	36.9	47.5	9.8	4.9		.8	100.0 (122)
Utilities	72.2	27.8					100.0 (18)
Financial intermediaries	86.0	12.0		2.0			100.0 (50)
Investment companies	85.7	14.3					100.0 (7)
Trade	55.9	26.5		5.9	11.8		100.0 (34)
Other	60.0		40.0				100.0 (5)
Total	51.8	36.2	5.4	4.3	1.6	.8	100.0 (257)

1996	Country of control						
Industrial sector	Canada	US	UK	Other European	Asian-Pacific	Other	Total % (N)
Resources	92.3	7.7					100.0 (26)
Manufacturing	60.6	25.0	2.9	5.8	4.8	1.0	100.0 (104)
Utilities	96.9	3.1					100.0 (32)
Financial intermediaries	70.0	14.0	4.0	10.0	2.0		100.0 (50)
Investment companies	87.5	12.5					100.0 (8)
Trade	53.3	23.3		3.3	20.0		100.0 (30)
Other	87.5	12.5					100.0 (8)
Total	70.9	17.4	1.9	4.7	4.7	.4	100.0 (258)

and financial deregulation recomposed the group of leading corporations in a way that loosened the national corporate network.

As for the former, when we focus on our Top 250 we find the same trend toward a cosmopolitan cross-penetration of capital as we did for the economy as a whole (see Table 4.2). In 1976 the American presence, although no longer at its post-war peak, was striking: 36 per cent of all top corporations were American-controlled, followed at some distance by interests based in Britain (5 per cent). American interests were particularly evident in resources and manufacturing; Canadian capitalists had their strongest presence in the transportation-communication-utilities and financial sectors—a pattern consistent with Clement's (1977) account of 'continental corporate power'. Very few major corporations were controlled by interests outside the North Atlantic triangle.[8] The pattern of national control still showed traces of North-Atlantic investment and trade circuits reaching back to the nineteenth century.

By 1996 the American presence was diminished but still substantial. Of the 258 major corporations 17 per cent were controlled by American interests, compared with 71 per cent controlled in Canada and 2 per cent controlled in Britain. Canadian capitalists registered their greatest gains in the control of domestic industrial firms in all three of the broad sectors.[9] The other interesting change concerns the national control of financial intermediaries, in which an increased foreign presence was claimed primarily by European interests. Overall, we find a resurgence of Canadian capitalists' control of big industry, a general decline in the American presence, and a shift in the locus of foreign control from the North Atlantic triangle to a somewhat more cosmopolitan pattern. Whereas the number of Anglo-American-controlled firms *dropped* sharply, from 107 to 50, the number of foreign-controlled firms controlled elsewhere *increased* moderately, from 17 to 25—12 in industry, 6 in finance, 7 in trade (6 of them Japanese-controlled). Although the continental-European presence grew slightly, the most evident shift in foreign control had to do with increased control of capital by Asia-Pacific interests.

Considering now the foreign investments *of* large Canadian corporations, Table 4.3 categorizes our Top 250s according to the extent to which they operated subsidiaries in foreign countries ('transnational status') as well as the country in which controlling interest was held ('country of control'). In constructing the former categorization, I followed Niosi's (1985) criterion for defining a Canadian multinational (transnational) corporation—that it have operations in at least five countries (including Canada)—and made two further distinctions.[10] Within the transnational corporate sector, I distinguish between firms with operations in 5–9 countries and those with operations in 10 or more. Within the sub-transnational corporate sector, I distinguish between 'national' firms (no foreign subsidiaries), 'continental' firms (subsidiaries only in the US), and near-transnationals (operations beyond the US but in fewer than five countries).[11]

The table shows a distinctive pattern of transnationalization. In both years, only one-fifth of large corporations was purely 'domestic': based in Canada, controlled by interests in Canada, and without any foreign subsidiaries. In the two intervening decades, however, the proportion of 'national' companies fell while the propor-

TABLE 4.3

Largest Canadian Corporations Cross-Classified by Country of Control and Transnational Status (%)

1976 (N=231)			Country of control				
Transnational status	Canada	US	UK	Other European	Asian-Pacific	Other	Total
National	19.9	28.1	1.3	2.6	1.3	.4	53.7
Continental	6.1	1.3	2.2	.9		.4	10.8
Near-TNC	9.1	7.4	.4	.9			17.7
TNC: 5-9 countries	4.3	2.2	2.2				8.7
TNC: 10+ countries	7.8	1.3					9.1
Total	47.2	40.3	6.1	4.3	1.3	.9	100.0

1996 (N=217)			Country of control				
Transnational status	Canada	US	UK	Other European	Asian-Pacific	Other	Total
National	19.4	13.4	1.8	2.8	3.2		40.6
Continental	12.9	.9		.9		.5	15.2
Near-TNC	15.2	3.2	.5	.5	1.4		20.7
TNC: 5-9 countries	9.7	.9					10.6
TNC: 10+ countries	12.4	.5					12.9
Total	69.6	18.9	2.3	4.1	4.6	.5	100.0

tion of TNCs rose, as did the proportion of firms with purely continental operations. In both years most foreign-controlled companies—themselves subsidiaries of TNC parents—did not engage in extensive foreign direct investment. The changes reviewed earlier in foreign control of large corporations carry two implications here: (1) as the developing continental market rendered branch-plant production for a 'Canadian' market obsolete, many domestically oriented firms controlled in the US disappeared from the Top 250, while (2) there was an increase in the complement of domestically oriented firms controlled in the Asia-Pacific region. In place of the branch-plant subsidiaries, Canadian-controlled companies with exclusively continental investments doubled as a proportion of the sample, indicating a tendency towards North American investment strategies among some major Canadian interests. Most strikingly, in a *transnationalization of domestically controlled corporate capital* the number of TNCs controlled in Canada overtook the number of national companies controlled in Canada. Relatedly, while a good many Canadian-based TNCs and near-TNCs had been controlled in the US (or Britain)—a pattern described by Clement (1977) as 'go-between' investment—by year end 1996 nearly all large corporations with extensive transnational reach were controlled by Canadian capitalists.

Looking more specifically at the composition of the transnational sector, we can distinguish financial institutions from non-financial (hereafter 'industrial') firms. Relatively few financials qualified as TNCs, even in 1996,[12] but what stands out is the presence of all six major chartered banks among the eight TNC financials of that year. The assets of these eight ranked them among the 10 largest financials of 1996. Clearly, only the very largest Canadian financial institutions had embraced full-fledged transnationalization.

Among the non-financial corporations there was considerable shifting over the two decades: only 11 of the 42 TNCs of 1996 were already TNCs in 1976. Six of these longstanding TNCs were among the 11 industrials with the greatest transnational reach in 1996.[13] However, *all five of the 'newcomers'*—firms that had catapulted from non-transnational status in 1976 to the ranks of the 11 most transnational industrials of 1996—were in the high-tech and communications sectors, suggesting that Canadian transnationals had begun to outgrow the label of 'technological imitators' that Niosi (1985:170) ascribed to them in the mid-1980s.[14]

In sum, the recent transnationalization of investment did recompose the Top 250, but in a way that only partly fitted the motif of capitalist disorganization. The resurgence in domestic control of big industry ran against the grain and provided a possible basis for a strengthened national network. But the increasingly cosmopolitan sources and destinations of investment, the increased foreign control in finance, and the increasing transnational reach of domestically controlled corporations and banks were possible bases for a looser network, or a cleavage between transnational and national capital. I will explore these possibilities in section 3 below.

b. Financial deregulation

If transnationalization served to recompose the Top 250, with possible implications for the corporate network, much the same can be said of financial deregulation. Given permission, as of 1987, to own securities dealers, chartered banks were quick to acquire most of the country's major investment banks, after which they absorbed several trust companies, confirming their dominance in the financial sector. In 1976 the six biggest banks claimed 57.5 per cent of the assets of the 50 largest financial institutions. By 1996 they claimed 59.7 per cent. The number of trust companies in our Top 50 dropped in the same period from 10 to 2. The centralization of capital that resulted from deregulation transformed the sector, converting intercorporate network relations into intra-corporate hierarchies. For instance, as banks devoured trust companies, directorate interlocks across the pillars of the financial sector disappeared into incipiently universal banks. The entry of foreign banks—another effect of deregulation—brought a further compositional change. Here the question is whether foreign-controlled banks participated in the Canadian corporate network or were hooked into intra-corporate hierarchies leading back to their parents. By 1996, the end of the 'pillars' also meant more direct competition between banks and life insurers, in place of the long-standing cooperation and coordination across separate spheres of financial intermediation that had been encouraged by the state-mandated division of financial spoils.[15] Concomitantly, a vigorous credit-union movement had come of age, fuelled partly by consumer dissatisfaction with the retail services provided by banks. Owned by their members, credit unions elect directors who typically have no linkages to the corporate elite. Our 1996 Top 50 included six credit unions, compared with none in 1976. All these developments may have led the financial sector—long the integrated centre of Canada's corporate network—to lose some of its coherence after the 1980s. Below, we assess the structural impact of changes to the financial sector, after first exploring the implications of reforms in corporate governance.

c. Corporate governance reforms

The reforms reviewed earlier altered several board practices that in the past actually produced interlocking directorates. Corporations were encouraged to shrink their boards, and directors were encouraged to limit their directorships. These changes promoted a sparser network. In view of the importance placed on outside directors as custodians of shareholder value, we will maintain the distinction introduced in Chapter 3 between two kinds of interlocking directorships. When an *officer* of one company sits on the board of another, (s)he creates a *primary* interlock between the companies: a relation in which that officer can be said to *represent* his or her home company on the board of another company. Research has shown primary interlocks to be particularly stable and not infrequently related to inter-corporate ownership ties between the interlocked companies (Ornstein, 1984): the network of primary interlocks reflects relations of influence, control, and coordination. Conversely, when an outside director of one firm also sits as an outside director of another, (s)he creates a *secondary* interlock, in which case it can be difficult to trace influence, control, or coordination.[16] The network of secondary interlocks or outside directorships is not so much a product of instrumental behaviour in the accumulation process as it is an unintended consequence. In the remainder of this chapter we will explore changes to the corporate network and hence to the structure of finance capital, by distinguishing between these kinds of interlocks and by attending to the three aspects of capital disorganization discussed above.

In Table 4.4 we can see some of the effects of the governance reforms. Over the two decades the mean size of corporate boards decreased by two. *This drop was attributable to the decreased complement of officers on corporate boards.* In 1976 boards averaged five directors who were officers in some dominant firm. By 1996 the average number of such directors was only three. It is these directors who generate primary interlocks through their multiple directorships.

This shift away from 'inside directors' had structural ramifications visible in Table 4.5, which distinguishes between directors who were officers of dominant corporations and those who held only outside directorships in the latter. In 1976, of the

TABLE 4.4
Average Board Size and Composition

	1976	1996
A: Mean N of directors who were officers in some Top 250 firm	5.06	3.13
B: Mean N of directors who were not officers in any Top 250 firm	8.21	8.17

2398 people who were directors of one or more of the largest companies, just over a third were officers of at least one firm. By 1996, there were fewer corporate directors, 2135 in all, of whom only a quarter were officers. In both years, one-fifth of directors held multiple directorships, and most of the network was carried by 'big linkers'—directors of four or more dominant companies. In 1976, nearly three-quarters of all ties in the network were carried by 129 big linkers, of whom 68 were officers in dominant corporations. These 68 made up less than three per cent of all directors but accounted for well over a third of all interlocks—896 in all. In contrast, the 1996 network included only 28 officer-big linkers, who collectively carried nearly 600 fewer interlocks. Thus the net loss of 649 interlocks was attributable largely to a sharp decline in extensive interlocking by corporate officers.

In this way, the corporate governance reforms made not only for smaller boards populated with fewer officers, but for a *network knitted together mostly by outside directors*. The density of primary interlocks fell from 0.01262 to 0.00676, a drop of nearly 50 per cent. The density of secondary interlocks fell less steeply, from 0.0419 to 0.0307.

d. The changing position of banks: disentangling the financial sector

Corporate governance reforms had particularly significant impacts on bank boards. In 1976, the boards of the five major chartered banks were extraordinarily large, and as we saw in Chapter 2, they brought together the core members of the corporate elite. Table 4.6 shows that bank boards were composed of many officer-directors, placing banks at the heart of the network of primary interlocks. By 1996, banks had adopted the new governance norms, slimming their boards and removing most of their own officer-directors.[17] Moreover, with the new emphasis on 'unrelated direc-

TABLE 4.5
Distributions of Directors and of Interlocks Carried

Year	Type of Director	Number of Directorships Held			Total
		1	2–3	4 or more	
A. Distribution of directors					
1976	Non-officer	1269	234	61	1564
	Officer	638	128	68	834
	All directors	1907	362	129	2398
1996	Non-officer	1303	230	54	1587
	Officer	406	114	28	548
	All directors	1709	344	82	2135
B. Distribution of interlocks					
1976	Non-officer	0	372	651	1023
	Officer	0	204	896	1100
	All directors	0	576	1547	2123
1996	Non-officer	0	364	624	988
	Officer	0	182	304	486
	All directors	0	546	928	1474

tors', the few bank officers who remained on bank boards were no longer particularly welcome on the boards of their clients. The impact of all this is evident in the disappearance of such primary ties between the five biggest banks and the Top 200 non-financial operating companies. In 1976 there were 97 outgoing primary ties, each of which took a bank officer onto the board of an industrial firm. In 1996 there were only seven! However, officers of industrial companies continued to serve as bank directors, as the total number of such primary ties declined more gently. And, although the mean degree of primary interlocking plunged, the decline in the degree of secondary interlocks was far less sharp. The Royal Bank's board illustrates the trend. It shrank from 50 to 31, and instead of five RBC officers the 1996 board included only the bank's CEO. The Royal retained just one outgoing primary tie to a non-financial firm, but the smaller board still had 7 incoming primary ties and was directly linked via secondary interlocks to 39 industrials.

Deregulation and centralization of capital within the financial sector also loosened interlocks *among* financial institutions. With the collapse of the state-regulated pillars and the banks' absorption of investment dealers and trust companies, there was a shift from network to hierarchy in the organization of financial capital, resulting in fewer institutional relations among the remaining financial institutions. In conjunction with the governance reforms that removed most officers from bank boards, this change meant less interlocking among financials, especially via their officers. In 1976, officers of the five big banks sat on a total of 26 directorates of

TABLE 4.6

Five Biggest Banks: Board Size, Composition, and Interlocks with the 200 Largest Non-Financial Corporations

Bank	Year	Board size	N of bank officers	Outgoing primary ties	Incoming primary ties	Degree of primary ties	Degree of secondary ties
Royal Bank of Canada	1976	50	5	14	12	25	57
	1996	31	1	1	7	7	39
Canadian Imperial	1976	53	10	32	10	38	45
Bank of Commerce	1996	33	3	1	3	4	41
Bank of Montreal	1976	53	10	27	7	31	53
	1996	28	2	2	3	5	31
Bank of Nova Scotia	1976	38	6	7	6	16	34
	1996	27	2	1	5	7	23
Toronto-Dominion	1976	38	5	17	10	21	39
Bank	1996	24	2	2	8	9	22
Totals/Means	1976	46.4*	7.2*	97	45	26.2*	45.6*
	1996	28.6*	2.0*	7	26	6.4*	31.2*

* Mean values, averaged across the five banks. The other totals are sums.

other financial institutions. By 1996, not a single primary interlock of this sort existed! Similarly, the disappearance of trust companies as a distinct 'pillar' meant that over the two decades 15 primary interlocks involving trust companies were reduced to one. Although credit unions were entering the Top 50, they did not establish primary interlocks with other financial institutions.[18] The very few primary interlocks remaining within the financial sector knitted together the boards of financial institutions that were linked by intercorporate ownership, several of them members of the Brascan enterprise group. Overall, the density of primary interlocks within the financial sector plummeted from .029 to .007. The density of secondary ties fell less steeply from .071 to .029. Rather than sitting on the boards of other large financial institutions, Canadian bankers had either absorbed those institutions or come to compete directly with them. Thus a key accomplishment of deregulation—the creation of universal banks—brought *a more fragmented network of financial institutions*, which weakened the position of bankers while it disentangled the web of large financial institutions that had long been at the core of the Canadian corporate power structure.

Yet even if by 1996 the major banks were no longer quite at the centre of the network of primary interlocks,[19] in the network of secondary interlocks they ranked first, second, fourth, twelfth, and eighteenth in degree, and the two transnational life insurers ranked sixth (Sun Life) and seventh (Manulife). This suggests that despite the effects of governance reforms and deregulation, leading transnational financial institutions had not disappeared from the Canadian network of outside directorships. Nor were these financial institutions the only transnationals centrally positioned. In fact, among the 27 most central corporations in the secondary interlock network were 18 TNCs—10 of them transnational industrial corporations. This suggests a continued interweave of financial and industrial interests in the context of intensified transnationalization—which brings us back to the issue of transnational investment.

3. The Structural Impact of Transnationalization

a. Foreign-controlled companies

One way of revealing the structural impact of transnationalization is to employ categories from our earlier compositional analysis to compare the density of interlocking within and across *sectors* of the corporate network. From the standpoint of a given country transnational investment both *emanates from* the 'national economy' and is *directed into* it. Considering the latter issue first, Figure 4.1 shows the density of primary and secondary interlocking *within and between* four sectors of the corporate network: (1) the *domestic financial* sector (financial institutions controlled in Canada), (2) the *domestic industrial* sector (non-financials controlled in Canada), (3) the *foreign financial* sector (foreign-controlled financial institutions), and (4) the *foreign industrial* sector (foreign-controlled non-financials). As we saw earlier, between 1976 and 1996 the second and third of these expanded in their complements of large firms.

In the top panel, we can see that the density of primary interlocking fell within and across all four sectors. But *by 1996 foreign finance was especially detached from the*

FIGURE 4.1
Sectoral Density of Interlocking, Distinguishing Country of Control and Economic Sector

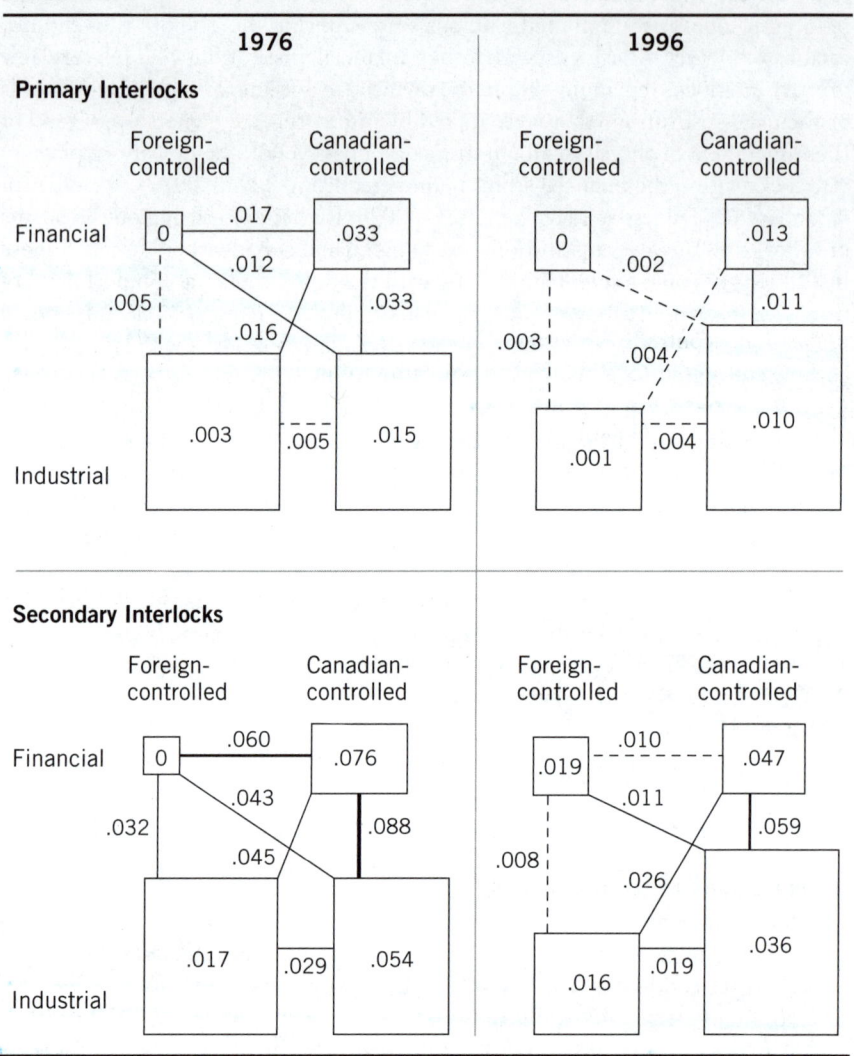

Values within boxes indicate the density of interlocking within the sector; values on lines and line thicknesses indicate the density of interlocking across sectors; areas of boxes are roughly proportional to the number of firms in the sector.

network. Foreign-controlled financials had increased in number but had not established primary ties in Canada. Primary interlocks involving domestically controlled financials were also much less evident in 1996, and as we have seen, the financial sector was less densely interlocked, in great part because deregulation and capital centralization had altered its composition. Considering only domestically controlled firms, *the density of primary ties between financials and industrials fell by two-thirds,* largely as a result of the governance reforms, a drop from 120 such inter-sectoral ties to 52.

Densities also fell in the network of secondary ties, shown in the lower panel of Figure 4.1. But in 1996 domestically controlled companies retained a great many ties. Again, foreign finance showed little tendency to establish interlocks. In sharp contrast, the domestic financial sector continued to be densely interlocked via outside directorships, both internally and with domestic industry. The density of the links between domestic finance and foreign industry was not inconsiderable in either year. Yet the financial-industrial axis in 1996 remained largely 'domestic' in terms of its locus of control.[20] Although the density between domestic finance and domestic industry fell from .088 to .059, the actual number of interlocks linking these sectors decreased only marginally (from 319 to 291), as a similar number of financial-industrial interlocks became distributed across an enlarged sector of domestically controlled industry.

Thus, although the financial sector came to include more foreign-controlled companies, this form of transnationalization did *not* produce a local network of foreign banks and domestic industry. And, although governance reforms weakened all segments of the primary interlock network, the centre of gravity of secondary interlocks shifted towards domestic financial and industrial interests.

b. Canadian investment abroad

How does Canadian investment *abroad* appear in the network? In Figure 4.2 the sectors are defined by contrasts between transnationals and sub-transnationals on the one hand and financial institutions and industrials on the other. If the density of primary interlocking among TNCs is any indication, in 1976 Canadian-based financials and industrials were already 'organically linked in their internationalization'. The changes in corporate governance made for much less extensive interlocking between these sectors; yet *even in 1996* the densest segment of the primary network was the interface between financial and non-financial TNCs. On the other hand, the sub-transnational financial sector became particularly detached from the network of primary ties. By 1996, it was the eight financial TNCs that appointed industrial executives to their boards, and the clear preference was for them to link up with other TNCs.

The network of secondary interlocks shows a rather different pattern. There was only a small drop in interlocking between TN finance and TN industry. In both years roughly one quarter of all possible ties across these sectors existed—by far the highest density of any segment. The transnational industrial sector also remained densely interlocked, and interlocking among TN financials actually increased. Thus by 1996 the *entire transnational sector was highly integrated through secondary ties*. One additional segment of the network merits mention, namely the interface between the eight transnational financials and the large category of industrials that remained sub-transnational in 1996. One-tenth of all these pairs of firms shared outside directors, pointing up the crucial integrative role that the eight financial TNCs had come to play for both transnational and non-transnational industrial capital. Because of the sheer increase in the number of TNCs, by 1996 ties within the transnational sector accounted for an increased share of the total number of secondary interlocks (16.1 per cent, compared with 9.6 per cent in 1976), while ties within the sub-transnational sector accounted for a decreased share (39.7 per cent, compared with 46.3 per cent). In effect, the network's centre of gravity had shifted somewhat towards a *transnational sector organized around financial-industrial interlocking*.[21] However, the transnational sector continued to be interlocked with the sub-transnational sector, particularly through transnational banks and life insurers.

FIGURE 4.2
Sectoral Density of Interlocking, Distinguishing Transnational Status and Economic Sector

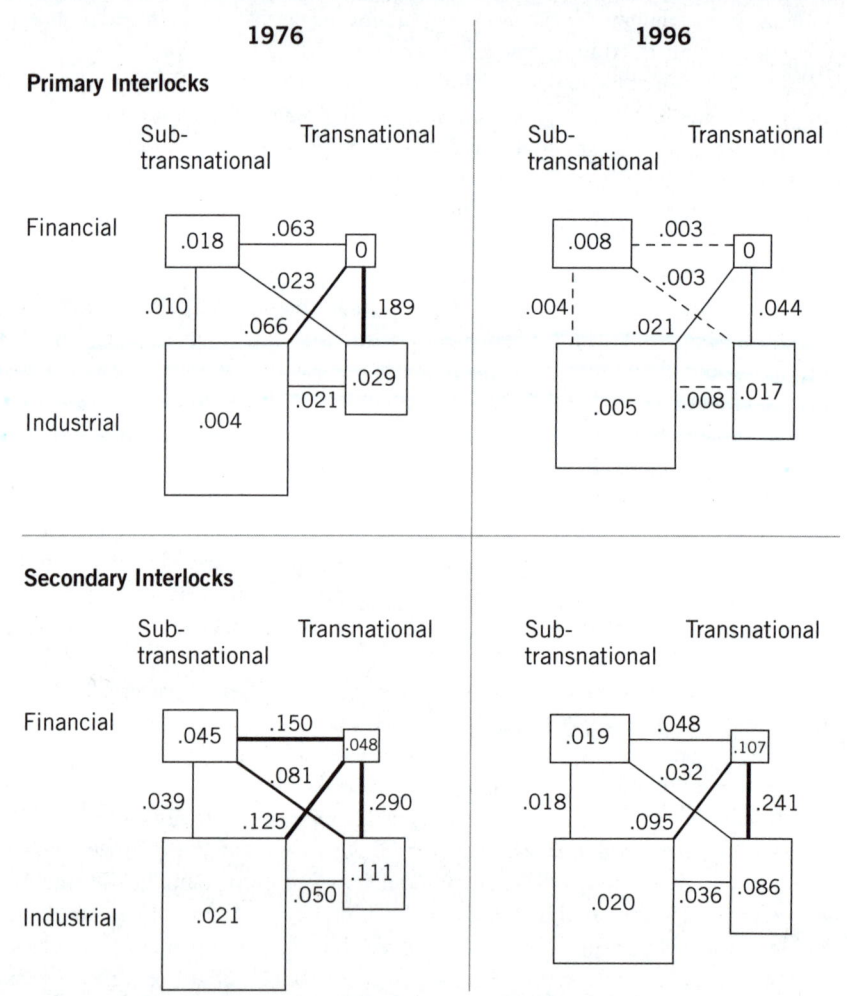

Values within boxes indicate the density of interlocking within the sector; values on lines and line thicknesses indicate the density of interlocking across sectors; areas of boxes are roughly proportional to the number of firms in the sector.

c. Mapping the transnational sector

Figure 4.3 concretizes some of these findings by mapping the 1996 network of transnational corporations, with financial institutions enclosed in boxes and primary interlocks shown in bold. Of 51 TNCs, the 44 shown in the sociogram formed the dominant component of the network, which overwhelmingly represented capital based in Canada. Only one of the 44 was foreign-controlled.[22]

The companies in the sociogram are heavily interlocked, with a density of 0.187. However, certain TNCs are clearly more central than others: the Royal Bank is directly tied to 17 other TNCs, while the forestry companies Cascade and Quebecor are each tied to only two. To highlight this difference, the centre of the TNC network is marked off from its margin by a closed curve.[23] Most of the 18 firms on the margin are tied predominantly to companies in the centre, with the notable

FIGURE 4.3
The Network of Canadian TNCs, 1996

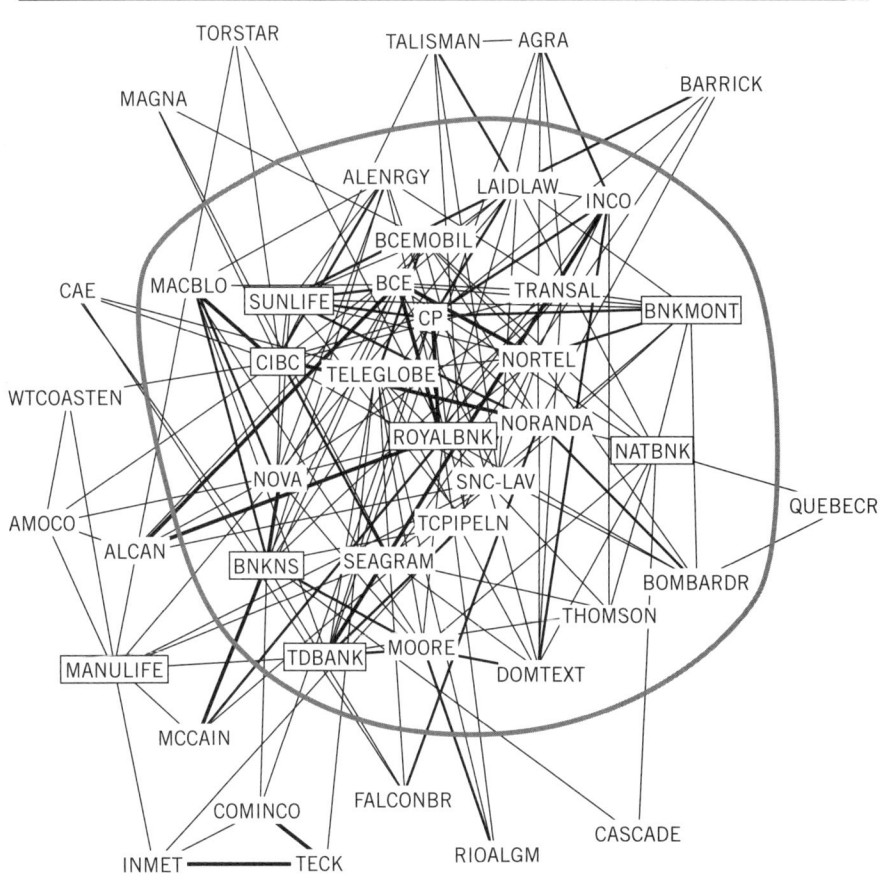

Primary interlocks are bolded; financial institutions are in boxes; the closed curve separates the centre from the margin.

exceptions of Alcan and Manulife (the latter of which shares outside directors with nine other TNCs, five of them on the network's margin). Among the 26 corporations in the centre, the density is a whopping 0.348. Included in the dense centre are seven transnational financial institutions and 19 transnational industrials, with especially strong representation of IT-communications companies,[24] the oil-gas-energy sector,[25] and a mixed set of manufacturers.[26] Two major mining firms—Inco and Noranda—are in the centre, and seven more are positioned on the periphery, along with three other oil-gas-energy firms.[27]

Although much of the TNC network has the character of an emergent formation, with companies such as Bombardier and SNC-Lavalin having risen in economic status after the 1970s, some Canadian TNCs have been at the apex of the economy for many years, and certain ties between firms also have a long history. For instance, in 1996 Canadian Pacific and Sun Life shared four outside directors, a number that closely resembles the mean number of directors these firms shared over the entire 1946–76 period (Carroll, 1986:130). Such stable, institutionalized relations attest to a *persistence* of organized capitalism, even in the context of compositional and structural transformation.[28]

CONCLUSIONS

John Scott (1997:312), following Lash and Urry, has argued that recent globalization and the disarticulation of national economies have disorganized corporate power: 'national capitalist classes are being increasingly fragmented along the lines of the globalized circuits of capital and investment that they are involved in.' Our analysis lends only modest support to this claim. The increasingly cosmopolitan cross-penetration of investments fits the motif of 'disorganization', yet a domestic accumulation base for the Canadian corporate elite has remained intact. After the mid-1970s, capitalists based in Canada dramatically increased their control of big industry and continued to expand abroad through a growing number of transnational corporations and financial institutions, while foreign interests penetrated the financial sector. Moreover, the distinctive pattern of transnational investment in and from Canada was not itself a 'disorganizing' factor. Foreign control of industry peaked around 1970, just when left-nationalist critics were beginning to label Canada the 'world's richest underdeveloped country' (Levitt, 1970), and thereafter fell as capitalists based in Canada repatriated control of some corporations (with the assistance of nationalist policies in the late 1970s) and US-based direct investment increasingly went to Europe and the Far East (Dicken, 1992:62–7). Financial deregulation did open the door to a greater foreign presence in the financial sector. The financial TNCs that expanded their Canadian operations remained detached from the domestic network, rendering it looser than it might otherwise have been. But this source of network disorganization was minor compared with the other factors we have explored.

The main impact of changes in transnational direct investment was to bolster the size of two (overlapping) sectors: the domestically controlled industrial sector and the transnationalized sector (which has developed under predominantly domestic control). Although density fell, the basic architecture of the network—the concentration of interlocking along a financial–industrial axis—did not change. However, the network's centre of gravity shifted towards interests *based in Canada but operating on a transnational scale*—the Canada-based segment of what Robinson and Harris (2000) call the 'transnational capitalist class'. The network became centred more around a core of transnational banks and corporations, controlled by capitalists based in Canada and interlocked mainly through outside directorships. Although TNCs were at the core, the boards of transnational banks included many outside directors of firms whose operations remained sub-transnational. 'Transnational finance capital' has radiated from Canada in a way that has *not* disorganized the national network, but has *embedded* it more extensively in a circuitry of global accumulation. In this, Canadian corporate power resembles globalizing Swiss capital; there is no evidence of any 'disarticulation' of national economic power.

The main reasons for the loosening of intercorporate ties were more immediate than the transnationalization of investment. They had to do with state policies and especially governance reforms within the business community. Both developments were in step with neoliberal initiatives elsewhere. Financial deregulation, a multilateral initiative since the 1994 Uruguay round of GATT reforms (Braithwaite and Drahos, 2000), was intended to make the Canadian financial sector more competitive by letting firms diversify (and banks universalize) while opening up the home market to foreign-based institutions. Corporate governance reforms, championed in the Anglo-American business systems since the mid-1990s and more recently adopted by the OECD and imported into continental Europe (Nooteboom, 1999), sought to bolster shareholder rights as a means of improving performance under the pressure of heightened global competition. In Canada, part of the rationale was to prevent any recurrence of the financial scandals that had tarnished Canadian capital in the eyes of international investors and to persuade managers to accept the discipline of dividends and share value regarded as performance indicators.

The emergent structure of corporate capital places transnational corporations at the centre of a looser network of information flows across outside directorships. 'Leaner-meaner' bank boards are still important meeting points for directors of both TNCs and sub-transnationals, even if new centres of financial capital—institutional investors such as pension funds—have gained a greater presence in an era of fetishized 'shareholder value'. In a globalizing world, investment capital is highly mobile, and the pressure to attain maximal profitability is severe. Commercial banks are less keen to tie up funds in long-term loans to industry—their own sensitivity to the bottom line leads them elsewhere. Moreover, with deregulation Canadian banks have more options. As owners of the leading investment banks they regularly buy corporate securities in a transaction-based rather than relationship-based credit nexus. With the internationalization of their operations, their assets increasingly include speculatively-held currencies.[29] As banks pursue international financial transactions, the basis for *nationally bounded* financial–industrial relations weakens. Part of the circuitry of financial capital is transposed to an international field. Non-financial corporations also have more options for financing in the new era, including the issuance of commercial paper (i.e., disintermediation).[30] The relations between commercial banks and corporations become looser and more episodic, with syndicated bought deals replacing long-term loans.[31] The old nationally organized financial–industrial axis, whose backbone was long-term bank loans to corporations, fades a bit as bankers come to play less of a role on corporate boards in the new governance framework.

For Lash and Urry (1994:286), the notion of the end of organized capitalism seems to imply the end of one of organized capitalism's criterial attributes: finance capital. Our analysis, by contrast, suggests that *a major rearrangement of finance capital* may be under way. This is intimated in the formation of transnational finance capital and the loosening of financial–industrial relations, but also in a blurring of industrials and financials, as the former come to engage more directly in financial functions: issuing commercial paper, holding financial assets, and even retooling themselves into financial–industrial powerhouses—most spectacularly in the case of GE Capital in the US (Curran, 1997).[32] Such an organic integration of industrial and financial capital might contribute to a weakening of interlocks between 'industry' and 'finance', but should not be confused with the end of finance capital as a form of capital integration.

II

The Spatial Terrain

Chapter 5

Westward Drift: The Shifting Geography of Corporate Power

In this chapter and the two that follow we consider Canada as a distinct site of capital accumulation and explore the spatial terrain of Canadian corporate power. Ever since Harold Innis wrote of centre and margin in his final ruminations on the fur trade in Canada (Innis, 1956:385–6), the contrast between powerful metropole and dependent hinterland has figured prominently in Canadian studies. The most vivid depiction was no doubt Davis's (1971) multi-layered master narrative of Canadian history and society as a story of metropolis versus hinterland, played out in the relations between Canada's regions, in the relations between Quebec and the dominant Anglo presence, and in the relations between Canada and the American hegemon. Some have questioned this approach to placing Canada within the world system (Carroll, 1985; Resnick, 1989). Others point to the unstable nature of the categories themselves, as uneven capitalist development can result in peripheralization of the core, or colonization of relatively undercapitalized sites within the core (Cox, 1987; Palmer, 1994). As Brym (1985) points out, one of the basic issues in these debates has to do with the character of the Canadian capitalist class, and indeed this character is the subject of a good part of the analysis in the middle chapters of this book, which work from the 'inside' outward. As Figure 5.1 suggests, we begin by examining the spatial distribution of the Canadian corporate network (line A); then in Chapter 6 we will shift to consider the linkages between Canadian and American corporations (as in line C), as part of a 'continental' network (lines A, B, and C), before finally locating the Canadian network within a developing global corporate network that reaches well beyond North America (line D; Chapter 7).

Despite the recognition, since Innis, of the importance of spatial relations, what we might call the 'geography of corporate power' within Canada has not been systematically charted.[1] This chapter maps the changing network of large Canadian corporations in the half-century following the Second World War, using the location of corporate head offices as a window on the geography of corporate power. Head-office location matters broadly in the political economy of corporate capitalism, in a number of ways. As De Smidt points out, 'a head office is the decision center of a firm, the home base of management. Hence, cities with a concentration

FIGURE 5.1
Schematic Representation of National and International Corporate Interlocks

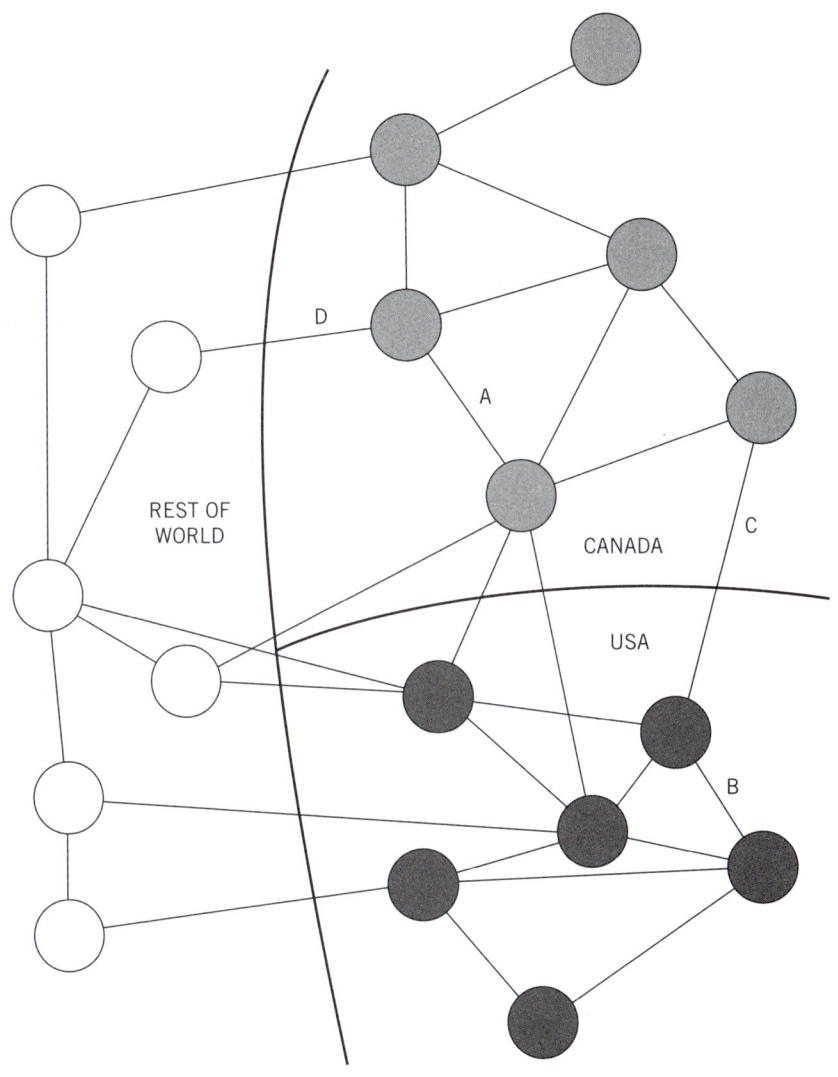

KEY: A = an interlock between corporations based in Canada; B = an interlock between corporations based in the US; C = a 'continental' interlock between Canadian and American corporations; D = an interlock between a Canadian corporation and a corporation based in the rest of the world.

of head offices may be considered management centers' (1991:148). Urban zones that attract and retain major corporate offices tend to reap benefits in the form of employment and investment, even if new business structures have often meant a decentralization of management activities and an increase in the contracting-out of corporate services (Marshall and Raybould, 1993). Particularly in the era of the 'global city' (Brenner, 1998), the fate of any given locality is tied to its success in the inter-urban competition not only for investment funds but over the siting of corporate command centres (Beaverstock and Smith, 1996).

Head office also matters specifically in the structuring of the corporate elite. A company's head-office location has an obvious bearing on its access to directors. Large metropolitan centres offer head offices 'ease of interorganizational face-to-face contacts, business service availability, and high intermetropolitan accessibility' (Pred, 1977:177). The tendency in advanced capitalism for major corporate head offices to gravitate to the largest metropolitan areas has meant that corporate elites tend to be highly clustered within a relatively small number of urban zones—the command centres of the world system and of national economies within it. In this way, the spatial pattern of corporate head offices has imposed 'a marked centralizing influence' on the space economy (Coffey and Bailly, 1992:865). The well-researched case of the US provides a good example. Numerous studies have identified New York as the hub of a spatial network of interlocking directorates that also includes semi-national subnetworks, particularly around Chicago, and various regional groupings (Sonquist and Koenig, 1975; Green and Semple, 1981; Bearden and Mintz, 1987; Kono et al., 1998).

In Canada, corporate power has also had a characteristic geography, expressing the rise of key urban centres and tracking the westward expansion of capitalism. Canada's business class has had a recognized spatial dimension—captured in Creighton's (1956) image of British North America as a 'commercial empire of the St Lawrence' organized around the staples trade, with Montreal as the centre of gravity throughout the nineteenth century, and, later, with Toronto and Winnipeg growing in importance as settlement and capital moved westward within the framework of the National Policy (Easterbrook and Aitkin, 1956). In the first decade of the twentieth century a distinctive network of corporate capital was consolidated among the directors of large firms born of the merger movement and based mainly in Montreal and Toronto, favoured sites for the command centres of Canada's anglophone business elite (Piedalue, 1976). Piedalue's study shows a corporate network broadening in the first three decades of the twentieth century to include the country's major financial institutions, railways, hydroelectric and telegraph/telephone companies, and mining/manufacturing companies. Although by 1930 the network was somewhat segmented, with one large cluster of firms based in Montreal and a smaller group based in Toronto, the entire set of corporations formed a single component.

In their analysis of the corporate network as of 1958, Park and Park (1973) emphasized the leading role of the Bank of Montreal as a hub for the country's major capitalist grouping, with the Royal Bank (also based in Montreal) and the Toronto-based Bank of Commerce serving as lesser hubs of more diffuse groupings. Indeed, what Clement (1975:63) has termed the Toronto–Montreal axis continued as the backbone of Canada's corporate elite in the post-1945 era. Niosi's (1978:170–1) analysis of the head offices of large Canadian corporations in the mid-1970s led him to conclude that the Canadian capitalist class was 'largely concentrated in Toronto and Montreal' (1978:170–1), yet also pan-Canadian through its effective control of smaller firms nationwide. In my own interpretation, the Toronto–Montreal axis has been central to a bloc of finance capital: an intercorporate structure involving the symbiosis of financial institutions and industrial corporations, which has been reproduced across the decades even as the particular individual directors and corporations have changed with promotions and retirements, mergers and takeovers, and the like (Carroll, 1986; Carroll and Lewis, 1991).

This axis of corporate power is the historically sedimented product of developments specific to Canada, such as the movement of capital and of head offices out of the Maritimes (Brodie, 1997:251–2) and the formation of a state-mandated system of branch banking. The former constituted a chapter in the dynamic of uneven development that has shaped Canada in various ways. The latter, in allowing chartered banks to operate at the retail level in all parts of the country, set up the preconditions for a financial apparatus far more centralized than its counterpart in the US, where interstate banking was prohibited (Kauffman, 1992). The purpose of this chapter, however, is not to rehearse the formation of Canada's business system, but to map its post–World War Two trajectory, and in this regard a key question must be the fate of the Montreal–Toronto axis.

We can readily point to four political-economic developments that may have transformed Canada's spatialized configuration of corporate power in distinctive ways. First, the three decades following the Second World War brought a consolidation of 'organized capitalism'. This meant not only the *persistence of finance capital*—of the strong institutionalized relationships between big industry and high finance—but also the *further centralization of strategic control over capital* in the form of large, multidivisional corporations in which plant-specific, operational aspects of management became subordinate to corporate strategies issuing from metropolitan head offices (Chandler, 1962). In itself, this tendency would presumably favour the emergence of one city—presumably Toronto—as *the* strategic centre for corporate capital based in Canada, a potential 'global city'.

However—and this is our second point—tendencies towards such a centralization of command have been continually undone by the uneven development of capitalism itself. In the Canadian case, the post-war era brought a countervailing trend: a dramatic shift of capital westward, with the growth of large forestry and mining firms in BC and, after oil was struck at Leduc in 1946, of the Calgary-centred 'oil patch'. Even within the logic of the staples thesis, by the end of the 1970s it was plausible to speak of a 'prairie capitalism' spurred on by an entrepreneurial Alberta government and industries bidding for major corporate power:

> The rise of arriviste regional bourgeoisies and the decline of established capitalist core areas involve a complex struggle for ascendancy and power waged at the level of the state and politics as much as in the realm of economics and if the trends of the past decade are a reliable economic guide, power has shifted with the economic centre of gravity toward the West, particularly toward Alberta (Richards and Pratt, 1979:247).

Along similar lines, Niosi saw in the 1970s and 1980s a sharpening conflict, with 'the emerging regional bourgeoisies being pitted against the indigenous bourgeoisie, which is becoming increasingly concentrated in Ontario' (1981:34).

A third, related post-war development revolved specifically around the emerging politics of Quebec nationalism, beginning in the mid-1960s. This meant on the one hand promotion of a Quebec-based business community through such provincial vehicles as the Caisse de Dépôt (Niosi, 1981), but on the other a flight of corporate head offices from Quebec in the wake of the Parti Québécois's rise to political power. These countervailing tendencies might have been expected to alter the ethnic composition of the Quebec-based corporate elite segment, and (depending on their relative strengths) possibly its size.

Finally, rising levels of foreign, mainly American, direct investment in the 1950s and 1960s expanded the 'comprador' element in Canada's corporate elite (Clement, 1975), which tended to concentrate both in the Toronto–southwestern-Ontario corridor of branch plants as well as in the Calgary-based oil patch, where a bias against public investment made large-scale direct investment and ownership by giant foreign companies inevitable (Richards and Pratt, 1979:87). In the 1970s, however, the weakening of American hegemony ushered in a 'renaissance of Canadian nationalism' (Niosi, 1981), supported by policies such as the Foreign Investment Review Agency, and a weakening of the comprador element, followed more recently by a strong tendency towards continental integration under the Free Trade agreements of 1989 and 1994 (Blank and Haar, 1998). The shifts in foreign control, then, constitute a fourth development that we need to keep in mind in mapping the formation of Canada's corporate network.

Mapping the Spatial Distribution of the Corporate Network

To follow the corporate network's development over half a century it was necessary to depart from the research strategy followed in the rest of this book. Available data from my earlier research (Carroll, 1986) allowed for the analysis of only 103 dominant corporations for 1946. Thus for consistency's sake we have restricted ourselves to a subset of our Top 250s for 1976 and 1996, selected so that as a group they match the 1946 Top 103, and categorized as to head office and other relevant features. Wholly state-owned corporations (e.g., the Canadian National Railway prior to its privatization) were excluded, to match the 1976 and 1996 samples to the 1946 one, which included only private-sector entities. For each year, the largest 23 financial institutions, ranked by assets; the largest 74 non-financial corporations ('industrials'), ranked by assets; and the six most important investment companies (each owning strategic blocs of shares in other Top 103 firms[2]) were selected. These cross-sections give us three windows on the structure of corporate power in the post-1945 era: the immediate post-war context; the mid-1970s, at the height of 'organized capitalism' and in the early stage of both the weakening of American hegemony and the recent pattern of multilateral globalization; and 1996, after a period of globalization and in some respects 'disorganization'.

THE SHIFTING CORPORATE GEOGRAPHY

Before examining the network of corporations in its spatial aspect, let us consider the changing spatial distribution of the corporate command centres themselves. Figure 5.2 provides a summary of the westward movement, graphing the number of firms headquartered in each city or region in 1946, 1976, and 1996. As we read across the time-axis, the changing height of the bars reflects the consolidation of corporate power in Toronto in the first three decades, the decline of Montreal and of other sites east of Alberta, and the rise of the west, particularly in the last two decades. The graph also distinguishes between financial institutions and other firms, and indicates no appreciable weakening of the Toronto–Montreal axis so far as the location of financial power is concerned.

In 1946 Montreal was the favoured location for head offices in general (33 in all), followed closely by Toronto (31). The diffuse region of Southwestern Ontario, extending from Hamilton–Niagara westward to Sarnia–Windsor, was home to 13 head offices, including industrial companies based in Hamilton, Windsor, and

FIGURE 5.2
Spatial Distribution of Corporate Head Offices, 1946–1996

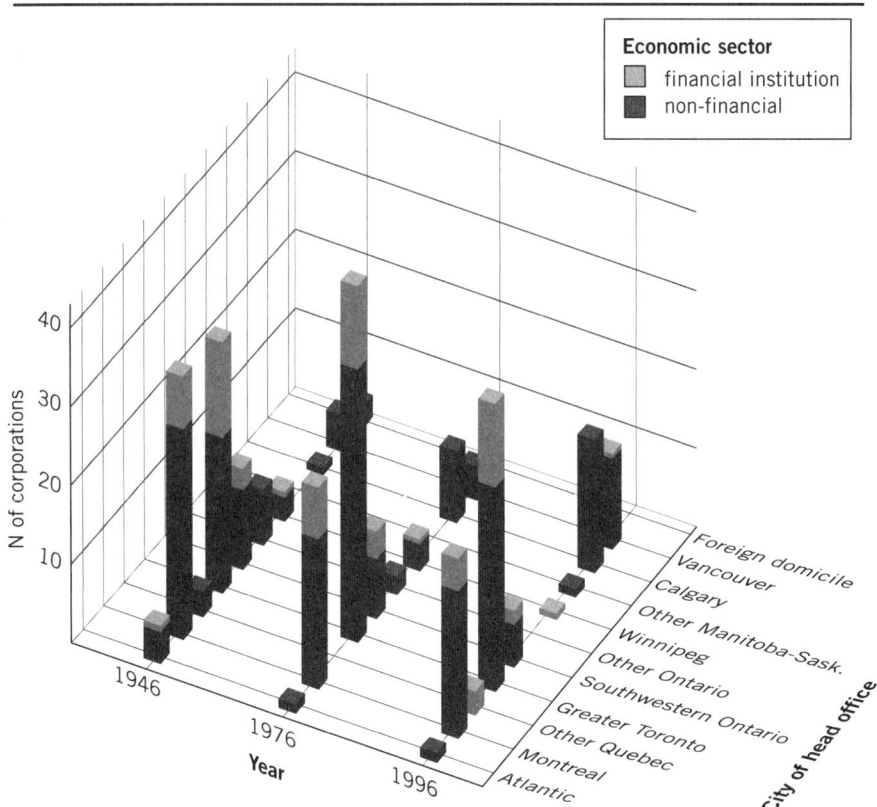

Sarnia and financial institutions based in London and Kitchener. The corridor stretching from Montreal to Windsor housed 77 head offices. Although these were the major locations, a number of head offices were sited in other parts of Ontario (seven in all, including E.P. Taylor's Argus Corp., located in Peterborough, as well as six industrial companies located in Northern Ontario towns such as Sault Ste Marie, Sudbury, and Timmins). Five firms had their head offices in the Atlantic provinces, including the Bank of Nova Scotia (Halifax) and four forest-sector concerns sited in smaller towns such as Bathurst, New Brunswick, and Cornerbrook, Newfoundland. Three firms in the pulp-paper and closely associated hydroelectric sectors were sited in Quebec City. Cities west of Ontario had no profile in the Top 100, with the exceptions of Winnipeg and Vancouver, each of which hosted four head offices. Calgary claimed only one head office—that of meat-packer Burns Foods. Two companies with primarily Canadian operations but head offices elsewhere, including the Hudson's Bay Company, were large enough to qualify for the Top 103.[3] It is also evident, from the shading of the vertical bars in the figure, that most of the country's major financial institutions were based in Montreal (7) and Toronto (11); Winnipeg was the only western city hosting a major financial institution.

By 1976 a number of shifts are apparent. Consistent with the characterization of the first three post-war decades as a period of consolidation, major corporate head offices were no longer sited in the hinterland towns of Atlantic Canada and northern Ontario. Even Halifax lost the Bank of Nova Scotia to Toronto, and Quebec City ceased to be a host for large corporate offices. Perhaps the most dramatic development was Toronto's confirmation as the centre of gravity for corporate capital, housing 46 headquarters—20 more than Montreal. As sites for the command of financial capital, the profiles of the two cities remained unchanged, so the shift in stature had purely to do with the siting of industrial headquarters. Calgary's dramatic rise from obscurity also involved a sectorally specific pattern of capital accumulation. In 1976 all nine of the corporations based in Calgary and Edmonton[4] were industrial companies, and seven of them were oil and gas producers. Calgary had become a second-tier centre in one of the country's most dynamic industrial sectors.

Looking more closely, and recalling that the period from the 1940s to the early 1970s saw the expansion of a comprador bourgeoisie, coincident with the expansion of US-based capital in an era of American global hegemony, it is striking how the ascendance of Toronto and Calgary was implicated in the growth of foreign-controlled industry. In 1946, the 31 Toronto-based corporations included six non-financials controlled in the US and one controlled outside North America. By 1976 fully 15 of the 48 Toronto-based companies were controlled in the US and another five were controlled outside North America. In the same year, all seven of the Calgary-based oil and gas firms were controlled in the US.

In the two decades following 1976 some of the trends already evident continued. Montreal's position slipped further, not only as a host for industrial companies but now also for financial institutions such as Sun Life, whose move to Toronto in the wake of the PQ's electoral victory of 1976 telegraphed the corporate elite's verdict on Quebec independentism, a verdict echoed after the 1995 Referendum when Bank of Montreal Chair Matthew Barrett remarked that the bank would, in the case of separation, move its head office from Quebec. In contrast, Calgary attracted a greater share of industrial command centres, so that by 1996, Montreal's total of 23 head offices placed it not far above Calgary's 17, and substantially below Toronto's 38. The redistribution of head offices westward in this period was extraordinary. Toronto's net loss of eight head offices was matched by Calgary's gain, but corporate headquarters also continued to drain from southwestern Ontario, while the marginality of the Atlantic and northern Ontario regions was confirmed,[5] and the number of head offices in Vancouver tripled. The rise of Vancouver as a power centre coincided with the eclipse of Winnipeg, which by 1996 retained only one headquarters. Indeed, only Quebec City bucked the westward trend: by 1996 it was home to three financial institutions, compensating for Montreal's net loss of three, so that the corridor from Quebec City to London continued to house nearly all of the country's leading financial institutions.

The westward shift in corporate head offices was thus a shift in the command centres of *industry, not finance*: high rates of accumulation and massive concentration of capital in the oil and gas, forestry, and mining sectors of Alberta and British Columbia meant a shifting geography of corporate power in the industrial but not the financial sector. The one financial institution headquartered west of Winnipeg in 1996, the Hong Kong Bank of Canada, based in Vancouver, was a subsidiary of a British TNC—a fact that raises the issue of foreign control in the corporate geography of 1996.

The twenty years following the mid-1970s were a complex period. In the first decade, American hegemony in the world capitalist system weakened somewhat while Canadian-based corporate capital came of age, strengthening the position of Canadian capitalists in both their home market and the world system (Resnick, 1989). Yet in the second decade, the Conservative government's turn from liberal nationalism to 'continental neoliberalism' (Carroll, 1990), including the conversion of the Foreign Investment Review Agency into Investment Canada and the free trade treaties of 1989 and 1994, seemed to portend a 're-compradorization' (Ratner, 1994), which might be expected to show its effects in the composition of the country's leading corporations.

Consistent with Chapter 4's analysis of the Top 250, in the Top 103 we find a *net decrease* in foreign control of the largest industrial companies after 1976.[6] In that year, 32 of the Top 103 were controlled by interests in the US (an increase of 6 from 1946), and 13 were controlled outside North America (an increase of 7 from 1946). By 1996, only 12 firms were controlled in the US and a further 6 were controlled outside North America. In absolute terms, Toronto continued to host the most foreign-controlled corporations (7, including 2 financial companies owned respectively by Ford and General Motors), but in relative terms Vancouver's 4 foreign-controlled firms accounted for one-third of its complement of major head offices.[7] Of the 4 urban centres, Montreal had the smallest comprador element (1 US-controlled and 1 British-controlled firm). Significantly, Calgary's top corporations, all controlled in the US in 1976, had been for the most part Canadianized by 1996: 12 of the 15 leading companies headquartered there were controlled by Canadian capitalists; one each was controlled in the Netherlands, Hong Kong, and the US.[8]

Over the half-century we find first a consolidation of corporate headquarters in major metropolitan zones, the decline of Montreal and the increased importance of Toronto and Calgary—both of which became sites for an expansive comprador element with the US-centred wave of accumulation around consumer goods and resource commodities. The later two decades witnessed a further shift westward, to Calgary and Vancouver, a further attrition from Montreal, southwestern Ontario, and Winnipeg, and a general decline of the comprador element, although it retained some presence in Toronto. These developments meant the ascent of the far west as a locus for top corporate management. In 1946 the ratio of corporations based in the far west to those based in Montreal–Toronto was .078. By 1976 it was .181; in 1996 it was .475. The overall spatial distribution of head offices became *simplified* around four metropolitan centres in two quite distinct regions, which together housed 90 per cent of major corporations in 1996. The one constant in all these shifts was the location of major financial institutions in the Montreal–Toronto area (with some internal shifting from the former to the latter), extending eastward as far as Quebec City and westward as far as London. The rise of the west as a locale for the command of corporate capital was an industrial phenomenon. It did not disturb or displace the eastern-based and indigenously controlled financial sector.

TRENDS IN THE VOLUME OF INTERLOCKING

The industrial character of the west's rise suggests that despite fractional tensions of a regional nature, the shift westward may not have involved a dramatic transformation in elite social organization. The persistence of certain features of organized capitalism that we noticed in Chapter 4 has relevance here. Despite the recent streamlining of bank boards and other changes associated with corporate governance reform, we found an enduring financial–industrial axis at the heart of the Canadian corporate network. If governance reform, deregulation, and the increasing transnationalization of Canadian-based finance capital have not dramatically disorganized the national network, the westward shift in corporate power domestically might be seen in a similar light, as contributing to a recomposition rather than a decomposition of finance capital. By implication, we might expect to see the rise of the west as a matter not so much of an emerging 'western' network, cohering on the basis of geographical propinquity, as of a westward *extension* of the Toronto–Montreal axis of finance capital, with interlocks predominantly linking the western-based firms back to the heartland and its financial sector. By the same reasoning, Montreal's decline as a host city for head offices may have been mitigated by its continued relative centrality in the network of corporate power, via venerable financial institutions such as the Bank of Montreal and Royal Bank of Canada.

To map the network of interlocking directorships spatially, we calculated the *relative volume* of interlocking within and between major cities—the proportion of shared directors between companies headquartered in each pair of cities, expressed as a percentage of all interlocking directorships. Table 5.1 presents a matrix of intra-

and inter-city volumes, arrayed from east to west. Within each cell, the relative volume of shared directors for a pair of cities is shown at three points in time. For instance, the entry '4.2' at the intersection of the 'Atlantic' column and the 'Montreal' row indicates that in 1946 4.2 per cent of all directorship interlocks in the entire national network linked firms based in Atlantic Canada with firms based in Montreal.[9]

In 1946 Montreal was unrivalled in its centrality, and for reasons well beyond the sheer number of head offices sited there. Of the 824 interlocks that made up the entire network at that time (the network's total volume), 35.0 per cent stitched the Montreal-based companies into the dense centre of the network. Equally evident is Toronto's secondary status: only 12.7 per cent of all interlocks linked Toronto-based companies to other Toronto-based companies, the same proportion as linked Toronto firms with Montreal firms. Interlocks connecting corporations based outside Montreal and Toronto were rare. Instead, most of the interlocking 'beyond' the two metropoli drew outlying firms *into* the Montreal–Toronto bloc. Companies based in the Atlantic region and southwestern Ontario tended to interlock with companies based in Montreal, while those based in northern Ontario tended to link with Toronto.

By 1976, the total number of interlocks had grown to 1018—a proliferation of intercorporate ties consistent with the consolidation of organized capitalism—but Montreal was no longer the core city. Its 138 interlocks accounted for less than one-tenth of the total, whereas interlocks among Toronto-based companies represented one-quarter, as did ties linking Toronto- to Montreal-based firms. The volume of interlocking within the Toronto-Montreal bloc represented 64 per cent of the total volume of interlocking in the network, compared with 60 per cent thirty years earlier. Beyond that central bloc, the most notable set of interlocks—7.6 per cent of all ties—linked firms based in southwestern Ontario with those headquartered in Toronto, although a few dozen ties also extended westward from Montreal and Toronto to Winnipeg, Calgary, and Vancouver, and a small handful had been established among firms based in the far west.

In the entries for 1996 one can see a proliferation of ties among far-west firms, yet the network remained substantially organized around the Toronto–Montreal core. Between 1976 and 1996 the overall volume of interlocking decreased to 719, for reasons explored in depth in earlier chapters. But the rise of Calgary and Vancouver is unmistakable. Interlocks centred in Montreal continued to constitute about a tenth of all ties, and the relative volume of interlocking in Toronto actually dropped to 21.1 per cent. Interlocks within the Toronto–Montreal bloc accounted for slightly less than half of all interlocks in the national network—still the largest concentration of intercorporate governance ties, but a major decline from the 1976 zenith. In comparison, the 50 interlocks *among* firms based in the far west represented only 7 per cent of the total. Although a regional network had emerged in the far west, the dominant pattern was for western firms to interlock with companies based in Toronto and, secondarily, Montreal. Taken as a whole, 181 east-west ties accounted for one-quarter of the total. The 21 interlocks among Alberta-based corporations, for instance, were overshadowed by the 94 ties linking

TABLE 5.1
Relative Volume of Interlocking within and among Cities, 1946–1996

Year	City/region of head office	Atlantic	Montreal	Other PQ	Toronto	SW Ontario	Other Ontario	Winnipeg	Calgary/ Edmonton	Vancouver	Total*
1946	Atlantic										7.0
1976											0.8
1996											1.3
1946	Montreal	4.2	35.0								68.7
1976		0.1	13.6								52.3
1996		0.6	10.6								42.8
1946	Other PQ	0.1	2.2	0.1							2.7
1976			0.4	0.1							1.0
1996											
1946	Toronto	2.1	12.7	0.2	12.7						39.3
1976		3.9	25.0		25.3						65.2
1996		0.6	16.6	0.3	21.1						62.2
1946	SW Ontario	0.1	6.4		3.3	0.5					11.2
1976			4.0		7.6	2.2					15.7
1996			3.6	0.1	6.3	1.0					12.0
1946	Other Ontario	0.2	4.1		5.9	0.5	1.0				12.5
1976			1.3		9.8	0.1					2.6
1996											
1946	Winnipeg	0.2	1.2		1.3	0.2	0.5	0.4			4.2
1976			3.2		2.4	0.7		0.6			7.7
1996			3.1		0.3						3.6
1946	Calgary/ Edmonton		0.4		0.1	0.6	0.1	0.5	0.2		0.5
1976			2.3		1.5	2.5	0.3	0.3	2.9		5.7
1996			6.3		13.1						27.4
1946	Vancouver	1	0.7		0.4	0.5	0.2		0.1		1.5
1976		1	2.8		2.1	0.3	0.1	0.3	0.6	0.9	7.4
1996			1.8		4.0				2.4	1.7	10.3
1946	Foreign domicile										
1976			1.7		0.5	0.1		0.4			2.7
1996											

* Totals indicate the percentage of interlocks for which at least one firm was headquartered in the indicated city.

Calgary–Edmonton to Toronto and the 45 ties extending to Montreal. In this sense, the 1996 network was still centred on Toronto and Montreal: most interlocks either occurred within the Toronto–Montreal zone or linked firms sited elsewhere to this core region. The regional network of far-west corporations did not constitute an indigenous centre of corporate power at the close of the twentieth century. The network remained centred on the Toronto–Montreal axis, but major spokes reached westward to new sites of corporate command.[10]

THE NETWORK OF EASTERN AND WESTERN METROPOLI, 1996

The volume of interlocking gives some sense of the shape of the network, but a more concrete analysis can illuminate other features relevant to the spatial organization of corporate power. Of particular interest here are the 181 interlocking directorships that in 1996 linked corporations based in Montreal or Toronto with those based in the far west. A closer look shows that these involved 42 firms based in Montreal or Toronto (29 in Toronto alone) and 27 far-west firms. All told, the east-west network included more than two-thirds of the entire Top 103.

Let us consider first the 'eastern' side of this bipartite network.[11] Fully 68 per cent of the ties involved Toronto-based firms, while 32 per cent involved firms based in Montreal. Financial institutions were heavily involved on the eastern side of the network. Twelve of the eastern companies were financial institutions, and these firms participated in 45 per cent of all the east-west ties. The big five banks alone were involved in 52 interlocks; two major life insurers (ManuLife and Sun) in another 16. These seven were the very same companies that our analysis in Chapter 4 showed to be fully transnational in their investments. In all, they provided 38 per cent of the ties between the far west and the Toronto–Montreal bloc. Among the non-financials sited in the east, a few venerable corporations account for many of the interlocks: Montreal-based Canadian Pacific Limited (11) and BCE (5), Toronto-based Brascan (7) and its affiliate Noranda (7). Comprador elements based in the east, however, were marginal in the bipartite network: five eastern-based companies under foreign control were interlocked with far-west firms, but in total they accounted for only 8 per cent of the ties linking the eastern and western metropoli.

Now let us consider the same 181 interlocks from the western side. In 1996, 59 per cent of the 27 far-west firms were based in Calgary–Edmonton, with the remainder headquartered in Vancouver. But 77 per cent of interlocks involved Calgary–Edmonton companies; and most of the interlocking linked Calgary with Toronto. All but one of the 27 far-west firms were industrials, and six were foreign-controlled. In all, foreign-controlled, western-based companies participated in 15 per cent of the 181 interlocks, including 11 ties involving US-controlled firms and 16 ties involving other foreign-controlled firms. Significantly, a very few companies, mainly Calgary-based, accounted for most of the ties to the east: Norcen alone claimed 32 ties, followed by Petro Canada (15), TransCanada PipeLine (14), and Nova (13). These four energy companies participated in one-third of the entire east–west volume of interlocking.

100 *The Spatial Terrain*

Mapping the Network Core, 1996

By 1996, then, the ties between major eastern and western centres were highly concentrated among a small set of companies. Moving to a more concrete analysis still, Figure 5.3 maps the most centrally positioned companies in 1996. Each firm shared one or more directors with at least 15 other Top 103 corporations. In all, 26 firms met this criterion—eight based in Montreal (including two financial institutions), 13 based in Toronto (including seven financial institutions) and five based in Calgary (all in the petroleum-based energy sector).

What Figure 5.3 shows is a single, integrated network, with nothing in the way of regional cleavage. All but two of the 21 corporations based in the east share directors with one or more of the Calgary five, and although four of the Calgary firms form a connected subnetwork, Norcen has links only to the east.[12] Among the other four Calgary-based companies, TransAlberta Utilities is the hub, but in addition to its links to Nova, TransCanada PipeLine, and PetroCanada it is interlocked with a host of eastern financial institutions and with industrial corporations like BCE and Inco, which have long been at the centre of the Canadian corporate network (Carroll, 1986:131).

There can be no doubt that the basic pattern in this densely-interlocked network core is one of *integration along a financial–industrial axis*, with the financial function (along with a good deal of industry) continuing to be located in the east. Indeed, one can see that in 1996 each of the five Calgary-based industrials was directly interlocked with three of the five big banks and with at least one of the five other financial institutions in the network, rendering the bank boards central meeting points for oil-patch directors.[13] At the same time, there is no evidence of compradorization at the network's centre. Only one of the 26 most central corporations—General Motors Canada—was foreign-controlled in 1996.

Also noteworthy is the substantial overlap between companies in Figure 5.3 and companies in Figure 4.3—the network of Canadian-based TNCs charted in the last chapter. Fifteen of the 26 most central companies in the east-west network (seven of them financial institutions) numbered among the 44 transnational corporations that make up a connected network at the centre of Canadian corporate capital. All but one of these 15 (Manulife) were located within the densely-connected core of that network of Canadian-based TNCs. By 1996, then, companies that were central in holding together the east-west axis of finance capital also tended to be the most centrally positioned transnational corporations in Canada's corporate network. This is further evidence in favour of the conclusion reached in Chapter 4, that finance capital emanating from Canada has become transnationalized without disorganizing the 'national' network.

The Inner Circle: A New Alignment of Finance Capital

How, finally, has this regional realignment been manifested in the structure of the corporate elite? For the Top 103 firms we consider in this chapter, the entire 1996

FIGURE 5.3
Sociogram of 26 Centrally Positioned Corporations, 1996

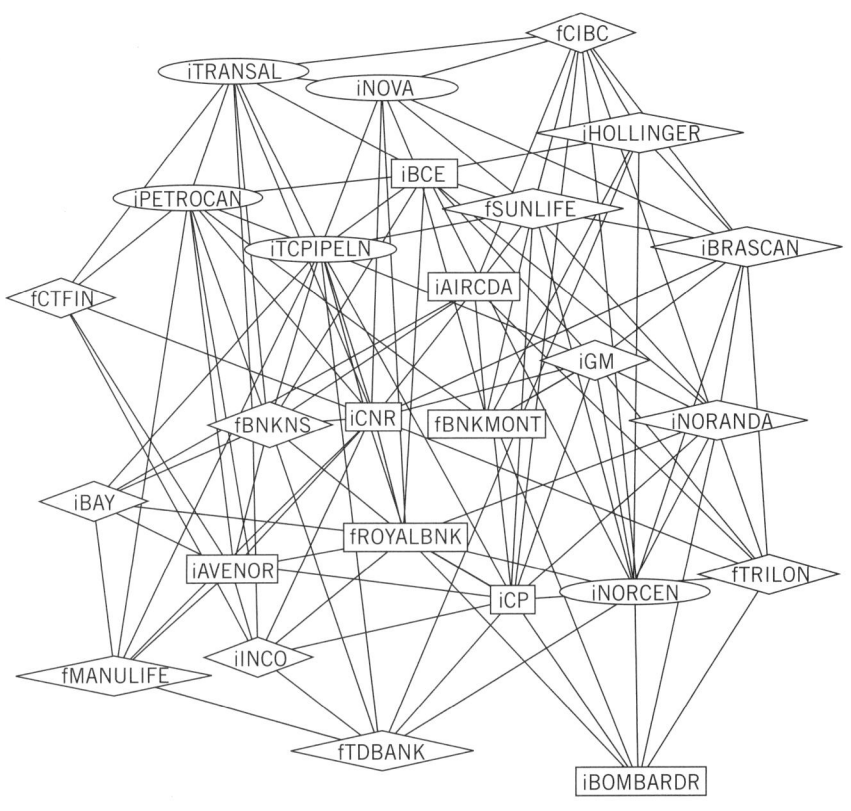

Firms based in Montreal are in boxes; firms based in Toronto are in diamonds; firms based in Calgary are in ovals. An 'f' at the beginning of a point's name indicates a financial institution; an 'i' at the beginning indicates a non-financial corporation.

network was created by 237 individual directors, who on average carried 3.0 interlocks.[14] These directors are cross-classified in Table 5.2 by the economic sectors and major metropolitan areas in which they participated via their corporate affiliations. With regard to the regional pattern of corporate affiliations, shown in the table's rows, the largest single category is the 96 directors whose companies were all based in the Toronto–Montreal zone. These make up 41 per cent of the 237 directors. However, members of this 'eastern establishment' carry only 1.88 interlocks each, on average: they are *not* the key networkers who stitch together the corporate elite. The second largest regionally defined category is made up of 73 directors of corporations based in *both* the eastern and western metropoli. It is *these* directors who are the most well-connected, carrying an average of 5.43 intercorporate ties. In stark contrast, very few of the 237 directors are affiliated with companies based exclusively in the west, and those who are carry very few interlocks.[15] There is no evi-

TABLE 5.2
Inner-Circle Members Cross-Classified by Region and Economic Sector, 1996

Region(s) in which directors participate		Sector(s) in which directors participate			Total
		Industrial firms only	Financial institutions only	Nonfinancial firms and financial institutions	
Toronto–Montreal only	N	35	1	60	96
	Mean	1.83	1.00	1.92	1.88
East–west (Tor/Mont to Cal/Ed/Van)	N	13	0	60	73
	Mean	3.77		5.78	5.42
Far West only	N	16	0	0	16
	Mean	1.31			1.31
Other	N	6	8	38	52
	Mean	1.83	1.00	2.71	2.35
Total	N	70	9	158	237
	Mean	2.07	1.00	3.58	3.03

'N' refers to the number of directors with directorships in the sectors and regions indicated; 'means' refers to the average number of corporate interlocks carried by directors of a given type.

dence of a cohesive far-west capitalist fraction detached from the east. Instead, a separate tabulation shows that of the 50 interlocks that knit the western firms into a subnetwork, 29 are carried by directors who have at least one corporate affiliation in the eastern metropoli. The regional network that had emerged by 1996 with the shift of corporate command centres westward was simply a segment of a national network that entailed extensive east-west interlocking.

If we consider now the sectoral pattern of corporate affiliations, most of the 237 directors were 'finance capitalists' in Zeitlin's (1989) terms: they directed financial institutions *together with* major nonfinancial corporations. Fully 158—two-thirds of the total—manifested this pattern, and it was these directors who engaged in most of the interlocking.

Finally, the most dramatic contrast is between the 16 exclusively 'far-west' directors (who had no directorships with major financial institutions and carried few interlocks) and the 60 finance capitalists who directed both eastern and western companies, averaging nearly six interlocks. The latter 60 directors—integrating through their multiple directorships both east and west, both industry and finance—were the most significant players in the spatialized network of corporate power. Although they made up only a quarter of its individual members, they carried nearly half of the entire 1996 network.[16]

CONCLUSION

Our analysis of shifts in the location of head offices and in interlocking directorships suggests that each of the four developments discussed earlier contributed to the recomposition of corporate power in the context of a five-decade-long shift westward.

As the notion of organized capitalism suggests, head-office locations were consolidated into a very few metropolitan command centres, so that by 1996 the network had been simplified into a bipolar configuration with two major urban centres and two lesser ones in the far west. Although nearby secondary centres like London, Quebec City, and Edmonton were home to a few head offices and thereby figured peripherally in the national network, there was by 1996 very little involvement of such places. However, after the 1970s there was no cumulative trend for Toronto to increase its stature as central metropolis. As Calgary became an attractive site for corporations based in the Alberta energy sector, several major firms such as Shell Canada and Suncor shifted their head-office locations from Toronto to Calgary, enhancing the basis for a western subnetwork.

Indeed, there was a dramatic movement of industrial head offices westward, tracking the flow of capital. Yet directors with far-west affiliations tended to link only moderately with other far-west firms; most of their links were with corporations based in the Toronto–Montreal heartland, where the major sources of finance—both financial institutions and stock exchanges—continue to be housed.[17] It is also worth noting that although regional forward-linkage growth strategies were to some extent successful in diversifying the industrial composition of the west, in 1996 most large 'high-tech' communications companies were based in the east.[18]

Quebec nationalism also left its mark, in two distinct ways. The threat of economic instability associated with the independentist project provoked a retreat by old money to Toronto (and even to Calgary with Canadian Pacific's move from Montreal in 1997). However, the nationalist project also meant the rise of new Quebec-based companies to economic prominence—the financial institutions of Quebec City, the Caisse de Dépôt in Montreal with its various strategic shareholdings in mainly Quebec-based concerns, and such industrial corporations as Bombardier, Donohue, Groupe Vidéotron, and Quebecor. The recomposition of Montreal-based corporate capital involved both *a decline in Montreal's national profile and an upswing in the French-Canadian presence*. Over the half century, the number of corporate-elite members directing Quebec-based firms fell from 129 to 115—but the percentage of such directors who could be categorized according to surname as French Canadian jumped from 12 per cent to 31 per cent. These results support the thesis proposed by Niosi two decades ago, that the French Canadian bourgeoisie has arisen not as a 'national bourgeoisie' interested in independence as a means to secure a home market, but rather as 'the French Canadian section of the Canadian capitalist class' (1981:68).

Finally, on the issue of foreign-based fractions of capital, the half-century divides into two periods. Over the first three decades the enormous international expansion of US-based capital enlarged the comprador element in Canada's corporate elite, in a spatially nuanced way. Part of Toronto's and Calgary's rise to prominence reflected high rates of industrial accumulation in the branch plants of Ontario and the foreign-controlled oil fields of Alberta. Yet the weakening of American hegemony and the robustness of Canadian-based capitalists meant that the trend of the first three decades was reversed in the latter two, with a net reduction of the comprador element at the top echelon of corporate power.

It is intriguing and perhaps paradoxical that, as of 1996, a predominantly 'national' corporate elite—arrayed east to west and linking industry with finance—governed major corporations in an economy whose trade and investment flows were increasingly moving north to south.[19] The image of 'silent surrender' drawn so vividly by Kari Levitt (1970) at the height of American hegemony—of Canadian capitalists literally selling out to American-based transnationals and in the process becoming a dependent class of branch-plant managers and coupon-clippers—is not sustained by our empirical analysis. But how stable the current configuration may be is unclear. Our analysis leaves open the prospect of re-compradorization through foreign takeovers—a possible longer-term implication of continental integration in conjunction with currency exchange rates that reduce the cost of Canadian corporate assets to US investors. We will take up this issue, among others, in Chapter 6.

Somewhat clearer is the answer to the question of whether the national network has undergone a regionalizing fragmentation, a balkanization. Despite a drop in the extent of interlocking, which we have analyzed in previous chapters, there has been no regional fractioning along the lines predicted by analysts such as Richards and Pratt (1979) a quarter of a century ago. Instead, the well-integrated centre of Canadian finance capital has stretched westward, incorporating Calgary and Vancouver as emergent sites. By 1996 the network's basic form could be described as an east-west structure carried primarily by finance capitalists, with directorships in both industrial and financial corporations. Across half a century, even as its contours were reshaped by the westward shift of command centres and the greater complement of French-Canadian corporate capitalists based in Quebec, the Canadian corporate elite largely maintained its cohesiveness. Neither Montreal nor Toronto retained the pre-eminence of earlier times, but their continuing dominance in finance (and also in a more diversified array of big industry) lent some institutional stability to the geography of corporate power while ensuring that, among major corporations, interlocks originating in the far west would for the most part terminate in the two eastern centres.

From a more international perspective, only Toronto could lay some claim to being a 'global city' by the close of the twentieth century. In a recent international study of some 3000 cities, Toronto was the only Canadian city ranking in the Top 50 in terms of its closeness to other major cities in the global network of parent corporations and their subsidiaries. Toronto ranked eleventh, behind the four leading global cities (Paris, Tokyo, London, and New York) and also behind San Francisco, Düsseldorf, Amsterdam, Munich, Chicago, and Stockholm (in that order), but ahead of centres like Zürich, Los Angeles, Madrid, and Dallas (Alderson and Beckfield, 2002).

As the twentieth century drew to a close, the Canadian corporate elite appeared well-integrated across the main urban centres of economic power, across the financial and industrial forms of capital, and across the Anglo–French ethnic difference.

This spatial, sectoral, and ethnic integration presented a structural basis for strong business leadership in both economic and extra-economic fields. Whether such corporate hegemony is ultimately compatible with a democratic way of life is another matter, which we will take up in our conclusion.

Chapter 6

Continental Connections: Toward a North American Corporate Elite?

Juxtaposed to the east-west axis of finance capital within Canada, which we explored in the previous chapter, has been the north–south pull of 'continental corporate power' (Clement, 1977). Since the signing of the 1989 US–Canada Free Trade Agreement, the question of the organizational impact of continental economic relations on the network of the largest Canadian and American corporations has if anything gained salience. Has there been a continentalization of corporate elites? Have we witnessed the formation of a North American capitalist class? The most important earlier study in this field concluded, on the basis of data from the early to mid-1970s, that continental connections 'reflect a pattern in which a segment of Canada's elite has been drawn into the inner circle of the U.S. elite' (Clement, 1977:179). This meant enhanced continental power for one Canadian elite segment, but a deepening dependency for Canadian society (179–80). Clement's thesis was that 'the financial-industrial axis is continental for Canada but national within the United States' (1977:179). Canadian financial capitalists participated in continental relations of allocative power, helping to fund the Canadian investments of American industrial capitalists, who participated in continental relations of strategic power through their control of branch plants. Clement's novel and influential study drew a picture of corporate power in a continental system that consisted of the world's major capitalist metropole and a secondary, developed yet dependent country. Our findings from previous chapters already cast doubt on this picture. If transnational finance capital has radiated from Canada in a way that has maintained a national corporate network, reaching westward with the emergence of Calgary and Vancouver as corporate command centres, then whatever north–south axis might exist may be quite secondary in importance. On the other hand, as continental economic relations have deepened in the wake of the free-trade agreements of 1989 and 1994, a blending of corporate elites may well have occurred. But the impact of free trade—the disappearance of tariffs, the increase in Canada–US trade, the rationalization of corporate structures—may run in the opposite direction. After all, if from the National Policy onward tariffs were intended to promote 'industrialization by invitation' (Naylor, 1975), then their removal should have eliminated much of the incentive for branch plants, and for a comprador elite.

Besides mapping the trend in continental elite formation, our analysis explores the possibility that in the post-FTA era *different kinds of continental connections*, consistent with both continental integration and a more globalized regime of accumulation, have emerged. With a weakening in American control of large Canadian firms, continental connections may be structured less along parent–subsidiary lines and more along the loosely organized financial–industrial lines we noted in Chapter 4. In a continental economic space we might expect such a shift, particularly among the transnational corporations.

Here, as elsewhere in this book, our empirical analysis has both a biographical and an organizational aspect. We consider the 'continental linkers' who serve simultaneously on American and Canadian corporate boards but also the cross-border network and the kinds of Canadian and American firms that participate in it. The objective is to situate Canada's corporate elite within a field of continental relationships. Although this chapter focuses on elite-level corporate interlocks, at its close we shall look at some of the other forms of corporate continentalism in light of changes in the corporate network.

NATIONAL AND CONTINENTAL NETWORKS: BASIC ARCHITECTURE

To conduct this analysis we identified the Top 250 American corporations of 1976 and 1996, exactly as we did for our Canadian samples, and gathered data on their directors.[1] We then merged the Canadian and American data in each year, verifying the names of apparent corporate interlockers, and proceeded to trace out the continental connections.

As a structure of corporate affiliations, the 509 dominant Canadian and American corporations for 1976 generated 7384 directorships (3409 in Canada and 3975 in the US). The analogous figure for the 512 corporations in 1996 was 6204 (2915 in Canada and 3289 in the US). However, our interest is in the directors who actually participate in interlocks, forming national corporate elites and possibly a continental elite. We limited the analysis to the corporate affiliations of those with two or more directorships in any of the continental 'Top 500': 3325 corporate affiliations in 1976 and 2544 in 1996. These directorships were held by 1209 people in 1976 and 944 in 1996. It is these interlocking directorships that we analyze.

The corporate affiliations can be categorized according to whether the incumbents are 'continental linkers'—directors of both a Canadian and American firm. In 1976, of the 1640 directorships in Canadian firms 270 were held by continental linkers, and of 1685 directorships in American firms 235 were held by continental linkers. By 1996, the corresponding values had fallen steeply, to 87 of 1252 Canadian directorships and 82 of 1292 American directorships. Continental interlocking appeared to wane in the closing decades of the twentieth century.

We have already commented in Chapter 4 on the general weakening of corporate interlocking in Canada, the reasons for it and its concentration particularly among primary ties formerly carried by bankers. Interestingly, Davis and Mizruchi found similar patterns in the American corporate network between 1982 and 1994, as did Barnes and Ritter (2001) between 1983 and 1995. Interpreting the declining centrality of American banks as part of the trend toward disorganized capitalism, Davis and Mizruchi concluded that as alternative forms of corporate financing developed in the 1980s and 1990s, banks' traditional monopoly on corporate lending evaporated. Banks responded by further internationalizing their lending and moving towards transaction-based finance, which does not involve directorate interlocks. As they shifted away from corporate lending, banks withdrew from their role as network centres, resulting in 'a more fragmented intercorporate network' in which banks, although still relatively central, were no longer able to knit together the corporate elite (1999:235).

In Table 6.1 we see clear evidence of a weakening in the American corporate network, which already in 1976 was somewhat more diffuse than Canada's. In the entire continental network the percentage of all pairs of corporations sharing one or more directors fell from 2.41 per cent to 1.75 per cent. The decline occurred both within national networks and between them. Interlock density in the American network was approximately two-thirds that of the Canadian network in 1976, and the thinning of ties continued south of the 49th parallel, though at a slower pace than in Canada. Compared with the American network, primary interlocks in Canada declined more precipitously, and what was a substantial difference in densities in 1976 became attenuated two decades later. The disappearance, with corporate governance reforms, of bankers on the boards of industrial corporations—a key structural transformation of the Canadian network—has no parallel in the US, which already had a looser organization of finance capital.[2]

The most revealing aspect of the table is that it shows the steepest decline occurring in continental connections. Compared to the national networks, continental connections were *quite rare in 1976 and extremely rare in 1996*. Already in 1976, only about five in every thousand pairs of large Canadian and American firms was interlocked, for the most part via shared outside directors. By 1996, primary continental connections had all but disappeared from the network, and the density of secondary continental connections had declined by more than half. The continental segment was just a remnant of its earlier form. Continental ties occurred at a rate of two for every thousand Canadian–American pairs—less than one-tenth the density of interlocking in either of the national networks. There is no evidence here

TABLE 6.1

Densities In and Between National Segments of the Continental Network

	1976			1996		
	Primary	*Secondary*	*All ties*	*Primary*	*Secondary*	*All ties*
Within Canada	1.262	4.195	5.019	0.676	3.071	3.514
Within US	0.892	3.096	3.712	0.629	2.667	3.146
Continental	0.122	0.432	0.519	0.040	0.168	0.204
Entire network	0.592	2.011	2.409	0.342	1.501	1.747

NOTE: Densities are expressed as percentages of pairs of firms in a given category whose directorates were interlocked according to the stated criterion, and are calculated on the basis of all corporations in each national sample, including isolates. Ns: for 1976, 257 Canadian and 252 American firms; for 1996, 258 Canadian and 254 American firms.

of US–Canada elite integration by way of board interlocks. Moreover, most continental connections were carried by outside directors rather than corporate insiders, and this bias grew greater over time. By 1996 the continental segment consisted mainly of a sparse collection of overlapping outside directorships. If anything, the tendency has been the reverse of that predicted by Wallace Clement (1977:181–2):

> It can be anticipated that as the operations of U.S. branch plants in Canada mature and become established, more of the executives will be recruited from and trained in the branch plants, and more members of the indigenous elite will be drafted into their board rooms. . . . the U.S. and Canadian elites are becoming increasingly integrated with one another upon a mutually reinforcing power base.

If Table 6.1 provides an overall sketch, to fill in the details we need to consider the actual continental connections in each year. In 1976 the primary lines in the continental network were overwhelmingly expressions of American strategic control. There were 100 primary continental interlocking directorships, some of which functioned as multiple-director interlocks between firms.[3] Of those 100 ties 66 involved executives of US-based firms serving as outside directors of Canadian firms, 10 involved executives of both a Canadian and a US firm, and 24 involved Canadian executives sitting as outside directors of American firms.

However—consistent with Clement's (1977) claim that Canadian capitalists do not serve on American boards in the exercise of strategic control—none of the last set involved strategic control of US firms by Canadian capitalists. Indeed, in four of those 24 cases the control relationship went the other way.[4] The other 20 mostly involved executives of Canadian-controlled firms serving in advisory capacities south of the border.[5] Clearly, in 1976 Canadian capitalists had not extended their control of major corporations into the US.

The exact opposite held for the other 76 continental primary connections, of which 69 involved American strategic control. This is the hierarchical structure of command that so concerned Canadian dependency scholars in the 1970s. Nevertheless, by 1996 the number of primary continental links had plummeted to 26. Only 17 represented relations of US–Canada intercorporate control, and five of these were 'go-between' in nature.[6] By 1996, then, *only a dozen primary lines* could be considered part of a transnational corporate governance structure internal to US-based TNCs.[7]

Similar inferences can be drawn from a close analysis of secondary interlocks. In 1976 the 253 lines of this type, connecting 105 Canadian corporations with 92 US firms, were often associated with American strategic control. In all, 111 of the 253 lines linked US-controlled Canadian companies to American-based firms, though not necessarily to the parent firms.[8] Another 18 secondary continental links connected Canadian firms controlled outside North America to American firms, some of which were themselves controlled outside North America.[9] By 1996, however, only five of the 90 secondary continental lines reflected US–Canada intercorporate control, and for one of these the US parent served as a go-between for a European controlling interest.[10]

Across the two decades, then, there was a dramatic attrition in continental connections, both primary and secondary. In 1976, 73 primary and 35 secondary connections followed clear intercorporate ownership ties between American parents and Canadian subsidiaries. By 1996, 12 primary and 4 secondary lines followed the same lines of ownership and control. Yet in many cases, the American parent continued to exercise strategic control. For instance, Coke, Xerox, Amoco, GE, Ford, and Bankers Trust had no interlocks with their Canadian subsidiaries. Cases such as these point not to a severing of continental capital relations but to *a different kind of continental management regime* within American-based TNCs. In other cases, including Goodyear, Weyerhaeuser, McDonald's, Sears, and Textron, the long-standing pattern of board interlocks between American parent and Canadian subsidiary continued into the late 1990s.

The other lines in the continental network did not involve the transnational control of corporate capital. These also decreased, from 218 to 99. By 1996 most of the remaining continental connections were weak, and some implied more globalized circuits of accumulation. Part of this decrease can be attributed to the thinning of corporate interlocks, in both countries. Part can be attributed to the decreased number of large Canadian firms under American control. And part may have to do with changes in the management regime both for the continental economy and for TNCs more generally—an issue we will revisit at the close of this chapter.

IN SEARCH OF THE CONTINENTAL CORE

The weakening of continental connections detailed above should not be mistaken for a sign that the network is disappearing altogether. It is true that by 1996 198 of the 258 leading Canadian corporations shared no directors with any of the 254 leading American corporations (up from 134 in 1976). Even so, most large Canadian firms remained 'reachable', at least indirectly, by leading American corporations. In fact, the numbers of large companies from both countries that participated at least indirectly in the continental network did not change much. In 1976, 467 corporations formed a single connected component with a diameter of seven and a mean distance of 2.988. In 1996, the dominant component—the largest set in which all points are ultimately reachable by all other points—contained 458 companies. Its diameter was nine and the mean distance between companies within it had risen to 3.408.[11]

Although the general trend was away from the highly organized system of continental interlocks, the movement in this direction was uneven. Among companies with one or more interlocks of any kind, the proportion involved in continental interlocking fell from 49.8 per cent to 26.7 per cent. However, there continued to be heavy continental interlocking among a relatively small set of companies. The continental segment became narrower in its immediate membership, yet there remained a (relatively sparse) network into which most large Canadian and American firms were drawn, typically through indirect ties.

Certain corporations even became more central in the continental segment. A serviceable way of identifying those key participants is through Anthonisse's 'rush'—an index of the extent to which a point lies *between* many other points in a network. The index can be defined for various subsets of points, which makes it especially useful for present purposes. The key participants in the continental network are not simply companies with interlocks that cross the national border, but companies that, within the network, lie *between a great many firms in both countries*. We therefore calculated the rush for American companies from the US into Canada, and for Canadian companies from Canada into the US. If we think of the entire continental network of 500-odd corporations as consisting of intercorporate 'flows' that are proportionate to the number of directors who directly or indirectly connect pairs of firms via the shortest available path, the 'rush' of a given point indicates the fraction of all flow that passes through that point. For our purposes, this means that a company with a high rush score lies on many of the shortest paths between Canadian and American companies, rendering it central in the continental network. If continentalism has a core, its inhabitants are listed in Table 6.2, along with their rush scores.

As one moves from the very centre of the continental network the scores decline quickly. The most central Canadian company in 1996, Nortel Networks, has a rush score five times greater than the 16th ranked Canadian firm, and ten times the rush score of the 30th ranked Canadian firm. Although the 30 most central firms from each country comprise less than 12 per cent of each Top 250, their rush scores account for more than half the sum of all rush scores in each Top 250. This group contains the crucial mediating nodes in the continental network.

On the Canadian side of the ledger, it is striking how the Royal Bank, pre-eminent as the most central company in 1976, was displaced two decades later by Nortel, whose rush score in 1996 was more than twice the Royal's. In fact, Canadian banks in general lost continental centrality over the two decades. In 1976 chartered banks held the three most central positions on the Canadian side of the network; by 1996 the three most central Canadian firms were industrial corporations. This is not to say that financial institutions moved to the margins. As in 1976, five of the ten most central Canadian corporations in 1996 were financials. But with the reform-induced weakening in financial centrality, the biggest Canadian banks lost their singularity as central nodes, in both the national and the continental network. In both years, the thirty leading participants in the continental network made up a cross-section of big industry and finance. There is certainly no support for the idea that the key Canadian players in corporate continentalism have been financial institutions or commercial firms. Nor have the most central Canadian companies been subsidiaries of US parents to any great extent. In 1976 only five of the core 30 were controlled by US-based corporations, and in 1996 only two were.[12]

Clement's distinction between 'the relationships of parent companies and branch plants and the direct connection from a U.S. dominant to a Canadian dominant, independent of foreign control' (1977:173) is highly relevant here. Among Canadian firms at the heart of the continental network, in both years, we find that most were independent of foreign control. Some of these companies have been controlled ultimately by wealthy families (such as the Bombardier-Beaudoins, Desmarais, and Bronfmans), others by constellations of interests (the banks and life

TABLE 6.2
Leading Participants in the Continental Network

	Canada		US	
1976				
Rank	Name	Rush	Name	Rush
1	Royal Bank	0.1138	Metropolitan Life	0.0936
2	CIBC	0.0660	New York Life	0.0434
3	Bank of Montreal	0.0402	General Motors	0.0389
4	Canadian Pacific	0.0379	Citicorp (F)	0.0388
5	Sun Life	0.0332	Chrysler	0.0316
6	Celanese Canada	0.0328	Continental Corp. (F)	0.0285
7	Power Corporation	0.0323	Caterpillar Tractor	0.0239
8	Inco	0.0310	Chase Manhattan Bank	0.0215
9	Abitibi	0.0308	Union Carbide	0.0198
10	Toronto-Dominion Bank	0.0282	Equitable Life	0.0192
11	Simpson-Sears	0.0258	Chemical Bank	0.0172
12	Brascan	0.0233	Uniroyal Inc.	0.0167
13	Bell Canada	0.0218	A T & T	0.0166
14	Canada Life	0.0201	Bankers Trust	0.0159
15	Can Perm Mortgage	0.0199	International Paper	0.0157
16	Bombardier	0.0182	US Steel	0.0156
17	Iron Ore Co. of Can.	0.0181	General Electric	0.0148
18	Northern & Central Gas	0.0146	Eaton Corp.	0.0146
19	Genstar	0.0134	Celanese Corp.	0.0143
20	Seagram	0.0134	Prudential Life	0.0140
21	Great-West Life	0.0122	Standard Brands	0.0135
22	Massey-Ferguson	0.0122	Beatrice Foods	0.0130
23	Pratt Whitney	0.0120	Mutual of New York	0.0126
24	Mercantile Bank	0.0118	First Chicago Corp (F)	0.0124
25	Investors Group	0.0118	Kraft Inc.	0.0122
26	TransCanada PipeLine	0.0112	B.F. Goodrich	0.0122
27	Imperial Life	0.0111	J.P.Morgan	0.0117
28	Cominco	0.0108	United Airlines	0.0112
29	Northern Telecom	0.0105	Consolidated Foods	0.0108
30	Consolidated-Bathurst	0.0100	American Motors	0.0104
1996				
Rank	Name	Rush	Name	Rush
1	Nortel Networks	0.1290	Prudential Life	0.0720
2	Avenor	0.0684	Amoco	0.0552
3	Imasco	0.0596	Ford	0.0532
4	Toronto-Dominion Bank	0.0590	Textron	0.0481
5	CIBC	0.0521	Honeywell	0.0458
6	Bank of Montreal	0.0493	American Express	0.0450
7	Seagram	0.0485	Bell Atlantic	0.0277

TABLE 6.2 continued
Leading Participants in the Continental Network

Rank	Name	Rush	Name	Rush
8	Royal Bank	0.0462	General Electric	0.0266
9	Manulife	0.0461	Allied Chemical	0.0242
10	Sears Canada	0.0457	Ingersoll-Rand	0.0224
11	Laidlaw	0.0354	Northrop Grumman	0.0212
12	Power Corp.	0.0317	American International	0.0212
13	Molson	0.0314	Massachusetts Mutual Life	0.0212
14	Canadian Pacific	0.0290	May Department Stores	0.0209
15	Canada Life	0.0269	Woolworth Corp.	0.0196
16	United Dominion Indust.	0.0252	GTE Corp.	0.0187
17	Sun Life	0.0231	Westinghouse	0.0184
18	Weyerhaeuser Canada	0.0208	Coca-Cola	0.0177
19	Inco	0.0204	Nynex Corp.	0.0177
20	Rio Algom	0.0195	Morgan Stanley	0.0172
21	CT Financial	0.0194	McDonalds	0.0163
22	Rogers Communications	0.0190	Ashland Inc.	0.0161
23	Barrick Gold	0.0185	Chase Manhattan Bank	0.0157
24	Thomson Corp.	0.0172	Sears	0.0156
25	Noranda	0.0170	Bankers Trust	0.0154
26	Hollinger	0.0160	Bank of New York	0.0147
27	Nova	0.0152	Xerox	0.0145
28	Bank of Nova Scotia	0.0143	Pharmacia & Upjohn	0.0144
29	Teleglobe	0.0134	PPG Industries	0.0143
30	Bombardier	0.0133	Goodyear	0.0142

insurers, Canadian Pacific, Inco). The stability of membership in this most continentally connected section of the Canadian corporate network is also striking. Thirteen firms appear on both Canadian lists, and eight of the 15 most central companies of 1976 (four of them banks) continued to rank among the top 15 in 1996.

On the American side there are several parallels, as large financial institutions like Metropolitan Life, New York Life, and Citicorp were by 1996 displaced from pre-eminence by the likes of Amoco, Ford, and Textron. However, the most continentally central US company in 1996 was still a financial institution, as were two others in the top 15. Although large financial institutions contributed some stability to the membership of this network core, only four companies appear on the American list in both years.[13] By 1996 the key American corporations in the continental network were transnational industrials. But the most telling contrast between the two sides of corporate continentalism is the continued presence of American companies with subsidiaries in Canada.[14] In 1976, 13 of the core 30 were American parents of dominant Canadian companies. By 1996, the American parents numbered 11. While Canadian subsidiaries of American parents were on the margins of the continental network, certain American parents were central, as they interlocked not only with their Canadian units but with other leading corporations in both countries. Conversely, the marginality of the Canadian subsidiaries stems from their lack of 'betweenness'. As operating branches of TNCs, these firms have tended to have small, introverted boards that do not necessarily overlap with the boards of local corporations. For instance, in 1996 Canadian subsidiaries of Compaq, Goodyear, A&P, and Ultramar all shared directors with their respective parents but were completely isolated from the Canadian network. The parent–subsidiary relation did not lead to other links in a chain of interlocking; hence these companies had rush scores of zero. This peripherality was typical for wholly owned subsidiaries of US-based firms, whose mean rush scores were barely distinguishable from zero in both 1976 and 1996.[15] Among such corporations the degree of direct continental interlocking fell from 1.3 to 0.46 over the two decades. The practice of appointing directors of the parent TNC to oversee the Canadian subsidiary, common in the 1970s and earlier, was no longer conventional by the late 1990s, suggesting the emergence of a different regime of transnational management.

The continental network has been an amalgamation of the two kinds of relations noted by Clement, both of which have declined in number if not significance. Parent–subsidiary ties have generated a flagging number of *introverted* cross-border interlocks. As corporate governance reforms have taken hold and as banks have lost some of their structural centrality, other forms of elite recruitment and intercorporate relations have generated a sparser network of more *extroverted* continental ties. Figures 6.1 and 6.2, which show all interlocks among the firms listed in Table 6.2, mainly map the latter kinds of continental connections. It is clear that the vast majority of interlocks connect Canadian firms with each other and American firms with each other, that virtually all of the thick, multiple-director interlocks occur among firms domiciled in the same country, and that across the two decades the national and continental segments of the network have become sparser.[16]

Within this core of the continental network, companies sharing the same national domicile are heavily interlocked. However, few ties span the national border[17]—with four noteworthy exceptions. In 1976 the boards of Metropolitan Life and the Royal Bank were key meeting points for members of the continental elite. Metropolitan Life had a social circle of 15 corporations that included seven Canadian companies and featured a double-director interlock with Power Corporation—the only thick cross-border interlock in either year. The Royal Bank's social circle included 14 Canadian and eight American firms (with thick ties to nine of the Canadian companies). In 1996, British-controlled but Toronto-based Imasco had a social circle of nine companies, five of which were American-based. Finally, Nortel's 1996 social circle included nine Canadian corporations (with double-director ties to the Bank of Montreal, the Royal Bank, and Noranda) and six American firms including Bell Atlantic, Westinghouse, and two financial institutions.

The late 1990s was a period of exponential growth for Nortel, and although the dot.com bubble had burst by 2001, relegating Nortel to penny-stock status on the NYSE by July 2002, in the late 1990s Nortel was positioning itself to take full advantage of opportunities in the continental economy as part of its program of

FIGURE 6.1
Interlocks Among Companies Most Central in the Continental Network, 1976

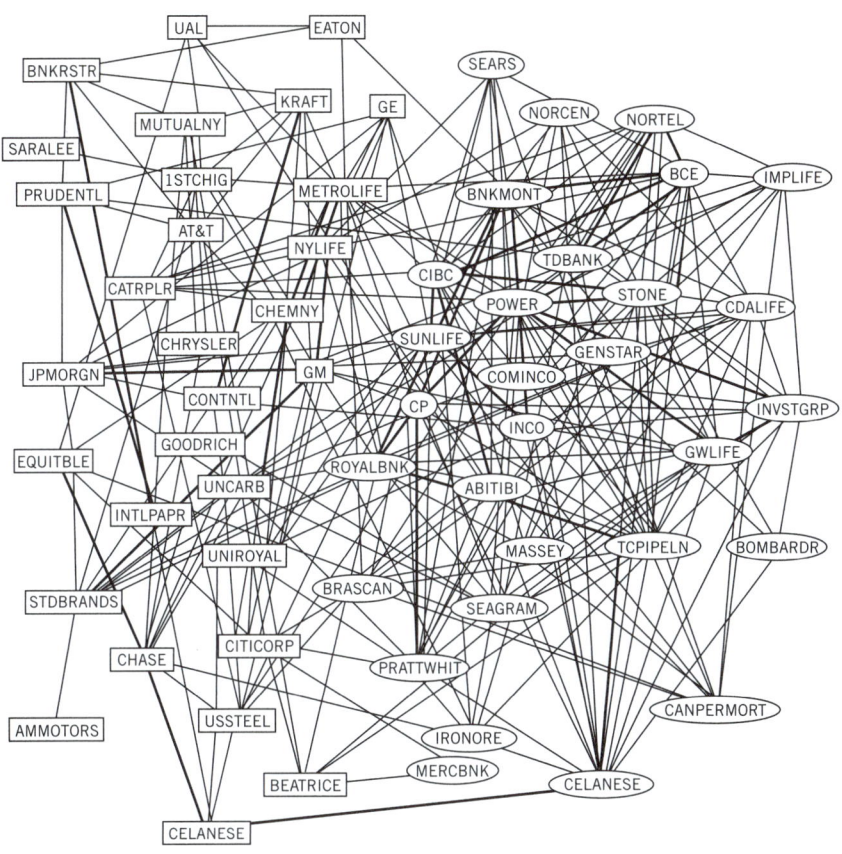

Canadian firms are in ovals; American firms are in boxes. Line thickness indicates the number of shared directors.

global expansion. Although its head office remains in Brampton, Ontario, Nortel moved its executive offices to Dallas in the 1990s, having had a major manufacturing presence there since the 1970s. Perhaps Nortel heralds a new form of corporate continentalism, distinct from the US-controlled branch plants that formed part of what Jenson (1989) aptly termed Canada's 'permeable fordism' during the post-1945 era. By 1996 some other major Canadian-controlled firms also shared directors with Top American financial institutions. Seagram's board was interlocked with three major American financials, Inco's with two. Most of the continental ties involving Nortel, Seagram, and Inco were secondary interlocks, carried by outside directors.

These kinds of cross-border ties seem compatible with the weakly organized financial–industrial relations that have come to prevail with the 'disorganization' of

116 *The Spatial Terrain*

FIGURE 6.2

Interlocks Among Companies Most Central in the Continental Network, 1996

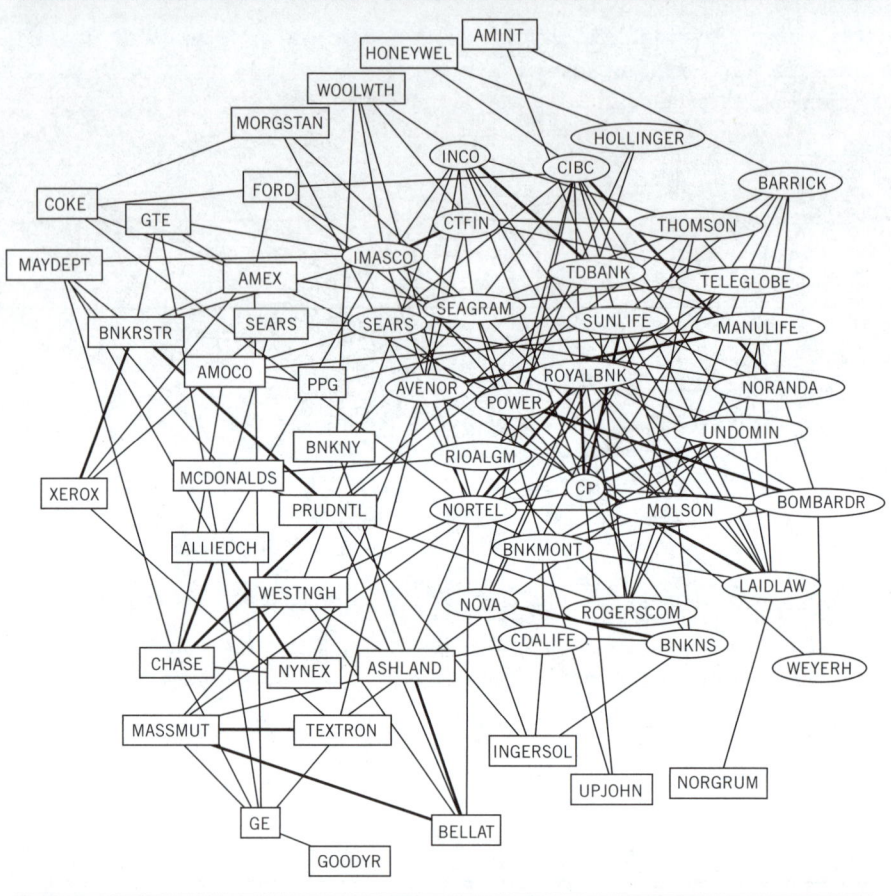

Canadian firms are in ovals; American firms are in boxes. Line thickness indicates the number of shared directors.

national capitalisms. In a world where fictitious capital washes across national borders at the speed of light, having well-connected members of the American corporate elite on board can improve business 'scan'—knowledge across a whole range of firms and industries—and facilitate the well-timed financial transactions that fuel competitiveness. Such arrangements may present the face of the future for some of the very largest Canadian-based corporations. There is some evidence, then, of a shift from the pattern discerned by Clement (with some exaggeration) in the mid-1970s—in which parent–subsidiary relations provided the basic architecture for a continental network grounded in unilateral strategic control—to a corporate continentalism in which Canada's finance capitalists come to operate effectively in a North American space, in the process shedding much of whatever it was that founded their claim to being 'Canadian'.

In general, however, Figures 6.1 and 6.2 reveal more of a continuing structural integrity in the national networks than they do a cumulative process of continentalization. On balance, a *decline in continental ties* among these select companies is what stands out most clearly. By 1996, the frontier between the Canadian and American segments was traversed by 44 thin ties, compared to the 214 ties (26 of them thick) that linked the 30 Canadian firms and the 92 ties (11 of them thick) that linked the 30 American firms.

SECTORAL PATTERNS IN CORPORATE CONTINENTALISM

Two questions arise from this analysis of the most central companies. First, what have been the overall patterns of interlocking among the entire 500-odd corporations, taking into account structurally relevant features such as industry and location of head office? Second, which directors have actually carried the continental connections and what has been the pattern of their involvement? These are the concerns of the remainder of this chapter.

For initial guidance on the first question we can again consult Wallace Clement (1977:179), who argues that the continental network has manifested a distinct sectoral pattern:

> A continental elite connecting the sectors of greatest strengths can be said to exist, although it would be wrong to say that the entire elite is a continental one. The exchanges, because of the particular historical development of each nation, occur in such a way that they are mainly from Canadian finance to U.S. manufacturing and from U.S. manufacturing to Canadian finance—from strength to strength.

With a larger sample and a longitudinal design, can Clement's thesis on the *sectoral specificity* of continental connections be sustained? In Table 6.3 we compare mean degree of interlocking within and between national segments of the continental network. Four findings stand out.

1. Consistent with earlier observations, the degree of interlocking within Canada is greater than that within the US, and the degree within each country is much greater than between them. While the Canada–US difference narrows somewhat, the disparity between national and continental connections increases over the twenty years.
2. In 1976, *within* the Canadian national network, financial institutions, investment companies, and communications-utilities were heavy interlockers and commercial firms were marginal. Canadian commercial companies were also least involved in cross-border interlocking, and investment companies (Power, Brascan, Anglo-Canadian Tel) and resource companies (Iron Ore, Falconbridge, Inco) were most continentally interlocked. Contrary to Clement's claim, Canadian financial institutions were on average not particularly interlocked with US-based corporations.
3. In 1976, *within* the American national network, financial institutions were by far the most central, and investment, resource, and commercial companies the least. As for continental connections, it was not the US manufacturing sector

TABLE 6.3

Mean Degree of Interlocking Within and Between National Segments of the Continental Network

	1976			
	Canada		US	
	National	Continental	National	Continental
Resources	11.62	1.81	5.46	1.69
Manufacturing	10.86	0.95	8.94	1.18
Utilities	17.72	1.39	8.77	0.69
Financial inst.	19.58	1.18	13.74	1.44
Investment co's	20.00	2.71	0.50	3.00
Commercial	6.97	0.88	5.80	0.44
Total	12.80	1.12	9.32	1.15
	1996			
	Canada		US	
	National	Continental	National	Continental
Resources	9.65	0.46	4.50	0.17
Manufacturing	8.46	0.52	9.65	0.49
Utilities	13.88	0.31	7.06	0.21
Financial inst.	10.24	0.42	8.88	0.52
Investment co's	8.75	0.25	3.00	0.00
Commercial	4.52	0.31	4.12	0.45
Total	9.02	0.42	7.96	0.43

but the resource companies and financial institutions that tended towards continental linkage.[18] This pattern is not easily reconciled with Clement's account from the same period. Canadian financial institutions were not particularly integrated with the American network, nor were American manufacturers especially connected with the Canadian network.

4. By 1996 the prominence of financial institutions in both national networks had diminished. In Canada the communications-utilities sector was the most central, and in the US manufacturing companies were. Except for the commercial sector in both countries and the resource and investment-company sectors in the US (all of which continued to be relatively marginal to the national networks), sectoral differences in degree of interlocking had plunged. The same decline is evident in the continental segment of the network, particularly on the Canadian side. From the American side, financial institutions, manufacturers, and commercial firms were the most continentally connected, averaging roughly 0.5 interlocks with Canadian firms.

These figures do not show the actual structure of corporate interlocking across sectors of the continental economy. As a direct test of Clement's thesis that the financial–industrial axis has been national for the US but continental for Canada, we replicated his analysis, focusing on the manufacturing and financial-intermediation sectors that are crucial to the hypothesis. In Figure 6.3 it is clear that, at least at the level of interlocking directorates, no continental financial–industrial axis existed either in 1976 or in 1996. The minuscule size of the cross-border densities between financials and manufacturers refutes the notion of a continental axis between Canadian financials and US-based manufacturers. What is more interesting, however, is the way that *the pattern of densities within Canada comes to resemble the American network*, as ties weaken between financial institutions and manufacturers and among financial institutions. Although the persistence of family-controlled corporate groups in Canada may mitigate matters, it appears that corporate governance reforms have harmonized the shape and form of the Canadian corporate network to the American norm of loosely structured interlocking (which Scott (1997) has termed the Anglo-American pattern of polyarchic financial hegemony).

A CONTINENTAL CORPORATE ELITE?

Our analysis thus far has focused mainly on corporations themselves, but each such tie involves a distinctive set of personal corporate affiliations. Who have been the key players in the continental network, and how does viewing the corporate elite in the context of US–Canada relations alter our picture? In Figure 6.4 directors of two or more dominant corporations are grouped in several categories. The entire set of interlocking directors numbered 1209 in 1976 and 944 in 1996, a decrease of one-fifth that reflects the move towards leaner boards and less bank-centred interlocking. Most directors had multiple corporate affiliations in only one of the two countries, and these types grew as a proportion of the entire continental elite. By 1996, 94.1 per cent of all individuals with two or more major North American corporate directorships participated in only one of the national corporate networks, up from 85.6 per cent in 1976. Most of this gain occurred at the expense of another distinct type: directors of one major Canadian and one major American corporation, whose numbers fell from 112 to 29. Other categories of continental linkers also decreased as a proportion of the entire set of directors. By 1996, individuals with multiple directorships on both sides of the border—the strongest candidates for a continental elite—disappeared entirely as a type.[19] At the level of individuals the trend has been towards *less* continentalism.

Besides the five fully 'continentalized' corporate directors of 1976, there have been two types of major players in the continental network: (1) those serving on multiple boards in one country and one further board in the other—the people who contribute directly to the close 'betweenness' of certain corporations in the continental network—and (2) those simply directing one major corporation in each country. The former are members of one country's corporate elite, with one additional directorship reaching into the other country. The latter are singularly 'continental' linkers. Within each type, in Table 6.4 we make two further distinctions having to do with nation and class: (1) between directors whose main affiliation is with a Canadian concern, directors whose principal affiliation is with an American concern, and directors mainly affiliated with concerns based outside of North America, and (2)

FIGURE 6.3
Densities of Interlocking Within and Between Four Segments of the Continental Network, 1976 and 1996

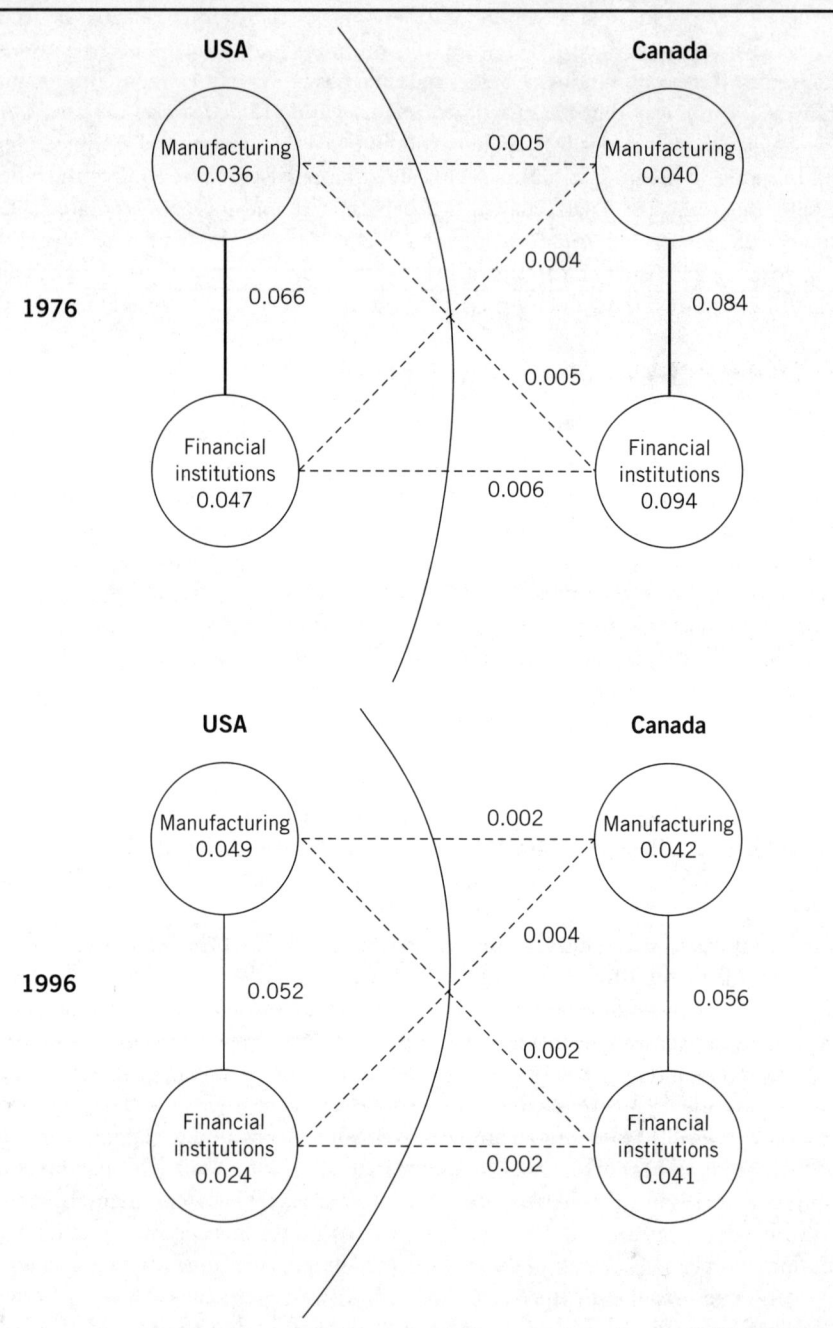

FIGURE 6.4
Continental Elite Grouped by Pattern of Corporate Affiliations

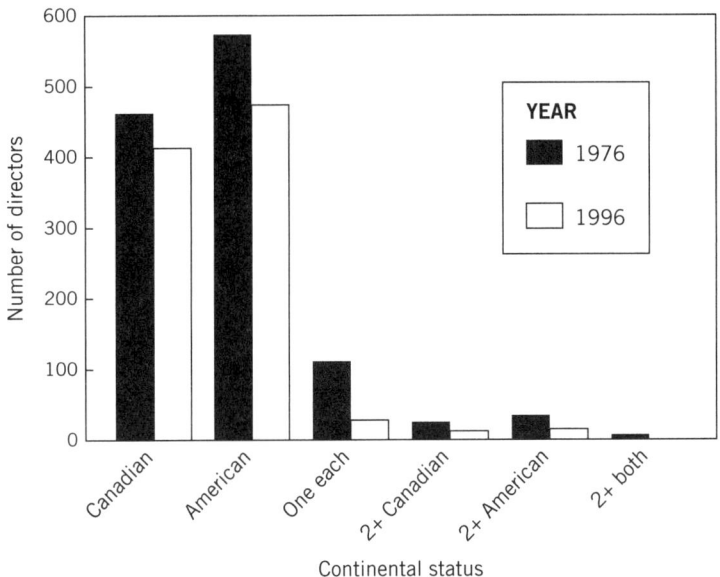

Key
Canadian: Directors of Canadian companies only
American: Directors of American companies only
One each: Directors of one Canadian and one American company
2+ Canadian: Directors of two or more Canadian and one American company
2+ American: Directors of two or more American and one Canadian company
2+ both: Directors of two or more Canadian and two or more American companies

between directors whose main affiliation positions them as financial capitalists, as non-financial (industrial) capitalists, or as advisors to corporate capital.[20]

It is evident that the directors bridging the border with single directorships on each side have been industrial capitalists affiliated mainly with American-based corporations. What we have here, particularly in 1976, are the managers of American transnational industrial capital: individuals at the centre of complexes of strategic and operational control based mainly in the US. Very few corporate advisors or financial capitalists manifest this pattern of interlocking, and comparatively few Canadian industrialists sit on an American board. Interestingly, by 1996, at which point the number of American-based industrialists with one directorship in each country had dropped from 84 to 15, six industrialists affiliated with globalizing firms based in Europe and Japan made up a subgroup within this type.

American-based industrialists also predominated among directors with multiple affiliations in the US and single affiliations in Canada, and by 1996 the relatively

TABLE 6.4
Types of Continental Linker, Cross-Classified by Class and Nation

Type of continental linker	Primary national affiliation	Class position			Total
		Financial exec	Industrial exec	Advisor	
1976					
One directorship in each country	Canadian	1	9	2	12
	American	3	84	5	92
	Other		5		5
Multiple in US, one in Canada	Canadian		1		1
	American	5	27		32
Multiple in Canada, one in US	Canadian	6	6	6	18
	American		4	1	5
	Other	1			1
Multiple in both countries	Canadian	2	1		3
	American		2		2
Total		18	139	14	171
1996					
One directorship in each country	Canadian		5	2	7
	American	1	15		16
	Other		6		6
Multiple in US, one in Canada	Canadian		1		1
	American	1	10	3	14
Multiple in Canada, one in US	Canadian	1	3	6	10
	American	1		1	2
Total		4	40	12	56

NOTE: Three individuals in 1976 could not be classified by class position, because biographical information was missing.

few American-based financial capitalists had been largely replaced by corporate advisors also based in the US. This type of continental interlocker represents an extension of the American corporate elite into Canada.[21] What stands out is the decline in strategic control as the fulcrum for this type of continental connection. By 1996 there were only five directors of multiple American corporations whose single directorship with a Canadian firm formed part of a parent–subsidiary relation.[22] Twenty years earlier, among the 33 directors of multiple American and single Canadian firms 23 were participants in a parent–subsidiary relation.

Finally, there is the type of continental connection involving members of the Canadian elite who sit on one major American board. After 1976 these also decreased, leaving only a dozen continentally connected members of the Canadian corporate elite. Further, the number of American-based capitalists in this category dropped from four to one. By 1996 James A. Parke, a vice-president with GE Capital (US) and a director of both GE Capital Canada and the Royal Bank, was the sole American-based capitalist who, according to our network criterion, belonged to Canada's corporate elite. However, corporate advisors gained profile within this type, as the number of capitalists fell from 17 to 5 while the number of advisors held steady at 7. In this sense, too, continental connections had become less significant in the actual control of corporations. Of the seven advisors, three were retired executives of chartered banks and one was a retired industrialist. *Éminences grises* had come to play a greater role in the developing continental network. By the same token, Canadian-based financial capitalists became less evident.[23]

In general, financial capitalists withdrew from the continental network, their total numbers declining from 18 to just four. Yet amid a disintegrating continental network corporate advisors nearly held their own. As to nationality, judged by principal affiliation, the predominance of Americans faded somewhat, particularly as many parent–subsidiary linkages disappeared. By 1996, 32 of the 56 continental linkers were American-affiliated (down from 131 in 1976), 18 were Canadian-affiliated (down from 34), and six were affiliated with businesses outside of North American—the last being executives in Japanese- and European-based transnational enterprises. The continental network of 1996 was a sparse collection of cross-border ties, relatively few of which entailed the strategic control of corporate capital, carried by forty executives in predominantly non-financial, US-based corporations, plus a dozen corporate advisors and a smattering of financial capitalists.

As a final note, it bears mention that corporate continentalism has been an overwhelmingly male preserve. In 1976, few women had gained entry to the corporate elite, whether American (3.3 per cent women) or Canadian (0.7 per cent), and not a single woman was involved in any type of continental interlocking. By 1996, women made up greater proportions of the domestic segments of the continental network (11.9 per cent of the American corporate elite and 9.2 per cent of the Canadian elite were women); yet only one woman was engaged in continental interlocking.[24]

Conclusions

Perhaps the most remarkable finding from our mapping of the continental network is the massive decline in the kinds of parent–subsidiary interlocks that have been taken as definitive of the relation between Canadian and American corporate elites. Part of the decline is simply a consequence of falling levels of American strategic control at the higher reaches of Canada's corporate economy, a trend we noted in earlier chapters. But even when we factor that decline into the picture, it is remarkable that by 1996 only a dozen primary interlocks between large American and Canadian corporations could be considered part of transnational corporate governance structures internal to US-based TNCs. What this finding suggests is a transition, or perhaps several interrelated transitions, in the structures and practices of transnational corporate management. While our data do not provide a basis for causal inferences, several speculative explanations for the disappearance of continental connections can be tentatively advanced.

Transnational corporations have not only been agents of globalization; they in turn have been reshaped by it. Their own internal structures have become more globalized as part of the broader process they have led. The mostly US-based TNCs that expanded into Canada and other countries before the mid-1970s typically had an organizational design that centred on the US market. 'International operations' were hived off as a separate division, with a vice-president who could well serve on the boards of key foreign subsidiaries. In the wake of the Second World War, American capitalists were hesitant to invest in Europe until the successful launching of the European Economic Community. Accordingly, their Canadian subsidiaries attracted massive levels of investment in the late 1940s and 1950s, and close directorate-level ties were established to provide oversight. The resulting network, consisting mostly of executives of the US parent sitting on the board of the Canadian subsidiary, was still intact when Clement conducted his research in the early 1970s, and we see evidence of it also in 1976. Yet the subsequent deepening of globalization brought more global organizational forms, as foreign operations of American TNCs became more complex. In many instances, the Canadian subsidiary became simply one of many units. In some, more global structures meant greater integration at head office and the further reduction of foreign subsidiaries to the status of operational units (Clarkson, 2002: 216). In others, it meant increased autonomy for foreign subsidiaries in managing day-to-day needs and possibly even world product mandates, with procurement and production linked into the most efficient global arrangements for the enterprise. For a number of TNCs, formal, board-level oversight by the parent firm appears to have given way to informal means of communication. In a highly globalized corporate structure, the practice of placing representatives of subsidiaries on the parent's board (and vice versa) becomes unwieldy, and the growth of information technology has offered alternatives to elite-level interlocks. As Bettis and Hitt (1995:7) point out, 'telecommunications and computer networks are altering the way managers work and interact, more effectively integrating overseas subsidiaries and alliances with headquarters executives....'[25]

The widely heralded shift from 'ethnocentric' to 'geocentric' regimes of transnational management (Robock and Simmonds, 1989), which has also been part of recent globalization, may have played some role in the thinning of elite-level continental connections. As described by Heenan and Perlmutter (1979), under the ethnocentric regime typical of American TNCs in the 1950s and 1960s, key positions in subsidiaries were filled with personnel from the home country of the parent company. However, as corporate capitalists came to appreciate the commercial value of integrating local knowledge and talent into their business strategies, TNCs shifted toward 'geocentric' policies, which are sensitive to local contexts and concerned to mobilize talent on a meritocratic basis, without prejudice as to nationality. In Canada American TNCs continued to appoint officers from the parent to the board of the Canadian subsidiary into the 1970s; the disappearance of such directed primary ties by 1996 may be in part a reflection of the end of that practice and the adoption of more open recruitment policies. [26]

At the same time, to the extent that free-trade agreements have converted Canadian subsidiaries into units within each TNC's North American operations, much of the impetus for board-level connections between the American-based parent and the Canadian-based subsidiary has disappeared. After all, within an incipiently integrated North American economic space, subsidiaries in Canada are not much different from subsidiaries in, say, California.

These speculations aside, we have shown empirically that there has been no cumulative tendency towards the kind of tightly knit continental elite, underlain by unidirectional relations of strategic control, that Canadian dependency analysts anticipated in the 1970s. Instead, cross-border ties have loosened even more dramatically than have ties within each national network. This is not surprising, in the post-NAFTA era. As the branch plants producing for a protected Canadian market are reconfigured or decommissioned, much of the rationale for the kinds of continental connections observed by Clement in the 1970s disappears. But the weakening of elite-level connections should not be mistaken for a surge in 'Canadian independence'. Indeed, with a deepening of north-south economic relations, other forms of corporate continentalism may take the place of elite-level 'continental connections', as in the use of email and intranet communications to integrate business practices and strategies across the regional and national divisions of a North American enterprise. With the consolidation of a North American economy, the social relations that used to exist at the level of corporate strategy (the board of directors) might be transposed to the operational level—across different units or divisions of companies, some sited in Canada, some sited south of the border. The trend (noted in Chapter 5) for major Canadian corporations to move their executive offices to the US while retaining a titular head office in Canada (as in Nortel's relocation to Dallas) is a form of continentalism that is surely more fateful than elite-level interlocks. So, for that matter, is the integration of capital markets, as the largest Canadian firms come to be listed on US exchanges, and to reckon their financial results in US dollars. Thus it is also not surprising that in 2000, five of the ten largest equity financings in Canada were underwritten by four US-based investment banks, and two-thirds of the $164 billion in Canadian merger-and-acquisition activity involved a deal with a US company (Maclem, 2001).

Considerations such as these provide a context in which to interpret elite-level continental connections that involve loosely structured financial–industrial integration. Such ties link leading corporate capitalists and advisors from both sides of the border as they serve on directorates such as those of Nortel, Seagram, Inco, and Textron. These companies, of course, are not simply major players in a continental economy. They are full-fledged TNCs. Our analysis of the continental network brings us to the brink of placing Canada's corporate elite within a fully global context.

Chapter 7

The Canadian Corporate Elite in the Global Power Structure

In a globalizing world, the issue of how the Canadian corporate elite fits within the transnational network of corporate power looms larger and larger. Interest in the apparent emergence of a transnational capitalist class has grown since the 1970s, when Richard Barnet and Ronald Müller published *Global Reach: The Power of the Multinational Corporations* (1974) and Steve Hymer provisionally declared that 'an international capitalist class is emerging whose interests lie in the world economy as a whole system of international private property which allows free movement of capital between countries' (Hymer, 1979:262). This issue has gained salience as scholars such as Robinson and Harris (2000) and Sklair (2001) have observed the formation of a fully transnational capitalist class (cf. Gill, 1995; van der Pijl, 1998). Yet, curiously, precious little systematic research has explored the structural contours of global corporate power as a network of interlocking directorates, and no study has attempted to situate Canada within the global corporate network.

Since much of this chapter breaks new ground in the sociological analysis of the Canadian corporate elite, let us lay out an analytical agenda consisting of several empirical questions. What, to begin, has been the predominant pattern of relations linking Canadian corporate boards into the global network? Have Canadian-based corporate boards linked principally to the US and only marginally to Europe, the Asia-Pacific, and other regions? Is Canada's corporate elite 'regressing' to dependent, hinterland status, as in Kari Levitt's (1970) 'Silent Surrender' thesis? The latter position has been echoed more recently by Peter C. Newman:

> globalization guarantees no level playing fields. It has been advertised as a natural marketing phenomenon, promising to increase business and multiply profits for all concerned. Instead, globalization turned out to mean Americanization, period (1999:53).

Alternatively, is the corporate continentalism we depicted in Chapter 6 simply a 'special case' of globalization, as the Canadian network becomes more embedded in a transnational formation? How extensively does the global network reach into the Canadian network, and vice versa? Are transnational interlocks largely the preserve of a few Canadian TNCs or major enterprise groups? At the level of individuals, what roles do Canadian capitalists play in the global network, compared to corporate advisors, and in what ways do members of the Canadian corporate elite (both functioning capitalists and organic intellectuals) participate in the global network of elite policy-planning groups? Such groups, themselves interlocked with global corporations, arose in the twentieth century in attempts to organize and promote a general transnational capitalist interest in 'free markets'—to extend the reach of corporate power into global politics (Gill, 1990; Van der Pijl, 1998; Robinson and Harris, 2000; Sklair, 2001). What presence have members of the Canadian corporate elite achieved in such transnational political initiatives?

In this chapter we trace the elite-level relations between dominant Canadian corporations and other major global companies. Available data allow only a very selective longitudinal analysis of changes in the transnational participation of Canadian corporate directors. This is the focus of the first section. For 1996, a fuller range of data allows an extensive analysis in the chapter's middle sections. Finally, in anticipation of the discussion of the corporate elite's political and cultural power that will occupy our final chapters, we consider that elite's participation in a global policy-planning network that revolves around such peak organizations as the World Economic Forum and the International Chamber of Commerce.

Canadian Peak Corporations in the Global Network, 1976 and 1996

The first major study of the network of global corporations was conducted by Meindert Fennema of the University of Amsterdam, and published in 1982. Fennema's data refer to the early-to-mid-1970s, just around the high point of American hegemony in the world capitalist system. In constructing his sample of the world's largest firms, he found that a simple size-based criterion would have meant drawing a sample of overwhelmingly US-based companies, offering little scope for the analysis of transnational interlocks (1982:249). Two decades later, however, corporate capital had accumulated and concentrated in western Europe and Japan to such an extent that the size of the largest corporations domiciled there had reached parity with the largest in the US. Fennema's 1976 sample, which is our empirical starting point, consisted of the largest 135 non-financial corporations (industrials) and largest 41 banks headquartered in eight countries or regions of the world, selected by size but with a quota for each stratum.

Our network analysis begins with an examination of change in the ways that Canada's very largest, 'peak' corporations have been embedded in the global network. Here we draw on Fennema, whose 1976 sample included the four largest Canadian financial institutions (all of them chartered banks) and seven largest non-financial corporations, enabling us to situate these peak corporations within the global network. Recently, Fennema and I extended his original study by constructing a sample of the 176 leading world corporations of 1996, matching the same numbers of corporations for each domicile (Carroll and Fennema, 2002:416).

Among our findings several stand out. The twenty years following 1976 bore witness to a massive decline in the international dominance of US-based corporations. In 1976 the 26th-ranked American industrial had revenues 30 times the size of the 26th-ranked Japanese corporation. By 1996 the 26th-ranked Japanese firm was *slightly larger* than the 26th-ranked US company. The transnational network itself became only slightly more integrated over the two decades, and by 1996 was carried more by outside directors than by corporate insiders. This led us to conclude that transnational interlocks tend to be vehicles for the formation of a transnational business community—for the exercise of class hegemony—more than they are relations of strategic control—a thesis consistent with the evolution of the continental network traced in the previous chapter. Although there was some loosening in national networks, the further development of transnational interlocking did not lead them to fragment. There was no dramatic shift from national to transnational interlocking. We also found that leading banks, though central to most national networks, were not exceptionally central transnationally—whether in 1976 or 1996. However, by 1996 a core group of two dozen well-connected European and North American corporations (including three banks) had been consolidated. Ensconced in that cluster of transnationalized corporate boards were two Canadian firms—Seagram and the CIBC.

It is worthwhile to pursue this longitudinal comparison in greater depth, and Figures 7.1 and 7.2 provide the appropriate snapshots. Each sociogram features 11 Canadian 'peak corporations' as well as any non-Canadian firm that shared a director with one or more of the Canadian 11 in the given year.[1] Comparing the two sociograms, we can note some changes in how the top tier of Canadian corporate capital has been embedded in the global network.

Overall, with the general thinning of corporate interlocks both domestically and internationally, the number of participants in the global network of 176 firms decreased from 317 people holding 733 corporate directorships in 1976 to 268 people holding 628 directorships in 1996, although the number of corporations actually linked into the network by one or more director changed only slightly (increasing by one to 145 in 1996). The Canadian segment of the network, shown in the figures as a set of intercorporate ties, was made up of 44 people holding 98 directorships in 23 corporations in 1976 and 28 people holding 70 directorships in 22 corporations in 1996. The principal reason fewer people participated in the Canadian segment in 1996 was the thinning of ties among Canadian-based firms.[2] Fewer individuals participating in interlocks, however, did not mean fewer ties between Canadian and foreign-based corporations. In both years, the 11 Canadian firms were involved in 15 such ties. However, the destination and nature of the ties shifted. In 1976 the 11 Canadian companies interlocked with 6 American firms (five of them parents of Canadian subsidiaries), three firms based in Britain and three firms based on the European continent. The 11 foreign-based firms of 1996 included two American companies, seven firms based in France, one based in Belgium (Fina) and one firm with dual citizenship, based in the Netherlands and UK (Unilever). Only one of the American-based companies, Ford, was parent to a Canadian branch plant.

Looking specifically at Figure 7.1, we find thick, dense ties among most of the Canadian firms. The function of several transnational interlocks in the strategic and operational control of foreign-owned subsidiaries is clear enough. In 1976, Ford Motor Company CEO Lee Iacocca sat on the board of Ford Canada, and Ford

Vice-President W.O. Bourke directed Ford's Canadian and German subsidiaries, creating a triadic structure. C.D. Shepard, an executive with Gulf Oil Corporation, chaired the board of Gulf's Canadian subsidiary, while Gulf Canada CEO J.L. Stoik also was an executive in the American parent. Gulf Canada was itself linked into the Canadian network via the CIBC, whose board provided seats for three Gulf Canada directors. However, alongside these ties were connections of a looser sort, in which the CIBC figured prominently. D. Barran's outside directorships with the CIBC established ties between the bank's board and the boards of three European companies on which Barran sat as an outside director—Midland Bank, British Insulated Callender's Cable (both British), and Royal Dutch Shell (based in the Netherlands and Britain). CP CEO Ian Sinclair was an outside director of the Amsterdam-Rotterdam Bank, providing a further portal into the European elite.

FIGURE 7.1
Interlocks Among Peak Canadian and Top International Firms, 1976

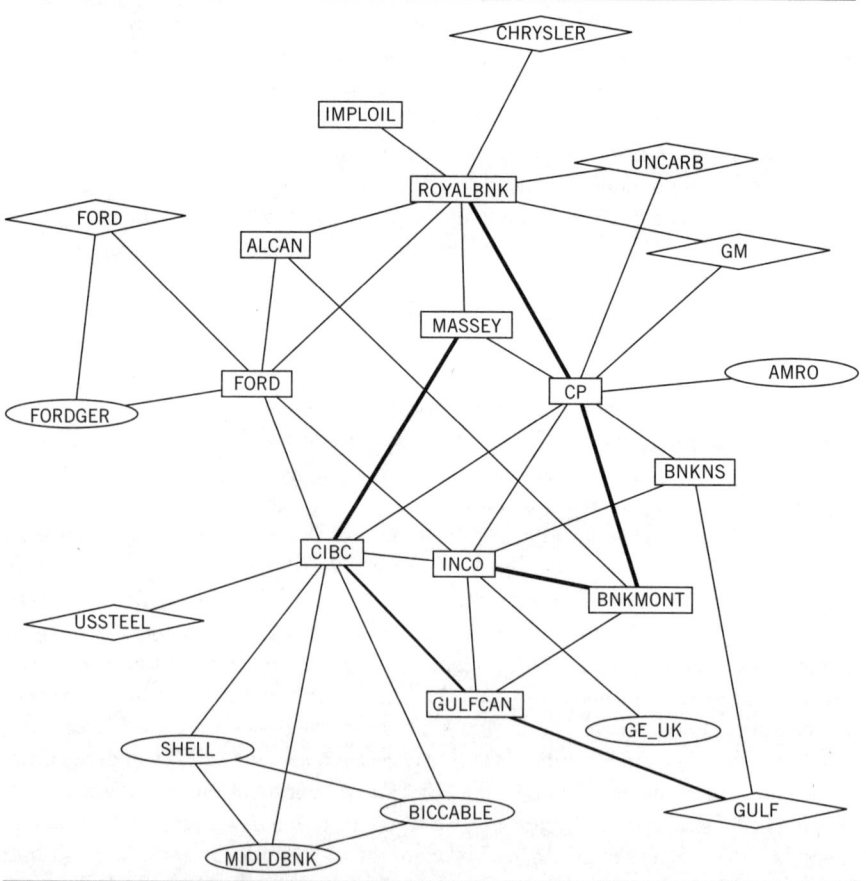

Canadian firms are in boxes; American firms are in diamonds; European firms are in ovals. Line thickness indicates the number of shared directors.

FIGURE 7.2
Interlocks Among Peak Canadian and Top International Firms, 1996

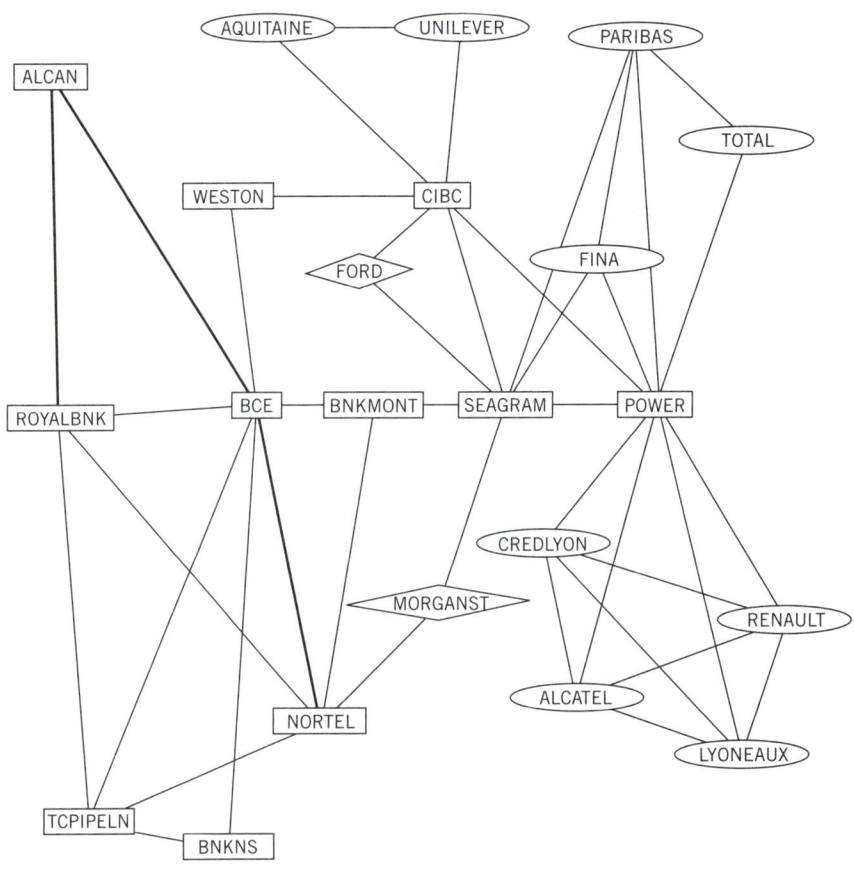

Canadian firms are in boxes; American firms are in diamonds; European firms are in ovals. Line thickness indicates the number of shared directors.

In general, the analysis of the transnational ties around the 11 peak Canadian firms shows the latter to have been focused largely on continental connections in 1976, with only a few tentative overtures toward Europe.

Two decades on, the transnational ties around the 11 peak Canadian firms had a more European tilt and a less tentative content, almost entirely as a result of Paul Desmarais's extensive European investments. The remaining connections into the US were not vehicles of American strategic control. In fact, although in the interests of providing an exact longitudinal comparison, Figure 7.2 does not show Ford Canada, a wholly-owned subsidiary,[3] by 1996 the board of US-based Ford Motor Company had no interlocks either with Ford of Canada or with Ford Credit Canada, also a Top 250 Canadian corporation. The American parent's two links into the Canadian peak network were weak ties carried by corporate advisor Marie-

Josée Kravis, who sat on the boards of Seagram and the CIBC. Except for those two firms and the Desmarais group, the peak Canadian-based firms were largely detached from the global network, but heavily interlocked with each other. Three banks (Royal, Montreal, Nova Scotia) and four industrials (BCE, Nortel, TransCanada PipeLine, Alcan) formed a closely connected group. With the partial exception of the CIBC, whose board in 1976 was also the most internationalized, *the banks continued to serve primarily as hubs for domestic Canadian firms*, a pattern identical to the situation for other countries in the larger global network. The 31-member Royal Bank board, for instance, was a meeting point for eight directors from Alcan, TransCanada PipeLine, BCE, and Nortel.

The full, bi-modal picture of the peak network of 1996, in Figure 7.3, reveals precisely who carried each corporate interlock and (in bold lines) whether the individual held an inside position in any of the 22 firms. In the cross-directorships linking Nortel and Seagram to US-based Morgan Stanley—carried respectively by Paul Oreffice (retired chair of Dow Chemical USA) and Seagram treasurer and vice-chair Robert W. Matschullat—we find examples of loosely structured financial–industrial relations, as both Nortel and Seagram came to locate more of their executive functions in the US.[4] The CIBC's ties to European industrials are carried as outside directorships by Bertrand Collomb, CEO of Groupe Lafarge. Meanwhile, corporate lawyer and former Ontario Premier William Davis carried secondary links among the CIBC, Seagram, and Power Corporation. For many years the Power and Seagram boards had been strongly interlocked by a reciprocal arrangement under which Paul Desmarais sat on the Seagram board and Charles R. Bronfman on the Power board, and Davis's outside directorships in 1996 reinforced this deeper alignment.

Nevertheless, it is the collection of ties around Power Corporation that deserves particular scrutiny.[5] As we saw in Chapter 3, by the late 1990s Paul Desmarais Sr, and to a lesser extent his sons Paul Jr and André, were themselves influential capitalists on the European scene. Indeed, through his holdings in Bertelsmann Desmarais had become a major investor in European multimedia. But his key positions in Europe, indicated in the pattern of interlocking in Figure 7.3, have been strategic control blocs (held in partnership with the Frère family of Belgium) in Belgian-based Petrofina and French-based Paribas, on whose boards he sat in 1996. Transatlantic coordination of business strategies was further facilitated by Paribas Chair Michel Francois-Poncet's directorship with Power Corp., while Jean Peyrelevade, CEO of Crédit Lyonnais and director of several major French corporations, furnished the Power board with additional business scan in its European ventures. Just as Nortel, Seagram, and Inco, whose rather continental social circle were noted in the previous chapter, are not in any sense representative of large Canadian industrials, Desmarais's turn to Europe is not in itself typical of globalizing business practices at the top of Canada's corporate hierarchy. Yet these cases offer glimpses of the way the top corporations and capitalists based in Canada now operate in a world of economically permeable national borders. In so doing, they re-pose the question whether any coherent 'nationality' can be meaningfully ascribed to such concentrations of capital. In any case, our longitudinal comparison

FIGURE 7.3
Individuals in the Network of Peak Canadian and International Firms, 1996

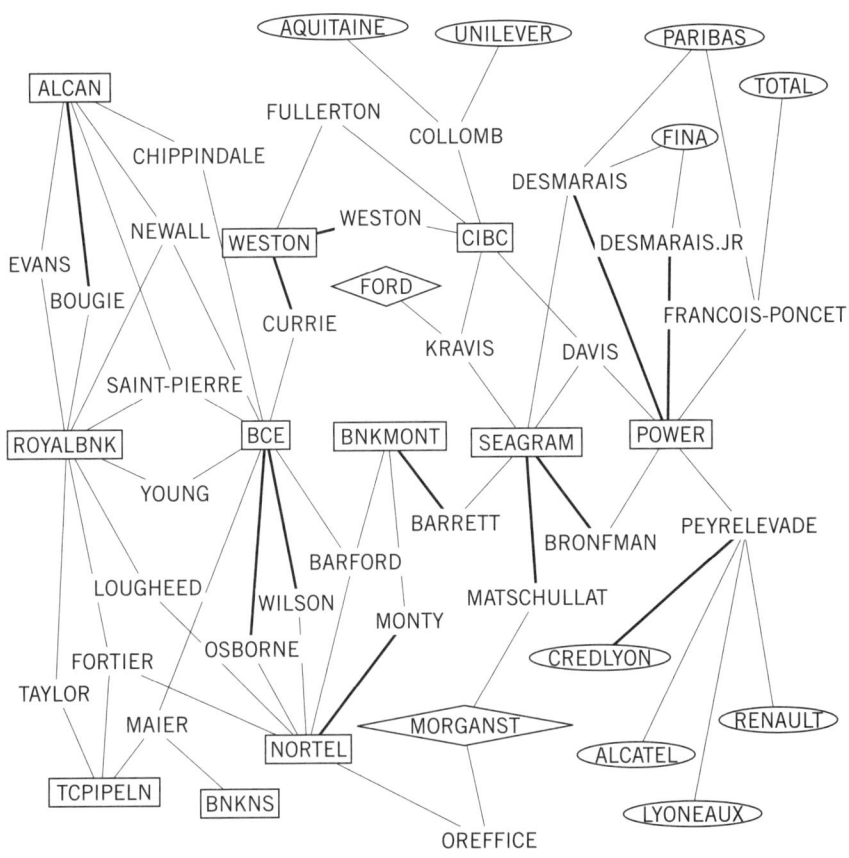

Canadian firms are in boxes; American firms are in diamonds; European firms are in ovals. Line thickness indicates the individual held an executive position in the firm.

of peak corporations suggests that the weakening of continental interlocking based in American strategic control was matched by an increase in the strategic control relations that draw Canadian corporate power into Europe.

CANADIAN CORPORATE POWER IN THE GLOBAL NETWORK, 1996

For more recent times, we can map a more complete network of interlocks carrying Canada's elite into the global arena. Our international data for 1996 derive from a study I conducted with Colin Carson (Carroll and Carson, 2003), in which we probed the global network of 350 dominant companies and five policy-planning groups. The sample included all of the Top 176 firms that were the focus of the previous section, but it was drawn in such a way that the world's 210 largest industrial companies (ranked by revenue) and 90 largest financial institutions (ranked by assets) were selected, together with 50 companies (40 industrials and 10 financials) headquartered in countries and regions—particularly on the semi-periphery of world capitalism (countries such as Brazil, South Africa, and Turkey)—that otherwise would be thinly represented.

The interlocks among Canada's Top 258 corporations and the Global 350 (12 of which were members of the Canadian Top 258) may be said to form a Canada-global network. The density of interlocking in this network and the numbers of firms participating in it give an overall sense of its integration and scope. Among the entire set of companies, the density of interlocking is .01154. About one in a hundred pairs of firms is interlocked. One quarter of all interlocks involves an executive in one (or both) of the firms: the density of such primary interlocking is 0.00288. But the most interesting densities are those between Canadian and foreign-based corporations. In keeping with the general pattern Fennema and I found in the global network, these are much lower than densities within the Canadian network. Recalling from Chapter 2 that our Top 258 showed an overall density of 0.03514, the density of interlocking between the Canadian Top 258 and the 338 non-Canadian companies in our global sample is only 0.00085. The comparable figures for primary interlocks are 0.00679 within Canada and 0.00023 between Canada and the rest of the world. In all, just 74 interlocking pairs of boards (20 of them involving the sharing of an executive) hook the Canadian corporate elite into the transnational business community.

Yet if the ties are sparse when considered as a proportion of all possible links, they still pull most of the 596 companies into a dominant component of 480 corporations. Alongside this connected network of 220 Canadian and 260 non-Canadian corporations are (1) 10 smaller nationally-based components and transnational dyads, detached from the Canada–global network and accounting for a total of 25 firms, and (2) 91 entirely isolated companies, 36 of which were based in Canada. It is interesting, in this global perspective, to note that 24 of the Canadian isolates were under foreign control in 1996, as were the two Canadian-based companies belonging to smaller components.[6] Other Canadian isolates from the Canada–global network tended to be either state-controlled (six in number) or organized as cooperatives or credit unions (three in number). In effect, virtually all large corporations under the control of Canadian capitalists were connected into the global network either directly (by transnational interlocking) or indirectly (through their ties to Canadian corporations with global interlocks).

DIRECT INTERLOCKS IN THE CANADA–GLOBAL NETWORK

Let us first consider the direct linkages—the transnational interlocks between Canadian boards and the boards of foreign companies. As of year-end 1996, 29 of our Canadian Top 258 shared one or more directors with a foreign-based company numbering among our Global Top 338. These transnational interlocks established board-to-board ties to 46 foreign corporations, forming a bipartite network[7] of

74 Canada–global interlocks. The 29 Canadian corporations included, of course, the three Desmarais-controlled companies making up the Canadian wing of the Desmarais-Frère group. However, other enterprise groups we analyzed in Chapter 3 were conspicuously absent. The Caisse de Dépôt's mandate of national development virtually precludes it from extensive participation in transnational interlocking. Even within Canada, as we have seen, it has mostly played a passive investment role, rarely seeking board representation where it takes up minority positions. The Brascan-Edper group—Canada's largest corporate empire—also showed no elite-level ties to the Global 338, even though it contained two major Canadian transnationals. In fact, most of the 51 TNCs in our Canadian Top 258 *did not participate* in transnational directorate interlocks, and among the 29 Canadian participants, companies with no foreign subsidiaries outnumbered transnationals by 11 to 8. All but one of the former were wholly owned subsidiaries of TNCs based outside Canada—the exception, ironically, being Power Corporation. Among the Canadian TNCs participating in transnational interlocks were six companies with operations in ten or more countries (the CIBC, Toronto-Dominion Bank, Inco, Nortel, Seagram, Thomson Corp.) and two companies with operations in five to nine countries (Barrick Gold and Manulife). As for nationality of control, 14 of the 29 were controlled by foreign interests (six Japanese, five American, and three European). Most of the 29 were headquartered in Montreal (six) or Toronto (16, six of them subsidiaries of foreign TNCs). Vancouver was the base for four firms, all of them foreign-controlled subsidiaries (BC Tel, Mitsubishi Canada, Itochu Canada, and Hong Kong Bank of Canada).

The transnational interlocks were structured as a dominant component consisting of 13 Canadian and 23 foreign firms, four smaller components, and nine dyads. Figure 7.4 displays the larger formations.[8] In these groupings the tendency for Japan-based TNCs to establish primary interlocks with their Canadian subsidiaries and affiliates is again evident in the cluster of two Canadian and four Japan-based corporations (see upper right corner). This entire set of interlocks was carried by Susumu Miyamoto, president of Mitsui Canada and a managing director of Shoko Chukin Bank, an affiliate within the Mitsui *keiretsu* in Japan. A few other parent-subsidiary relations were also evidently cemented by primary interlocks, as in Royal Dutch Shell's relation with Shell Canada and British-based HSBC Holdings' relation with Hong Kong Bank of Canada. Not unexpectedly, the major concentration of primary interlocks united the Canadian and European sides of the Desmarais-Frère empire. With the exception of Honda's link to its Canadian subsidiary, the only multiple-director interlocks in the entire transnational formation are contained within the Desmarais-Frère group.[9]

These details aside, what really stands out in our survey of all the interlocks linking the Canadian corporate elite into the larger world system is (1) the complete absence of interlocks leading to corporations located on the semi-periphery of capitalism; and (2) the dearth of 'continental' (US–Canada) interlocks, which appear no more important in the elite structure than do interlocks to Europe. The first observation simply shows the Canadian corporate elite to be a typical formation of world capitalism's centre. Elsewhere (Carroll and Fennema, 2002; Carroll

FIGURE 7.4

Interlocks Between 258 Top Canadian and 338 Top Global Companies, 1996

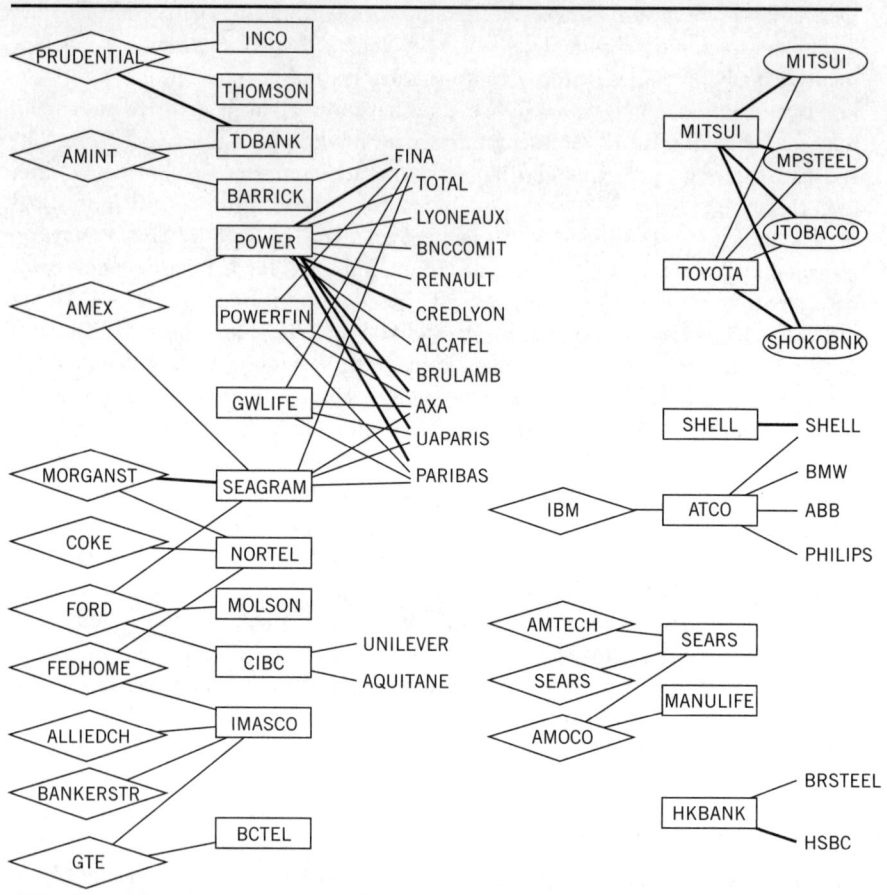

Canadian firms are in boxes; American firms are in diamonds; Japanese firms are in ovals; European firms have no enclosing shape. Line thickness indicates the number of shared directors.

and Carson, 2003) my colleagues and I have shown that the global corporate network excludes directors based in countries outside the triad of western Europe, northern North America, and Japan-Australia. True to form, every line linking major Canadian boards to corporate directorates elsewhere stays well within the triad, with 28 extending to the US, 34 to Europe, and 12 to Japan. The leading directors of Canadian corporations are part of a system of *collective imperialism* in which decisions are made at the top of the centre, and consequences are endured at the bottom of both the centre and the periphery (the latter having no effective voice even at elite levels). The second observation cautions us against the all-too-common belief—refuted in the previous chapter—that 'continental connections' have become or are becoming the main axis of elite formation. What seems more accurate is a suggestion I made some years ago:

while there is no doubt that a 'continental elite' of leading Canadian and American capitalists exists, it can perhaps be most fruitfully viewed as a segment of a larger, international network that has developed with capitalist cross-penetration in the post-Second World War era (Carroll, 1985:42).

Many of the transnational interlocks that pull Canada's corporate elite into the European and American corners of the triad are thin, secondary ties created when two firms share a single outside director. Such relations certainly contribute to a transnational business community, but they do not likely reflect relations of control over capital. If we recall the concept of allocative power, and its typical locus in large financial institutions controlling credit, it is striking how many interlocks from Canada to both Europe and the US involve at least one financial institution. On the American side, Prudential, Amex, Morgan Stanley, Federal Home Loan, and Bankers Trust are all prominent in the dominant component. On the European side sit the affiliates of the Desmarais-Frère group, as well as HSBC. Within Canada we find the Toronto-Dominion Bank, Power Financial, Great West Life, and the CIBC all participating in transnational interlocks. Some of these ties may facilitate the kinds of international financial transactions that the world's largest corporations now rely on as an integral part of their self-expansion. In contrast, relations with Japan are of a focused, strategic-instrumental character, expressing the internal relations of transnational business enterprise.

MAPPING THE CANADA–GLOBAL SEAM

From a network perspective, of course, the bipartite structure in Figure 7.4 gives us only part of the picture. We need to consider the interlocks that integrate each side of the Canada–global divide. In Figure 7.5 we display the entire network of interlocks among the transnationally connected Canadian companies and the European, American, and Japanese firms with which they were interlocked in 1996. The network is clearly organized along spatial lines, with the companies linking mainly to other firms headquartered in the same country. Even though we have included only the most transnationalized Canadian boards, there are extensive ties among the Canadian corporations, the major exceptions being wholly owned foreign-controlled subsidiaries.[10] In particular, Japanese-controlled companies located in Canada are quite marginal to the Canadian corporate elite. Among the 26 Canadian corporations in the dominant component, Seagram appears to be the most central. Its extensive ties within Canada are complemented by links into the US and France. Power Corporation has the most interlocks, but many of them link the Power board to other companies under the same strategic control. The two regions of fairly dense transnational interlocking involve the Power Corp.-Paribas group, most of whose interlocks spill across the Canada–Europe divide, and a more diffuse collection of ties between several leading Canadian companies (Toronto-Dominion, Inco, Imasco, Thomson, Barrick, and Seagram—themselves interconnected) and their American counterparts (Prudential, Bankers Trust, Allied Chemical, American International, GTE, and American Express—also interconnected). Although Figure 7.5 includes only the small subset of foreign companies with ties to Canadian corporations, other transnational linkages are apparent. IBM, for instance, interlocks not only with Canada-based Atco but with four major European TNCs located in three different countries.

Figure 7.5 does not indicate the extent to which transnational interlocks *ramify* within the wider Canadian corporate elite as well as in other sectors of the global network. For example, it does not show the many companies that occupy central locations in Canada but do not have any transnational directors on their boards. Given the centralized shape of corporate networks, there is reason to expect that some of these may, in integrating the national elite, also bring firms in the national network closer to foreign corporate boards, thus making indirect contributions to

FIGURE 7.5

Interlocks Among 69 Canadian and Foreign-based Companies Comprising a Dominant Component, 1996

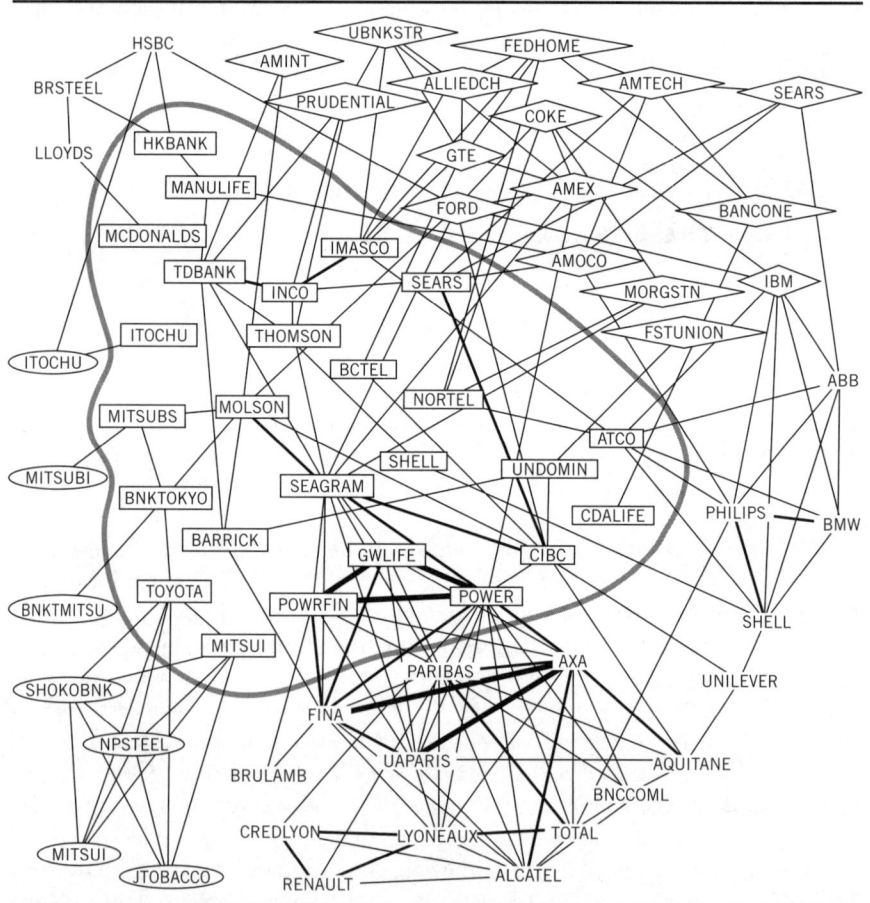

Canadian firms are in boxes; American firms are in diamonds; Japanese firms are in ovals; European firms have no enclosing shape. Line thickness indicates the number of shared directors.

transnational elite integration. For instance, a bank board may have no directors with transnational affiliations, yet may count among its members several directors of companies whose boards include transnational directors. As we saw in Chapter 6, a useful indicator of the extent to which a corporation contributes to the structural integration of two network segments is Anthonisse's rush. The analysis of rush provides a summary of which companies do the most to integrate the Canadian corporate elite into the global corporate network. A high rush score means that a company lies on many of the shortest paths linking Canadian companies to firms based in the rest of the world (ROW). Such companies integrate the field of transnational interlocking by bringing Canadian and foreign corporations closer together in the social space of the global network. Which corporations, Canadian and non-Canadian, lie directly on the seam between Canadian capital and global capital?

Table 7.1 lists the 30 Canadian and 30 foreign corporations that scored highest in Canada–ROW rush. Both the Canadian and foreign segments contain a fair number of financial institutions (10 in Canada, including five of the country's six major chartered banks; 13 in the ROW segment), which lie between many other corporations in the Canada–global network. On the Canadian side, most of the 30 companies are controlled by capitalists based in Canada, four are controlled in Japan, two in the UK (Imasco and Hong Kong Bank) and one in the US (Sears). On the ROW side we again find no compelling evidence of continentalism as the central organizing principle behind the Canadian corporate elite's insertion in the global network. At the seam between Canadian and global corporate power, the US presence is not much greater than that of Japan, and less extensive than that of Europe, which accounts for 14 of the 30 most central firms. In fact, considering the rush into Canada's Top 258 for all 90 US-based companies in our Global 338, the mean score (0.00586) is not much higher than the mean for the 73 Japan-based firms (0.00517), and lower than the mean for the 25 French-based firms (0.00601) and nine Dutch-based firms (0.0141).

The Dutch example is worth drawing out, given that smaller Western European countries like the Netherlands, Belgium, and Switzerland host a number of large corporations engaged in extensive transnational interlocking, and lying between a great many firms in the global (and particularly European) network (Carroll and Fennema, 2002). For instance, Unilever's high rush score reflects the fact that it is well-connected in the global network beyond Canada (with ties to six British companies, three Dutch, two American, and one French) and is also directly linked to the most central corporation in the Canada–global network, the CIBC (whose interlocks within Canada extend to 42 companies). Much the same can be said of Belgian-based Fina, interlocked with two Belgian companies, 11 French, one Dutch, and one German. However, although the Fina board is interlocked with Power Corp., Power Financial, and Barrick Gold (the last via former Canadian Prime Minister Brian Mulroney, who in 1996 directed major corporations in Canada, Europe, and the US),[11] these companies are not nearly as central within Canada as the CIBC; hence Fina's lower rush score compared to Unilever's.

In the cases of Prudential, the most central foreign firm on the seam between Canadian capitalism and global capitalism, and third-ranked Bank of Tokyo-

TABLE 7.1
Rush Scores for the Most Central Firms in the Canada–Global Network, 1996

Corporations based in Canada		Corporations based elsewhere		
1. CIBC	.1424	Prudential Ins Co. of Amer.	USA	.0787
2. Molson	.1293	Unilever N.V.	NETH	.0716
3. Power Corp.	.1009	Bank of Tokyo-Mitsubishi	JAPN	.0639
4. Seagram	.0802	Amoco Corporation	USA	.0599
5. Bank of Tokyo-Mitsubishi	.0729	Petrofina	BELG	.0538
6. Royal Bank of Canada	.0724	AXA (AXA-UAP)	FR	.0401
7. BC Gas Inc.	.0716	Ford Motor Co.	USA	.0346
8. ATCO Ltd.	.0698	Mitsubishi Corporation	JAPN	.0328
9. Mitsui & Co. (Canada) Ltd.	.0664	American Express	USA	.0323
10. Toronto-Dominion Bank	.0597	Nippon Steel Corp.	JAPN	.0317
11. Manulife Financial	.0522	Union des Assur. de Paris	FR	.0313
12. Imasco Ltd.	.0448	HSBC Holdings	UK	.0277
13. Sears Canada Inc.	.0447	Honda Motor Co., Ltd.	JAPN	.0253
14. Bank of Montreal	.0414	Kansai Electric Power	JAPN	.0232
15. Northern Telecom Ltd.	.0407	Banco Santander S.A.	SP	.0230
16. Mitsubishi Canada Ltd.	.0358	Royal Dutch/Shell	NETH	.0223
17. Canadian Pacific Ltd.	.0342	The Coca-Cola Co.	USA	.0196
18. Power Financial Corp.	.0324	Inst. Banc.s.P. di Torino	ITAL	.0192
19. Barrick Gold Corp.	.0317	First Union Corp.	USA	.0191
20. Honda Canada Inc.	.0281	Marubeni Corp.	JAPN	.0184
21. United Dominion Industries	.0279	BMW	GER	.0179
22. National Bank of Canada	.0279	ABB Asea Brown Boveri Ltd	SWIT	.0168
23. Hongkong Bank of Canada	.0252	Philips Electronics	NETH	.0164
24. Great-West Lifeco	.0241	RTZ-CRA Group [Rio Tinto]	UK	.0161
25. Thomson Corp.	.0215	American International Grp	USA	.0156
26. Inco Ltd.	.0208	Bankers Trust New York	USA	.0153
27. Bombardier Inc.	.0193	Fortis	NETH	.0153
28. Noranda Inc.	.0184	Banca di Roma	ITAL	.0153
29. National Trustco Inc.	.0179	Xerox Corp.	USA	.0145
30. Avenor Inc.	.0159	Meiji Life Insurance	JAPN	.0143

Mitsubishi, we have foreign-based financial institutions that are relatively central in their respective national networks but also linked to key Canadian companies. Prudential's interlock with the Toronto-Dominion board alone means that a Prudential director—namely TD CEO Richard M. Thomson—is in contact (via the TD board) with directors from 28 Canadian companies. Bank of Tokyo-Mitsubishi is linked, through its Canadian subsidiary, to Molson, placing Art Hara, a director of the bank's Canadian subsidiary, in touch with directors from 17 Canadian companies. The Japanese connection in turn contributes significantly to Molson's own centrality in the Canada–global network. Like the CIBC, which has direct interlocks with relatively central corporations in both Europe and the US, the Molson board shares a director with the Ford (US) board yet is also positioned on the seam between the Japanese and Canadian segments, affording it high centrality in the Canada–global network.

Indeed, provided that a company lies between a number of corporations on both sides of the Canada–global seam, its board may have no direct transnational interlocks yet still register a relatively high rush score. That is, the corporate boards may draw companies into the transnational network without having a transnational composition. For instance, the Bank of Montreal's board had no directors of any Global 338 corporations in 1996, yet it placed 14th in rush by virtue of its many interlocks with other Canadian corporations, some of them (such as Seagram and Nortel) relatively cosmopolitan, but most of them connected only to the bank and other Canadian companies. The Bank of Montreal remains a meeting point for well-connected corporate directors, some of them affiliated with globally linked companies, others not. Along with other boards, relatively rich in rush yet not directly linked to foreign firms, the Bank of Montreal helps to integrate the cosmopolitan and local segments of the Canadian corporate elite.

In view of these indirect contributions, it is worth exploring the extent to which the global network reaches into the Canadian network, and vice versa. To this end, we mapped the network of foreign corporations scoring highest in transnational rush, along with the firms linked to them on both sides of the Canada–ROW divide. The task was simplified by the nearly complete lack of connection in the global network between Japanese and Euro-American corporations. Although the 132 European-based firms in our Global 338 were connected to the 90 US-based companies by 45 interlocks, there were only two interlocks linking the European corporate elite to the 73 Japanese-based companies in our Global 338, and only one interlock linking American and Japanese companies![12] As Fennema and I have discussed elsewhere (2002), at the close of the twentieth century the transnational business community was still overwhelmingly centred on the North Atlantic.

LINKS TO JAPAN AND EUROPE

Given the disjuncture between Japanese and Euro-American corporate boards, and the fact that we have already analyzed the Canada–US segment of the global network in Chapter 6, we can divide the remainder of our transnational mapping project between the Canada–Japan and Canada–Europe segments. To explore the reach of transnational interlocks into national and regional corporate networks, we first selected for each segment those foreign (Japanese or European) companies with Canada–ROW rush scores greater than 0.01, indicating their relative centrality in the Canada–global network. This yielded 13 Japanese and 20 European firms. We then added Canadian-based firms that interlocked directly with any of these central Japanese or European companies—a total of five firms for the Canada–Japan segment and nine for Canada–Europe. Lastly, we added any companies within the social circles of the firms already selected and thus connected into the transnational network at one remove. For the Canada–Japan segment this procedure resulted in a set of 10 Canadian and 44 Japanese corporations, all of them forming a single component. For the Canada–Europe segment it brought us 91 Canadian and 88 European firms, 174 of them forming a dominant component and the other five forming a minor component. The difference in scale is instructive. *Interlocks linking European corporate capital into Canada penetrate much more deeply into the actual social organization of the Canadian corporate elite than do Canada–Japan interlocks.* While a great many Canadian boards connect with European firms directly or at one remove, very few Canadian companies are linked into the Japanese corporate network in the same way.

This difference is amplified by the actual patterning of ties. All five of the Canadian firms whose boards interlocked with the 13 Japanese companies were subsidiaries of Japanese TNCs, and rather marginal to the Canadian network. At the close of the twentieth century, ties between Japanese and Canadian segments of the global network continued to be weak and remarkably shallow. In contrast, Canada–Europe interlocks connected companies central in their respective 'home' networks. The resulting interpenetration of corporate elites on both sides of the Atlantic is reminiscent of the continental connections traced in Chapter 6.[13]

Regional clustering in the European segment was also evident. In the component made up of 174 European and Canadian companies were only two of 13 large Italian companies, and none of four large Spanish corporations. On the other hand, the component did include a majority of companies based in northern Europe.[14] In 1996 the Canada–Europe network took in most of the large companies of northwestern Europe, which were themselves densely interconnected, forming the core of European corporate capital. However, British firms kept somewhat to their own rather loosely knit national network, and were linked to the rest of Europe via the boards of Dutch/British Unilever as well as British Petroleum, British Telecom, and National Westminster Bank.[15] Incidentally, British firms were also the most tied to US-based companies.[16]

Transnational Elite Integration: Canada within the Triad

How does the integration of continental Europe's corporate elite compare with that of other segments of world capitalism's centre? Considering all 81 dominant companies domiciled in the northwestern corner of the European continent,[17] the mean degree of interlocking, 7.605, is actually higher than the average among the 90 US-based companies in our Global 338 (6.533). That is, *the corporate elite of northwestern Europe is more socially integrated than the American corporate elite*. This finding confirms that the formation of a European business community was well advanced by the late twentieth century (cf. Carroll and Fennema, 2002; van Apeldoorn, 2002). On the other hand, the 73 largest Japanese corporations show a mean of only 3.014. However, the organization of Japanese corporate capital differs from the Euro-North American pattern, so that the density of directorate interlocking actually underestimates the extent of intercorporate integration.[18] By contrast, we find a mean of 8.171 among the 50 largest Canadian non-financials and 20 largest

Canadian financial institutions. The comparison with the European segment is complicated by the fact the latter includes not one but a whole range of countries, some bigger and some smaller than Canada. Nevertheless, we can safely conclude that at the close of the twentieth century, as in the early 1980s (Ornstein, 1989), and despite corporate governance reforms and other changes, the Canadian corporate elite remained relatively cohesive compared to corporate elites in other regions of world capitalism's centre.

A simple but illuminating way of placing Canada within the triad of advanced capitalist countries is to map the total numbers of inter-regional interlocks, as in Figure 7.6. For the sake of the comparison, the calculations are based on the 70 largest Canadian firms just mentioned, so that the total pool of companies based in Canada is roughly similar to the numbers of American (90), continental European (88), and Japanese (73) firms in our Global 338 (though substantially greater than the number of British-based firms [34]). We should keep in mind, however, that except for the dozen largest companies, many of the 70 Canadian firms are substantially smaller than firms based in other triad countries. The sociogram shows that overall, the 70 largest Canadian companies were more heavily interlocked with continental European firms than with American firms, although the difference was not great. No ties connect these 70 largest Canadian firms with the Japanese corporate network, and only two ties extend from Canada to the UK. The British, American, and continental European segments are very weakly linked to Japan, via one interlock each, and more densely interlocked with each other and with Canada, forming a North Atlantic network. But the lion's share of interlocking occurs within each national or regional segment of the triad. Inter-regional ties are sparse.

The basic structure of transnational interlocking embeds Canadian corporate capital within the global system by means of three types of relations: the Desmarais-Frère empire, bilateral ties between foreign-based TNCs and their Canadian subsidiaries, and 'weak ties' involving either a large financial institution (whether based in Canada or elsewhere) or an organic intellectual. France and Belgium figure prominently in the first type of relation. Japan is singularly involved in the second type. The US is particularly prominent in the second and third types. Among the three types of ties, only the first is clearly indicative of an 'outward' thrust of corporate power. Most relations of strategic control point 'inward', whether they emanate from Europe, Japan, or the US. In part, however, this asymmetry derives from our methodology, which has included a much larger set of Canadian firms (some of them wholly owned subsidiaries) than firms based in each other country of the triad.[19]

The same asymmetry is observable at the level of individual directors. Taking all Canada–global interlocks, only 33 individuals were directly involved in linking Canadian boards to foreign ones in 1996, and only six were actually members of the Canadian corporate elite as we have defined it.[20] The other 27 each directed one Canadian and one or more foreign firms. Three of the 27 were involved in the Desmarais-Frère empire, 11 carried bilateral parent-subsidiary ties (four US-to-Canada, two Europe-to-Canada, five Japan-to-Canada), and 13 (11 of them directors of major financial institutions) spanned independent firms. Leaving aside the

FIGURE 7.6
Number of Interlocks Within and Between Key Countries and Regions of the Triad, 1996

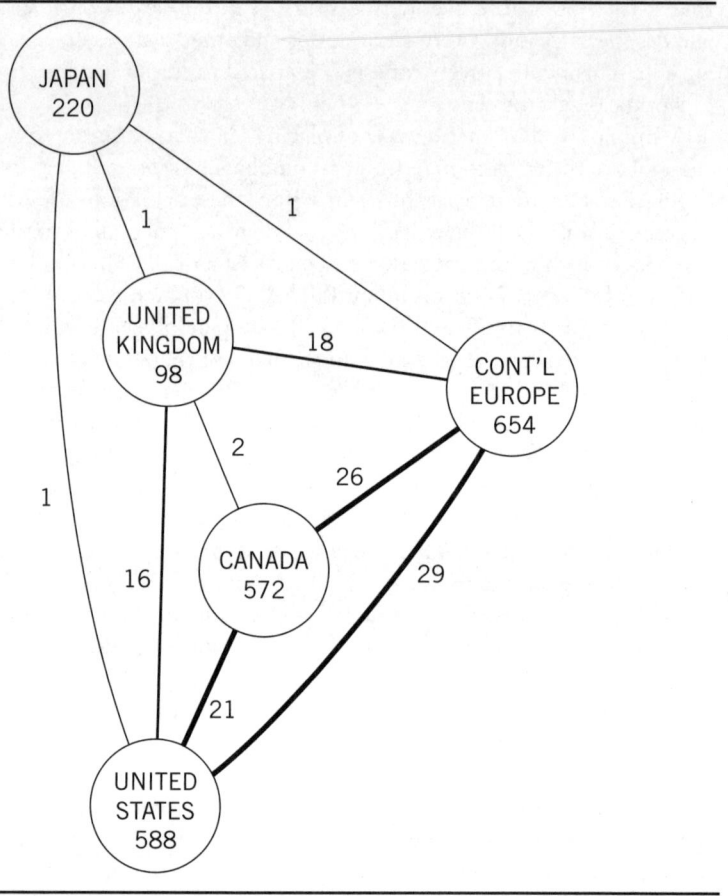

fact that Marie-Josée Kravis was the only woman among the 33 transnational linkers participating in the Canadian network, what is striking is the very small numbers of Canadian-based directors who participate in the global network. Of the 82 big linkers who (as we saw in Table 4.5) carried 62.7 per cent of the national network in 1996, only one—Paul Desmarais—was a transnational interlocker.

Relative to the incidence of interlocking within the national network, transnational interlocking was clearly no more than a sideline for Canada's corporate elite at the close of the twentieth century. With the exception of the Desmarais-Frère group, the tendency was for directors based elsewhere to hold one directorship with a dominant Canadian corporation, whether as part of a relation of transnational strategic control or for a less transparent motive. This pattern is consistent with the notion that Canada's position in world capitalism is that of a smaller middle power.

The Canadian corporate elite has maintained a robust accumulation base, and as of 1996 the total stock of foreign direct investment from Canada to ROW outweighed the total stock of foreign investment in Canada (Burgess, 2002:199–203). Yet at the level of directorate interlocks, most of the ties linking Canadian corporations into the global network appear to reach from Europe, Japan, and the US into Canada, not vice versa.

THE ROLE OF GLOBAL POLICY-PLANNING GROUPS

Corporate boards have not been the only vehicle of global capitalist integration in which members of Canada's corporate elite have participated. As Colin Carson and I have shown elsewhere (2003), the relatively sparse and thin ties that compose the global corporate network are complemented by a series of connections to the global policy-planning groups and fora that have arisen since the second decade of the twentieth century. Table 7.2 summarizes our detailed characterization of the five key groups: the International Chamber of Commerce (ICC), the Bilderberg Conference, the World Economic Forum (WEF), the Trilateral Commission (TC), and the World Business Council for Sustainable Development (WBCSD). These groups promote variants of neoliberal ideology, with the International Chamber of Commerce being the most free-market–oriented and the World Business Council for Sustainable Development the most inclined to blend its embrace of the world market with prescriptions for regulatory restraints on capital's relationship with nature. They also differ in organizational form, specific constituencies, and geopolitical reach, as indicated in the table (for details see Carroll and Carson, 2003). These five groups have come to occupy distinct niches in a field of neoliberal policy formation that has become more complex and extensive since the latest wave of globalization began to build in the early 1970s.

Our analysis of governance-level interlocks among the policy groups, and between them and the Global 350 corporations (including a dozen peak Canadian firms), revealed a highly centralized network. Of the 622 corporate directors making up the global corporate elite, 91 belonged to the Trilateral Commission, 40 belonged to the World Business Council for Sustainable Development, 18 were regular attendees at the Bilderberg Conference, 15 were on the Council or Foundation Board of the World Economic Forum, and 4 served on the Executive Committee of the International Chamber of Commerce. Within the wider network an *inner circle* of 105 corporate capitalists and advisors knit the policy groups together and embedded them in a corporate-policy network extending unevenly to most major corporations in the triad. The global corporate-policy network provides an additional layer of elite social organization, pulling together key business leaders from countries of the centre, and thereby reducing distances between the national networks in a way that reinforces the tendency for Europe and North America to form the network's centre. Our main finding, that a global corporate elite has formed, and that global policy groups have been instrumental in its formation, supports claims by Sklair (2001) and Robinson and Harris (2000) that a 'transnational capitalist class' took shape amid the globalizing initiatives of the late twentieth century.

TABLE 7.2
Classification of Five Leading Transnational Policy Groups

	Neoliberal variant	Agenda priorities	Organizational form	Core membership	Geopolitical reach
International Chamber of Commerce Est. 1919 Paris headquarters	free-market conservative	corporate self-regulated, global *laissez faire*	transnational business organization; government lobbyist; linking to locals	7,000 corporations from 130 countries	Global: corporations and regional committees worldwide, including the Americas, Europe, the Middle East, Africa, and the Asia Pacific
Bilderberg Conference Est. 1952 Geneva origin	neoliberal structuralist	economic order amongst 'Heartland' states	secretive policy-planning and elite consensus-seeking forum	115 national and international corporate, govt., military and academic elite; no set membership	North Atlantic 'Heartland': draws elite representation from Western Europe and North America
Trilateral Commission Est. 1973 Washington, Paris, and Tokyo headquarters	neoliberal structuralist	economic order amongst 'Triad' states	policy-planning and elite consensus-seeking forum; research task forces; discourse producer	350 national and international corporate, media, academia, public service, and NGO elite	'The Triad': draws elite representation from North Atlantic, Japan, ASEAN
World Economic Forum Est. 1971 Geneva headquarters	neoliberal structuralist	'global' economic order	combined elite transnational business organization, and policy-planning and consensus-seeking forum; research task forces; discourse producer	1,000 top transnational corporations	Global: draws elite representation from Western Europe, Central and Eastern Europe, Africa, North America, Latin America, Asia, and Oceania
World Business Council for Sustainable Development Est. 1995 Geneva headquarters	neoliberal regulationist	'global' environmental and economic reform	combined elite transnational business organization, and policy-planning and consensus-seeking forum; research task forces; discourse producer	123 top transnational corporations	Global: draws elite representation from Western Europe, Central and Eastern Europe, Africa, North America, Latin America, Asia, and Oceania

My study with Colin Carson included only the 12 peak Canadian corporations that numbered among the Global 350 of 1996. We found that five of the 105 members of the inner circle were based primarily in Canada, including Paul Desmarais Sr (who was both a transnational linker and member of the Trilateral Commission) and Conrad Black (director of one Global 350 firm [the CIBC] and a member of both the Trilateral Commission and Bilderberg Conference). It is instructive to ask how the entire Canadian corporate elite—an assemblage of 426 interlocking directors of Canada's 258 largest firms—figures in the global corporate-policy network. In Table 7.3 the global corporate-policy network is extended to include all members of the Canadian corporate elite, yielding a set of 20 individuals.

Major shareholders predominate on the list, more so than in the elite as a whole, where as we saw in Chapter 2, they account for only one in ten members. Clearly, Canada's wealthiest capitalists, with strong representation of the Edper-Brascan and Power Corporation interests, have been heavily involved in transnational business activism. Four reigning CEOs also number among the 20, so that 14 of the 20 rank among Canada's major corporate capitalists. Among the advisors, two are former CEOs in dominant Canadian corporations, two are corporate lawyers (namely the former Canadian Ambassador to the UN Yves Fortier and former Canadian Ambassador to the US Allan Gotlieb), one is a (quasi) academic advisor, and one is a consultant.

The Trilateral Commission stands out as the favoured global policy group for the Canadian elite—partly reflecting the Commission's size compared to the other groups,[21] but also expressing the priorities of an elite that looking westward sees Japan, looking eastward sees Europe, and looking southward sees the US. Indeed, according to Newman (1998) the TC has to some extent *supplanted* the private clubs as a mechanism for cultural integration at the top tier of the corporate elite. Although in general Table 7.3 shows affiliations as of 1996–7, we have included André Desmarais's membership in the Trilateral Commission, as of 1998, to illustrate the continuing and quasi-dynastic character of the Desmarais family's involvement in global governance, alongside global accumulation. Similarly, a number of sporadic Bilderberg attendees are listed for the sake of completeness.[22]

Applying more stringent membership criteria, five individuals drop out of the Canadian segment of the global corporate-policy network, leaving 15 corporate directors who sat on multiple Canadian corporate boards and on at least one global policy board in 1996–7.[23] These 15 tended to be very well-connected in the Canadian network. Nine were big linkers directing four or more major Canadian corporations in 1996. In the aggregate, they directed 53 Canadian, four European, and two American companies. Their affiliations with the global policy groups put a good number of Canadian corporate directorates in contact with major transnational sites for policy formation.

In addition to these fifteen, two European-based corporate directors, each with a single Canadian directorship, also participated in the global policy-planning network. Cornelius Herkstroter, president of Royal Dutch-Shell Group, was a director of Shell Canada and also on the Council of the World Economic Forum.

TABLE 7.3
20 Canadian Corporate Elite Members and their Global Policy-group Affiliations, 1996

Name	Policy groups	Principal affiliation	Class
Conrad Black	TC, Bilderberg	Hollinger/Southam	major shareholder
André Desmarais	TC*	Power Corp.	major shareholder
Paul Desmarais	TC	Power Corp.	major shareholder
Fredrik Eaton	Bilderberg***	Eaton	major shareholder
Trevor Eyton	ICC	Edper/Brascan, Senate	major shareholder
David Kerr	WBCSD	Noranda (Edper/Brascan)	major shareholder
Harrison McCain	TC*	McCain Foods Ltd.	major shareholder
James Pattison	TC	Jim Pattison Group	major shareholder
Edward Rogers	Bilderberg**	Rogers Communications	major shareholder
Ronald Southern	TC	Atco	major shareholder
Jacques Bougie	TC	Alcan	CEO
Paul Gagné	WBCSD	Avenor Inc.	CEO
Michael Phelps	TC	Westcoast Energy Inc.	CEO
Lynton Wilson	TC, Bilderberg**	BCE	CEO
Marshall Cohen	TC	formerly Molson	*éminence grise*
Yves Fortier	TC	Ogilvy Renault	legal advisor
Allan Gotlieb	TC, Bilderberg**	Stikeman, Elliott	legal advisor
Marie-Josée Kravis	TC	Hudson Institute	academic advisor
Maureen Sabia	Bilderberg***	Maureen Sabia International	consultant
William Turner Jr.	WEF	formerly Power Corp. group	*éminence grise*

KEY: ICC: International Chamber of Commerce, TC: Trilateral Commision, WBCSD: World Business Council for Sustainable Development, WEF: World Economic Forum.
* Membership as of 1998 but not in 1996
** Attended in 1996 but not in 1997
*** Attended in 1997 but not in 1996

Bertrand Collomb, CEO of Lafarge, a French-based TNC not large enough to qualify for our Global 338 (and 1997 'manager of the year', according to *Le Nouvel Économiste*) was a director of Aquitaine and Unilever as well as the CIBC. But beyond these corporate affiliations Collomb was one of the most politically active of transnational capitalists. In 1996–7 he sat on both the Trilateral Commission and the Council of the World Economic Forum, was a regular attendee at the Bilderberg Conference, and served on the 13-member Executive Committee of World Business Council for Sustainable Development.

The 17 Canadian and European corporate directors and their organizational affiliations are shown in Figure 7.7. In all, 63 corporate boards (nine of them foreign-based) and five global policy groups are linked into a single component by the directors' multiple group affiliations. However, 46 of the corporations and one policy group (the ICC) have only single ties into the network.

Consistent with Peter C. Newman's characterization, the Trilateral Commission is by far the most central organization. It is a meeting point for a dozen directors of major Canadian corporations, including TC North American Deputy Chair Allan Gotlieb, who in 1996 sat with fellow Commissioner Conrad Black on the Hollinger board. The CIBC, followed by Brascan, is the most central corporation. Its four policy-group affiliated directors not only link the CIBC to corporate boards in Europe and the US, they also meet each other on the TC while linking the bank's board to three other global policy groups. Brascan's three directors with global policy-group affiliations compensate somewhat for the lack of interlocks between Brascan-affiliated corporations and major foreign-based companies. Unlike the Desmarais family, the Brascan group has globalized its capital within specific TNCs owning smaller foreign subsidiaries that do not appear in our list of top global corporations. But its board is well ensconced within the global policy-planning network, with Brascan chair Senator Trevor Eyton serving on the Executive Board of the International Chamber of Commerce, Noranda CEO David Kerr serving on the Executive Committee of the World Business Council for Sustainable Development, and Conrad Black doing double-duty with both the Trilateral Commission and the Bilderberg Conference.

Bertrand Collomb is the most central individual in the policy-planning network. A key Euro-capitalist, he sits with Black on the CIBC and the TC and attends at Bilderberg. Collomb also serves on both the CIBC and TC with Marie-Josée Kravis, whose full-time position as Senior Fellow and executive board member at the Hudson Institute provides another link between the Canadian corporate elite and the world of international policy-planning. Once a financial analyst for Power Corporation before becoming special assistant to two successive federal cabinet ministers, Kravis also belongs to the Washington-based Council on Foreign Relations, along with four other members of the Canadian corporate elite.[24] Collomb's seat on the World Business Council for Sustainable Development puts him in touch with Avenor CEO Paul Gagné and Noranda CEO David Kerr, and he meets William Turner, Jr, and Cornelius Herkstroter on the World Economic Forum Council. All of these ties reinforce a certain worldly political solidarity among members of Canada's corporate elite, but the example of Bertrand Collomb is especially illuminating. Through Collomb's directorship the CIBC board not only gains an influential contact in the European business community. It also benefits from the strategic insights of one of global capital's most politically active leaders. This is how global policy-group affiliations create solidarities that lift a section of Canada's business community out of its national context and onto a global political plane. Were we to analyze the entire global corporate-policy network, we would note many more such ties (see Carroll and Carson, 2003). Widening the lens beyond the world of corporate capital, we would begin to notice connections between the corporate elite and political leaders such as Jean Chrétien, Paul Martin, and Mike Harris, all of whom attended the 1996 Bilderberg Conference.

FIGURE 7.7
Elite-level Ties Among Top Canadian Companies and Five Leading Global Policy-Planning Groups, 1996

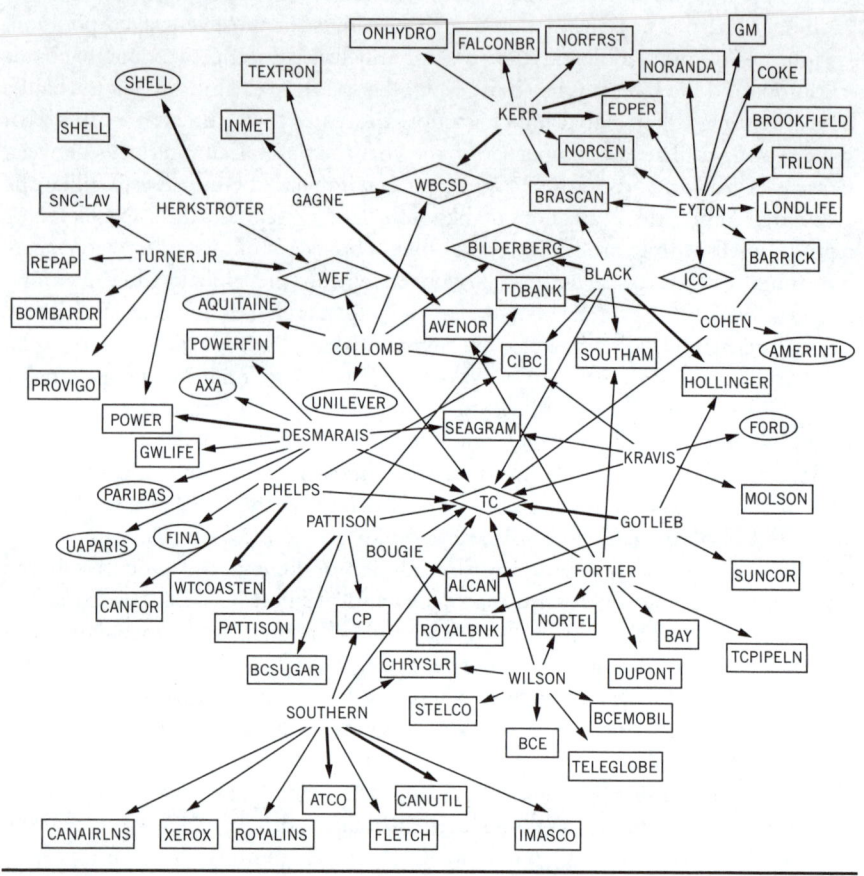

Canadian firms are in boxes; policy groups are in diamonds; foreign companies are in ovals. Thick lines indicate that the person held an executive or inside position in the organization. KEY: TC=Trilateral Commission, WEF=World Economic Forum, ICC=International Chamber of Commerce, WBCSD=World Business Council for Sustainable Development; BLDRBERG=Bilderberg Conference.

CONCLUSIONS

With this chapter we have completed our mapping of Canadian corporate power within the space of Canada, across the space transected by the 49th parallel, and over the globe (which in practical terms means the triad of developed capitalist countries, where virtually all of the socially connected corporate boards are sited). Our analysis of the global corporate network suggests a more multilateral engagement since the mid-1970s on the part of the Canadian corporate elite. The disappearance of many 'continental connections' based in American strategic control of

Canadian firms and the emergence of the transatlantic Power-Frère group are striking developments. Consistent with our findings in Chapter 4, Canadian banks continued to serve as hubs for domestic firms, suggesting that as it became more transnationalized, Canadian finance capital retained a definite national focus. Even so, a good many of the mostly secondary interlocks linking Canadian corporations to Europe and the US involve at least one financial institution, and these weak ties may facilitate the international financial transactions that are central to corporate business in a globalizing world.

Although at the seam between Canadian and global corporate power the American presence is not much greater than that of Japan, the overall pattern of interlocking is consistent with Van der Pijl's (1984) notion of an 'Atlantic ruling class'. Very few directorships are shared between major Japanese corporations on the one hand and European or American companies on the other. Moreover, the ties that hook Canadian companies into the Japanese corporate network are operational extensions of the corporate power of Japanese TNCs, exercised through Canadian subsidiaries. There has been very little integration of actual corporate elites. In contrast, interlocks to Europe (itself a highly integrated field of corporate power) are more profuse and they penetrate more deeply into the Canadian network, resembling the continental connections charted in the previous chapter. The case of Canada supports the conclusion Colin Carson and I reached: the global network is built on national corporate networks and centred in Europe and North America, even if participation of Japanese and other corporate directors on policy boards like the Trilateral Commission pulls the elites of world capitalism into a transnational formation.

Compared to the practice of interlocking among Canadian corporations, transnational interlocking was at the close of the twentieth century no more than a sideline for Canada's corporate elite, involving a mere half dozen of its 400-odd members. And, with the important exception of Paul Desmarais's empire, Canada's corporate capitalists had not established themselves as leading players in the global network. All this suggests that the Canadian corporate elite was positioned globally in a manner commensurate with Canada's location as a middle power in the world capitalist system; however, it also suggests that the 'disorganizing' impact of globalization on the elite's social organization was modest.

Finally, we charted the Canadian corporate elite's participation in five key global policy groups that function as organizations of transnational capitalist governance. Some of Canada's leading corporate capitalists are involved in the global network of transnational business activism—particularly in the Trilateral Commission which brings together business leaders and key intellectuals from Europe, North America, and the Asia-Pacific. Certain of Canada's major corporations, while not well-connected in the global network of corporate interlocks, are ensconced in the parallel network of corporate-policy ties. These ties reinforce a worldly solidarity among members of Canada's elite, and the participation of Canadian directors mobilizes in the pursuit of transnational neoliberalism important human resources that have accumulated within the Canadian corporate power structure. The policy boards at the heart of this parallel network, however, are not command centres for the accumulation of capital. Rather, they are fora for the exercise of the other form of corporate power I distinguished in this book's first chapter: the leadership in political and cultural affairs that, when successful in persuading vast masses of people, we call hegemony. The question of hegemony, particularly the transitions in the Canadian corporate elite's reach into civil society, is the focus of our next two chapters.

III

The Hegemonic Terrain

Chapter 8

Consolidating a Neoliberal Policy Bloc

WITH MURRAY SHAW

From the mid-1970s through the mid-1990s, neoliberalism became a persuasive policy discourse in liberal democracies such as Canada. The Keynesian project that had framed the post-war era—attempting 'to unite the principle of continued private control of the investment and production processes of a capitalist economy with public demands for a change in the market-determined pattern of employment and income' (Wolfe, 1984:47)—was largely supplanted by a market-driven approach to governing capitalism. The shift away from Keynes reflected not only the enhanced structural power that globalization and increased capital mobility gave to investors, but a complex configuration of problems associated with the Keynesian paradigm, some of which (like the fiscal crisis of the state) became evident in the 1970s, others of which (like the rising wage bill relative to productivity) were recognized by the late 1980s. Proceeding from the premises of monetarist economic theory, neoliberalism introduced sweeping measures to widen the scope of markets in social life. These included deregulation, privatization, regressive tax reforms, erosion and dismantling of social services, campaigns of state deficit- and debt-reduction, the opening of doors to foreign investment, and attacks on trade-union rights.[1] What the policies of neoliberalism have in common is a commitment to 'the principle of corporate private property, and its defence and advancement' (Teeple, 2000:6)—a commitment whose rationality seems self-evident in a context of heightened international competition, not only among firms but among states seeking the new investments that power local economies. Integral to the rise and consolidation of neoliberal hegemony were the emergence of new centres of class-wide business activism and the retooling of established policy institutes along neoliberal lines. Following on the previous chapter's analysis of the network that embeds the Canadian corporate elite within the global field of neoliberal policy formation, this chapter examines in greater depth the elite-level relationships between Canada's largest corporations and five Canadian policy groups on the neoliberal right. Our analysis is built around four theses that may help to concretize the ways in which hegemonic corporate power reaches into civil society to influence both the substance and the common sense of political policy. These four theses converge on a view of neoliberalism as a political and cultural accomplishment—a *hegemonic project*, in Jessop's (1983) terminology.[2] They are as follows:

1. We view neoliberal policy groups as crucial *organizations of organic intellectuals*, 'deputies' or members of the capitalist class entrusted with the activity of 'organising the general system of relationships external to ... business itself' (Gramsci, 1971:6).³ As we noted in Chapter 2, such intellectuals are 'organic' in a double sense: they are 'organizers' of an advanced capitalist way of life, and their intellectual work is functionally predicated on the dominance of capital in human affairs. The agency of leading corporate capitalists in governing neoliberal policy groups is an important expression of the organic relationship between the business of capital accumulation and the politics of policy formation.
2. Policy groups can be characterized as *sites for the construction of political discourses that circulate in the form of various texts and have influence not only in business and government circles but in news media and popular culture*. Such discourses represent bids for hegemony because they lay out programs and strategies that define the 'national interest' in a given policy domain. The key issue is how a *neoliberal discursive field*—an ensemble of producers and consumers of texts enunciating neoliberal perspectives (research reports, speeches, press releases, news stories, and the like)—has come to provide *cultural resources for political-economic transformation*.
3. Constructing a new hegemony requires social organization. Inhabiting a space in civil society with ties to big capital, the state, and the media, neoliberal policy groups form a critical component of that apparatus. These groups need to be analyzed as *embedded elements of a social network*, within which neoliberal business activism has taken shape. Ties between the corporate world and the world of policy groups—and the direct participation of corporate directors in policy-group work—make it possible to conduct a continuing conversation in which political frames can be aligned and adjusted, effecting a moving consensus between functioning capitalists and their organic intellectuals (Useem, 1984; Domhoff, 1998). On this score, we analyze the network of neoliberal policy groups and large corporations, interlocked at the level of their governance boards, and consider the relative importance of the policy groups in knitting the corporate elite into a political-cultural community.
4. Finally, the corporate-policy group (PG) network as a whole can be considered in terms of its *distinctive organizational ecology*—the interdependent types and specializations that characterize the entire field of policy groups, including innovative new organizational forms (Hunt and Aldrich, 1998). The key issue is how each group has come to occupy a *distinct niche* in an emerging organizational ecology that has entailed a shift to *business activism*. This shift is evident in two changes in the field of policy groups. On the one hand, since the early 1970s various 'advocacy think-tanks' have emerged, either through transformation of traditional policy groups or as newly minted organizations. Unlike traditional policy research institutions such as the Conference Board, advocacy think-tanks are not driven by a desire to advance scholarly research. On the contrary, their primary motivation is to engage in policy advocacy. In short, they do not covet attention in the scholarly community, but are deeply committed to imposing their ideological agenda on the electorate (Abelson and Carberry, 1998:538).

On the other hand, 1976 saw the formation of the Business Council on National Issues, a cross-sectoral peak organization dedicated to business activism, explicitly seeking to construct a policy consensus not simply for bankers or manufacturers, but for the entire *haute bourgeoisie* (see Dobbin, 1998; Langille, 1987).

In Canada it is widely recognized that the turning point in consolidating neoliberalism was the imposition of North American free trade, a 'policy Trojan horse' intended to oblige the state to conform to strict market principles (Bradford, 2000:67). By creating a North American zone, the trade deals of 1989 and 1994 placed Canadian locations in competition with investment sites in the US, unleashing (according to Jackson, 1999) powerful pressures to 'harmonize' Canadian standards and programs with the lowest common denominator. The terrain of public policy shifted as market-oriented approaches to 'rationalizing' social programs, taxation rates, and regulations gained credibility. The reality of free trade, in conjunction with energetic campaigns by new right forces such as the Reform Party of Canada, the National Citizens Coalition, and the Canadian Taxpayers Foundation, helped to make neoliberalism the political currency of the day, so that by the 1990s even policy groups that had participated in the Keynesian consensus in the 1960s were exponents of the new liberalism.

THE FIVE POLICY GROUPS

A similar discursive migration—from Keynes to Friedrich Hayek—characterizes the first two of the five policy groups we will examine here. The Conference Board of Canada dates to 1954, when the New York-based Conference Board (formed in 1916) opened an office in Montreal to serve clients based in Canada (Lindquist, 1998:128). In 1971 the Canadian operations were moved to Ottawa and thereafter grew rapidly, providing research, conferencing, and information services to business clients in the areas of 'organizational strategies and practices, emerging economic and social trends, and key public policy issues' (Conference Board of Canada, 1999a:1). The Conference Board is now the largest think-tank in Canada, and unlike others it conducts research using its own in-house staff (Lindquist, 1998:131, 133). Its mandate to develop and disseminate knowledge and information tends to distance it from specific policy recommendations (Conference Board of Canada, 1999a:i, ii). Within the ecology of neoliberal policy work, the Conference Board's niche is to provide a nodal point for policy research, linking into academia, the state, and corporate capital in many different ways, but without an explicit goal of either *advocacy* or *consensus formation*. More than any other group, the Conference Board is a think-tank plain and simple.

The group has long focused on issues of 'organizational effectiveness'—'one of the most critical determinants of our nation's productivity' (Conference Board of Canada, 1999a:i). However, whereas in the Keynesian era effective management strategies were aimed at promoting profit in conjunction with full employment and buoyant aggregate demand, by the 1990s the broader context within which 'organizational effectiveness' was promoted had led the Board to specify its 'mission': 'to help our members anticipate and respond to the increasingly changing global economy' (Conference Board of Canada, 1999a:1). Indeed, in the 1990s international competitiveness became a central theme, in terms both of productivity and of the need for Canadians to adjust their expectations to meet the new realities of global competitive pressures. Commenting on the 1999 report 'Performance and Potential', in which Canada's performance was compared with six countries across 40 socioeconomic indicators, Board President James Nininger stated that 'regrettably, we find ourselves lacking. . . . The truth is that Canada is only in the middle of the pack, when we compare ourselves with our peers. We can, and must, do better' (Conference Board of Canada, 1999b). The proposed solution is to improve productivity both in the administration of social programs and in organizational management strategies, thereby boosting performance without triggering inflation. The report comes out strongly in support of the devolutionary Social Union framework—widely perceived by its critics as a threat to national standards and universal entitlements—as a way of increasing the efficiency of social programs and government accountability by 'establishing performance indicators in social programming that will change how government administers taxpayers' money' (1999b:2). In the area of organizational management, the development of a more 'flexible' working population is seen as a way to decrease the unit labour costs that are damaging the competitiveness of Canadian industry (Conference Board of Canada, 1998:6).

The Conference Board is not an advocacy think-tank. Rather, there are two senses in which it now occupies a *moderate niche* within the neoliberal policy spectrum. First, the many texts it produces offer a nonpartisan and technocratic perspective on public issues, organized mainly around discourses of public-choice political analysis and neo-classical economics—the ideological toolkit of neoliberalism. Second, a broader social agenda is reflected in its strategies for meeting the challenge of globalization with a more flexible and productive work force. At the heart of the Board's prescription is the restructuring of organizational, social, and economic policy to enhance the competitiveness and profitability of capital.

The C.D. Howe Institute (CDHI) is described on its web-page as an independent, nonprofit economic and social policy research institution, with a mandate to provide balanced, well-reasoned, and comprehensible analysis of issues of national interest to governments, the media, and the Canadian public. Much of the CDHI's work provides input to policymakers, recommending, 'where appropriate, particular policy options that, in the Institute's view, best serve the national interest' (C.D. Howe Institute, 1995:2) and consists of short-term policy analysis, carried out by a small in-house staff of economists, with contributions from external academics and business economists (Ernst, 1992:115). In addition to the Annual Policy Review and the 10 to 15 policy studies it publishes each year, the CDHI maintains standing committees of business leaders and professionals who organize and participate in conferences and speaking engagements (1992:116).

The CDHI's predecessor was the Private Planning Association of Canada (PPAC), founded in 1958 by Canadian members of the Canadian American Committee (CAC), a group of business and labour leaders from Canada and the US whose aim was to 'seek out and reduce the basic causes of friction in U.S./Canadian relations'

(Ernst, 1992:117). While the PPAC's main goal was reduction of Canada–US trade barriers, policy statements from the 1960s indicate acceptance of Keynesian macroeconomic policy and 'a cautious stance toward Canada–U.S. free trade and the elimination of Canadian tariffs' (1992:118). Owing to a lack of resources, in 1973 the PPAC merged with the C.D. Howe Memorial Foundation, which provided a $2 million endowment, and the CDHI was formed. In keeping with the corporatist design of its predecessor, the board of the new group included not only a plethora of corporate directors, but also some labour leaders, such as Joe Morris, president of the Canadian Labour Congress.

Since 1973, however, there has been a shift in the CDHI's policy stance that reflects the emergence of a vigorous business agenda in Canada. In the early to mid-1970s its policy recommendations took for granted the value of Keynesian demand management and programs such as Unemployment Insurance. But by the time of its 1983 submission to the Macdonald Royal Commission on the Economic Union and Development Prospects for Canada, the CDHI had for the most part rejected Keynesian fiscal policies. Arguing that Keynesian measures for stimulating economic growth were no longer feasible in the face of global competition, CDHI discourse in the early 1980s began to emphasize that 'the central goal of economic policy must be to encourage adjustment' (Dobson, Lipsey, and Smith, 1983:7).

The CDHI's embrace of neoliberalism is reflected in changes in its positions toward free trade with the US and Unemployment Insurance. Election of the Mulroney Conservatives in 1984 'pushed the CDHI toward a harder neoconservative line' (Ernst, 1992:129), and by 1985 it was trumpeting free trade as the only realistic option for Canadian economic policy. Along with a major study (Lipsey and Smith, 1985), lobbying efforts by staff were instrumental in convincing many senior federal ministers and bureaucrats to support a free-trade deal with the US. In its 1986 policy review, deficit reduction superseded full employment as a core macroeconomic goal, and in the same year the CDHI reversed its earlier opposition to the Fraser Institute's plea to dismantle the Unemployment Insurance system (Ernst, 1992:129–32). Throughout the 1990s the CDHI continued to maintain a high profile, endorsing such measures as North American free trade, the privatization and decentralization of government services, an end to universality in social programs, and the introduction of a 'social union' framework to devolve authority to the provinces within a fiscal framework of reduced federal funding.[4]

The Conference Board and C.D. Howe Institute have take similar routes into their current 'mainstream' niches in the organizational ecology of neoliberal policy work. Both had roots in the era of Keynesian consensus, when they brought together business leaders, technical experts, and labour leaders around an agenda of cautious, continentalist corporatism, suited to the distinctively 'permeable' fordism that prevailed at the time (Jenson, 1989). Although the Institute's shift to neoliberalism began as the post-war order unravelled in the mid-1970s, it was the question of US–Canada Free Trade in the 1980s that truly crystallized its new position. By the late 1980s, the CDHI was extolling the benefits of deregulated markets, the virtues of the self-reliant individual, and the dangers of the overweening, debt-plagued state. Meanwhile, the Conference Board was reframing its strategies for organizational effectiveness along the lines of more flexible labour relations and decentralized, targeted social programs—the leaner, neoliberal state. By the 1990s, the boards of these groups, which in the past had included labour representation, could be described as centres of corporate consensus formation, well suited to a neoliberal policy agenda.

The Business Council on National Issues (BCNI)—recast late in 2001 as the Canadian Council of Chief Executive Officers—occupies a unique position in this organizational ecology. Unlike the other groups, the project of the Council is primarily one of consensus-formation. It is less a 'think-tank' than a shadow government—an executive committee of 150 top CEOs—devoted to managing the common affairs of Canada's corporate elite. Beyond providing a single voice to enunciate the claims of corporate capital, the BCNI endeavours to make that voice heard both in state practices and in public discourse through lobbying efforts with the federal government and high-profile forays into the public sphere. In contrast with the think-tanks, whose media work tends to wear a veneer of objectivity in the popular imagination, the BCNI is transparently a creature of the corporate elite, and its persuasiveness in popular discourse depends on its effectiveness in constructing a general interest capable of bringing the people in line with the needs of capital.

The BCNI was formed in 1976 to address concerns that the corporate elite needed to find a way to represent its broad range of interests as a coherent hegemonic project. Canadian corporations had long depended on state support, but this relationship had deteriorated badly by the 1970s; and as corporations had come to be regarded as vehicles for a wealthy interest group, their public image had declined (Dobbin, 1998:165). Poor public image, a government often critical of the business community, labour unrest, and a changing international political economy created the context in which two corporate leaders, Alfred Powis and W.O. Twaits, decided to form an organization whose purpose would be to boost the image and influence of corporate interests. Canadian corporations had until this point been slow to respond to global economic developments, and were torn between protecting their short-term interests and collaborating with government on long-term economic strategies (Langille, 1987:48).

The BCNI bears a strong resemblance to the Business Roundtable in the United States (Langille, 1987:49–50). Membership is by invitation, and consists of '150 chief executives of leading Canadian companies representing every sector of the economy' (BCNI web page). The Council's mandate is 'to ensure that Canadian chief executives play an influential role in the international financial, trade, investment, environmental and foreign affairs domains' (Langille 1987: 49–50). Its structure consists of an executive committee and policy committee (providing overall direction), a secretariat (providing support and research services), and the general membership (serving on committees and task forces; D'Aquino, 1991:194). BCNI task forces resemble 'a virtual shadow cabinet'—covering specific portfolios such as National Finance, International Economy and Trade, Taxation, Competition Policy, Federal–Provincial Relations, Foreign Policy and Defence, Education, and Corporate Governance (Langille, 1987:55). Task-force findings and recommendations are forwarded to the executive committee, which carries 'the Council's message to governments, to key opinion moulders, to specific constituencies, or to the public at large' (D'Aquino, 1991:195).

Since the 1970s the BCNI has advocated the reduction of government presence in the economy and the opening up of Canada's borders to investment. In the 1990s, the fiscal crisis faced by the state provided a pretext for urging restraint and deregulation, and in the late 1990s, when that crisis was alleviated, the Council responded with a rhetorical shift from the state deficit to global competition as the looming threat to national well-being. In the lead-up to the 1988 'Free Trade' election, the BCNI played a major behind-the-scenes role in funding and seconding personnel to a front group, the Canadian Alliance for Trade and Job Opportunities, which it established in 1987 to build a broad basis of public support for the Canada–US FTA (Fillmore, 1989). In 1999, with North American free trade in place, the Council launched its Canada Global Leadership Initiative, to address its concerns that Canada's position in the global economy would deteriorate rapidly unless action were taken to further reduce corporate and personal tax rates and restrain government spending. At its Summit 2000 meeting the BCNI issued a report envisaging a future in which Canadians and their enterprises would attain the coveted status of 'world leaders' rather than 'regional followers'—attracting the big corporations, head offices, cutting-edge technology, and rich people whose ideas and money would create prosperity and in the process pay most of the government's bills. Through lower corporate and personal income tax rates, the report claimed, 'we must make Canada a compelling place for Canadians and foreigners alike to invest their money in our people and ideas, and to build growing global enterprises' (Business Council on National Issues, 2000:15). This example shows that the BCNI does not simply respond to government policy initiatives. It anticipates issues and delivers its recommendations to policy-makers and the media while initiatives are under consideration (Langille, 1987:55). As Dobbin (1998) notes, since the days of the Trudeau Liberals, governments and prime ministers have come and gone, but 'the BCNI, the voice and organizational embodiment of corporate rule, is a permanent presence' (1998:168).

From its home base in Vancouver, the Fraser Institute (FI) has actively struggled to secure a hegemonic position for 'free market' principles in the economic, political, and social domains of Canadian society. The Institute's formation dates from 1973, when founder and director Michael Walker, then working for the federal finance department, managed to persuade T. Patrick Boyle, vice-president of MacMillan Bloedel, and 15 mining executives to invest $200,000 in the FI's 1975 start-up (Scott, 1994:109). Since that time, Institute revenues and membership have grown steadily, with annual income rising from $825,736 in 1983 to $3,253,846 in 1997, and total membership (corporations, foundations, individuals) increasing from 521 in 1983 to more than 1200 in 1997 (Fraser Institute, 1983:17; Fraser Institute, 1997:25). Along with its recently formed east-coast cousin, the Atlantic Institute for Market Studies (see below), the Fraser Institute is the most advocacy-oriented of our five policy groups. Much as the BCNI has been modelled after its American sister organization, the FI is a close replica of American advocacy think-tanks such as the American Enterprise Institute. Funded privately by large corporations, the FI's sources and methods of fundraising resemble those of its American counterparts (Havemann, 1986:15).

Neoliberal advocacy is at the heart of the FI's project. Its *Annual Report* for 1997 states that its mandate is to provide 'an alternative to well-intentioned but misguided and conventional views about the appropriate role of government in the economy' (4). Ideologically, the FI draws on a combination of 'neoclassical economics and libertarian rhetoric' (Havemann, 1986:15) as in the works of Milton Friedman and Friedrich Hayek. FI discourse has consistently represented the market economy as a self-regulating entity, the natural processes of which are distorted by any form of government interference—whether rent control, unemployment insurance, environmental regulation or medicare. The distorting effect of unemployment insurance on the mechanisms of the market economy has been a favoured topic since the mid-1970s, as the Institute has argued that UI creates a 'disincentive to work' that actually leads to high rates of unemployment (Grubel and Walker, 1978).

The FI's activities consist of generating publications and holding conferences that are accessible to both policy-makers and the general public. Executive Director Michael Walker claims that 'the work we do is global. Our books are distributed to 52 countries . . . in August we are holding a meeting of economic advisors and analysts from 40 countries' (in Brunet, 1999:5). The Reform Party (re-launched in 2000 as the Canadian Reform Conservative Alliance) has drawn extensively on the FI for its policy positions and critiques of government policy. Despite the striking parallels between FI views and Reform Party platforms, and the winning of a Reform seat in Vancouver by Institute economist and SFU professor Herbert Grubel, Michael Walker has denied any 'overlap' between the Institute and the Reform Party (Lorinc, 1994:12). While there may be no formal link, the Reform Party has over the years been a faithful consumer of FI ideas. Dobbin (1998:194) points out that 'during the 1993-97 Parliament . . . twenty-two of the fifty-one Reform MPs drew on Institute materials for their speeches.'

These instances of political influence notwithstanding, the FI has had less immediate influence at the federal level than the more 'mainstream' policy institutes. If, as Evert Lindquist (1990:34) states, the policy-relevance of a think-tank's output can be assessed in terms of its 'amenability' or 'contestability' vis-à-vis the goals of its target audience, the FI's output has tended towards contestability. Yet what the FI has lacked in direct influence has been mitigated by its success in 'pushing the limits of acceptable political discourse well to the right, and in creating more space and legitimacy for neoliberalism' (Cameron, 1997:13). The FI has made the greatest inroads into political discourse through the popular media, a forum in which

> the institute has moved from the fringe to the centre . . . shifted from [being] a comic example of ultra-right hyperbole to the representation of reason. . . . No longer is its almost daily reference in the media prefaced with 'right-wing think-tank'. . . . the Fraser Institute is now as respectable as the Conference Board and the C.D. Howe Institute (Hackett and Zhao, 1998:157).

Hackett and Zhao state that 'the news uncritically transmits the Institute's dubious assumptions, categorizations, and polemical language' (1998:157). A study of business news over the Canadian Press wire service found that over a one-year period 'the Fraser Institute was quoted in 140 stories, while the left-wing Canadian Centre for Policy Alternatives was quoted in 16' (1998:158).

While the FI has not had the direct policy input enjoyed by more mainstream groups, it has played a pivotal role in the dissemination of a neoliberal agenda through its media presence, publications, public conferences, and student programs.[5] Indeed, it has served as the vanguard in the effort to construct neoliberal hegemony. Its full-blooded advocacy of the free market and minimal state—widely dismissed in the 1970s as lunatic-fringe ranting—directly inspired the first experiment in neoliberal state transformation: the Social Credit 'restraint program' of 1983 in British Columbia.[6] Its growing influence throughout the 1980s and 1990s in federal parties of the right—first the Mulroney Tories, more recently the Reform Party/Canadian Alliance—helped to place neoliberalism at the centre of political debate; its proactive strategy of co-opting a stable of academics into an expanding publication program while engaging in tactful 'media penetration' has brought neoliberal ideology from the margins to the centre.

Finally, the most recent addition to the field of neoliberal policy groups is the Atlantic Institute for Market Studies (AIMS), an advocacy-style group formed in 1994 'as an independent, non-partisan, social and economic think-tank based in Halifax'. Its self-declared mission is 'to broaden the debate about realistic options available to build our economy' (Atlantic Institute for Market Studies, 1997/98:1). In its ideological discourse, mandate, structure, and *modus operandi*, AIMS is a smaller, east-coast version of the Fraser Institute. Its 1998 board of directors was made up of 24 Atlantic-based members, two directors based in Toronto (including its chair, Purdy Crawford, also chair of Imasco), and single directors based in Montreal and Calgary. In its first years of activity, AIMS organized conferences, published books, and produced a monthly newsletter that became regularly cited in local media. Its pro-market interventions included a critique of regional development subsidies for Atlantic Canada and advocacy of 'market solutions' to problems in the fishery, rural development, environmental protection, and higher education. AIMS also instigated a movement for 'charter schools' which has since taken on grass-roots appeal—an example of what its President has called 'planting seeds' that take root and 'continue to sprout and grow' throughout society (Atlantic Institute for Market Studies, 1997/98:7).

Taking into account all five groups, it is clear that by the mid-1990s the neoliberal project had established a firm organizational base in the policy-formation field. A collection of corporate-funded groups had been invented or re-tooled to facilitate the work of organic intellectuals committed to free-market ideology. The neoliberal formation had evolved a complex organizational ecology, with niches ranging from the Conference Board's 'pure think-tank' emphasis through the BCNI's consensus-formation project to the Fraser Institute's tenacious advocacy. This discursive field was well developed in both academia and the media, and encompassed a rich spectrum of authors and genres—from press releases and conferences to in-depth policy research papers, all asserting that, in a globalizing world, increased market discipline is essential medicine for the nation's economic ills. We now turn to the third component of neoliberal hegemony distinguished earlier: the interorganizational relations that knit these policy groups together with many of the largest Canadian corporations into a social network, at the upper echelons of corporate governance and elite formation.

MAPPING THE CORPORATE–PG NETWORK

Since the pioneering work of C. Wright Mills (1956), sociologists have documented 'the avenues of contact and channels of communication' between sections of the corporate elite that provide a structural base for business leadership in society (Clement, 1975:255). The most studied case is the US, where Burris (1992), Domhoff (1998), and Dreiling (2000) have researched the network of policy groups tied through directorate interlocks to each other and to the largest corporations. In Canada studies have focused more anecdotally on policy groups as elite fora with particular ties to corporate capital (Clement, 1975; Dobbin, 1998). In the 1980s two projects of network analysis examined the corporation–policy-group network and found a substantial volume of interlocking between corporate and policy boards between 1946 and 1976 (Fox and Ornstein, 1986:492–3) and between 1976 and 1986 (Carroll, 1989). However, these studies did not attempt to trace the corporate–PG network in any detail.

Our intention here is to provide such an analysis for 1976, when the neoliberal bloc was just forming, and two decades later. Our samples of major corporations are the same Top 257 companies of 1976 and the Top 258 of 1996 employed throughout this study. However, defining the constituents of the neoliberal policy network posed a problem. All five of our neoliberal policy groups have maintained strong ties to Canada's corporate elite, both in funding and in governance relations; strictly speaking, however, in 1976 only the Fraser Institute qualified as an unequivocally neoliberal organization. Its ideological role in the context of that time was very much that of Thatcherism *avant le lettre*. Two of the groups—the Conference Board and CDHI—had roots in the Keynesian welfare state formation of the 1950s and 1960s and only later became neoliberalized. Even the BCNI's commitment to neoliberalism was rather vague in 1976, its formative year. As an emerging site of class-wide business activism, it was neoliberal more in practice than in theory.[7] For comparative purposes our network analysis includes all extant groups in both years, even though only two of them—the Fraser Institute and BCNI—could actually have been described in 1976 as nodes of an incipient neoliberal policy network. However, by the mid-1990s a neoliberal policy bloc, providing sites for such business activism from coast to coast, had clearly been consolidated. Below we explore its changing topography as a social network.

Like the network of corporate interlocks, the corporate–PG network operates at two distinct levels: those of the organization and the individual. Key players at either level can have a major influence on the shape and form of the network. In 1996, David Kerr, CEO of Noranda, sat on seven dominant corporate boards and two policy boards (BCNI and CDHI)—generating a total of 21 direct intercorporate ties and 14 corporate–PG ties. In the same year, the BCNI—which is explicitly constituted as a roundtable of leading CEOs—included 100 directors of Canada's largest corporations, who as a group populated the boards of 120 dominant corporations, rendering the Council a sociometric star.

In Table 8.1 we can see that in 1976 a total of 241 people sat on one or more of the four extant policy boards. Two decades later, in 1996, 262 people sat on one or more of five boards. In both years a majority of policy-group directors also directed one or more leading corporations, and 22 of them sat on multiple policy boards. Most of these 22 were also corporate directors, and in 1996 six of them directed three policy groups each, forming a closely-knit network core. The many corporate affiliations of these individuals confirm that the governance of neoliberal policy groups is largely the work of the corporate elite. They also underline the fact that most policy-group directors are organic intellectuals operating at the highest level of the capitalist class.

However, Table 8.1 also shows the consequences of the thinning of corporate interlocking for the corporate–PG network. By 1996 a great number of policy-group directors held no major corporate directorships, and a smaller number were members of the corporate elite, with directorships in multiple dominant corporations.[8] In Table 8.2 we can see the impact of a sparser corporate network on the composition of the policy boards. In both years, the preponderance of directors of the BCNI, CDHI, and Conference Board were affiliated with one or more leading corporation. However, by 1996 the BCNI included fewer members of the corporate elite, as CEOs became less involved in directing multiple firms. This pattern holds for other policy groups, except that the Fraser Institute's board grew as CDHI's shrunk, with the latter showing a sharper fall in corporate directors but an increase in directors of multiple policy groups. In both years ties *among* policy groups were

TABLE 8.1

Directors in the Corporate–Policy Group Network

N of policy-group directorships held	N of corporate directorships held			
	0	1	2 or more	Total
		1976		
1	92	54	73	219
2	1	1	16	18
3	0	1	3	4
Total	93	56	92	241
		1996		
1	122	67	51	240
2	3	3	10	16
3	0	2	4	6
Total	125	72	65	262

TABLE 8.2
Size and Composition of Policy Boards

	Size of board	N of corporate directors	N of corporate elite members	N of policy-group linkers
1976				
BCNI	142	101	66	20
C.D. Howe	55	34	26	8
Conference Bd	36	27	25	15
Fraser Inst.	34	13	8	5
1996				
BCNI	151	100	53	21
C.D. Howe	29	21	16	11
Conference Bd	36	23	18	14
Fraser Inst.	48	12	9	3
AIMS	26	11	5	1

carried mainly by directors of the more 'moderate' groups: the BCNI, CDHI, and the Conference Board. By 1996, more than a third of CDHI and Conference Board directors were affiliated with at least one other neoliberal policy group.

In these findings we can identify another organizational implication of corporate governance reforms. As Table 8.3 suggests, with the relative decline in the banks' centrality (last row), the BCNI's 120 direct ties to major corporations in 1996 became more integral to elite integration than were its 128 corporate ties in 1976. The diminished prominence of bank boards as meeting points for the corporate elite may actually have amplified the importance of the BCNI as a site where prominent CEOs may forge a policy consensus. In the process the BCNI became a particularly crucial place for reconfirming a consensus of values and world view. For CDHI and the Conference Board, the overall decrease in corporate interlocking appears to have had more impact. Their boards have tended to include corporate 'big linkers' who direct four or more large firms, but as the corporate network became sparser, the number of ties carried by such linkers was reduced. Both CDHI and the Conference Board show sharp drops in degree of interlocking with corporations. The Fraser Institute and AIMS—the advocacy think-tanks—are, in fact, the only groups that registered gains in the numbers of corporations with which they shared directors. For AIMS those gains came with the establishment of a presence in the higher circles of the corporate elite. For the Fraser Institute, they suggest increased centrality in the corporate–PG network.

According to one index of centrality, which views networks as webs of communication, this is indeed the case. As we saw in Chapters 6 and 7, Anthonisse's rush assesses the extent to which a point lies on the shortest paths between other points in the network. It may be interpreted as the sum of the proportions of flows that pass through a given point, a measure of 'betweenness'. Table 8.4 shows rush scores for each policy group and for five major chartered banks.[9] The Fraser Institute

TABLE 8.3
Number of Corporations Interlocked with Each Organization

	1976	1996
BCNI	128	120
C.D. Howe	76	43
Conference Bd	62	32
Fraser Inst.	21	23
AIMS	—	23
All corporations (mean)	12.8	9.0
Five largest banks (mean)	59.0	34.8

TABLE 8.4
Rush Scores for Five Policy Groups and Five Big Banks

	1976		1996	
	Rush score	Rank among all organizations	Rush score	Rank among all organizations
BCNI	.2916	1	.4241	1
C.D. Howe	.0720	2	.0212	9
Conference Bd	.0302	7	.0363	2
Fraser Inst.	.0055	49	.0172	13
AIMS	—	—	.0081	40
Royal Bank	.0677	3	.0328	5
CIBC	.0576	4	.0330	4
Bank of Montreal	.0518	5	.0335	3
TD Bank	.0399	6	.0201	10
Bank of NS	.0192	9	.0225	7

moves from a quite peripheral score to one not far below that of CDHI, whose centrality drops from second to ninth highest among the 260-odd organizations, mainly as a result of its having adopted a smaller board with fewer corporate linkers on it. AIMS's score and rank for 1996 resemble the Fraser Institute's for 1976, when as a newly minted group its board also had a more regional base. With the exception of CDHI, the policy groups gained centrality. In the sparser network of 1996 they are star-like nodes that integrate the network, particularly the BCNI, whose score increases by 45 per cent. In contrast, although the banks remain relatively central in the network, their rush scores tend to decrease, in the Royal's case by over 50 per cent, indicating a reduced proportion of overall communicative 'flow' passing through their boards. Still, if the policy groups gained centrality, bank boards remained important meeting points in the corporate-PG network. Indeed, in 1996

TABLE 8.5
Number of Shared Directors Among Neoliberal Policy Groups

	BCNI	C.D. Howe	Conference Bd	Fraser Inst.
1976				
C.D. Howe	6			
Conference Bd	14	3		
Fraser Inst.	4	1	2	
1996				
	BCNI	C.D. Howe	Conference Bd	Fraser Inst.
C.D. Howe	10			
Conference Bd	14	4		
Fraser Inst.	2	3	0	
AIMS	1	0	0	0

the five banks and five policy groups accounted for eight of the ten most central positions in the entire network.

An important part of any corporate–PG bloc is the set of ties *among the policy groups*, (see Table 8.5). Already in 1976 there was substantial sharing of directors among the groups, mainly by virtue of the BCNI's omnibus board. In the ensuing two decades, despite decreases in corporate interlocking, the number of ties among the policy groups actually increased slightly, from 30 to 34, as BCNI maintained its interlocks with the other groups and established one tie to AIMS, while CDHI increased its ties to three of the groups. However, the interlocks between the Fraser Institute and Conference Board disappeared. These changes rendered the core of the policy network—BCNI, CDHI, and the Conference Board—more integrated, but also—intriguingly—split the hard-line Fraser Institute and the more soft-line Conference Board, with BCNI and CDHI jointly mediating between them by receiving directors from both.

As a final aspect of our network analysis, Figures 8.1 and 8.2 map the inner circle of the corporate–PG network. This inner circle consists of 22 individuals who in 1976 or 1996 directed two or more policy groups.[10] Their organizational affiliations appear as lines, while corporations appear as rectangular nodes and policy groups appear as diamond-shaped nodes. In these sociograms we can observe the roles played by key organic intellectuals in integrating the governance of corporations and neoliberal policy groups.

In 1976, we find the founders of the BCNI, Messrs Powis and Twaits, sitting not only on the BCNI but on the Conference Board and, in Twaits's case, the CDHI. In the same year, Powis was president of Noranda Mines and a director of BC Forest Products, Gulf Canada, and Sun Life, and Twaits was a director of Alcan Aluminum, the Royal Bank of Canada, Abitibi Paper, Ford Canada, and Norcen. Other key corporate directors were L. Lodge, president of IMB Canada, and James Black, president of The Molson Companies and director of Mutual Life—both of

FIGURE 8.1
Network of Directors of Two or More Policy Boards, 1976

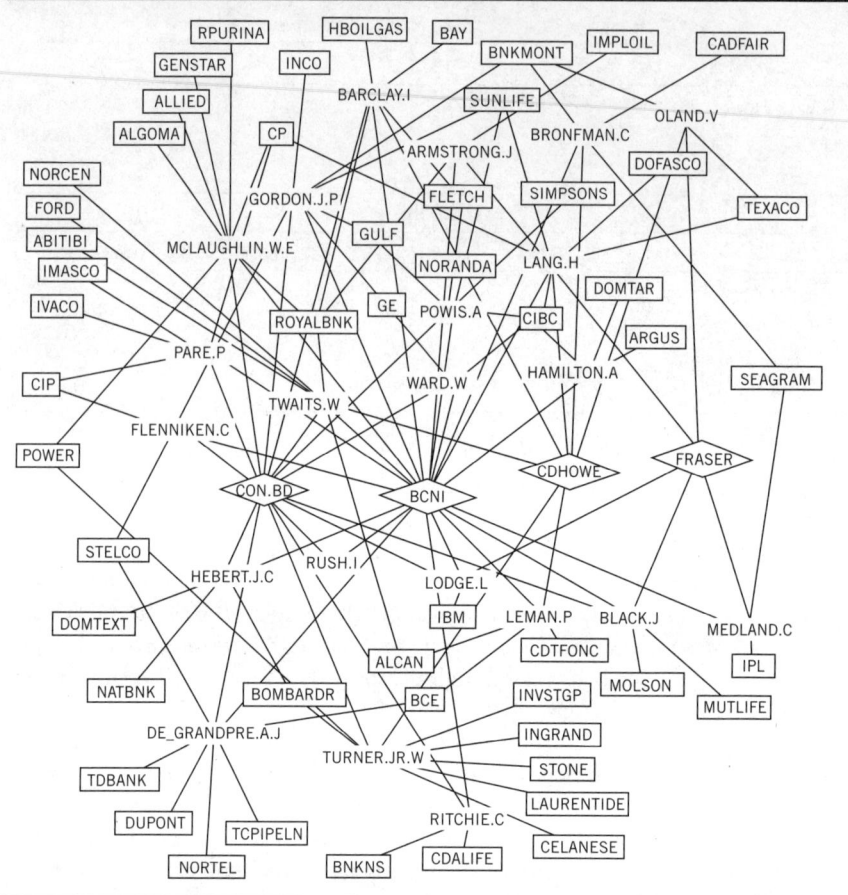

Firms are in boxes; policy boards are in diamonds; individuals have no enclosing shape. KEY: CON.BD = Conference Board of Canada; BCNI = Business Council on National Issues; CDHOWE = C.D. Howe Institute; FRASER = Fraser Institute.

whom were affiliated with the BCNI, Conference Board, and FI. Each of Canada's three largest banks—the Royal, Montreal, and CIBC—was a meeting point for several policy-group linkers. Fully 14 of the 22 linkers sat on bank boards.

By 1996, two banks—the Royal and the Toronto-Dominion—were still meeting points, but banks' overall structural prominence had been reduced,[11] and other firms such as Canadian Pacific Ltd., Sun Life, BCE, and Alcan were no longer meeting points for several policy-group linkers. This decline in the integrative role of banks and other corporations renders the policy groups particularly central. The BCNI, CDHI, and Conference Board appear as a constellation of sociometric stars radiating ties to discrete sets of corporations. And although the Fraser Institute no longer shares directors with the Conference Board, its interlocks with CDHI have strengthened,[12] while the three most central policy groups—BCNI, CDHI and the

FIGURE 8.2
Network of Directors of Two or More Policy Boards, 1996

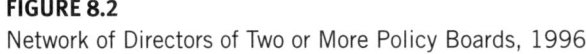

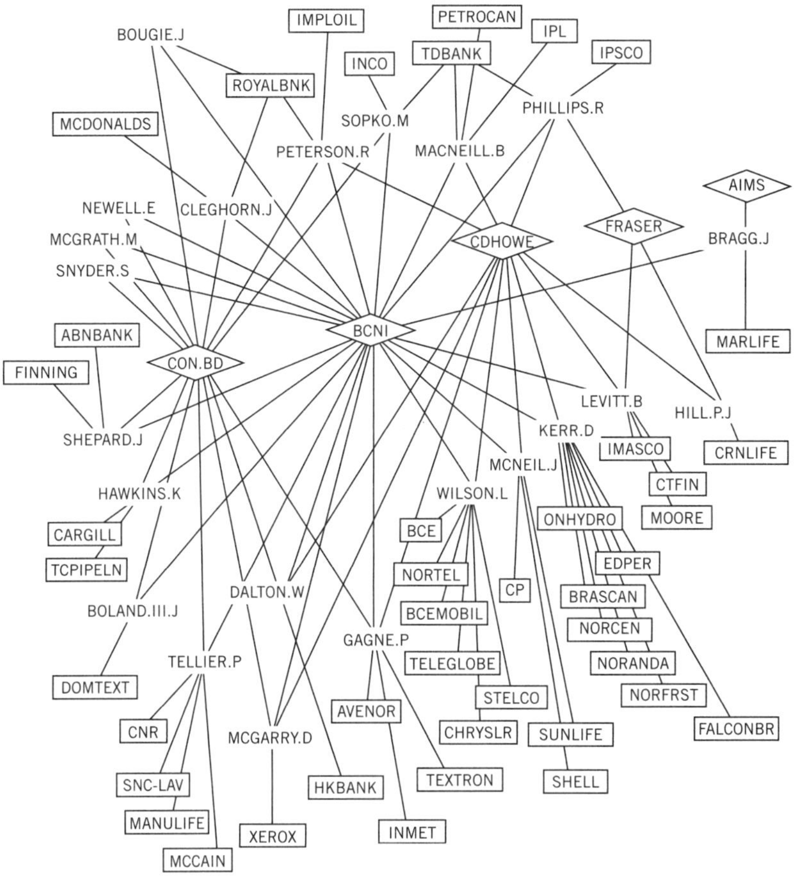

Firms are in boxes; policy boards are in diamonds; individuals have no enclosing shape. KEY: CON.BD = Conference Board of Canada; BCNI = Business Council on National Issues; CDHOWE = C.D. Howe Institute; FRASER = Fraser Institute; AIMS = Atlantic Institute for Market Studies.

Conference Board—are knit together by four leading corporate capitalists, each sitting on all three boards and epitomizing the integrative role of organic intellectuals in organizing both the accumulation of capital and the administration of life beyond capital's immediate circuitry.[13] In short, at the heart of the corporate–PG network we find a tightly integrated inner circle.[14]

THE CORPORATE–PG NETWORK AS A HEGEMONIC STRUCTURE

Our starting point in this chapter was a fourfold conception of the role policy groups have played in the formation of a neoliberal hegemonic project. How, in these terms, may we grasp this process as a cultural and structural transformation?

Culturally, we have traced the emergence of a neoliberal discursive field in the various reports, books, press releases, conference documents, and other texts that issue from the policy groups and in the ongoing communicative practices—conferences, media strategies, consultations with state officials, and so on—that help to maintain a persuasive presence in civil society and the state. The groups have taken different routes to the present consensus, and the resulting discursive field is not homogeneous. In organizational terms, comparing 1996 with 1976 we find a developing division of labour among distinct policy groups that occupy particular niches in neoliberalism's organizational ecology. The shift in hegemony from Keynes to Hayek has occurred in some cases within ongoing organizations and in others with the emergence of new species of policy groups, as plain think-tanks have been joined by advocacy think-tanks and the consensus-forming BCNI. This organizational ecology yields a richer discursive field than would a monocultural or statist configuration. It offers possibilities for nuanced debate and diverse action repertoires, all within the perimeter of neoliberal discourse. An important sign that hegemony has been achieved is the ability to control the agenda by delimiting the spectrum of feasible policies—the common-sense of state politics.

Much of the agency for neoliberal consolidation in the realm of our five groups has been supplied by corporate capital's organic intellectuals, a small subset of whom we have considered here. It is striking how extensive the direct participation of leading corporate directors has been in governing policy groups and how tightly knit the inner circle of policy linkers had become by 1996. However, such participation in itself is not a function of neoliberal hegemony: in fact, it dates back to the Keynesian era. Moreover, the *actual work* of policy think-tanks is accomplished not by corporate capitalists but by their 'delegates'—staff, academic associates, and the like—who likely share the same world view and have the skill sets and the time required to execute technical functions. What is new about neoliberalism is not the representation of big business on policy boards *per se* but the heightened level of business activism in the field of public policy—both in the formation of advocacy think-tanks (financed and governed from their inception by corporate capitalists) and in the highly integrative BCNI, a kind of senate of corporate capital in which leading executives actively discharge an intellectual function in the political field, not as representatives of their particular business sectors, as in previous times, but as leaders in the 'business community'.

Similarly, although directorate interlocking is not new, the consolidation of neoliberalism has transformed the corporate–PG network. At a time when the intercorporate network has become sparser and bank boards less integrative elite meeting points, we find an expanding neoliberal corporate–PG network, in terms of both organizational and individual participants. The increasing structural importance of these policy groups in the life of the corporate elite is worth pondering in view of the tendency toward more internationalized accumulation. In a globalizing capitalism where mobile financial capital has gained importance, rendering capital relations sparser and more fleeting, nationally oriented policy groups may gain importance as places where common visions and strategies can be forged. The Canadian policy groups coexist with their transnational cousin organizations—the

Trilateral Commission, World Economic Forum, Bilderberg Conference, etc. Although some of Canada's leading corporate capitalists participate in the latter groups, effective business leadership may require that the transnational viewpoint be counterbalanced by a continuing commitment to national politics. In a globalizing world, it may actually become *more* important for the corporate elite to shape politics in the national arena—to lead in the construction of a collective identity that blends national pride with a disciplined cosmopolitanism of free trade, as we have seen in the recent BCNI Canada Global Leadership Initiative. Inspired by that venture, BCNI president Thomas D'Aquino's book *Northern Edge* (2001) is one example of the effort to construct such a collective identity. Exhorting Canadians to find the 'will to win' in a world of sharp global competition, D'Aquino and his co-author argue that in addition to its resources, people, skills, technology, and infrastructure, Canada can offer global investors

> the world's most successful multicultural society. As multinational companies serving the global market evolve into increasingly multicultural institutions, the diversity and tolerance of Canadian society could become our unique selling proposition, the key characteristic that will make us stand out as the preferred alternative amid many attractive possibilities.
>
> A society that works, an economy that works, the home of choice for global champions: we have the makings of a compelling brand (D'Aquino and Stewart-Patterson, 2001:331).

Yet even as D'Aquino and his colleague were extolling the Canadian 'brand', the BCNI was in the process of repackaging itself as the Canadian Council of Chief Executives. The removal of 'national issues' from the group's own identity signalled the increasingly global, and continental, arena in which the Council strives to promote a 'Canadian' brand.

Finally, and as another marker of neoliberal consolidation, it is worth commenting on the position of the Fraser Institute. Consigned to the margins both of political discourse and of the corporate–PG network in 1976, the FI has become more interlocked with large corporations, more centrally positioned as a meeting point for corporate directors, and more interlocked with the board of the CDHI—a 'centrist' group whose policy framework had by the 1990s come closer to that of the FI. Without moderating its positions to any great extent, the FI has moved from the periphery more to the centre, as 'market solutions' have become political common sense and as the neoliberal bloc has become more integrated.[15]

What is missing from this organizational ecology, from this corporate–PG network, and from the discursive field of neoliberalism in Canadian politics, is capital's antithesis. As analysts like Robert Cox (1987) have pointed out, the new hegemony is not very effective in providing concessions and benefits, material or symbolic, to 'the people' and relatively exclusivist. In the post-war era of class compromise, corporatist groups such as the Conference Board and CDHI co-opted labour leaders onto their boards, but the contemporary neoliberal bloc contains what network analysts call a 'structural hole' where organized labour used to be. Not surprisingly, the very consolidation of a neoliberal policy network has provoked the formation of a counter-network around labour and its allies. In consequence, the arena of policy groups in Canada is now largely split along left-right lines, as corporate-funded groups jostle with such alternative organizations as the Canadian Centre for Policy Alternatives, the Parkland Institute, and the National Anti-Poverty Organization, in a struggle to frame issues and organize political practice.[16] But that is a topic for another investigation. In the meantime, it is worthwhile at this point to note another way in which corporate power reaches into civil society: namely, through corporate political contributions.

A Note on Corporate Political Contributions

Arguably, the mobilization of business activism within neoliberal policy-planning groups has been the most important means by which the Canadian corporate elite has formed and exercised its collective will in recent decades. However, the elite's influence extends into civil (and political) society in other ways. The well-known traffic in both directions between the corporate elite and the political elite is an obvious example (Clement, 1977; Olsen, 1980), and in previous chapters we have occasionally noted points of contact between corporate and state elites that include organizations as different as the Bilderberg Conferences and the Senate of Canada. However, three decades after the famous debate between Ralph Miliband and Nicos Poulantzas, it is equally well established that the political power of the capitalist class does not reside in personal connections between capitalists and the state. Liberal democratic states have *relative autonomy* from the dominant class (Poulantzas, 1976)—which is precisely why elite attempts to mobilize public opinion, through policy groups and the like, are so important.

Besides the policy group, a crucial civil agency for the formation of political projects, and indeed for the formation of governments, is the political party. If elite-level interlocks between corporations and policy boards represent one way in which corporate power extends into civil society, monetary donations to political parties represent quite a different way. In contributions, *corporate power takes an allocative form*, as surplus value is redirected from capital accumulation into political activity. As Cohen and Rogers (1983:61) point out, capitalist democracies are ultimately systems of highly unequal class power, and one reason can be found in the 'enormous fixed and liquid assets' that capitalists and corporations control—accumulated reserves that lower the costs of political action. Indeed, one of the key political advantages that capitalists enjoy over workers is the liquid form that their prime resource—capital—takes (Offe and Weisenthal, 1980).

The question of whether corporate political donations have an impact on government decision-making has been a recurrent issue ever since 1872, when the Pacific Scandal brought down Sir John A. Macdonald's Tory government (Canadian Democracy and Corporate Accountability Commission, 2002:32). In 1974 the Elections Expense Act required disclosure of all contributions exceeding $100 to registered political parties, and since then it has been possible to examine the extent and pattern of corporate donations. In his path-breaking work on this issue, Wallace Clement described the symbiosis between large corporations and the mainstream political parties in the following terms:

> The fact that Canada's top corporations give, and the two major political parties receive, such large donations reflects the ideological affinity between them. For the corporations, they are a form of 'insurance' and leverage enabling them to keep avenues of access open. For political parties and politicians, they defray the costs of campaigning. To 'bite the hand that feeds them' would certainly jeopardize their ability to be re-elected (1977:244).

Subsequent studies have endeavoured to account for differences in levels of corporate contributions and explored the relationship between party donation and subsequent government contracts, with Wearing and Wearing (1990) reporting that foreign-owned firms are less inclined to contribute money to Canadian parties and Wearing (1987) reporting only idiosyncratic associations between donations and contracts. Brooks and Stritch (1991) discern both a long-term trend in the motivations behind corporate donations, away from the patronage that characterized the early Canadian state, to a more subtle form of influence, and a more recent shift from corporate towards individual donations (defrayed by tax credits made available through the 1974 Act) as a major source of party financing. While parties like the Bloc Québécois, New Democratic Party, and Reform Party have been heavily financed by individual contributions, for the two bourgeois parties that until 1993 had dominated federal politics for over a century, corporate contributions 'still account for close to half of the total contributions during election years, and roughly 40–50 percent between elections' (Brooks and Stritch, 1991). For our purposes the central issue—shared with recent research programs such as Ferguson's (1995) and MacDermid's (2001)—is how we might understand corporate political donations as an expression of *allocative power*. The empirical questions, therefore, are *how much* Canada's largest firms contribute; where they direct *their contributions*; and whether *the positioning of companies* within the structure of corporate power helps to determine the amount and destination of contributions.

Our data come from the 'Registered Party Fiscal Period Return' document issued annually by Elections Canada. Since election years see the most intense efforts at party mobilization, we chose to examine the record of corporate contributions in the election years closest to our data for the Top 250 corporations: 1979, when the Tories formed what proved to be a short-lived minority government, and 1997, when the Liberals formed a second majority government.[17]

Table 8.6 shows the basic results, with amounts in 1997 dollars. Although a federal party, the BQ has voluntarily adhered to legislation in Quebec banning corporate (and union) contributions. Thus no corporate contributions were made to the BQ in 1997. Donations to the NDP, which only began to accept corporate money in the 1980s, remained minuscule through 1997, although Suncor had by then adopted the nonpartisan policy of giving equal amounts to every major political party. In 1979 only two of our Top 257 gave any funds to the federal NDP. In 1997 the NDP received funding from 14 dominant corporations, totalling $44,883—16.3 per cent

TABLE 8.6
Corporate Political Contributions in 1979 and 1997

	1979		1997		
	Liberal	PC	Liberal	PC	Reform
N of corporations contributing	142	145	136	117	71
Sum of contributions ($000s)	3,550	3,859	2,537	2,089	795
As % of all business donations	75.6	52.0	22.6	32.5	41.6
As % of all donations	30.1	20.4	14.5	19.0	9.0

Elections Canada: Registered Party Fiscal Period Returns.

of its total business contributions but only 0.3 per cent of its overall contributions. In contrast, the Liberal and Progressive Conservative parties continued to receive the lion's share of major corporate contributions through 1997. However, those contributions were smaller than eighteen years earlier when reckoned in constant dollars, and represented less of each party's total financial support from both business and all sources. Moreover, the Reform Party, which became the Official Opposition following the 1997 election, also claimed a share of major corporate donations, totalling just under $800,000 (less than 10 per cent of its total financial support base). What stands out in Table 8.6 is (1) the declining financial dependence of major bourgeois parties on contributions from big business and (2) the shift from a pattern of basically even-handed support for the two bourgeois parties to a more diverse pattern that favoured the incumbent Liberals in 1997.

Among the 156 Top corporations making political contributions, certain firms were major donors (see Table 8.7). In 1979 the largest donor was Power Corporation, followed by the Bank of Nova Scotia, CIBC, and the Bank of Montreal. The top three donors accounted for 9.7 per cent of the grand total. In 1997 the top three corporate donors, accounting for 13.0 per cent of the total political contributions from all dominant firms, were the Bank of Montreal, Royal Bank, and Toronto-Dominion Bank. The concentration of corporate contributions among the very biggest donors increased somewhat over time. In 1979 the 39 corporations that each gave at least $50,000 (1997 dollars) to federal parties accounted for 67.3 per cent of all contributions from dominant corporations. In 1997 the 37 companies that each contributed at least $50,000 accounted for 71.5 per cent of the total. Nortel ranked among the top five donors in both years, giving $228,371 (and ranking fifth) in 1979 and $202,939 in 1997 (ranking fourth).

Indeed, the leading corporate donors in both years were in most cases the largest financial institutions and industrial corporations, predominantly under the control of Canadian capitalists. Companies under state control, directly or indirectly, did not make political contributions, although (Caisse-controlled) Provigo gave $5000 to the Liberals in 1997 and Canada Post gave a token $210 to Reform in the same year. Foreign-controlled firms donated in smaller numbers and amounts than firms controlled by Canadian capitalists.[18] Many foreign-controlled companies remained disengaged from Canadian federal electoral politics, just as they were largely disengaged

TABLE 8.7
Top 20 Contributors to Political Parties, 1979 and 1997

	1979		1997	
1	$232,801	Power Corporation of Canada	$248,772	Bank of Montreal
2	231,763	Bank of Nova Scotia	231,900	Royal Bank of Canada
3	230,130	Canadian Imperial Bank of Commerce	230,407	The Toronto-Dominion Bank
4	229,502	Bank of Montreal	202,939	Northern Telecom Ltd
5	228,371	Northern Telecom Ltd	192,070	Midland Walwyn Inc.
6	226,110	Royal Bank of Canada	182,427	Canadian National Railway Company
7	226,110	Toronto-Dominion Bank	162,940	Canadian Imperial Bank of Commerce
8	226,110	Inco Ltd	141,330	BCE Inc.
9	209,527	Gulf Oil Canada Ltd	138,376	Rogers Communications Inc.
10	186,247	Noranda Mines Ltd	127,540	Canadian Pacific Ltd
11	159,864	Domtar Ltd	123,158	Bombardier Inc.
12	158,277	Canadian Pacific Ltd	120,881	The Molson Companies Ltd
13	141,974	Kaiser Resources Ltd	112,646	The Bank of Nova Scotia
14	141,441	Canada Cement Lafarge Ltd	98,089	Power Corporation of Canada
15	141,273	Alberta Gas Trunk Line Company Ltd	93,209	Imasco Ltd
16	135,666	Dominion Foundries & Steel Ltd	86,977	Dofasco Inc.
17	130,805	Canada Packers Ltd	85,572	Southam Inc.
18	130,043	Steel Company of Canada Ltd	84,000	Imperial Oil Ltd
19	101,456	Simpsons-Sears Ltd	80,599	Pratt & Whitney Canada Inc.
20	98,064	John Labatt Ltd	80,000	Agrium Inc.

NOTE: Amounts are expressed in 1997 Canadian Dollars.

from the corporate network. Indeed, centrality in the corporate network was itself a correlate of companies' political donations. The Pearson correlation coefficient between size of total donation and the number of firms with which a corporation shared directors was 0.630 in 1979 and 0.566 in 1997. The 50 most central companies in the Canadian corporate network accounted for 55.5 per cent of all major corporate donations in 1979 and 58.3 per cent in 1997.

The overall levels of corporate donations are in a sense less interesting than the patterns of contributions to one party or another. Previous research has established that the Canadian corporate elite has tended to contribute in nearly equal measures to the two leading bourgeois parties, at least until the 1980s (Clement, 1977; Wearing, 1987), and this is indeed what we find for the 1979 election year. In that year, all but 29 of the 156 dominant corporations that made a political donation gave to both the Liberal and Progressive Conservative parties; 16 gave exclusively to the Tories and 13 gave exclusively to the Liberals. Of the 127 that donated to both, 67 companies—many of them quite central in the corporate network—gave equally to the Liberals and Tories, within a 10 per cent differential. Thus, although large companies sometimes differed as to *preferences*, the vast majority of large corporate donors recognized the *worthiness* of both parties, and with that the value of a political order centred around two strong bourgeois parties, both 'congenial towards corporate enterprise' (Brooks and Stritch, 1991:291). Moreover, this 'investment in two-party domination' (ibid.), which we might call the *norm of bipartisanship*, was particularly evident among the central members of the business community. While just under half of all dominant corporations contributed to both the Liberals and Tories, 44 of the 50 most central corporations did so. In contrast, Table 8.6 indicates that smaller companies (outside the Top 250) allocated a far greater total value of funds to the Tories ($3.562 million) than to the Liberals ($1.145 million) in 1979. The base of support for the Conservatives was stronger in the middle ranks of the capitalist class.

By 1997 the longstanding bipartisan corporate consensus had become frayed. Nine years earlier, in the election of 1988, corporate Canada had deserted the Liberals when Liberal leader John Turner had openly criticized the proposed Canada–US Free Trade Agreement. Through the BCNI and its Canadian Alliance for Trade and Job Opportunities, the corporate elite campaigned heavily for the re-election of the Mulroney Tories and the passage of the FTA. Chaired by David Culver (president of Alcan and chair of the BCNI in 1987), the Alliance was heavily interlocked with the BCNI via other luminaries like BCNI president Tom D'Aquino (who served on the Alliance's executive committee), and functioned as a political action committee that encompassed all the business organizations in the country that supported free trade. In what Fillmore (1989:14) describes as 'the largest lobbying and public relations effort in Canadian history', and what we might call a well-timed exercise of allocative corporate power, the Alliance and related pro-free trade forces spent $6.5 million in the last three weeks of the campaign, compared to less than one million by the critics of free trade. These efforts managed to turn around a public opinion that had threatened to defeat the Tories and, with them, free trade.[19] If the election of 1988 marked something of a breach in the long tradition of bipartisanship, the election that followed in 1993 further complicated matters. The massive Tory defeat at the hands of the Liberals reduced the Conservative caucus to a rump group, while the neoliberal-populist, western-based Reform Party nearly gained Official Opposition status. By the time the Liberals stood for re-election in 1997, not only had a neoliberal policy bloc been fully consolidated, but the field of neoliberal party politics had become divided among three parties. The incumbent Liberals had won their neoliberal stripes in ratifying NAFTA within weeks of assuming office late in 1993, reneging on one of their core campaign promises, and then launching a single-minded war against 'the deficit' that continued throughout their term of office (McQuaig, 1995; Workman, 1996). The Tories, although much diminished in Parliament, retained an electoral base from Ontario eastward, and had Conservative tradition on their side. The upstart Reform Party had articulated the most coherent neoliberal agenda from within Parliament, but its highly regional base disturbed the logic of national corporate bipartisanship. How, then, would big corporate money ante up in 1997?

Among the 156 dominant corporations that made contributions in 1997, the most common pattern was to donate to all three bourgeois parties, though typically not in the same amounts. In all, 58 firms made three-way donations, but in only seven of these cases were the amounts given to the three parties within 10 per cent of each other. The next largest group consisted of 43 companies that maintained the traditional norm of bipartisan support for the Liberals and Tories. The incumbent Liberals received exclusive donations from 30 companies, the Tories from 12. Reform was the exclusive beneficiary of only four donations from big business, including two foreign-controlled donors (Gulf Canada Resources and Lafarge Canada). Two corporations favoured Reform while making smaller contributions to the Liberals.[20]

Overall, however, the tendency was for corporate donors to favour the incumbent Liberals, who were widely expected to win the election, and did so handsomely. Of the 156 top corporate donors, 87 favoured the Liberals, 31 the Tories, and 22 both the Liberals and Tories in preference to Reform. Only seven companies favoured Reform, either donating exclusively to it or donating at least 10 per cent more to Reform than to any other party. In 1997, the prospect of Reform's shedding its self-limiting trope of 'western alienation' still looked dubious to Canada's corporate elite, and the pattern of corporate donations reflects that doubt. Many of the biggest donors, themselves well-connected within the corporate network, continued to give even-handedly to the Liberals and Tories. These were companies like the Royal Bank, CIBC, Canadian Pacific, Bank of Montreal, Noranda, Manulife, Imasco, and Inco, each with links to 20 or more other corporations and embodying old, Montreal–Toronto money. The contributions from these remnants of the Canadian Establishment continued to reproduce the hegemonic pattern of post-war bipartisanship.[21] Corporations that gave to all three parties also tended to be most central in the network; whereas firms donating to only one of the two traditional parties on the right were more marginal.

Thus the structurally central corporations under the control of Canada's major capitalists contributed the most to political parties. And although their donations in many cases acknowledged the opening toward right-wing populism that Reform presented, they strove to keep up the tradition of supporting two strong bourgeois parties—an established formula for hegemonic political management in Canada.²² With continuing electoral disappointment for the Tories in 1997 and Reform's ascension to Official Opposition status, corporate funds appear to have been reallocated between Reform and the Tories. By 2000, another election year, the motif of corporate bipartisanship had been reworked. The refurbished Canadian Reform Conservative Alliance took in $19.6 million in donations (35 per cent from corporations); the incumbent Liberals drew $26.5 million (45 per cent from corporations); and the Tories managed to attract only $4.8 million. In keeping with their status as general managers of the largest aggregations of money-capital, Canada's big five banks were at or near the top of the list of donors to all three bourgeois parties, contributing $683,000 to the Alliance, $467,796 to the Liberals, and $404,663 to the Progressive Conservatives (Baxter and Naumetz, 2001). If the concentration of capital is a basic organizational feature of the economy, it also shapes the allocation of funds to the major pro-business parties. Just as a tiny proportion of all corporate shareholders owns a large proportion of all shares, the bulk of party revenues comes from a small population of wealthy individual and corporate donors. The Chief Electoral Officer has reported that in 2001 45 per cent of Liberal Party revenues came from only 3 per cent of donors (Freeman, 2002).

Responding to public concerns about corporate power in party politics, in January 2003 the federal government introduced a political financing bill that would ban corporate (and union) donations to political parties and impose an annual limit of $1000 on corporate donations to candidates, riding associations, and nomination race candidates. Likely to take effect in January 2004, Bill C-24 would create a system of public financing for political parties, based on the number of votes won in the previous election (conferring an immediate advantage on the ruling Liberals). Although the new legislation would restrict the exercise of allocative power by corporations, Aaron Freeman of Democracy Watch, an Ottawa-based citizens' group, pointed out that the more permissive limit on individual donations would advantage the wealthy. It was also unclear whether loopholes in the act might allow corporations to donate through multiple shell companies (Freeman 2003). At the time of writing (July 2003), the political financing bill had been referred to a parliamentary committee for amendment before passage, likely in 2003. If the bill becomes law, it will be interesting to monitor the ways and means through which the corporate elite endeavours to maintain its persuasive influence in Canadian party politics. We can expect the wide disparities in political contributions among corporations to narrow somewhat: it would not be legal, for instance, for the big banks to drop $683,000 into Canadian Alliance coffers, as they did in 2000. But it is possible that corporate funds could be redirected in innovative ways. For example, the proposed $1000 ceiling on each corporation's donation to a specific candidate means that a given company could without much difficulty spread $50,000 among 50 politically worthy individuals. The new legislation could thus engender a more micro-managed allocation of funds, although to be politically effective this would require the sort of concerted action that Canada's business community displayed in the 'free trade' election of 1988.

Whether through active involvement of corporate directors in neoliberal policy groups or through corporate funding of pro-business parties, Canada's corporate elite exercised a crucial political influence in the closing decades of the twentieth century. In the transition from a state-centred Keynesian policy paradigm to a market-driven neoliberal framework 'that gives content and shape to the heightened internationalization or globalization characteristic of our times' (McBride, 2001:13), the agency of the corporate elite was an important factor in shaping specific outcomes, most notably the election of 1988, but also in reshaping the political terrain itself.

Chapter 9

Integrating Corporate and University Governance for a Globalizing World

WITH JAMES B. BEATON

Beyond the world of policy groups and political parties, the corporate elite's reach extends into key institutions of civil society, including universities. In a globalizing world where market relations are in the ascendant, 'higher education takes on a new strategic role as a central source of a national or regional territory's global competitiveness, its capacity to attract and retain both a skilled workforce and corporate investment' (Kurasawa, 2002:336). High levels of literacy, skill, professional expertise, and research and development have become recognized as competitive levers in the struggle to attract and retain investment, jobs, and income. At the same time, corporate elites have expressed a growing interest in universities both as 'incubators' for the 'human capital' in which knowledge-workers invest themselves and as 'catalysts' for 'stimulating innovation and the growth of new industries' (D'Aquino and Stewart-Patterson 2001:13, 181). Humanists committed to a liberal-arts conception of the university will recoil from this sort of objectifying language. Yet the manifesto that D'Aquino and Stewart-Patterson present in favour of 'marrying smart economic policies with core Canadian values' (2001:21) exemplifies the new role that corporate capital has defined for higher education in the knowledge-based, technology-driven economy of the twenty-first century. With increasing interest have come a broadening and a deepening of the reach of corporate power into higher education. As the voices of corporate capital become more resonant within the university's practice of governance, teaching, research, and so on, academe is becoming corporatized and universities are becoming key ancillaries in the production process (Noble, 2001; Newson and Buchbinder, 1990).

In this chapter we map some of the connections that link the corporate elite to Canada's universities and related organizations. One site where the voice of corporate capital may hold sway is the university board of governors, the highest level of authority within Canadian universities.[1] Although research studies have established a pattern of cross-membership between university boards of governors and corporate boards of directors, they have relied on data from the 1970s and earlier (Useem, 1981; Ornstein, 1988). Here we compare the network of corporate–university ties in 1976, when the trend towards globalization and the neoliberal political project were both just beginning to build, with the 1996 configuration.

Our objective is to map the structure of corporate–university relations at the level of governance boards, as a means of highlighting the changing architecture of capitalist-class power in the field of higher education. First, however, we need to consider the context of contemporary relations between corporations and universities.

Globalized Capital and Higher Education

It is well known that the rise of neoliberalism and the internationalization of economies have strengthened the power of corporate capital and weakened the ability of states to regulate business and maintain social services. As global markets act to discipline the state in its practices, public institutions such as universities model their operations on business principles that are increasingly detached from democratic accountability. The privileging of markets has increased the acceptance of corporate ideals in organizing both society and public institutions (Gill, 1995).

Although neoliberal regimes may reduce their activities in the areas of social welfare and economic redistribution, they still promote economic development through supply-side policies. These policies mark a shift towards what Jessop has termed the Schumpeterian workfare state (1993). Higher education plays a role in this scenario. Key activities such as research and skills development are viewed as strategic components of the competitive economic base needed to attract globally mobile investment. The flows of capital and labour power that wash over national boundaries are aspects of an increasingly reflexive accumulation process appropriating new forms of knowledge and technology and new subjectivities, a process that surrounds and penetrates academe (Lash and Urry, 1994). With globalization, market-relevant disciplines and professions become the favoured ones, intellectual property rights become a strategic resource, and relationships tighten between corporations and state agencies responsible for research—hence the apt phrase 'academic capitalism' (Slaughter and Leslie, 1997).

The importance that business and government place on research, development, and training turns universities into centres for profit, and current efforts to strengthen the relationship between universities and business must be understood in that light (Newson and Buchbinder, 1990:367). As Noble (2001) argues, one of the most significant recent changes in universities has been the identification of the campus as a site of capital accumulation, a place for creating or enhancing the profit-making capacity of individuals, businesses, or the country itself. Within this neoliberal discourse, the products of universities—knowledge and credentialed labour-power—are *commodities* that flow into circuits of capital accumulation in a tendentially international economy, improving prospects for local and national competitiveness. In short, the current transformation of higher education conforms closely to the neoliberal norm that public institutions are best operated on market principles.[2]

Within the prevailing framework, the state has been reducing its role in funding higher education while enacting policies that promote private-sector partnerships. These changes mark a profound reversal of the pattern in the Keynesian era, when the state expanded its funding and actively promoted the social and cultural benefits of higher education, alongside the economic benefit of 'human capital' formation. As they come to be viewed as sources of specific skills and technologies that can promote competitiveness on the supply side, and as they struggle to survive in an environment of reduced state funding, universities begin to mimic capitalist firms in competing for investment funds. Peter Godsoe, CEO of the Bank of Nova Scotia in the 1990s and a leading corporate activist on higher education, has argued that universities must compete, and that the market rather than the state should determine their success (1996). In accordance with this neoliberal vision, universities have tried to refashion their managerial practices and institutional arrangements along corporate-capital lines (Cassin and Morgan, 1992; Newson, 1992; Polster, 2002).[3] The focus of our analysis, however, is not on the internal practices that characterize neoliberal university administration, but on the links between the academic and corporate worlds at the highest levels of governance.

Corporate–University Linkages

From the inception of corporate capitalism, corporations have had relationships with universities; see, for instance, Veblen (1954); Noble (1977). Levels of influence, however, have varied, depending on the institution. Many of the newer universities in Canada were created in the post-war effort to build a 'human resource' base for the economy. The active role that corporate capitalists played in founding institutions such as York University was symptomatic of the broad consensus in the late 1950s and the 1960s that sheer expansion of higher education was in the national interest (Axelrod, 1986).

Since the transition to neoliberalism began in the 1970s, corporate–university linkages have encouraged a more direct integration of the university into capitalist production. With Newson and Buchbinder (1990), we can distinguish two types of linkages: (1) those formed as the university tries to break into markets (responses to *internal pressure*); and (2) those formed as outside corporations penetrate university boundaries, often in search of enhanced profit (responses to *external pressure*). The structural supports for corporate–university linkages include research funding bodies, third-party networks such as the Corporate Higher Education Forum, and inter-university networks such as the Centres of Excellence.

A form of corporate–university linkage not mentioned by Newson and Buchbinder but central here is the network generated by overlapping memberships on university and corporate governing boards. Newson and Buchbinder's internal–external distinction raises the question of whether it is the corporate elite whose reach has extended into university governance, or whether it is university administrators who have begun to reach into the corporate elite. Thus we may begin with a two-part research question:

1. Did the 1970s–1990s witness an increase in the representation of the corporate elite on university governance boards (an externally-based penetration of university governance)? And did the same period witness a greater tendency for leading university administrators to join the corporate elite (an internally-based reaching-out)?

The very nature of certain corporate–university links as 'business deals' would seem to favour the involvement of the senior level of university management with the senior level of corporate management. However, such an instrumental interest on the part of specific corporations and capitalists does not displace the broader, hegemonic interest that corporate capital has had in providing cultural leadership through university-board service.

Indeed, the changing social composition of governing boards is indicative of a shifting balance of power between intellectuals, administrators, and economic and political elites, as shifts in class power create opportunities for capital to transform the intellectual labour process. In the current era, corporate intellectuals such as Peter Godsoe have used a discourse that defines the university as a business organization, treating spending on universities as a social investment that yields quantifiable returns in the form of productive knowledge, technical innovation, and marketable skills. This form of cultural influence reinforces the material dominance of capital by privileging the standpoint of corporate capital (Barrow, 1990).

It is appropriate, then, to view corporate–university ties as instances both of bourgeois *class hegemony*—as leading capitalists participate in the direction of higher education—and of *instrumental domination* tied to particular corporate interests. Corporate participation in universities may or may not directly produce capital or realize surplus value, but a corporate presence on campus helps to legitimate capitalism as a way of life. Membership on a university governance board is always in part honorific; yet insofar as universities depend structurally on capital, the presence of a corporate official will exceed the symbolic, especially if the official participates in the direction of the university's finances.

There is significance, then, in the combination of capital's material and symbolic power in university governance, a combination that exemplifies the reach of the corporate elite into institutions of civil society. As university governors, corporate capitalists have input into the financial direction of the university, specifying the programs they or other moneyed interests would be willing to finance, and the type of research and graduates that universities should be producing.[4]

University Governance and the Corporate Elite

A number of sociologists have examined corporate–university linkages and their socio-political implications. In a study based on American data, Michael Useem (1981) differentiates the corporate elite according to several criteria such as economic sector (industrial, financial, etc.) and size. Useem finds that specific business strata have formed their own special relationships with other subsets of universities. For instance, high technology firms have interlocked with universities whose strong applied research traditions have yielded important commercial applications—an instance of ties stemming from what Newson and Buchbinder call 'external' pressure. Useem also suggests that indirect ties between business and universities are sustained through third-party organizations such as philanthropic foundations, which interlock with both corporations and universities.

Canadian studies confirm that overlapping memberships between governance boards and corporate directorates have a long history, particularly among elite institutions such as the University of Toronto, McGill, and Queen's, which have been integral to the intergenerational reproduction of the corporate elite itself. In *The Vertical Mosaic* John Porter observed that, 'as befits their status in Canadian academic life, McGill University and the University of Toronto have boards which positively glitter with stars from the corporate world' (Porter, 1965:300), and claimed that their participation on university boards bolstered upper-class solidarity. Nevertheless, he thought that corporate directors' presence on university boards was largely honorific—and that their role limited to extracting money from other members of the corporate elite. A decade later, Wallace Clement (1975:251) argued that university boards can act as fora for elite members to work out their common concerns, and that philanthropic activity such as university board service serves as good public relations for modern corporations. And for Paul Axelrod (1982) the corporate–university relationship seems to have been more a matter of cultural leadership than an overt attempt on the part of corporations to control research and teaching.

More recently, Ornstein (1988) has examined the interlocking between corporations and universities between 1946 and 1977. He reports that throughout the period there were enormous differences among universities in the extent of their board ties with major corporations; that the oldest and best-endowed universities had the most extensive ties; that the big banks and other financial institutions (plus some industrial companies) were the main corporate contacts; and that Canadian-controlled companies were especially interlocked with universities—the last point suggesting that it is the 'indigenous' fraction of the Canadian corporate elite, not the 'comprador' fraction, that concerns itself with the direction of higher education in Canada. Finally, Ornstein provides evidence of a corporate withdrawal from university boards, beginning in the late 1960s and continuing for at least a decade, which in his view reflected the increasing state support for universities, demands for community representation, and eventual corporate disillusionment. Whether this trend continued beyond the 1970s—as state support wilted and as corporate activism around a neo-liberal agenda blossomed—is at present an open question.

Extrapolating from previous work, we may add four research questions to our initial query:

2. What kinds of corporate directors are active in university governance: functioning capitalists or advisors to corporations? industrialists or bankers?
3. Are certain schools—well-endowed ones that have historically played a central role in educating the upper stratum of the Canadian bourgeoisie—particularly likely to have corporate representation on their boards?
4. Are there differences in the degree to which sectors of corporate capital participate in university governance (for example, the big banks)? Do certain sectors of industry, particularly so-called high-tech industry, tend to link up with universities?
5. Are corporate–university ties supplemented by third-party ties of relevance to higher education and research? Do organizations such as the recently estab-

lished Canadian Foundation for Innovation provide further meeting-points for university governors and corporate directors?

With these questions in mind, we can map continuities and changes in the structure of corporate–university ties across two decades of neoliberal consolidation.

As in other chapters, our basic corporate data refer to the top corporations of 1976 and 1996, and the directors who carry the interlocks among the corporations—numbering 257 firms and 489 persons in 1976 and 258 firms and 426 persons in 1996.[5] We chose our sample of universities on the basis of a combination of total enrolment and regional stratification. The top 20 universities, by enrolment, were chosen for 1976 and 1996. With the exception of three universities the sample was identical in each year. We included all universities that ranked within the top 20 of either year, for a total of 23 institutions. To ensure representation of regions, Memorial University of Newfoundland, ranked 21st in 1996, was added. In all, then, 24 universities were included in the study: three from Atlantic Canada, four from Quebec, 10 from Ontario, four from the prairies, and three from BC. Relying on biographical handbooks as well as university calendars, we recorded the positions of all the corporate-elite members who served on the governance boards of the 24 universities in 1976 or 1996.[6]

Corporate-elite involvement in university governance

We saw at the outset of this study that between 1976 and 1996, the corporate elite shrank by 12 per cent, from 489 people to 426. But despite this decrease, the number of elite members active on university boards—whom we call *university linkers*—remained constant, at 52. With one exception, noted below, the 52 corporate directors restricted themselves to one university board each. However, precisely because of their multiple directorships, their participation on university boards generates a complex network of corporate–university ties, which we will now explore.

Concerning the class positions of the 52 university linkers, Table 9.1 shows that in both years a majority of the university linkers were *functioning capitalists*, that is,

TABLE 9.1
University Linkers Grouped by Principal Occupation (%)

Class position	1976	1996
Top 250 executive	50	44
Other executive	35	25
Legal advisor	10	12
Academic advisor	2	6
Consultant	0	6
Éminence grise	0	6
State official	0	0
Other advisor	4	2
Total	100	100
N	52	52

insiders of corporations. But we also find a greater proportion of outside directors in 1996, and a greater range of occupations among them, including academic advisors, consultants, and *éminences grises*. Such organic intellectuals—corporate advisors implicated in the accumulation process as well as university governance—may be said to mediate the relation between corporations and universities.[7] Most important, the three academics serving on university and corporate boards in 1996 were presidents of their respective institutions.[8] In 1976 university presidents did not serve on multiple corporate boards; by 1996 chief administrators at three universities had joined the corporate elite proper.

Another way to view the network is to consider which economic sectors of corporate capital are 'represented' on university boards by executives. Here our cases include all the university linkers who held an executive position in a corporation, whether the firm was in the Top 250 or outside it. Table 9.2 shows a definite shift in representation, away from industry towards capitalist investment. Executives in investment companies, who control operating companies through ownership of strategic blocs of share capital, might well be considered prime candidates for university governance, as these beleaguered public institutions turn to private funding sources.

Table 9.3 shows which governance boards tended to have the most extensive corporate representation. In the first two columns are the numbers of corporate linkers who participated in the governance of each university in 1976 and 1996. While four universities had no such linkers in either year, and therefore are not listed (Memorial University of Newfoundland, University of Ottawa, University of Saskatchewan, and University of Victoria), York and McGill both had five or more in both years, and Dalhousie and Toronto also had several. Thus three long-established schools, including the major elite anglophone universities in Montreal and Toronto, have maintained a range of corporate connections via their governing boards. York's strong ties to corporate capital date from its inception as a project behind which Toronto-based capital mobilized in the late 1950s (Axelrod, 1982).

TABLE 9.2

University Linkers Grouped by Economic Sector of their Home Corporation (%)

Economic sector	1976	1996
Primary industry	12	3
Manufacturing	34	20
Utilities/communication	10	14
Commerce	7	9
Financial intermediation	24	23
Investment companies	10	31
Property development	2	0
Other	0	0
Total	100	100
N	41	35

TABLE 9.3
Corporate Linkers and Corporate Contacts for University Governing Boards

University	Linkers (N) 1976	Linkers (N) 1996	Corporations (N) 1976	Corporations (N) 1996
York	8	9	31	25
Montreal	1	9	3	19
McGill	5	5	19	20
Toronto	4	3	9	11
New Brunswick	0	3	0	8
British Columbia	0	3	0	7
Alberta	0	3	0	11
Dalhousie	6	3	17	6
Queen's	9	2	33	10
Concordia	2	2	4	4
Calgary	2	2	4	10
Simon Fraser	0	2	0	5
McMaster	8	1	23	2
Western Ontario	3	1	12	2
Guelph	1	1	3	2
Waterloo	1	1	4	10
Ryerson	1	1	3	9
Laval	0	1	0	2
Manitoba	0	1	0	2
Carleton	1	0	3	0
Bipartite density*			0.0338	0.0331

NOTE: Includes two university affiliations for Peter C. Godsoe (Dalhousie and UWO) in 1996.
*Proportion of all university–corporation pairs that are actually interlocked.

Yet there has also been an interesting *redistribution* of ties. In 1976, only 14 of the 24 universities had corporate interlockers on their boards. By 1996, 19 governance boards had recruited members of the corporate elite. This suggests a transition from a corporate–university network focused on the boards of a few key universities in the heartland of post-war corporate capital, and at the heart of the Canadian bourgeoisie as a social class, to a more dispersed network that takes in a *greater range* of schools and of regions.

The University of New Brunswick (UNB) illustrates the shift. In 1976 its governors were local municipal leaders and the like. By 1996, however, there were three corporate linkers on the UNB board, who among them created direct contacts with eight major corporations. Similarly, the boards of UBC, SFU, and Alberta all lacked any corporate representation in 1976, but included several members of the corporate elite, carrying ties to various corporations, by 1996. And while Université de Montréal had only one member of the corporate elite on its board in 1976, its nine corporate-elite members in 1996 created direct ties to 19 major corporations, ensconcing the board within the Montreal segment of the corporate elite. Across the decades we find that (1) the network becomes *more inclusive* of universities in Western Canada (Calgary, UBC), eastern Canada (UNB), and Quebec (Montréal, also Laval); and (2) except in the cases of York, McGill, and Toronto, there is *considerable shifting* in the extent to which members of the elite participate on the boards of specific university boards.

Sectoral differences in corporate–university interlocking

We now turn to the possible differences between sectors of corporate capital in university governance. We may think of the number of corporations to which a university is tied as the size of its social circle in the bipartite network of corporations and universities.[9] Table 9.3 showed how social circles vary in size from one university to another. The same is true of corporations. In 1976, 150 of the 250 Top firms had no university linkers[10] on their boards; by 1996, that number had risen to 161. The Royal Bank of Canada led all corporations, with board ties in both years to six different universities, including (in both years) York, McGill, and Queen's. A total of 16 corporations in 1976 and 15 corporations in 1996 each had ties to three or more universities, and the changes in the nature of these well-connected companies are instructive. In 1976, 11 of the 16 were financial institutions, including all five big chartered banks. Yet by 1996 only six of 15 were financial institutions, and although three of the chartered banks maintained a strong presence as meeting-places for university linkers, leading financial institutions lost centrality overall.

In a more systematic analysis of sectoral differences, we considered the mean number of universities with which corporations had board-level ties and found a striking decline in the prominence of financial institutions (see Table 9.4). In 1976, the 50 leading financial institutions were on average interlocked with 1.34 of the 24 universities—far more than other companies. By 1996 their average was indistinguishable from several other sectors. In a similar vein, we compared the mean number of ties to universities for Canadian-controlled and foreign-controlled companies. In 1976, Canadian-controlled firms had substantially more directorate ties

TABLE 9.4

Mean Number of University Contacts for Top 250 Corporations Grouped by Economic Sector

	1976	1996
Resources	.52	.85
Manufacturing	.49	.54
Utilities-communication	.83	.84
Financial intermediation	1.34	.82
Investment companies	.71	.87
Trade	.27	.30
Real estate	.00	
Other	1.00	.38
All companies	.65	.64
Eta^2	.128	.035

TABLE 9.5
Mean Number of University Contacts for Top Industrial Corporations Grouped by Nationality of Control and Level of Technological Intensity, 1996

Locus of control	Level of technology		
	Hi-tech	Lower-tech	Total
Canada	1.38 (21)	0.62 (97)	0.75 (118)
Foreign	0.00 (8)	0.44 (36)	0.36 (44)
Total	1.00 (29)	0.57 (133)	0.65 (162)

NOTE: Ns are in parentheses

to universities, but by 1996 this difference had attenuated somewhat. Interestingly, US-controlled firms also showed a drop in their already sparse ties to universities, suggesting that economic continentalization has not been propelling American-controlled corporations toward increased contacts with Canadian universities.[11]

As a final aspect of our analysis of sectoral differences, we considered how many board-level ties to universities had been established by corporations that could be classified as 'high tech' by 1996. Since there is no standard for such a classification, we relied on two general lists: a tabulation of the 50 top R&D companies of 1996 and a recent OECD classification of manufacturing sectors by technology-intensity.[12] The former indicated that of the 162 industrial corporations in the Top 250 of 1996, 22 had particularly extensive R&D expenditures for 1996, while the latter identified 17 industrial firms in high-tech sectors. Together these lists yielded a rough approximation of a high-tech category composed of 29 companies. The relevant comparison group for this category is the remaining 133 industrial corporations of 1996, whose technology intensity was no doubt quite mixed. Table 9.5 indicates that by 1996 the 29 high-tech firms had indeed established more board-level ties to universities than had other large industrial corporations. But what is most striking is the difference between Canadian- and foreign-controlled companies in this area. In the foreign-controlled category, high-tech firms had no university ties; yet among firms under domestic control, the high-tech companies had considerably more ties to universities than their lower-tech counterparts. It was companies controlled by Canadian capitalists—such as Nortel Networks, Bombardier, and CAE Inc.—that had established board-level ties to major universities by 1996. This difference is not surprising when considered alongside our earlier observations. Foreign-controlled high-tech companies—such as Pratt & Whitney Canada, IBM Canada, and General Electric Canada—are for the most part wholly owned by their parents. We noted in Chapters 3 and 6 that such companies often have small, introverted boards, and that the continental network between American parents and Canadian subsidiaries has weakened substantially in recent decades.[13]

Mapping the core of the corporate–university network

Tabulations such as the ones we have just presented shed light on some of the patterns in corporate–university interlocking, but they do not show us the shape of the network itself. To produce such a map, we first examined the entire bipartite inter-

FIGURE 9.1
The Big Block of Corporations and Universities, 1976

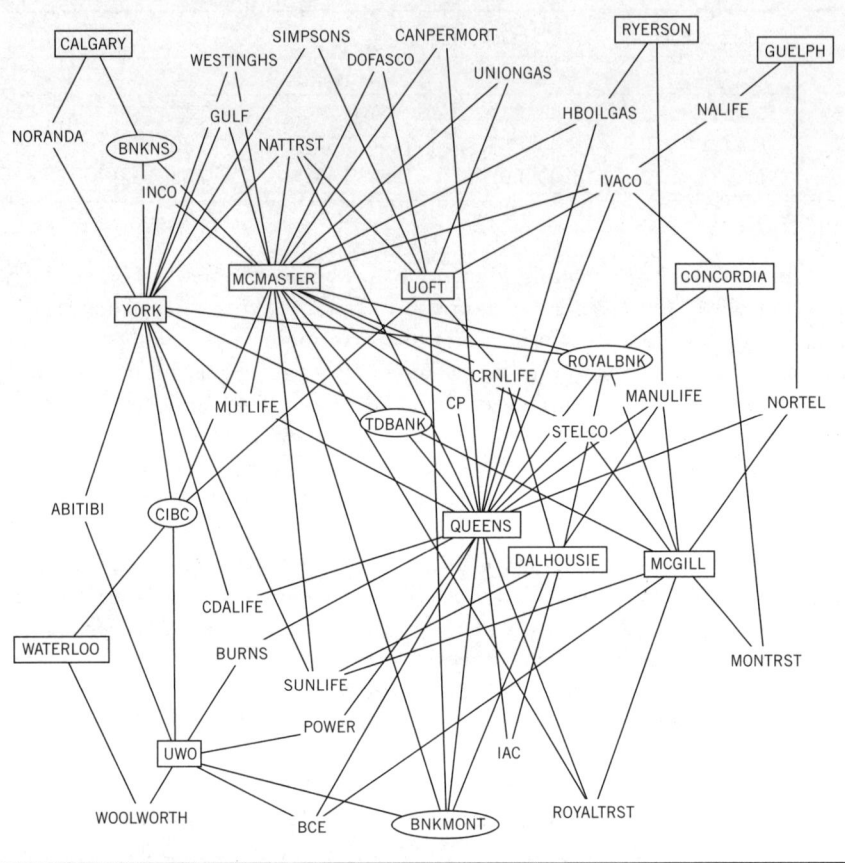

Universities are in boxes; banks are in ovals; other firms have no enclosing shape.

organizational network of corporations and universities, whose points are organizations and lines are interlocks between corporations and universities. We next considered how many of the organizations formed a *dominant component*—the largest set in which all points are ultimately reachable by all other points. In 1976, 12 universities and 101 corporations formed a component of 113 organizations, and two other universities were members of smaller separate components (Carleton, linked to three firms, and Université de Montréal, linked to three firms). In 1996, 18 universities and 95 firms formed a dominant component of exactly the same size, and McMaster formed a separate component with two firms.

To see which universities and corporations were located at the heart of the network at each point in time, we next narrowed the focus to the organizations that belonged to the *biggest block* within each dominant component.[14] For 1976 the

Integrating Corporate and University Governance for a Globalizing World 191

FIGURE 9.2
The Big Block of Corporations and Universities, 1996

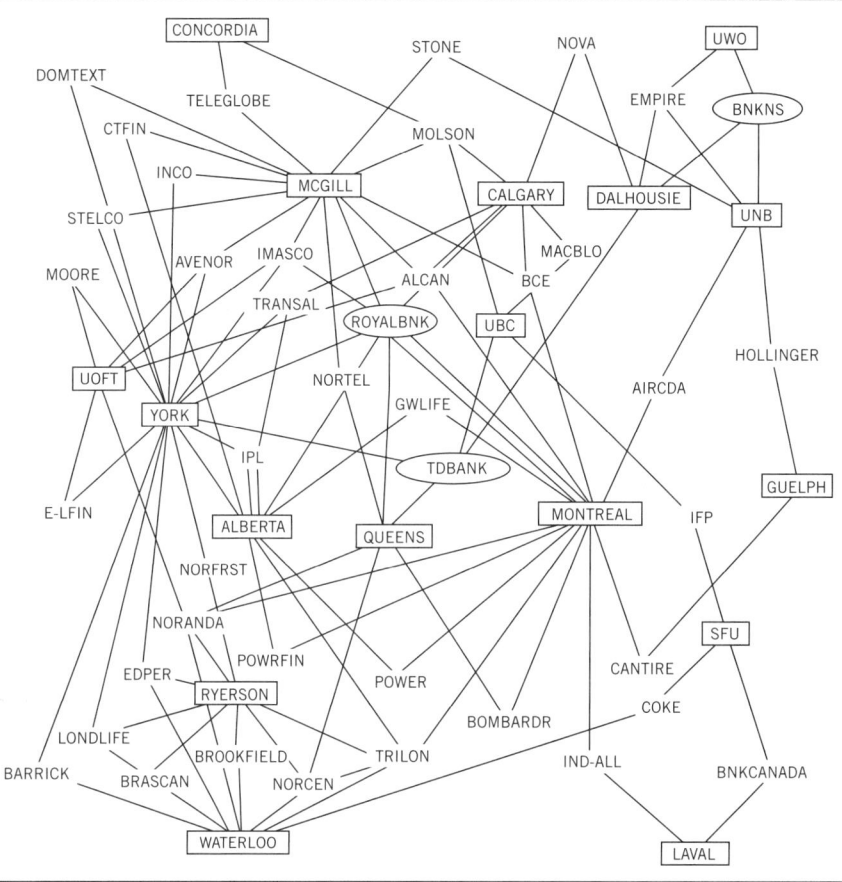

Universities are in boxes; banks are in ovals; other firms have no enclosing shape.

biggest block consisted of 45 organizations (12 universities and 33 firms). For 1996 the corresponding block consisted of 59 organizations (including 17 universities and 42 firms).[15] Although the big block expanded over the two decades, it became sparser in the process. In 1976 the big block of 45 organizations contained 94 lines, for a bipartite density of .237—meaning that nearly a quarter of all the pairs of universities and corporations within it were directly tied through board interlocks. In 1996 the big block contained 109 lines, for a bipartite density of .153. By 1996, more universities and corporations had been drawn together into an integrated block, but any corporation–university pair within this larger formation was less likely to be interlocked than were corporation–university pairs in the smaller, tighter 1976 block. We have mapped the interlocking directorates that form these bipartite graphs in Figures 9.1 and 9.2.

In 1976 (Fig 9.1) York, McMaster, Queen's, McGill, and Toronto ('UOFT') held central positions, as did several banks and leading financial institutions, which served as bridges between multiple universities in the bipartite network—particularly those located along the Toronto–Montreal axis. The York board alone included directors of four of the big five banks as well as three life insurers and a trust company, but was also linked to five industrial corporations and one commercial firm within the block of 33 corporations. The Royal Bank board included governors from Montreal-based McGill and Concordia, Toronto-based York, Kingston-based Queen's, Hamilton-based McMaster, and Halifax-based Dalhousie.

By 1996 (Fig. 9.2), York, Montreal, McGill, Ryerson and Waterloo were centrally positioned, and several of the western-based universities, as well as UNB, had become integrated into the network. The Royal and Toronto-Dominion banks could still be described as bridges, providing meeting-points for university governors from institutions spanning east and west. Overall, however, banks and life insurers had come to play a less significant integrative role. Meanwhile, firms in the Edper-Brascan corporate empire supplied governors to several universities, knitting a set of companies and universities based in Toronto and southwestern Ontario into a complex of overlapping board memberships. Four insiders to the Edper-Brascan group were particularly important in this complex. Senator Trevor Eyton, chair of Brascan, of Edper-Hees and of Trilon, sat on the University of Waterloo board, while Jack Cockwell, president of Brascan and of Edper-Hees, sat on the Ryerson Polytechnical board—Waterloo and Ryerson being two of more technology-oriented universities in the country. William Dimma, an executive of Trilon, sat on the York University board, as did Timothy Price, president of Edper-Hees. All four were directors of London Insurance. Thus the York, Ryerson, and Waterloo boards all included executives from the Edper-Brascan group—a small world indeed.

Third-Party Organizations as Sites for Elite Integration

One additional factor of relevance to the network approach we have taken here is the emergence and growth of 'third-party' organizations that serve as elite fora on higher education and related issues. Two kinds of such organizations can be distinguished: those sponsored by and linked to the state, and those sponsored by corporate capital.

We were able to identify only one third-party organization for 1976: the federally sponsored Science Council of Canada, founded in 1966. For 1997 we identified the federally established Canadian Foundation for Innovation. Both groups were mandated to promote research serving the national interest. However, the Science Council had an advisory role while the CFI is a semi-autonomous granting agency with a substantial budget (initially some $800 million) in public funds. The particular framework within which each organization operated reflected the political-economic arrangements of the day. In the mid-1970s, neoliberalism was only emerging as a political paradigm, and a significant current of Canadian economic thinking—grounded in dependency theory—decried the immaturity of Canadian capitalism and embraced the ideal of 'autonomous' development. Spanning state and civil society, the Science Council participated in this discourse, advocating reduced foreign control and increased 'technological sovereignty' (Kates, 1977; 1978). It became an important site for producing and promoting the 'nationalist-inspired industrial strategy' that gained influence within the Liberal government of the late 1970s and early 1980s (McBride, 2001:43), but suffered crippling cuts to its budget in the Mulroney government's deficit-reduction campaign of 1985 and was finally dissolved in 1992 (De la Mothe, 1992).

The Science Council consisted mainly of leading academics. Of its 25 members in 1976, 16 were academics, five were executives in corporations,[16] and four were consultants; only one—Ottawa-based surgeon H. Rocke Robertson—was a director of two major Canadian corporations.

By 1997, however, economic globalization, the information revolution, and the ascendancy of neoliberalism had created a post-fordist, Schumpeterian context in which a more corporate-centred approach to funding science and technology 'made sense'. The concern was not to promote an independent national economy but to underwrite the specific kinds of research that would bring greater corporate profitability and competitiveness within the global economy. 'In contrast to traditional research-granting councils,' writes Polster (2002:285), the Canadian Foundation for Innovation

> is an 'independent corporation' many of whose directors are not appointed by government.... While bound by federal legislation and various funding agreements, this body has more autonomy from government than do the traditional granting councils. It also operates more like a private than a public agency, having a separate CEO and chair of the board and engaging in less consultation with relevant stakeholders, which allows for more streamlined and rapid decision-making.

Industry representation on the CFI ensures that state funds will reward those initiatives that corporate executives find promising from a business standpoint. Like D'Aquino and Stewart-Patterson, quoted at the beginning of this chapter, these executives see research as a catalyst for efficient commodity production.[17] Whereas the Science Council advocated a state-facilitated industrial policy, the CFI's founding president, J. Keith Brimacombe, endorsed 'the need to grow new businesses that add value to our abundant natural resources, and that create high quality, high paying jobs in Canada' and pointed approvingly to corporate CEOs' advocacy of a greater role for business (and implicitly a secondary role for the state) in shaping social development.[18]

In 1997 the 30 members and directors of the CFI included six members of our corporate elite plus ten other designated representatives of private-sector industry, and only seven academics. Since the CFI, with its partners, has the capacity to distribute billions of dollars in public funds, there is the potential for this corporate-dominated body to shape research priorities. In order to receive CFI funding for their projects, applicants must establish a 'partnership' with private-sector funding sources or research institutes. In obliging researchers to find 'matching funds' the CFI places the onus on researchers to convince moneyed donors—chiefly capitalist interests—of the value of their projects. The *allocative power* of corporate capital becomes a de facto steering mechanism for a significant segment of academic research.

Here, as in other instances of corporate influence on the general direction of research and higher education, the advantages for capital are more general, benefiting the capitalist class as a whole, than they are instrumental. Specific firms represented on CFI will not necessarily reap profits from research. But by exercising leadership in research and development, Canadian corporate capital strengthens its position in the global economy. It consolidates that 'decisive nucleus of economic activity' in the absence of which the hegemony of a dominant class collapses (Gramsci, 1971:161).

Corporate Organization

The emergence since the early 1970s of two corporate-sponsored policy groups parallels the development of corporate political activism more generally, which the previous chapter showed to be an important cultural force promoting neoliberalism. Like CFI, the National Council on Education (NCE),[19] an affiliate of the Conference Board of Canada, formed in the 1980s, had six members of the corporate elite among its 1996 membership—one of whom served at the time on the CFI.[20] The Corporate-Higher Education Forum (C-HEF),[21] formed in 1983 to enable a cross-section of senior executives to discuss issues of mutual interest and broad societal concern with an equal number of university presidents, included 12 members of the corporate elite among its 1996 membership, one of whom was also a member of the NCE.[22] Just as the Business Council on National Issues and the Fraser Institute, founded in the 1970s, have exercised growing influence in the framing of broad political issues in Canada, the NCE and C-HEF have contributed to the formation of a neoliberal consensus on higher education. In the late 1990s, C-HEF was particularly active in attempts to globalize elite discussion of the place of higher education in twenty-first-century capitalism. In 1998 it combined its annual general meeting with the third annual joint meeting of business–university fora from Canada, the US, and Japan, with participation from 'sister' organizations in Australia and Poland. Citing a 'severe shortage of expert learners for the knowledge economy' (Corporate-Higher Education Forum, 1998:2), the Assembly took as its theme 'Getting the Story Straight'. With Canadian panelists including university presidents and vice-presidents from Queen's, Windsor, New Brunswick, Calgary, Université du Québec à Montréal, and McMaster, and executives from the Royal Bank, LaFarge Canada, Syncrude Canada, and the like—and with international representation from the Chase Manhattan Bank, Fuji-Xerox Company, Toshiba America, etc.—the participants endeavoured to determine the most effective means of producing and deploying 'a new kind of worker'—the high-performance 'knowledge worker', defined as 'one who can move effortlessly from data to information to knowledge and make it useful' (1998:2).[23] In a globalizing capitalist world, such cosmopolitan assemblies may well become integral to bourgeois hegemony in higher education.

Meanwhile, in the specifically Canadian context of 1997, a total of 22 members of our 1996 corporate elite were active in one or more of the three third-party groups, one of which was the CFI. Three of the 22 were also governors of universities in our sample. By implication, the third-party organizations drew 19 additional members of the corporate elite into higher-education governance and planning. When compared to the single individual that linked the corporate elite to the Science Council in 1976, these numbers represent a substantial increase in the extent to which corporate capital now participates directly in influencing the national agenda for higher education/research. In 1976, 53 members of the corporate elite (11 per cent) were active in university governance or in third-party organizations. In 1996, 71 (17 per cent) were similarly active.

In Figure 9.3 we map the affiliations of the 22 members of the corporate elite who were active on one or more of the three third-party organizations in 1997. The network contains 82 points—22 people, 57 firms, and three third-party organizations (the last are enclosed in ovals). Twelve of the 22 were functioning capitalists, including ten executives of Top 250 corporations. Among the ten advisors to corporate capital we find four university presidents—David Strangway of UBC, Lorna Marsden of Wilfrid Laurier (more recently president of York University), J. Robert Prichard of University of Toronto, and Lloyd Barber, retired president of University of Saskatchewan—all members of the C-HEF. The sociogram highlights the integrative roles played by certain well-placed individuals. Strangway, as president of UBC until July 1997, served on two major corporate boards (including MacMillan-Bloedel), chaired the C-HEF, and belonged to the National Council on Education. John Evans, former president of University of Toronto, was in 1997 chair of Alcan Aluminum and Torstar Corp., chair of CFI, and a director of two other Top 250 firms, MDS Inc. and the Royal Bank. Purdy Crawford, chair of Imasco of its subsidiary CT Financial Services, director of six other major corporations (and a major force on the board of AIMS), was co-chair of the NCE, a governor of McGill University, and chancellor of Mount Allison University. Angus Bruneau was chair of two mid-sized corporations (including Fortis Inc.), a director of four Top 250 firms (including the engineering concern SNC-Lavalin Group), and a member of both the CFI and the NCE. Peter Godsoe, president of the Bank of Nova Scotia, was also a director of the Empire Company, a member of C-HEF, a governor of Dalhousie, and chancellor of the University of Western Ontario. The network map shows the extent to which third-party groups now contribute to the intertwining of corporate capital and higher education at the level of governance and policy-planning.

One further way of illustrating this intertwining is to focus on the corporate boards that serve as meeting places for various directors of third-party groups. As with university board memberships, so also with third-party memberships, the Royal Bank led the field as a site for elite integration. Its board included not only governors from five universities, but five additional members of third-party groups—two of them participants in C-HEF, two members of CFI, and one member of the NCE. The two Royal Bank directors who belonged to C-HEF—Allan Taylor (retired president of the Royal) and David O'Brien—also served on

FIGURE 9.3

Corporate Interlocks with Three Higher Education/Research Organizations, 1996

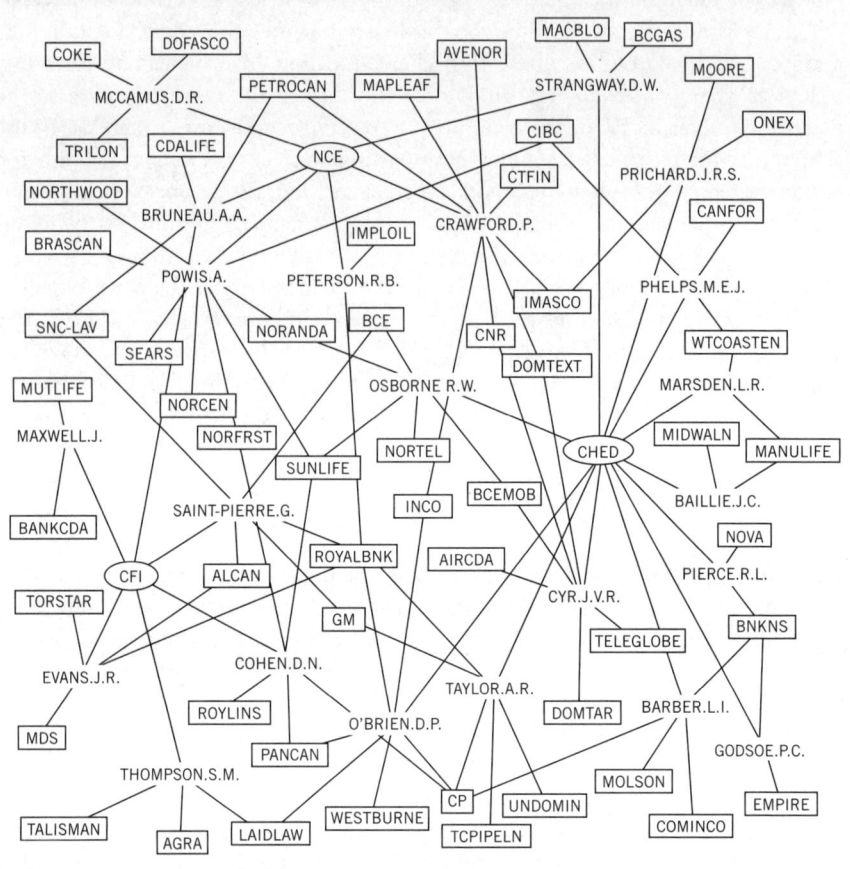

Corporations are in boxes; higher education/research groups are in ovals. KEY: NCE = National Council on Education, CFI = Canadian Foundation for Innovation, CHED = Corporate-Higher Education Forum.

the Canadian Pacific (CP) board (O'Brien being president), pointing up the strong link between the Royal Bank and CP, which reaches back many decades. But the CP board also included former University of Saskatchewan President Lloyd Barber (also a member of C-HEF) and corporate consultant Dian Cohen, a director of CFI as well as many corporations. Dian Cohen's directorship with Sun Life, meanwhile, put her into touch with both Alfred Powis (CEO of Noranda and a member of NCE) and Ronald Osborne (CEO of BCE and a member of C-HEF). Two other Royal Bank directors, John Evans and Guy Saint-Pierre, were both affiliated with the CFI. They also served on the Alcan board, and Saint-Pierre sat with Osborne on the BCE board.

This complex structure, which complements the network of corporate–university interlocks, creates a plethora of contact points among members of the corporate elite active in the third-party organizations, and a basis for consensus formation. The third-party groups thus make their own contributions to corporate hegemony on higher education and related issues.

Conclusions

In recapitulating this chapter's main findings and their substantive implications, three points merit emphasis. First, in connection with Newson and Buchbinder's distinction between the internal and external forces pushing toward corporatization, we have found no absolute increase in the corporate elite's presence on university boards; however, there is evidence of increased ties *emanating from inside universities*, as major university presidents become members of the corporate elite.[25] Such ties suggest *a deepening of corporate–university relations*, as chief executive officers of universities and corporations rub shoulders in corporate boardrooms and participate in a common managerial culture.

Second, although the overall extent of corporate–university interlocking remained stable across the two decades, there are several ways in which these relations became *more inclusive*, as the network came to span most of the country, to include most major universities, and to increase substantially the size of its central block. The increased number of organic intellectuals, who knit together universities and corporations through their participation in the governance of both, also points to greater integration, as do the many ties linking the corporate elite to emergent third-party groups, which provide new vehicles for business leadership in shaping higher education and research. All these indications point to *a broader class hegemony*, as the persuasive force of corporate-capitalist priorities makes itself felt in a wider range of areas, beyond the boards of a few elite institutions.

The new liberalism is indeed a move away from the elitist conservatism that was still evident in the 1970s. In the neoliberal world, all universities have equal potential as sites capable of assisting in the quest for international competitiveness, and most university boards now include one or more members of the corporate elite. A more inclusive hegemony might well be more persuasive in some quarters. On the other hand, those committed to different visions of higher education will likely resist any broadening of corporate involvement as anti-democratic. In March 1998, for instance, students at York University shut down a board of governors meeting, protesting against the preponderance of corporate representation rather than faculty and students on the York board, and calling for the removal of all corporate CEOs (Clarke and Schmidt, 1998).

Third, our analysis illustrates how corporate–university relations have evolved with the changing character both of the Canadian political economy and of the corporate elite. Neoliberalism figures heavily in these changes. State retrenchment has forced universities to launch massive fund-raising campaigns, and there can be little doubt that fundraising efforts have benefited from corporate representation on governing boards. By 1998, for instance, the University of Toronto had offset its 15.3 per cent cut in provincial funding with a $400 million campaign, spearheaded by executives from Northern Telecom, the Bank of Montreal, and other leading corporations (Cole, 1998).[26] Similarly, as the federal government shifted from a science council dedicated to a nationalist industrial policy to a corporate-dominated foundation that enables capital to set the agenda more directly, academics have been induced to form 'partnerships' with business as a condition for funding.

As for the structure of capital, the coming-of-age of a Québécois section of corporate business has helped to draw francophone universities into the national network, as firms such as Bombardier and SNC-Lavalin have risen to prominence and established elite ties both to other corporations and to academe. At the same time, changes in the world of finance and corporate governance have weakened the pre-eminence of chartered banks in directorate interlocking, and in corporate–university relations. However, the attenuation of financial institutions in the network of corporate–university governance should not be overstated, nor should it be mistaken for a weakening in the power of financial capital, upon which underfunded universities are increasingly dependent.

Meanwhile, since the 1970s new investment companies have emerged, some of whose executives have been recruited to university boards, possibly in appreciation of their prowess in raising and multiplying funds in the new framework of transaction-based finance. In other cases, university administrators have joined the boards of investment companies; an example is former University of Toronto president Rob Prichard's directorship with Onex Corp. The rise of high-tech companies adds a further nuance to the picture. Although, in general, executives in resource and manufacturing firms have come to play a less extensive role in university governance, by 1996 directors of domestically controlled high-tech companies showed an elective affinity for university boards. To some extent, indigenous high-tech companies have displaced financial institutions as the form of capital most visibly represented on university boards, perhaps because of perceived synergies between knowledge-intensive production within 'cutting-edge' corporations and the production of knowledge and skills within universities.

We find evidence here of a transition from an era in which the top layer of the capitalist class was represented in university governance predominantly by leading lights of banking and heavy industry, to one in which paper entrepreneurship and high-tech industry have a stronger presence. However, the changes should not be exaggerated. There are major banks whose directors continue to participate extensively in university governance, and in any case our analysis of intercorporate relations in Chapter 4 showed that as corporate capital has become more transnational, the financial–industrial axis has been maintained in a looser form among the transnationalizing firms. What seems clear is that universities are becoming more integrated into the world of corporate capital, as both sides of the university–corporate nexus respond to contemporary capitalism's reliance on neoliberal policy, technology-intensive production, and more globalized structures of accumulation.

IV

Conclusion

Chapter 10

Corporate Power and Neoliberal Democracy

The preceding chapters have told a story of corporate power in transition. In the last quarter of the twentieth century, Canada's corporate elite underwent a number of significant changes—some of them closely associated with recent globalization and its political handmaiden, neoliberalism, and all of them at least conditioned by those worldwide developments. Yet if the organizational, spatial and hegemonic terrains of corporate power were transformed, in some ways the scene remained familiar. Our task here is to integrate the empirical findings of our study into a perspective on the emerging form of corporate power that carried Canadian capitalism into a new century.

Corporate power is Janus-faced. It is ultimately rooted in the economic relations of advanced capitalism—the organization of life around a system of commodity production and exchange in which giant corporations and massive pools of money capital concentrate enormous social power in the control of the capitalist class's top tier, placing workers, communities, and states in a relation of unilateral dependence. This face of corporate power is inseparable from the accumulation of capital. In exploring it we have attempted to map the extra-market relations through which the largest corporations are linked together at the level of governance. Viewed from this angle, directorate interlocks, intercorporate ownership, and the like are traces of allocative, strategic, and operational forms of economic power that when considered in their entirety constitute a structure of finance capital.

Yet the exercise of corporate power is not simply a matter of commanding the heights of industry and finance. Its other face, no less important for elite organization and no less fateful for capitalist democracies, is cultural and political. In a way of life deeply marked by class inequality, by the juxtaposition of Rosedale and Regent Park, by the presence of homeless people living on the street within blocks of the First Canadian Place, the corporate elite must struggle to maintain hegemony. The consent of subordinates can never be taken for granted, and although much of the work of organizing that consent might be delegated to intellectuals of various stripes—in the media, policy planning, public relations, academe, etc.—the corporate elite, that small group at the apex of the dominant class, must exercise active leadership. This is not to say that the corporate elite, or the dominant class, 'controls' the political process and its outcomes. Fred Block's (1977) famous claim that 'the ruling class does not rule' is still entirely apposite, even after three decades of a neoliberal globalization that has diminished the relative autonomy of national states, which Block took for granted as he wrote in the closing days of the Keynesian class compromise.

Even if 'the ruling class does not rule,' business leadership *does reach* into civil society and into the institutions of the state, recruiting support for a world-view within which the interest of capital in profitable accumulation becomes universalized as the general interest of society, or even humanity. To reach effectively, to be a leading cultural and political force, the corporate elite must achieve and maintain a certain social cohesiveness as a business community—an internal basis of solidarity, with a shared perspective on what is to be done. In focusing on the various overlapping memberships that weave the corporate elite into a social network, our research has, of course, posed only a limited range of questions about accumulation and hegemony as forms of class power. What, then, have we learned?

Concentration of Economic Power

To begin with the obvious, large, increasingly globalized corporations concentrate enormous economic power in the hands of those controlling the business strategies of dominant firms. There are approximately one million incorporated businesses in Canada, yet the Top 25 enterprises account for 41.2 per cent of all business assets. Across all economic sectors, large companies (firms generally with assets greater than $25 million or annual revenue greater than $100 million) claim 79.4 per cent of all business assets (Statistics Canada, 2001:37, 44). The sheer concentration of corporate assets is not a new development, however. In Canada, capital has been highly concentrated, and a small elite of finance capitalists has wielded considerable economic power, ever since the era of the National Policy, under which the state facilitated investment in industrial capacity. Even at the dawn of the post-Second World War era, the largest corporate survival of the National Policy, the Canadian Pacific Railway, towered above all other corporations in the country, accounting in itself for one-tenth of total industrial assets (Carroll, 1986:65–6).

What was new in the ensuing half-century was the further *geographical concentration* of corporate head offices into a very few metropolitan command centres. Of course, even half a century ago Montreal and Toronto were the cities that mattered for the corporate elite (and particularly for the financial sector); yet a good many industrial corporations had their head offices and physical plants outside the Toronto–Montreal axis. As the century closed, the spatial organization of corporate power had been simplified into a bipolar configuration with two major urban centres and two lesser ones in the far west. Although nearby secondary centres hosted a few head offices and thereby figured peripherally in the national network, there was little involvement of outlying areas, and Toronto had decisively eclipsed Montreal as the country's corporate metropolis and terminus for many continental and transnational interlocks. Consistent with a consolidating organized capitalism, this shift in the locus of power meant the *further centralization of strategic control over capital* in the form of large, multidivisional corporations in which plant-specific, operational aspects of management were subordinated to extra-local corporate strategies issuing from metropolitan head offices.

In a globalizing world, the concentration of economic power cuts across national borders. Transnational investment is an important means through which capital becomes concentrated, and the most powerful corporations are transnationals whose multifarious holdings enable them to play one national or regional workforce (or state) off against another. In late twentieth-century Canada, transnationalization bore several meanings. In the financial sector it meant in part the entry of major European companies—though these did not establish elite-level ties to major Canadian companies. In industry the flagging presence of US-based TNCs was accompanied by an increased complement of subsidiaries of Japanese-based TNCs, again with little in the way of elite-level connections. Meanwhile, Canadian-based companies, both industrial and financial, continued their own process of transnationalization, an important aspect of economic concentration. By the closing years of the century, domestically controlled TNCs outnumbered large companies of purely 'national' scope and Canadian direct investment abroad outweighed foreign direct investment (FDI) in Canada. At the same time the corporate network became re-centred around a core of transnational banks and corporations, controlled by capitalists based in Canada. Although TNCs were central to this loose network, on the boards of transnational banks sat many outside directors of companies whose operations remained sub-transnational. We concluded that 'transnational finance capital' has radiated from Canada in a way that has *not* disorganized the national network but has *embedded* it more extensively in a circuitry of global accumulation. Following the Swiss example (Rusterholz, 1985), the Canadian network had become re-centred around an expanding sector of Canadian-based TNCs, both industrial and financial. In this transition, Canada's business community participated with other nationally based corporate elites in a global process of capital concentration and centralization. According to Peter Dicken, 1985 marked a major shift in the growth of world FDI to unprecedented levels, as FDI consistently outpaced world GDP. By the mid-1990s the advanced capitalist countries were the source of 92 per cent of world FDI. The same countries were host to three-quarters of all FDI in the world, underlining the fact that most transnational corporate investment takes the form of a cross-penetration of capital among developed national economies (Dicken, 1998:42–5).

AGENCIES OF STRATEGIC CONTROL

Corporate power is not wielded by a monolithic elite. It inheres in specific agents controlling capital concentrations and flows. At the higher reaches of the Canadian economy, family capitalism has not succumbed to the technocratic rationality of the managerial revolution; nor, by the late 1990s, had state capital been very widely privatized into new accumulation vehicles for capitalist investors. Major shareholders—wealthy families—have continued to make up a substantial fraction of the corporate elite, and family control at the 'ultimate' level actually increased after 1976 as more capitalist families resorted to intercorporate ownership as a means of control. By 1996 major shareholders were often central players in the network of thick ties knitting together strategically aligned firms. Yet at the same time the presence of institutional investors expanded, so that both a 'depersonalization of capital' and a 'repersonalization' seemed underway. If in Scott's (1997) view, depersonalization of control is one sign of a transition to 'disorganized capitalism', the robustness of family empires suggests that his thesis needs qualification in the case of Canada. The well-known tendency for many large Canadian companies to be controlled by other corporations continued through the 1990s, contributing further to the concentration of economic power. Major enterprise groups, organized around intercorporate ownership, associated capitalists, and thick interlocks, continued to claim space within the corporate network even if the specific companies and controlling agents changed. The larger of these ensembles—the Brascan and Power groups— became increasingly transnationalized, although in rather different ways. But even if major shareholders and institutional investors gained a bigger piece of the action, as US-based TNCs came to play a somewhat smaller role in the control of Canada's largest firms, the growth of credit unions and similar kinds of non-proprietary economic organizations at the margins of corporate power presented alternatives to that power, and member-elected directors of these organizations remained detached from the corporate elite. However, the 'social economy' of credit unions, wheat pools, co-operatives, and the like is enmeshed within a larger capitalist order that constrains the extent to which member-controlled economic organizations can flourish on the basis of an alternative set of values.

Despite neoliberalism's commitment to getting government off the backs of business, the Canadian state has continued to exercise agency in the control of corporate capital, with a slightly lower profile after the privatization of such crown jewels as Air Canada and the CNR. Certain ties between state enterprises and private-sector corporations even strengthened—notably in Quebec, which continued to follow an industrial strategy of sorts. In other cases, elite-level ties between state enterprises and the business community may have facilitated privatization initiatives. Whatever the case, the state has not renounced all agency in the economic field, and in some respects neoliberal programs to commercialize operations such as the post office have increased the state's 'presence' among the largest corporations, even if government-controlled firms remain on the whole marginal to the corporate network. However, with commercialization public-policy mandates become subordinated to the same exigencies of accumulation that apply to private-sector capitalists. In this 'partial privatization of state functions' (McBride, 2001:137) the market tends to colonize the 'public sector', with deleterious implications for the scope of democratic politics.

The ascension of institutional shareholding runs, as we have said, in the direction of 'depersonalization' of capital. But this tendency should not be confused with 'managerial revolution'. The pattern of strategic control shows clearly that no such revolution has occurred. At the apex of corporate power in Canada is a stratum of capitalists interested in expanding the social wealth they control, not professional managers committed to 'social responsibility', or some other mission conferring an ethical purpose.[1] One tangible result of the increased concentration of capital within investment funds was a more integrated network of intercorporate ownership, as the major institutional investors took significant minority positions in widely held corporations, shifting the constellations of interest atop many of the largest companies. In the late 1990s it was still rare for major funds to take seats on the boards of companies in which they held a substantial interest. But the future may well bring a proliferation of weak interlocks between the institutions and their investments, as part of the effort to press for 'shareholder value'. We do know that major pension funds have moved well beyond passive investment strategies. They have begun to acquire some of Canada's largest property-development companies, such as Cadillac Fairview (purchased by Ontario Teachers' Pension Fund Board in 2000) and Oxford Properties group (purchased by the Ontario Municipal Employees Retirement Board in 2001). Pension funds are now heavily involved in financing major corporate plays, such as Gerry Schwartz's purchase of Celestica Inc. from IBM Canada in 1996 (Newman, 1998:229) and Wallace McCain's purchase of controlling interest in Maple Leaf Foods in 1995 (Rubin, 1998). In effect, pension funds and other institutional investors have been morphing into financial conglomerates with wide-ranging investments that make it possible to exercise strategic control over corporate assets. The larger funds now number among the biggest single shareholders of chartered banks. In 1998 the Ontario Teachers Pension Fund had investments of more than $500 million in each of the Royal Bank, the Bank of Montreal, and CIBC (Rubin, 1998).[2] Not to be outdone, the banks have been acquiring some of the largest mutual funds, as in National Bank's purchase of Altamira Investment Services in August 2002 (Critchley, 2002). The enormous concentration of both allocative and strategic power that these developments portend is another facet of the drive for 'shareholder value', and another aspect of the emerging structure of finance capital in the twenty-first century. As we have seen, the movement towards improved corporate governance has been prodded by locked-in institutional investors insistent upon ever-expanding shareholder value. The motor for change has not been a market-driven, efficiency-enhancing process. Rather, 'realignments in corporate governance reflect the growing economic and political power of those who have accumulated financial assets . . .' (O'Sullivan, 2000:153). These realignments hold in varying degrees throughout the advanced capitalist world. In Canada the relatively small size of the share float in the local equity market, combined with federal regulations limiting the extent of foreign content in pension funds, has catapulted institutional investors into significant positions in a good many major corporations, further concentrating the control of corporate capital.

Corporate Governance Reform and the Recomposition of Finance Capital

Governance reforms have had the same two-faced quality as the corporate power they seek to regulate 'from within'. Arising out of heightened international competition, the frantic search for profit, and the financial crises and scandals that accompany this search, they have sought to pulverize traditional elite practices in the service of a 'higher morality' that, above all, portends even fatter financial returns. The reforms' impact on the structure of finance capital was dramatic, as interlocks involving corporate officers (and especially lower-level executives) disappeared from the network. Most significantly, bankers left the boards of industrial corporations and banks slimmed their elephantine directorates. This left a looser network of weak ties, in which the banks continue to figure prominently (particularly in the transnationalized segment) even if their boards are no longer quite the central hubs they once were. In Chapter 4 we concluded from this finding that corporate governance has operated in tandem with tendencies already in motion before the 1990s, in particular the trend away from relationship-based corporate finance and towards transaction-based finance, which the big banks provide most notably through their investment-bank subsidiaries.

As institutional investors accumulate corporate shares, a new financial–industrial axis seems to be emerging, one fully sanctioned by the new corporate governance framework. The recomposition of boards as strategic decision-making units for major and minor shareholders precisely reflects the shift from the 'patient money' of old-fashioned commercial banks to the more immediate, profit-sensitive style of the locked-in institutional investor in a frantically competitive environment. In the process, the constellations of interests atop major corporations shift away from salaried managers and bankers, and towards 'shareholders'—whether institutional or family-centred. As a quantitative norm that—with the incipient integration of stock exchanges—is potentially 'universal', shareholder value symbolizes the utopia of a fully rationalized, unitary capitalism in which transparent choices open themselves to professional investors operating in an information-rich field of global accumulation. 'Corporate governance' has in this sense been more than a movement for moral reform. It is an active part of what appears to be a transition to a new form of finance capital. A looser network, carried by outside directors, built more around information ties and business scan than around primary interlocks and patient money, and centred increasingly on transnational corporations, suits this new relation between finance and industry. Finally, the state has figured significantly in this transition. Deregulation has led not only to a more concentrated yet less socially integrated financial sector dominated by universal banks, but to increased involvement of institutional investors in equity markets, augmenting the power of funds within controlling constellations.[3]

VECTORS OF CORPORATE POWER

Capital, as David Harvey (1982) reminds us, never entirely escapes the material actualities it is anchored in. Even when it takes flight in fetishized forms—as hedge funds, futures, and derivatives—ultimately capital remains embedded in the spatialized relations that it helps to shape. Within Canada, the changing spatial terrain we have mapped has seen not only a concentration of corporate head offices in four major urban centres, but a *westward drift* of corporate power, tracking the flow of capital itself. Notably, Calgary rose from obscurity to become an important command centre for the energy/petrochemical sector. By the late 1990s, this reconfigured structure of finance capital continued to be centred on the Toronto–Montreal axis, home to most of the major financial institutions and many major industrial corporations, particularly in the high-tech sectors, but in contrast to the 1970s, let alone the 1940s, it now extended to the emerging command centres of Calgary and Vancouver. Still, the western cities remained for the most part industrial outposts. Reflected clearly in the network was the continued financial hegemony of Toronto and Montreal as sites of allocative power, and the vital role of 'finance capitalists' whose interlocking directorships stitched together industry and finance, east and west. And while Toronto ascended to the status of a second-tier global city, the Montreal-based segment underwent its own recomposition with the coming-of-age of a Québécois fraction integrated into the national network.

The north-south vector of corporate power is more difficult to characterize. As Stephen Clarkson (2002:214) has observed, 'there is no single template that can capture all corporate responses to continentalism.' We can safely say that the last quarter of the twentieth century witnessed no blending of Canadian and American corporate elites, at least not via interlocking directorships. Already sparse, 'continental connections' grew sparser. Canadian and American corporations are organized in two separate national networks, with very few ties traversing the border. Among the largest corporations, Canada–US interlocks are no more profuse than, say Canada–Europe interlocks. Moreover, across the two decades fewer firms and fewer directors participated in continental interlocks. In particular, interlocks reflecting US strategic control of Canadian companies disappeared from the network, in part because of the declining number of large American branch plants and in part because of changes in the structure of transnational management, about which we speculated at the close of Chapter 6.[4] By the later 1990s the continental network was a sparse collection of cross-border ties—relatively few of which entailed strategic control of capital—carried by perhaps threescore capitalists and corporate advisors. For some of the largest Canadian-based transnationals, such as Nortel, the sort of cross-border interlocking that was in play seemed compatible with the weakly organized financial–industrial relations that have come to prevail with the partial 'disorganization' of national economies. Although the financial–industrial axis remained predominantly national for both countries, there was some evidence of nascent north-south relations organized less around strategic control than around the allocative power of large financial institutions.

But if continentalism has been in decline at the level of corporate interlocking, in other ways it has been developing apace. Corporations rely increasingly on networked business processes, which Schiller and Mosco (2001:1) identify with the coming of cybercapitalism. The decline of continental directorship ties, particularly those linking American parents to their Canadian subsidiaries, may actually reflect more extensive networking at an operational level, as new communications technologies render the Canadian subsidiary simply one among various sub-units within a single economic zone. This interpretation is speculative; to assess its validity we would need to investigate recent changes in management practices within transnational corporations, which are beyond the scope of this study. Be that as it may, other examples of continental integration can easily be cited. Even though they remain domestically controlled, many of Canada's best-known companies are now run by Americans; and many of Canada's top capitalists themselves now have residences in Phoenix and other sunbelt cities (Newman, 1998:136, 141). Some Canadian corporations have moved their executive offices to the US, and their shares now trade on the NYSE and NASDAQ. Most major Canadian corporations own subsidiaries in the US, and between 1976 and 1996 there was a doubling of large Canadian firms with subsidiaries exclusively in Canada and the USA. Indeed, according to Bill Burgess 'it is Canadian investors who have been the more aggressive "continentalizers",' a state of affairs that hardly suggests a process of 'silent surrender'. Burgess goes on to note that levels of continental foreign direct investment between the US and Canada are comparable to levels among 14 western European countries. He concludes that Canadian economic integration with the United States is 'consistent with the broader pattern of interpenetration of "core" countries, however unequal in size and power' (2002:205).

Still, size and power do matter—which is why continental capital relations trouble those committed to a project of Canadian nationalism. Isaiah Litvak has summarized the problem nicely. Since the Canadian economy is one-tenth the size of the American, US acquisitions in Canada are quickly integrated, with some head-office functions transferred to the American operations. The corollary, however, is that Canadian firms are generally one-tenth the size of American firms. Thus when Canadian companies acquire US firms a 'reverse organizational outcome' is likely:

> successful Canadian MNCs with operations in the United States typically experience the phenomenon in which the Canadian portion of business pales in comparison to that in the United States. And, though the head office may be located in Canada, the US subsidiary normally acquires added decision-making powers because of the dominance of the US market, which accounts in many cases for the most substantial portion of Canadian MNCs' global revenues and growth (2001:7).

The changing perspectives of Canadian corporations with major stakes in the American economy raise the issue of corporate capital's 'nationality'—a question made more salient with the advent of North American free trade. As the agreements of 1989 and 1994 took effect, the east-west axis of Canada's home market, already frail due to decades of permeable fordism, was further eroded. In the later 1990s north-south trade flows grew by an estimated 10–11 per cent a year while east-west flows expanded by only 3 or 4 per cent annually (Scoffield, 1998:B4). What was consolidated in all this was an 'attitude change' among Canadian capitalists, a shift toward continental business strategies according to which companies were increasingly focused on north-south trading opportunities, and 'restructured their operations to take advantage of big US markets' (Scoffield, 1998:B4). Overall, trade—always a key aspect of capital accumulation in Canada—gained importance, rising from 25 per cent of GDP in 1991 to 41 per cent in 1997; and Canada's trade with the US increased from approximately 77 per cent in 1985–7 to 82 per cent in 1996–8 (Du Boff, 2001:43). Thus we find by the late 1990s a Canadian corporate elite whose social organization remained 'national' at the level of corporate governance, but whose business strategies were increasingly continental, if not more fully 'global'. This strategic orientation, combined with concerns about continuing US protectionism in the post-NAFTA era, has prompted calls from the C.D. Howe Institute for 'deeper integration' via customs-union or common-market-like arrangements (Dobson 2002). Ironically, the weakening of elite-level continental connections may coincide with and even reflect a deeper form of continentalism: an amalgamation of Canadian and American economies.

In conceptualizing continental relations it is crucial to keep in mind that regionalization is to globalization as a part is to the whole. We have suggested that the Free Trade agreements of 1989 and 1994 have had important implications for the structure of corporate power in North America.[5] But as Schiller and Mosco (2001:3) note, these are not simply regional agreements; they form an integral part of the globalization process. For instance, NAFTA provisions to protect foreign investors, enabling them to sue a government for compensation against regulations that retard their profits, were quickly picked up by the WTO as a new prospective norm for international governance. And, in integrating the North American market, NAFTA has stimulated an enormous inflow of foreign investment, further integrating the world economy. Driven by the complementary interests of American, Canadian, and Mexican corporate capital, 'NAFTA is part of, facilitates, and advances globalization—the restructuring of economic and financial capital through international flows of production, trade, investment, and assets' (Du Boff, 2001:58).

When we look beyond this continent to the global corporate network, for the most part we again find only sparse and weak ties connecting Canada's corporate elite to the rest of the world. To the close of the twentieth century, transnational interlocking remained no more than a sideline for Canadian corporate capitalists, most of whose network affiliations remained nationally organized. Most of the ties that did embed Canada within the global network reached from other countries into Canada, not vice versa. Still, the loose network we mapped for 1996 did contain one major transnational enterprise group based partly in Canada. The Desmarais-Frère empire—a Euro-Canadian partnership of two fabulously wealthy families—is a unique ensemble stitched together via family shareholdings, intercorporate ownership, and interlocking directorships that span the North Atlantic. Although other major transnational family empires can be cited—Li Ka-Shing's extensive holdings in southeast Asia and Canada come to mind[6]—the Desmarais-Frère group is by far the largest. Desmarais, however, is the only Canadian finance capitalist controlling a set of world-class corporations in other countries.

Apart from the Desmarais-Frère group, most of the interlocks joining Canadian corporations to the global network involve either the strategic control of Canadian subsidiaries by parents based in Japan or the US, or outside directorships that often feature a large financial institution on one side of the relationship, and that terminate in Europe or the US. The latter may facilitate the cross-border transactions that are an important aspect of transnational finance capital. With its interlocks extending primarily to the European and American networks, corporate Canada most closely resembles a middle power within an 'Atlantic ruling class' (van der Pijl, 1984). Canada's corporate elite is positioned in the centre of the global network, even if its status is secondary to the major Euro-North American powers—the US, the UK, Germany, and France.

As with continental connections, however, directorship interlocks represent only one aspect of global corporate power. There are several 'transnational practices' (the term comes from Sklair, 1995) that serve to knit the component parts of the world economy together—transnational strategic alliances, intercorporate ownership, collaborative ventures, subcontracting relationships, and so on (Dicken, 1998:223–40). Canada's top corporations have been busy enlarging their own transnational reach, and although their foreign branches do not rank among the world's largest corporations, there is a growing network of parent-subsidiary control relations extending from Canada to a wide range of countries. Some heirs to major family fortunes have also internationalized their investments. For instance, Charles Bronfman has invested heavily in Israel in recent years, and now chairs Israel's largest industrial conglomerate (Adams, 2002).[7]

What our mapping of the Canadian corporate elite within the global network reveals is, first, that Canada's corporate network is one of the most integrated. Second, and consistent with Dicken's (1998:193) observation that most transnational corporations remain nationally embedded, Canadian corporate capital has retained a predominantly 'national' base even as finance capital has become increasingly transnational in scope. Dense and thick ties tend to knit national corporate networks together, while a sparse set of weak ties links hands across the borders. This resilience of the national factor in elite organization urges us not to overestimate the disorganizing impact of recent globalization.

At the same time, however, there are structural forms of globalization that are not evident at the level of corporate elites, and since the early 1970s the elaboration of these forms has been fateful for world capitalism. Among the most important is growth in the volume of stateless, mobile financial capital—foreign-held portfolio investment. By 2000, the total stock of Canadian direct investment abroad had reached $301 billion, slightly more than the total stock of foreign direct investment in Canada ($292 billion). Yet if Canada had moved from being a net recipient to a net provider of foreign direct investment on the international scene, the figures on portfolio investment suggested a different story. The value of foreign bonds held in Canada ($35 billion) was less than one-tenth of the value of Canadian bonds held abroad ($381 billion), mostly in the form of state debt. This contributed to a net international investment deficit of $346 billion (Statistics Canada, 2001), placing stateless financial capitalists in a position of allocative power vis-à-vis the Canadian state. Insofar as neoliberalism constructs a conception of the general interest from the standpoint of transnational money-capital (Overbeek and van der Pijl, 1993:15), this shift in capital structure can be read as having provided somewhat of a practical economic basis for promoting neoliberal policies. The grave images evoked by a succession of finance ministers in the 1980s and 1990s—depicting the state deficit as Public Enemy Number One and warning Canadians of the international humiliation and effective trusteeship they would face if the debt was not brought under control—were the most visible political response to the global capital's enhanced structural power (Workman, 1996). But the discourse of fiscal crisis and neoliberal reform did not suddenly appear as a reflex of structural change. It was carefully assembled within policy groups, party committees, and academic conferences, and widely disseminated via popular and professional media. The corporate elite played an active role in this political-cultural construction project.

From a Culture of Leisure to a Culture of Activism

The corporate elite develops and maintains itself as a 'business community' in much the same way that any community does. There will be fractional divisions of interest and perspective over one matter or another, but communicative ties and joint activities continually recreate a collective sense of solidarity. If we think of the period from the 1970s through the 1990s as one of ongoing community development, what is striking is the extent to which the cultural basis for elite solidarity shifted from the sphere of leisure to that of activism.

In the early 1970s, private clubs, mainly in Montreal and Toronto, were the key sites for building class cohesion. They functioned as 'watering holes' for the old boys—places where leading businessmen and other elite professionals could relax together and discuss issues of common concern. Such clubs existed specifically to provide a space for comradely conversation among an exclusive membership, and leading directors of dominant corporations routinely belonged to several of them, knitting the elite into a centralized old boys' network. Before the Fraser Institute launched in 1974, with the BCNI following soon after, in 1976, the culture of solidarity that sustained the business community was primarily one of leisure, befitting an oligarchic elite. Corporate capitalists and their advisors did participate in policy groups such as the Conference Board, but these groups also included representatives of other parts of the society, such as labour. The venues they provided did more for class collaboration than for the development of an elite community. Sectoral organizations such as the Canadian Manufacturers Association played an important role in constructing and expressing the sectional interests of certain fractions of the business community, but were not suited for articulating the general interests of corporate capital. It was in the dense, centralized network of private clubs, and also on the capacious boards of the big five banks, that the elite found its collective identity as an exclusive 'confraternity of power'.

In the 1970s, as the 'golden era' of post-war boom and class compromise drew to a close, corporate elites created agencies of business activism—'councils', 'roundtables', 'institutes'—that brought leading capitalists and organic intellectuals together for explicitly political purposes. The Canadian case is no different from what Michael Useem (1984) found in his study of corporate business's proactive contribution to the rise of neoliberalism in Britain and the US. Indeed, the Anglo-Saxon world has 'led the way' in constructing and implementing the neoliberal paradigm. In Canada, business leaders recognized the need to legitimate a dramatic transition in the policy paradigm, from the Keynesian welfare state and associated state regulation of capital to the market-driven politics of neoliberalism. With the founding of the BCNI the corporate elite's basis for community began to shift from the sphere of leisure to that of political activism. As the elite mobilized for political action, a neoliberal policy bloc—a network of elite-level connections among half a dozen policy-planning organizations and Canada's leading corporations—was consolidated, and organic intellectuals such as Thomas D'Aquino and Michael Walker emerged as leading proponents of neoliberalism. In Chapter 8 we traced the consolidation of the bloc, noting how its diverse organizational ecology has made possible the development of a rich discursive field within which the vanguardist Fraser Institute has played a role complementary to that of the more mainstream groups. In this division of labour, business activism has mimicked social-movement activism. Typically, a movement develops as a collection of organizations, some practising a more flamboyant or extremist politics than others. The more extremist groups—and here the Fraser Institute comes to mind—attract the media coverage that puts political ideas into circulation, enabling more moderate groups to make similar claims from a more 'respectable' footing (Gamson and Wolfsfeld, 1993:122). The fact that by the 1990s the Fraser Institute was no longer being represented in the mainstream media as a marginal voice from the right confirms how effectively neoliberal business activism has managed to shift the terms of political discourse. The same holds, of course, beyond the arena of Canadian politics. Groups like the Trilateral Commission and World Economic Forum now constitute a transnational policy bloc that promotes neoliberalism both within nations and in the programs of supra-national agencies such as the WTO and IMF. The participation of Canadian business leaders in global policy groups has reinforced a certain worldly political solidarity within Canada's corporate elite, while contributing to the emergence of what Robinson and Harris (2000) call a transnational capitalist class (see Carroll and Carson, 2003).

In the field of corporate political party donations, the key transition was from a long-standing bipartisan corporate consensus to a more diverse pattern as of 1997. Although individual contributions came to make up a larger share of party financing, corporate capital's allocative power was not inconsiderable as it responded to the breakdown of the two-party system in the 1990s. Here the corporate elite's agency was necessarily less directive, more reactive, as the flow of funds favoured the incumbent party offering 'the greatest political and indeed economic return' for the contributor-investor (MacDermid, 2001: 19). Of course, the policy frameworks of governments and parties alike had, by the mid-1990s, been strongly conditioned by two decades of well-organized business activism. The CEO of the Business Council on National Issues, Thomas d'Aquino, summed matters up nicely:

> If you ask yourself, in which period since 1900 has Canada's business community had the most influence on public policy, I would say it was the last twenty years. Look at what we stand for and look at what all the governments, all the major parties . . . have done, and what they want to do. They have adopted the agendas we've been fighting for in the past two decades (quoted in Newman, 1998:151).

The new culture of business activism that d'Aquino personifies has extended to university governance boards. As the main sites for corporate head offices narrowed to just four major centres, the corporate elite's involvement in governing higher education actually *broadened* beyond the few traditional institutions responsible for socializing its sons and daughters. The corporate elite gained more of a national presence in university governance, and there was a complementary traffic in the other direction, as university CEOs joined the corporate elite. This networking has been about more than the accrual of status honour, which according to John Porter was the prime motive for such corporate elite involvement in the 1950s and 1960s. The corporate elite's interest in university governance reflects the new premium placed on both human capital and technological innovation in a period of knowledge-intensive capitalism in which local production is subordinated to the requirements of fierce global competition. A corporate presence in university governance and the dispensation of research funds redirects higher education and research to the needs of corporate capital, defining a trajectory along which they may be integrated as ancillaries to an extended form of (post)industrial accumulation.

These kinds of activism, whether in policy formation or in higher education and research helped to compensate for the loss of the integrative mechanisms formerly provided by the culture of leisure. As clubs lost their centrality, as bank boards slimmed to operationally optimal size, as the corporate-interlock network thinned, the corporate elite—and particularly its 'indigenous fraction', the directors of Canadian-controlled firms—traded traditional means of forging solidarity for activist work and the networks cutting across policy boards, university boards, the CFI, and so on. Indeed, these involvements did much more than compensate for the decline of the old boys' network. They significantly extended the reach of corporate power into civil society.

The Growing Importance of Organic Intellectuals

A more activist corporate elite relies extensively on an expanding corps of organic intellectuals. Our treatment of these advisors in Chapter 2 barely scratched the surface of the role they play. Because we chose to cast a narrow net, limiting our study to corporate directors with multiple affiliations to Canada's biggest companies, activists like Tom D'Aquino and Michael Walker do not even appear among the 400-odd members of our designated corporate elite. Nor do other advisors who sit on single corporate boards but may be heavily involved in other cultural and political domains. Yet from our limited data it is clear that intellectuals make up an important, and growing, element of corporate power. Even in the mid-1970s, beyond its core of functioning capitalists, the corporate elite included a varied assortment of advisors—retired corporate capitalists, lawyers, consultants, and so on—who lent their expertise to corporate business and in the process sometimes mediated between otherwise disjointed groups of associated capitalists. With the thinning of corporate interlocks—which also reduces the number of ties across enterprise groups—the contributions that such well-connected advisors make to elite integration become more critical. And as their numbers have grown, the division of labour has become more elaborate, offering directorates a greater range of specialized advisory and technical functions.

As higher education became increasingly integrated into the process of capital accumulation in the late twentieth century, academics—particularly university CEOs—made up an increasingly large fraction of the corporate elite. But the corporatization of universities has value beyond the economic domain. According to Antonio Gramsci (1971:10), one of the most important aspects of a dominant class's hegemony 'is its struggle to assimilate and to conquer "ideologically" the traditional intellectuals, but this assimilation and conquest is made quicker and more efficacious the more the group in question succeeds in simultaneously elaborating its own organic intellectuals.' In the modern west, the liberal-arts university has been the prime locale for 'traditional intellectuals' and for the pursuit of knowledge that is relatively independent of economic and political expediencies. As the priorities of universities become redefined—as a premium is put on commercial application of academic knowledge (Drakich, Grant, and Stewart, 2002:251–2)—Gramsci's imagery of assimilation and even ideological conquest seems apt.

Meanwhile, as outside directors have gained profile in the interlock network, the wisdom of retired capitalists (and retired politicians) has also been put to good commercial use on the boards of the largest corporations. In the 1990s, as their corporate affiliations cut across different enterprise groups, partly compensating for the decline of bank centrality, advisors such as former premiers Peter Lougheed and William Davis further integrated the elite. Many of the women recruited into the elite since the 1970s have also taken up advisory positions. If their widespread exclusion from high-level authority points up the resilience of male domination at the higher reaches, the ten-fold increase in the elite's female complement indicates a shift toward a culture of meritocracy.

DIVERSITY, MERITOCRACY, DEMOCRACY

With the advance of bourgeois society, aristocratic forms of closure have been rendered culturally archaic, and the years since the mid-1970s have witnessed an acceleration of that trend. We have characterized this period as one of *moral reform* within the corporate elite, of a transition in which ossified and oligarchic forms of closure gave way to greater diversity and openness. These democratizing developments went hand-in-hand with the development of business activism and the decline of the culture of leisure as the key basis for community. For instance, the elite came to engage with universities not selectively, as institutions of cultural closure, but generally, as the cultural factories producing technological invention and human capital. Catalyzed in the 1990s by financial scandals and the Dey task force, the new norms of corporate governance fit closely with a neoliberalized political environment of business self-regulation in an economic context of intensified global competition. They complement, at the highest level of capitalist authority, post-fordist transitions within the organization of work.[8]

In Chapter 2 we noted the cultural and structural implications of governance reforms. Driven by heightened international competition, financial deregulation, and the enhanced power of institutional investors, the reforms were meant to empower boards as independent, rational agencies. Open recruitment of directors would eliminate the dead weight of plutocratic cronyism and populate boards with dynamic, capable directors. Enhanced autonomy from management would help create conditions for effective discussion leading to rational strategic choices. Smaller, leaner boards following 'best practices' would further sharpen the competitive edge. The motives for reform were both pragmatic and moral. With improved governance Canadian business could restore its reputation on international financial markets (and reduce the cost of capital) and maximize 'shareholder value'. More broadly, the business community could shake off the taint of financial scams and scandals—from Confederation Life to Bre-X—and prove itself morally worthy of self-regulation. In an era of instability and crisis 'the ruling class feels itself under pressure to defend its social order as accountable and moral' (Gonick, 2002). Corporate governance reform has been on the front line of defence.

It would be difficult, however, to argue that these reforms had any demonstrable success in resolving capitalism's tendencies toward crisis and uneven development, and here the sorry case of Nortel provides a fine exemplar. Canada's best hope as a world-class transnational in the late 1990s, Nortel adopted the governance reforms of 1995 and proceeded to build shareholder value through a series of artful acquisitions that left it at the brink of bankruptcy when the dotcom-telecom bubble burst in 2000–1. Nortel's rise and fall demonstrates that aggressive pursuit of shareholder value is hardly a cure for capitalism's ills. In giving priority to the accumulation of paper assets and the narrow, short-term vision that focuses on quarterly financial results, the quest for shareholder value is part of the disease.

This is not to say that the new governance regime had no implications for elite organization. Among the most significant was a weakening of the interpersonal network that knits leading corporate directors into a business community. The life-world of the elite became less closely integrated via corporate cross-affiliations. The contraction of corporate directorates (especially bank boards) and the reduced number of directorships per director made the core of the network less of a densely woven old boys' network. A looser, less centralized network, with less representation of corporate insiders on directorates, may support more open communication among directors in the service of maximizing shareholder value. Yet even as the elite's social organization became less centralized, the banks retained a presence at the heart of the network, as most directors in the core of the interpersonal networks sat on the directorates of the big banks. In this way, the interpersonal network continued to consist of two tiers, structured around the hegemonic position of the big banks as 'general managers' of the 'social capital' (Marx, 1967:368, 402). With the weakening of the old boys' network came an increase in the numbers of women and non-British (but almost exclusively European) ethnicities at the upper echelons of corporate power. The corporate elite became less monocultural and less petrified, less a fixture of exclusionary corporate boards and private clubs and more diverse in composition, although its composition in terms of ethnicity and gender still contrasted sharply with that of the general population. By the late 1990s, the elite was regrouping around a Eurocentric multiculturalism that encompassed an emerging Québécois elite segment based primarily in Montreal. Although women remained almost a token minority consigned to the lower strata as advisors and vice-presidents, and almost entirely removed from continental and transnational interlocking, the elite's composition was becoming somewhat less patriarchal. In its social profile, educational credentials came to figure more importantly than exclusive club memberships, and advisors from academic and other fields of expert knowledge constituted a larger subgroup. In the world of private clubs a certain British hegemony persisted in muted form into the closing years of the century. Yet even more dramatically than the directorate network, the network of club memberships had contracted to a shadow of its earlier incarnation. With the decline of elite clubs as informal venues for community development came a further softening of stratification. Within the world of corporate business clubs lost their institutional centrality. These developments modernized the face of Canadian corporate capital, and provided for a more persuasive business leadership, more in tune with contemporary society.

CORPORATE POWER AND NEOLIBERAL DEMOCRACY

Multiculturalism, meritocracy, the reform of corporate governance—these are elements of an elite-level democratization that has curiously coincided with an increase in the importance of markets in people's lives resulting from both globalization and the implementation of a neoliberal policy paradigm. On the surface, this paradoxical medley seems consistent with the notion, championed by Francis Fukuyama (1992), of the 'end of history'. For Fukuyama, advanced liberal democracy—a system of free markets and liberal states towards which all human societies are evolving (1992:48)—is ideally suited to meet the human needs of self-esteem, reason, and desire. If this is true, by reinventing itself the business community is helping to usher in a higher form of democracy, within which individual liberty can coincide more exactly with economic efficiency and progress.

However, 'corporate democratization' has clear limits, some of which also constrain political initiatives that emanate from sources such as the liberal state. 'Multiculturalism', for instance, has been largely the project of the Canadian state. Prior to the 1960s, as John Porter knew, a modernist state discourse valorized the British group exclusively. But from the Report of the Royal Commission on Bilingualism and Biculturalism (1968) onward, the framework shifted to a new form of 'multicultural discipline.' Instead of trying to transform its Others through assimilation, the new discourse 'articulates them with regimes of rational-bureaucratic discipline' (Day, 2000:205). As ethnic difference is acknowledged and accommodated within larger social hierarchies that remain unchallenged, individual members of minority groups learn to accommodate themselves to the apparatuses of power. From the standpoint of ethnic and racialized minorities, this liberal multiculturalism is a co-optative tool for what Himani Bannerji (2000:27) calls the 'salad bowl corporate view of difference'. The modest growth of ethnic diversity within the Canadian corporate elite fits comfortably within this pattern. Lacking any political dimension, it does not question the history and legacy of colonization, but simply expresses the Eurocentric cosmopolitanism of an Atlantic ruling class.

By the same token, the structure of property ownership limits the scope for meritocracy. Mechanisms of closure associated with the old boys may have weakened after the 1970s, but the most powerful form of closure—ownership of capital—shows no sign of weakening, even if certain concentrated holdings now accumulate under the control of funds rather than families. In July 2002 the Toronto Stock Exchange reported a decrease in corporate share ownership among Canadians, reversing the upward trend that had been building since tracking began in the 1970s (Market Trend Canada, 2002). Ownership of most shares is extremely concentrated within a tiny segment of the population.[9] For the most part, corporate democratization is restricted to the principal actors within the business community itself, and extends only begrudgingly to minor shareholders, mainly as a by-product of the aggressive activism of institutional investors. At best, in broadening participation beyond the top tier of the capitalist class, corporate governance reform and related initiatives might give more sway to an incipient 'investor aristocracy'—the one-tenth of the population that holds stock portfolios of any size (Harmes, 1998:114).[10]

The stark limits to corporate democratization help to account for the hollowness of claims about the rise of 'popular capitalism' put forward by neoliberals in the 1980s. For the vast majority, excluded as they are from the business community, corporate democratization offers only a new regime of corporate power. However dramatic the shift *within the corporate elite* from oligarchy to democracy may have been (and in areas such as gender and ethnic representation the gains have been modest), it should not be mistaken for democratization of economic relations. Its political significance lies elsewhere. This transition seems integral to a new form of hegemony—a more porous elite social organization offering greater possibilities for the ruling class's reach into civil society, for civil society's reach into the ruling class, and thus for more effective business leadership. This is indeed what we have found in tracing the consolidation of a neoliberal policy bloc and the corporate elite's increasingly organic ties to higher education.

It is significant that the new regime of corporate power coincides with the turn to neoliberalism, a policy paradigm that has been identified with the hollowing-out of democracy. No longer so dependent on unique local configurations of labour and infrastructure, global capital enjoys enhanced allocative power (Bowles and Gintis, 1986). One result is 'a decline in the relative autonomy of the state from transient capitalist class will and ideology' (Ross and Trachte, 1990). What neoliberal democracy offers is a market-driven politics in which the mobility of investment shifts power from voters to capital, obliging states to serve the needs of global market forces.[11] This does not render states impotent, but it does constrain them to use power 'to advance the process of commodification' (Leys, 2001:3).[12] The market-driven politics that the corporate elite have spearheaded in Canada and elsewhere 'can lead to a remarkably rapid erosion of democratically-determined collective values and institutions' (Leys, 2001:4).

If neoliberal politics are market-driven, the transnational 'market forces' that drive them must be understood as expressions of class power. The enormous concentrations of capital that dominate the world market ensure that the shift in control over public affairs from citizens to markets affords at best '"a democracy of the few", of the rich and powerful' (Evans, McBride, and Shields, 2000:81). Petras and Veltmeyer (2001:70) exaggerate only slightly when they call these politics a 'new authoritarianism', distinct from the old-style militarism that denied electoral competition and individual liberty to those on the margins of world capitalism. The new authoritarianism, evident at both centre and periphery, combines formal features of liberal democracy with market-driven decision-making within elite transnational structures shielded from popular electorates. This helps explain a paradox in the 2002 UN Human Development Report, which bore the title 'Deepening democracy in a fragmented world'. Observing that since the 1980s a 'global shift from authoritarian to democratic regimes' has brought the world 'more democratic countries and more political participation than ever' (UN Development Programme, 2002:15, 14), the Report noted that 'people around the world seem to have lost confidence in the effectiveness of their governments—and often seem to be losing faith in democracy' (2002:63).[13] As welfare states and old-style authoritarian regimes give way to neoliberal democracy, the institutional trappings of democracy are put into place everywhere, yet popular electorates are disenfranchised. Strategic decisions are made elsewhere, 'in centralized headquarters by non-elected officials who rule by decree and without popular representation, deliberation or consultation' (Petras and Veltmeyer, 2001:158).

Liberal democracy, Ellen Wood reminds us, arose within modern capitalism in a long process whereby 'certain *political* powers were gradually transformed into *economic* powers and transferred to a separate sphere' as national states with 'an unprecedented *public* character' were forged (1995:36, 40). Standing apart from the economy, the state could 'belong to everyone' even as the class power of capital, mediated by markets and the pressures of competition, organized economic life (1995:40–1). In this way, 'democracy could be confined to a formally separate "political" sphere while the "economy" followed rules of its own' (1995:203). With recent globalization—with the transnationalization of finance capital and the elaboration of global elite governance structures—the sphere for liberal-democratic politics recedes. The transitions to neoliberal democracy that have accompanied recent globalization may carry quite different implications from those imagined by Fukuyama. 'If we are confronting the "end of History", it may not be in the sense that liberal democracy has triumphed but rather in the sense that it has very nearly reached its limits' (Wood, 1995:235).

Democratization in a substantive sense will have to await more coherent and sustained initiatives 'from below' that will champion human development, ecological well-being, and the expansion of public spheres beyond the narrow, elitist confines of neoliberal democracy. Whether the anti-corporate globalization protests that began to build in the mid-1990s and attained spectacular visibility in the 1999 'Battle in Seattle' can be translated into a cumulative movement for global democracy remains to be seen.[14] Meanwhile, Canada's corporate elite, both in its pursuit of profit and in its extensive cultural and political activism, continues to exert a dominant influence on the lives of those within its ambit. In a globalizing world, part of that ambit extends beyond state-defined boundaries. At several points in this study I have noted that the 'national identity' of corporate capital becomes ambiguous as capitalist practices become transnational. Against claims that globalization betokens a 'hollowing out of corporate Canada' (Arthurs 2000), the present analysis confirms the continued existence of a robust nationally organized business community. Yet that community, its business strategies, and its political vision are embedded within institutional structures of an increasingly global character. As I suggested in Chapter 7, the leading directors of Canadian corporations participate in a system of *collective imperialism* in which decisions are made at the top of the centre, and consequences are endured at the bottom of both centre and periphery.

The implications of corporate power in the international field are clear enough. Statistics on global corporate concentration cited at the beginning of this chapter earlier are reflected in massive and widening disparities in wealth and income worldwide. In 1960 the 20 per cent of the world's people in the richest countries had 30 times the income of the poorest 20 per cent. By 1997 the former's income was 74 times the latter's (Lee, 2002).[15] World inequality did not increase much from the mid-1960s to the early 1980s, but began to rise sharply as neoliberal policies were imposed worldwide, often at the insistence of the IMF and World Bank.[16] Anthropologist Wade Davis, who characterizes global disparities and dislocations as a 'ticking bomb', points out that behind the statistics are human lives of destitution and oppression. 'In reality, development for the vast majority of the peoples of the world has been a process in which the individual is torn from his past and propelled into an uncertain future only to secure a place on the bottom rung of an economic ladder that goes nowhere' (Davis, 2002).

Ultimately, in a globalizing world corporate power grows at the expense of workers, communities, and the ecosystem itself.[17] Recent transitions in the Canadian corporate elite give us a window—a view from the top—on a malleable structure of power that is also a contested terrain. In coming years, as the Canadian corporate elite's dominion becomes even more globalized and as other globalizing elites extend their reach further into Canada, we can expect its political vision to blend the 'national interest' with 'regional' North American and 'global' interests. It was not by chance that late in 2001 the Business Council on National Issues relaunched itself as the Canadian Council of Chief Executives, voicing a new commitment 'to the shaping of sound public policy in Canada, North America and the world'.[18] To contest corporate power, its critics in Canada will need to move well beyond the old preoccupation with 'the survival capacities of the Canadian state' (Clarkson, 2002: 420). The stakes are higher than ever before, and the struggle epochal. The ticking bomb can be defused only by transfiguring corporate power into economic democracy.

Appendix 1:
Internet Resources

The Internet is a crucial tool for researching large corporations, corporate power structures, and corporate-led political initiatives. In addition, it has become increasingly important as an organizing tool for groups and movements critical of corporate power and its implications for human and ecological well being. The websites listed below provide resources for both researching and resisting corporate power.

RESOURCES FOR RESEARCHING CORPORATIONS

'Citizen Portal on Brands and Corporations'. An extensive database on large corporations, their products, directors and executives, environmental policies, etc.
http://www.transnationale.org/anglais/

'Community Guide to Researching Corporations' (Aurora Institute). Lists many useful print and Internet sources, particularly for researching corporations based in Canada.
http://www.aurora.ca/publish/research.pdf

'DIY Guide: How to Research Companies' (Corporate Watch). A detailed guide for do-it-yourself investigative research on particular corporations. Very helpful.
http://www.corporatewatch.org.uk/publications/diy_research_2002.htm

'Internet Guide to Power Structure Research', by Val Burris (University of Oregon). A key resource for getting starting in social-network analysis of corporate power structures. Mainly American sources facilitate research into the backgrounds and social connections of individual members of the corporate elite, the internal power structure of major corporations and the political activities in which they are engaged, the role of foundations, think-tanks, and business associations in creating public policy, etc.
http://darkwing.uoregon.edu/~vburris/whorules/

'They Rule'. A website that allows you to create maps of the interlocking directories of the top 100 companies in the US in 2001. An updated version is planned.
http://www.Theyrule.net

In addition, various university libraries maintain websites that provide gateways to helpful resources on corporations in Canada and elsewhere. See, for instance, the company research site of York University's library:
http://www.library.yorku.ca/BG/publications/companyresearch.htm

ACTIVIST WEBSITES

'Adbusters'. A culture-jamming site that includes a jammer's gallery and various spoof advertisements that satirize corporate marketing campaigns.
http://www.adbusters.org/magazine/

'Friends of the Earth'. Website of a major international ecological group, presenting extensive analyses of the conflicts between corporate power and environmental and social well being. See especially the report *Clashes with Corporate Giants*, and the 'corporates campaign' page.
http://www.foei.org/

'Global Exchange'. Features material on transnational corporations, economic democratization, and anti-sweatshop campaigns. Highly recommended.
http://www.globalexchange.org/economy/

'McSpotlight'. A site maintained by The McInformation Network, an independent group of volunteers working from 22 countries on four continents. The group's mandate is to compile and disseminate factual, accurate, up-to-date information—and to encourage debate—about 'the workings, policies and practices of the McDonald's Corporation and all they stand for'. The site also features opposition to McDonald's and other transnational companies.
http://www.mcspotlight.org/

'Open Democracy'. Thoughtful discussion and analysis of issues surrounding the prospects for transition from global corporate rule to substantive democracy.
http://www.opendemocracy.net/

'Peoples' Global Action'. A network for spreading information and coordinating actions between grassroots movements around the world. PGA grew out of the international Zapatista gatherings in 1996 and 1997.
http://www.agp.org/

'Program on Corporations, Law and Democracy (POCLAD)'. A website devoted to 'instigating democratic conversations and actions that contest the authority of corporations to govern'. Contains various background analyses, focused mainly on the United States.
http://www.poclad.org/

'World Social Forum'. The democratic alternative to the World Economic Forum, WSF meets yearly, concurrently with the WEF, to debate 'alternative means to building a globalization in solidarity, which respects universal human rights and those of all men and women of all nations and the environment, and is grounded in democratic international systems and institutions at the service of social justice, equality and the sovereignty of peoples'.
http://www.forumsocialmundial.org.br/home.asp

'World Trade Organization (Yes Men)'. Culture-jamming site dedicated to satirizing the work of the World Trade Organization, described as 'the only international clique dealing with the universal rules of profit between lawmaking units. Its main function is to ensure that profit flows as smoothly, predictably and freely as possible.'
http://www.gatt.org/

ANTI-SWEATSHOP WEBSITES

The following sites focus on coordinated transnational campaigns to expose and resist corporate policies that prey upon especially vulnerable workers.

'Behind the Label'
http://www.behindthelabel.org/

'Maquila Solidarity Network'
http://www.maquilasolidarity.org/

'Nikewatch'
http://www.caa.org.au/campaigns/nike/index.html

'Sweatshop Watch'
http://sweatshopwatch.org/ (has excellent links)

CORPORATE WATCHDOG WEBSITES

The following sites present extensive information, often in article or case-study form, on specific corporations and corporate-led political initiatives.

'Corporate Europe Observatory'
http://www.corporateeurope.org/

'Corporate Watch'
http://www.corporatewatch.org.uk/

'Multinational Monitor'
http://multinationalmonitor.org/

Appendix 2:
A Note on Method

The research on which this book is based required extensive collection and processing of data on both large corporations themselves and their directors (including the latter's social-status characteristics). This appendix details the procedures used to build the database and analyze the data.[1]

IDENTIFYING THE LARGEST CORPORATIONS

The first step was to identify, for year end 1976 and year end 1996, the largest corporations in a given location. For the most part, this meant consulting lists of the largest corporations based in Canada, published by the *Globe and Mail Report on Business*, the *Financial Post*, and *Canadian Business*. From these lists the largest 50 financial institutions (ranked by assets) and the largest 200 non-financial operating companies (ranked by revenue) were selected. This method of determining the Top 250 matches the approach taken in the major comparative studies of corporate networks to date (Stokman et al., 1985; Windolf, 2002). Firms controlled by the state were included as long as they were bona fide commercial ventures and not simply government departments. Corporations owned entirely by a single shareholder were also included, provided the owner was not a corporation already in the sample. Thus wholly owned Canadian subsidiaries of foreign-based companies were included in the Canadian Top 250, as were corporations wholly owned by individuals. To the Top 250 we added any major investment companies—companies with no substantive operations, whose assets consist of corporate shares in other companies, including blocks of shares large enough to confer strategic control over one or more Top 250 company. This expanded the Canadian samples to 257 in 1976 and 258 in 1996. The sample employed in Chapter 5's analysis of the shift westward involves a 'Top 100' subset of these samples, and an analogous sample for year end 1946 (see the account of method in Chapter 5).

The sample of American-based corporations, analyzed in Chapter 6, was assembled using the same criteria used for the Canadian Top 250 and analogous lists from the American business press (primarily the *Fortune 500* but also lists published in *Business Week* and *Forbes*). Because investment companies have played less of a role in the strategic control of American corporations, only two investment companies in 1976 and four investment companies in 1996 were added to the basic Top 250 to complete the American samples. The global sample of the world's largest 350 corporations, analyzed in Chapter 7, was assembled through a somewhat more complex selection procedure that is detailed in Carroll and Carson (2003). Briefly, the global sample includes 100 large financial institutions (ranked by assets denominated in $US) and 250 large non-financial corporations (ranked by revenue denominated in $US); however, to ensure representation of corporations based on the semi-periphery of world capitalism, we defined regional strata and relaxed the selection criteria for certain strata.

CORPORATION-LEVEL DATA

For all corporations in the study, we coded the city and country in which the firm was domiciled in a given year as well as its assets, revenue, and industry (using the Standard Industrial Classification). Sources for these data included the annual ranked lists, manuals such as the *Financial Post Survey of Industrials*, and official corporate websites. For the Canadian Top 250 several additional variables were coded:

Country of control. The criteria used to assess the control of corporations were the same ones used in studies such as Scott's (1997). A firm was considered Canadian-controlled if the largest bloc of its voting shares was owned by Canadians, or if no identified interest held more than 10 per cent of voting shares. By these criteria, it is possible for a company to be Canadian-controlled even if a majority of its shares are dispersed among many foreign shareholders. It is also possible for a company whose shares are mostly held in Canada to be foreign-controlled, if a large block of shares is held abroad. In practice, these determinations are not difficult to make on the basis of reports in the business press and the Statistics Canada's *Intercorporate Ownership* (published occasionally since the 1960s). Data sources for determining a firm's country of control also included the *Financial Post's Survey of Industrials* (various years) and the lists of Canada's largest corporations, published annually by the *Financial Post*, *Canadian Business*, and the *Globe and Mail Report on Business Magazine*. Other aspects of corporate control, as presented in Chapter 3, were determined using these sources, supplemented with data from the search engine Lexis/Nexus.

Transnational status. As discussed in Chapter 4, top Canadian companies were categorized according to their status as transnational corporations. The source data were found in *Who Owns Whom, North American Edition* (New York: Dun & Bradstreet, 1977–88 and 1997), which lists all (majority-owned) subsidiaries and parents of corporations domiciled in Canada or the US, and indicates the national domicile of each subsidiary and parent firm.

Donations to federal political parties. The analysis in Table 8.7 of the leading 20 corporate donors to federal parties in 1979 and 1997 is based on data from Elections Canada: *Registered Party Fiscal Period Returns*. For recent years, these data can be downloaded from the Elections Canada website (http://www.elections.ca/).

High-tech status. As described in Chapter 9 (note 12), for 1996 two available listings of major corporations were consulted in order to identify 29 Canadian companies as particularly sophisticated in their use of technology.

Director-Level Data

For each year under investigation, the names and executive and board statuses of all members of the boards of directors of all sample corporations were recorded from reference sources including *Standard and Poor's Register of Corporations, Directors and Executives* (CD-ROM version, 1997), the *Financial Post Directory of Directors* (1977 and 1997 editions), the *Financial Post Survey of Industrials, Moody's International Manual, Moody's Industrials*, and corporate annual reports (both hard-copy and online). These data were entered into a file, with each name coded according to the format: 'lastname.firstname.middlename'. The file was sorted alphabetically, and sets of names that appeared to refer to the same person were verified using reference sources such as the *Financial Post Directory of Directors*, to confirm the corporate affiliations of each director. The Canadian corporate elite was operationalized as the set of directors with two or more Top 250 corporate directorships in a given year; an analogous criterion was used in defining the American corporate elite, analyzed in Chapter 6.

For each individual designated a member of the Canadian corporate elite, an extensive biographical search was conducted to establish the following social characteristics:

Gender. Where the first name did not provide an unambiguous indication, *Who's Who* sources (*Who's Who in Canada, Canadian Who's Who*, and *Who's Who in Canadian Business*) were consulted for clarification.

Ethnic background. The surname of each member of the Canadian corporate elite was checked against listings in various dictionaries of surnames.[2] In some dictionaries, names from the British Isles were traced back to earlier continental roots, but our categorization did not follow that lineage. Thus, for instance, a name found in an 'Irish' dictionary was considered to be an Irish name. As mentioned in note 4 of Chapter 2, our methodology provides only a crude indication of ethnic background.

Elite club membership. On the basis of listings in *Who's Who* sources, members of the Canadian corporate elite were categorized as to (1) the total number of club memberships they listed and (2) their membership status vis-à-vis each of the seven key clubs mentioned in Chapter 2 (namely the Toronto, York, National, St James, Mt Royal, Rideau, and Vancouver clubs).

Education, age, and principal occupation. These characteristics were also determined from *Who's Who* sources. The first-mentioned occupation in the biographical profile was taken as indicative of principal occupation, and the associated corporation (or other organization) was taken to be the primary organizational affiliation. However, occupancy of an executive position[3] in a Top 250 corporation was given precedence over the biographical sources. Thus an individual described as a corporate lawyer, who was actually president of a major corporation, was considered to be a corporate executive, primarily affiliated with that company.

Major shareholders in dominant corporations were identified on the basis of the sources used to categorize corporations by their country, mode, and type of control, which often identify the leading shareholder, supplemented by sources such as Niosi's (1978) listing for dominant shareholders as of 1976 and the list of the wealthiest Canadians published annually in the *Financial Post Magazine*.

Corporate directors who were not members of the Canadian corporate elite but who carried one or more continental interlocks (directing both a Top Canadian and Top American corporation) also received biographical treatment, using both Canadian and American *Who's Who* sources to determine principal occupation and organizational (and thus national) affiliation (as in Table 6.4). For the 1996 Canadian elite, affiliations with transnational policy boards were determined on the basis of complete listings that were either published in the annual report or made available by the organizations. The same types of sources were used to document the participation of the Canadian corporate elite on Canadian policy boards in 1976 and 1996. University calendars for the 1977–8 academic year served to establish the participation of the elite on university governance boards, circa year end 1976. For 1996 these affiliations were detected from listings in *Who's Who* sources. The difference in data sources very likely means that we have underestimated the extent of corporate–university governance ties in 1996. Finally, the participation of corporate-elite members in directing third-party higher-education and research organizations was documented from annual reports and official websites.

DATA ANALYSIS

Basic statistical analyses of data matrices depicting individual directors, individual corporations, and directors' corporate affiliations were conducted using the Statistical Package for the Social Sciences, version 10. Network analyses were carried out in stages. In the first stage the matrix of corporate attributes was input as point-level data and the matrix of directors' corporate affiliations was input as line data to GRADAP, the Graph Definition and Analysis Package, version 2.0 (Sprenger and Stokman, 1989). Although a second-generation network analysis program,[4] GRADAP remains unrivalled for its analytical power in dissecting bipartite directed graphs such as corporate networks—in large part because such analyses were designed into the program at its inception. Most of the sociograms featured in Chapters 2–9 were constructed by exporting sub-networks from GRADAP, importing them into UCINET (version 5, within which further structural analyses were conducted) and subsequently exporting the relevant data to KRACKPLOT (version 3), a network drawing program.[5] Certain sociograms (e.g., Figures 2.3 and 4.1) were drawn using Flow Charting PDQ Lite (version 1.1d, Keith Patton and William Patton, Sr., 1996). For explanations of the network-analytic terminology employed in Chapters 2–9, see C.J.A. Spenger and F.N. Stokman (1989) and Scott (1991, 2002).

Appendix 3:
Corporate Names and Abbreviations

The following table lists Canadian corporations that were in the Top 250 for 1976 or 1996 and that are shown in one or more of the sociograms in Chapters 3-9. The listing matches the most recent version of each corporation's name with the abbreviated version of the name used in the sociograms in Chapters 3-9. In all, 189 Canadian corporations are shown in the various sociograms in this book.

ABBREVIATION	NAME	IN TOP 250
ABITIBI	Abitibi-Price Inc.	1976/1996
ABNBANK	ABN AMRO Bank of Canada	1976
AGRA	AGRA Inc.	1976/1996
AGRIUM	Agrium Inc.	1976
AIRCDA	Air Canada	1976/1996
ALCAN	Alcan Aluminum Ltd	1976/1996
ALENRGY	Alberta Energy Co Ltd	1976
ALGOMA	Algoma Steel Inc.	1976/1996
AMOCO	Amoco Canada Petroleum Co. Ltd	1976/1996
ARGUS	Argus Corp.	1996
ATCO	ATCO Ltd	1976/1996
AVENOR	Avenor Inc	1976
BARRICK	Barrick Gold Corp.	1976
BAY	Hudson's Bay Company	1976/1996
BCE	BCE Inc. (formerly Bell Canada)	1976/1996
BCEMOBIL	BCE Mobile Communications Inc.	1976
BCGAS	BC Gas Inc.	1976
BCSUGAR	BC Sugar Refinery Ltd	1976
BCTEL	BC TELECOM Inc.	1976/1996
BNKCANADA	Bank of Canada	1976/1996
BNKMONT	Bank of Montreal	1976/1996
BNKNS	Bank of Nova Scotia	1976/1996
BNKTOKYO	Bank of Tokyo-Mitsubishi (Canada)	1976
BOMBARDR	Bombardier Inc.	1976/1996

Appendix 3: Corporate Names and Abbreviations 227

ABBREVIATION	NAME	IN TOP 250
BRASCAN	Brascan Ltd	1976/1996
BROOKFIELD	Brookfield Properties Corp	1976
BURNS	Burns Foods Ltd	1996
CADFAIR	Cadillac Fairview Corporation	1996
CAE	CAE Inc.	1976/1996
CAISSE	Caisse de depot et placement du Quebec	1976/1996
CANAIRLNS	Canadian Airlines Corp.	1976
CANCEMENT	Lafarge Canada Inc.	1976/1996
CANCORPMAN	Canadian Corporate Management Company Ltd	1996
CANFOR	Canfor Corp.	1976
CANINDUS	ICI Canada Inc.	1976/1996
CANPERMORT	Canada Permanent Mortgage Corp.	1996
CANRON	Ivaco Inc (formerly Canron)	1976/1996
CANTIRE	Canadian Tire Corp Ltd	1976/1996
CANUTIL	Canadian Utilities Ltd	1976/1996
CARGILL	Cargill Ltd	1976
CASCADE	Cascades Inc.	1976
CDALIFE	Canada Life Assurance Co.	1976/1996
CDTFONC	Credit Foncier Franco-Canadien	1996
CELANESE	Celanese Canada Ltd	1996
CHRYSLR	Chrysler Canada Ltd	1976/1996
CIBC	Canadian Imperial Bank of Commerce	1976/1996
CIP	Canadian International Paper Company	1996
CNR	Canadian National Railway Co.	1976/1996
CO-STEEL	Co-Steel Inc.	1976
COKE	Coca-Cola Beverages Ltd.	1976
COMINCO	Cominco Ltd	1976/1996
CP	Canadian Pacific Ltd	1976/1996
CRNLIFE	Crown Life Insurance Co.	1976/1996
CTFIN	CT Financial Services Inc (formerly Canada Trust)	1976/1996
DOFASCO	Dofasco Inc.	1976/1996
DOMINIONBRIDGE	Dominion Bridge Company Ltd	1996
DOMINIONST	Dominion Stores Ltd	1996
DOMTAR	Domtar Inc.	1976/1996
DOMTEXT	Dominion Textile Inc.	1976/1996
DUPONT	DuPont Canada Inc.	1976/1996
E-LFIN	E-L Financial Corp Ltd	1976/1996
EDPER	Edper Group Ltd	1976
EMPIRE	Empire Co Ltd	1976
EXPORT.DEVELT	Export Development Corp.	1976/1996
FALCONBR	Falconbridge Ltd	1976/1996
FINNING	Finning Ltd	1976/1996
FLETCH	Fletcher Challenge Canada Ltd (formerly BC Forest Products)	1976/1996

Appendix 3: Corporate Names and Abbreviations

ABBREVIATION	NAME	IN TOP 250
FORD	Ford Motor Co of Canada Ltd	1976/1996
FRASER	Fraser Companies	1996
GAZ.METRO	Gaz Metropolitain & Co., Limited Partnership	1976
GE	General Electric Canada Inc.	1976/1996
GENSTAR	Genstar Ltd	1996
GM	General Motors of Canada Ltd	1976/1996
GULF	Gulf Canada Resources Ltd	1976/1996
GWLIFE	Great-West Lifeco	1976/1996
HBOILGAS	Hudson's Bay Oil & Gas Company Ltd	1996
HKBANK	Hongkong Bank of Canada	1976
HOLLINGER	Hollinger Inc.	1976
HYDRO.QUE	Hydro-Quebec	1976/1996
IAC	IAC Limited	1996
IBM	IBM Canada Ltd	1976/1996
IFP	International Forest Products Ltd	1976
IMASCO	Imasco Ltd	1976/1996
IMPLIFE	Imperial Life Assurance Co. of Canada	1996
IMPLOIL	Imperial Oil Ltd	1976/1996
INCO	Inco Ltd	1976/1996
IND-ALL	Industrial-Alliance Life Insurance Co.	1976
INGRAND	Canadian Ingersoll-Rand Company Ltd	1996
INMET	Inmet Mining Corp.	1976
INVSTGRP	Investors Group	1996
IPL	IPL Energy Inc.	1976/1996
IPSCO	IPSCO Inc.	1976/1996
IRONORE	Iron Ore Company of Canada	1996
ITOCHU	Itochu Canada Ltd	1976
LABATT	John Labatt Ltd	1996
LAIDLAW	Laidlaw Inc.	1976
LAURENTIDE	Laurentide Financial Corporation Ltd	1996
LONDLIFE	London Insurance Group Inc (formerly London Life)	1976/1996
MACBLO	MacMillan Bloedel Ltd	1976/1996
MCDONALDS	McDonald's Restaurants of Canada Ltd	1976
MACKENZIE	Mackenzie Financial Corporation	1976
MAGNA	Magna International Inc.	1976
MANULIFE	Manulife Financial	1976/1996
MAPLEAF	Maple Leaf Foods Inc.	1976/1996
MARLIFE	Maritime Life Assurance Co.	1976
MASSEY	Massey-Ferguson Ltd	1996
MCCAIN	McCain Foods Ltd	1976
MDS	MDS Inc.	1976
MERCBNK	Mercantile Bank of Canada	1996
METHNEX	Methanex Corp.	1976
MIDWALN	Midland Walwyn Inc.	1976

Appendix 3: Corporate Names and Abbreviations 229

ABBREVIATION	NAME	IN TOP 250
MITSUBS	Mitsubishi Canada Ltd	1976
MITSUI	Mitsui & Co (Canada) Ltd	1976/1996
MLOEB	M. Loeb Ltd	1996
MOLSON	Molson Cos Ltd	1976/1996
MONTREALSAVINGS	Laurentian Bank of Canada (formerly Montreal City & District Savings)	1976/1996
MONTRST	Montreal Trust	1996
MOORE	Moore Corp Ltd	1976/1996
MULIFE	Mutual Life	1976/1996
NALIFE	North American Life Assurance Co.	1996
NATBNK	National Bank of Canada (formerly Banque canadienne nationale)	1976/1996
NATIONALDRUG	National Drug & Chemical Company of Canada Ltd	1996
NATTRST	National Trustco Inc.	1976/1996
NBPOWER	New Brunswick Power Corp.	1976
NORANDA	Noranda Inc.	1976/1996
NORCEN	Norcen Energy Resources Ltd	1976/1996
NORFRST	Noranda Forest Inc.	1976
NORTEL	Northern Telecom Ltd	1976/1996
NORTHWOOD	Northwood Forest Industries Ltd	1976
NOVA	NOVA Corp.	1976/1996
ONEX	Onex Corp.	1976
ONHYDRO	Ontario Hydro	1976/1996
PANCAN	PanCanadian Petroleum Ltd	1976
PATTISON	Jim Pattison Group	1976/1996
PETROCAN	Petro-Canada	1976
POWER	Power Corp. of Canada	1976/1996
POWERFIN	Power Financial Corp.	1976
PRATTWHIT	Pratt & Whitney Canada Inc.	1976/1996
PREMDOR	Premdor Inc.	1976
PRENOR	Prenor Group Ltd	1996
PRICECO	Price Company Ltd	1996
PROVIGO	Provigo Inc.	1976/1996
QUEBECR	Quebecor Inc.	1976
REPAP	Repap Enterprises Inc.	1976
RIOALGM	Rio Algom Ltd	1976/1996
ROGERSCAN	Rogers Cantel Mobile Communications Inc.	1976
ROGERSCOM	Rogers Communications Inc.	1976
ROYALBNK	Royal Bank of Canada	1976/1996
ROYALTRST	Royal Trust Company	1996
ROYLINS	Royal Insurance Co. of Canada	1976
ROYNAT	RoyNat Ltd	1996
RPURINA	Ralston Purina of Canada Ltd	1996
RUSSEL	Russel Metals Inc.	1976

ABBREVIATION	NAME	IN TOP 250
SEAGRAM	Seagram Co Ltd	1976/1996
SEARS	Sears Canada Inc. (formerly Simpson-Sears)	1976/1996
SEMITECH	Semi-Tech Corp.	1976
SHELL	Shell Canada Ltd	1976/1996
SIMPSONS	Simpsons Ltd	1996
SLOCAN	Slocan Group	1976
SNC-LAV	SNC-Lavalin Group Inc.	1976
SOUTHAM	Southam Inc.	1976/1996
STELCO	Stelco Inc.	1976/1996
STONE	Stone-Consolidated Corp. (formerly Consolidated-Bathurst)	1976/1996
SUNCOR	Suncor Inc.	1976/1996
SUNLIFE	Sun Life Assurance Co. of Canada	1976/1996
TALISMAN	Talisman Energy Inc.	1976
TCPIPELN	TransCanada Pipelines Ltd	1976/1996
TDBANK	Toronto-Dominion Bank	1976/1996
TECK	Teck Corporation	1976
TELEGLOBE	Teleglobe Inc.	1976
TELUS	TELUS Corp.	1976/1996
TEMBEC	Tembec Inc.	1976
TEXACO	Texaco Canada Ltd.	1996
TEXTRON	Textron Canada Ltd	1976
THOMSON	Thomson Corp.	1976/1996
TORSTAR	Torstar Corp.	1976/1996
TOYOTA	Toyota Canada Inc.	1976
TRANSAL	TransAlta Corp.	1976/1996
TRILON	Trilon Financial Corp.	1976
TRIMARK	Trimark Investment Management	1976
UNDOMIN	United Dominion Industries Ltd	1976
UNIONGAS	Union Gas Ltd	1996
WESTBURNE	Westburne Inc.	1976/1996
WESTINGHS	Westinghouse Canada Ltd	1996
WESTON	George Weston Ltd	1976/1996
WEYERH	Weyerhaeuser Canada Ltd	1976
WOOLWORTH	F.W. Woolworth Company Ltd	1996
WTCOASTEN	Westcoast Energy Inc.	1976/1996
XEROX	Xerox Canada Inc.	1976/1996

Notes

CHAPTER 1

1. The complex circuitry through which the economic surplus is appropriated, circulated, and consumed as surplus value is examined closely in the three volumes of *Capital* (Marx, 1967). For a more contemporary treatment see Harvey (1982).
2. For an especially clear exposition of Marx's theory of surplus value, as applied to 1970s American capitalism, see O'Connor (1974). Note that the tendency for capitalists to reinvest profits in expanded means of production is not without contradictions, issuing both from the increasing capital-intensity of production (which dampens the overall profit rate) and from the limitations that class exploitation places on the effective demand for the commodities that enlarged productions systems yield (Andrews, 2000).
3. Clement and Myles (1994:16–19) estimate, on the basis of survey data, that the capitalist-executive class made up 6.2 per cent of the Canadian population in the early 1980s.
4. As Gramsci put it, 'every social group, coming into existence on the original terrain of an essential economic function in the world of economic production, creates together with itself, organically, one or more strata of intellectuals which give it homogeneity and an awareness of its own function not only in the economic but in the social and political fields. The capitalist entrepreneur creates alongside himself the industrial technician, the specialist in political economy, the organisers of a new culture, of a new legal system, etc.' (1971:5).
5. Some leading Canadian studies include Ornstein's (1984) research on broken and reconstituted interlocks, which established that the more resilient ties are those involving executives and/or multiple shared directors, conditions which signal a close coordination of business strategies; Richardson's (1987) study of directorship interlocks and corporate profitability, which found a tendency for executives of relatively profitable non-financial companies to join the boards of financial institutions and for executives of financial institutions to join the boards of relatively underperforming non-financial companies; and Berkowitz and Fitzgerald's (1995) study of enterprise groups in the Canadian economy, which for 1987 identified 298 enterprises that through intercorporate ownership and interlocking directorates controlled 5396 legally distinct companies—a nearly five-fold reduction in the number of economic decision-making units since 1972.
6. Based on interviews with American and British directors, Useem developed the thesis that many corporate interlocks serve a 'scanning' function. In a complex and changing environment, corporate management is 'dependent on a continuous scanning or monitoring of new developments in government policies, labor relations, markets, technol-

ogy, and business practices ranging from stock option plans to charitable contribution schemes' (Useem, 1982: 209).

7. Examples of the former include Brian Mulroney (prime minister of Canada from 1984 to 1993) and Paul Martin (federal Finance minister for much of the 1990s). Mulroney, a corporate lawyer by background, was president of the Iron Ore Company of Canada before entering politics and after serving two terms at the helm of the Canadian ship of state became a director of corporations based in Canada, the US, and Europe. Martin was president of Canada Steamship Lines and a director of other firms before entering government. The recent traffic from elite positions in government to the corporate boardrooms includes John N. Turner, who shifted from government to the boardrooms in the 1970s, then re-entered government and parliament, only to return to corporate business after the Liberal electoral defeat of 1988. Prominent members of the Mulroney cabinet who went on to direct multiple large Canadian corporations include Michael Wilson, Barbara McDougall, and Don Mazankowski. In 1998, Peter Lougheed, former premier of Alberta was a director of 12 corporations. William Davis and David Peterson, former Conservative and Liberal premiers of Ontario directed 15 and 11 corporations, respectively. Frank McKenna, premier of Nova Scotia until the fall of 1997, directed six (Partridge, 1998).

8. Media studies have provided many insights on the role of mass media in accomplishing hegemony, a crucial issue not examined here. See Gitlin (1980); Curran and Gurevitch (2000).

9. With this formulation we follow Gramsci, who did not view the bourgeoisie and its organic intellectuals as mutually exclusive categories but recognized a considerable confluence: 'If not all entrepreneurs, at least an *elite* amongst them must have the capacity to be an organizer of society in general, including all its complex organism of services, right up to the state organism, because of the need to create the conditions most favourable to the expansion of their own class; or at least they must possess the capacity to choose the deputies (specialised employees) to which to entrust this activity . . .' (Gramsci, 1971:5–6).

10. The political dimension of recent globalization is effectively conveyed in Amoore and Dodgson's (1997) concept of neoliberal globalization, which has four defining characteristics: (1) the protection of the interests of capital and expansion of accumulation; (2) the tendency towards homogenization and harmonization of state policies and even state forms in the direction of protecting capital and expanding accumulation; (3) the elaboration of a layer of transnationalized institutional authority above the states, with the aim of penetrating states and re-articulating them to global capital accumulation; and (4) the exclusion of dissident social forces from the arena of policy formation, thereby insulating the neoliberal state forms against the societies over which they preside.

11. However, the state cannot simply take up the standpoint of global capital, but must also address the needs and aspirations of the citizenry, lest its hegemony be seriously compromised. This is why the full-blooded neoliberal policies advocated by groups such as the Fraser Institute have been typically watered down in Canadian public policy, as material and symbolic concessions to 'the people' are integrated into state budgets and programs.

12. In using network analysis to map these terrains, this book takes an 'architectonic' approach to corporate power. Our study highlights *structures* rather than the *practices* enabled by those structures. Ideally, one would prefer a fully triangulated methodology, combining structural analysis with ethnographies of corporate boards in action (as in Hill, 1995; Pettigrew and McNulty, 1995) and in-depth interviews with leading corporate capitalists (as in Useem, 1984; Sklair, 2001). All research has its limitations. What a mapping of the corporate network contributes is a systematic representation of 'traces of

power' (Mokken and Stokman, 1978) within the corporate elite (see Mizruchi 1996; Scott 1997).

Chapter 2

1. Porter's analysis of the composition of the elite relied on a sub-group of 760 persons for whom he was able to obtain biographical information, which he considered as both a sample of the entire elite and, because an elite is itself a hierarchy, as 'the most powerful of the 985' (1965:274).
2. For details on how the individuals were categorized see Appendix 2.
3. Between 1971 and 1991 the proportion of Canadians with 'non-charter' (non-British and non-French) backgrounds rose from 26.7 per cent to 27.6 per cent. Within the diverse group of those with 'non-charter' backgrounds, there was a massive shift in the population at large away from European predominance. In 1971 86.0 per cent had European origins; by 1991 only 55.7 per cent did. In contrast, within the corporate elite nearly all of the increase in non-charter group representation was accounted for by people with European backgrounds (see Table 2.1). The increase in Asian representation within the elite was quite modest in comparison with the increase in people of Asian background in Canada, whose proportion of the 'non-charter' population rose from 5.0 per cent in 1971 to 21.6 per cent in 1991. Figures for the general population have been kindly supplied by Peter Li. For details see Li (2003).
4. As detailed in Appendix 2, ethnic background was inferred from the surnames of members of the elite. The validity of this indicator (which represents only the male line of descent) becomes more tenuous as we move from the basic distinction between 'charter' and other groups to finer differentiations.
5. An analysis of participation in seven elite clubs showed a consistent tendency for the heavy participants to have British backgrounds. In 1976 (N=20) and 1996 (N=8) all corporate-elite members who belonged to four or more of the clubs had British backgrounds. Among corporate-elite members belonging to two or three clubs, the 'Brits' were also over-represented in both 1976 (when 87.8 per cent were British) and 1996 (74.5 per cent British). However, there were no clear patterns of differential club-participation among the other ethnic groups. We can say that in the world of private clubs a certain British hegemony persisted in muted form into the closing years of the century.
6. Namely, the St James and Mount Royal Clubs in Montreal, the National, Toronto, and York Clubs in Toronto, and the Rideau Club in Ottawa. See Porter (1965:304–5). Our analysis adds to these six the Vancouver Club.
7. In 1976 the Pearson correlation between age and number of club memberships was .150; in 1996 it was .175. For instance, in 1996 members of the elite aged 50 and younger belonged on average to 1.30 clubs while those over 65 belonged on average to 2.5 clubs.
8. Namely, Nancy Southern, daughter of Ronald Southern who in 1996 controlled both Atco Ltd and Canadian Utilities; Loretta Rogers, wife of communications mogul Ted Rogers, and Kathleen Richardson of the Winnipeg-based Richardson family, controlling shareholders in James Richardson & Sons Ltd.
9. It should be emphasized that Gramsci did not view the bourgeoisie and its organic intellectuals as mutually exclusive categories. (See note 9 of Chapter 1.) Although in this chapter we follow Niosi in equating corporate advisors with organic intellectuals, in Chapter 8 we shall have occasion to note the extent to which leading corporate capitalists themselves serve as intellectuals in governing the production of neoliberal policy prescriptions.

10. See Giuseppe Vacca's discussion, where he argues that 'the organic nature ... of the bourgeoisie's intellectuals of a new type stems first of all from the technical aspects of the fundamental productive functions of the modern bourgeoisie. A further function is to help to elaborate and build consensus around a bourgeois model of society. ... The organic nature of the link is inherent in the very formation of their specialized skills, as well as in the development of the particular functions of organizing the masses and the economy' (1982:62–3).

11. In assigning each individual to one of these categories it was necessary to establish an order of precedence, which follows the hierarchy of class power around which the corporate elite is stratified. Thus persons owning a major block of corporate shares were classified as major shareholders even if they were also CEOs (as many were). Persons who were CEOs in a Top 250 company but also executives in another firm were considered to be CEOs. Persons who were executives in a non-Top-250 firm but also practicing lawyers were considered to be executives in a non-Top-250 firm. In ambiguous cases we went with the first-mentioned position in the biographical profile.

An ambiguous class position is that of board chairs. These members of the elite do not occupy an executive status, but at a minimum they preside at board meetings and thus play a leading role in the strategic direction of the firm. Sometimes retired executives are recruited as board chairs, sometimes corporate lawyers are. In some ways, board chairs are organic intellectuals—organizers of corporate enterprise, whose actual remuneration may not be particularly higher than that of an elite professional such as a medical doctor. In other ways they resemble full-blooded corporate capitalists, and indeed may be retired CEOs. For present purposes, the status of board chair is treated as a kind of residual category. The other categories have precedence in the assignment of persons to class positions. People known to have some other calling (e.g., lawyers, academics, major shareholders) who also chair a Top 250 firm are *not* shown as chairs.

Note that in 1976 nine persons chaired major corporations but were executives in non-Top-250 firms (namely Donald Anderson, Ralph Barford, Alex Barron, J. Douglas Gibson, C. Malim Harding, J.P. Monge, H.J. Sander Pearson, John Howard Taylor, and Charles Burns). They have been coded under the latter affiliation. In addition, Walter Owen, Lt-Governor of BC, chaired Monsanto Corp.; R.M. Fowler, president of the CD Howe Research Institute, chaired BP Canada; and three legal advisors (Donald Byers, Fraser Elliott, and Joseph Jeffery) also chaired Top corporations in 1976. Similarly, in 1996 one senator, one academic advisor, three legal advisors, and nine executives in non-Top 250 firms chaired a Top 250 firm, and their principal affiliations have been taken as the first-mentioned status.

12. Moreover, the number of major shareholders who serve on only one top corporate board, and therefore do not meet the criterion for our corporate elite, also increased between 1976 (n=63) and 1996 (n=77). The personal control of major corporations—four decades after Daniel Bell (1961) heralded the breakup of family capitalism—continues to form one important aspect of class structure.

13. Betty Kennedy, a journalist and TV personality, directed both the Bank of Montreal and Simpsons Limited (and married Simpsons dominant shareholder Edgar Burton later in the 1970s). Louise Vaillancourt, president of the Hôpital Marie Enfant, directed the National Bank and Bell Canada. The third, Mitzi Dobrin, was a lower-level executive in Steinberg's Ltd and a member of the Steinberg family that owned controlling interest in the Montreal-based retailer.

14. The overall association in 1996 between our class categorization and gender is moderately strong, as indicated by a Contingency Coefficient of 0.336.

15. In all, 29.4 per cent fitted this description, and no Jewish members of the elite were presidents, CEOs, or chairs of Top corporations they did not control through ownership.

16. Taking all the corporate directors in each year (numbering 2,398 in 1976 and 2,135 in 1996), the average director served on a common board with 22.8 other directors of large corporations in 1976, while by 1996 the average director served with only 16.8 directors. In the interpersonal network, there were actually *fewer* points of interpersonal contact in 1996 than in 1976.
17. In 1976 the mean distance between members of the core group of 116 was 1.65. In 1996 it was 2.03. But in both years the core group's diameter was only 3.
18. In this context the degree is simply the number of contacts, that is, the number of other directors that a given director meets on one or more boards. The mean degree within a category is the mean number of such contacts among directors belonging to that category. Note that as a measure of networking across categories, degree is asymmetrical. In the table, we show the mean degree from the perspective of the column category. For instance, in 1996 members of the network's inner margin had on average 5.4 contacts in the network's core.
19. The eta^2 statistic is a measure of how much of a variable's variance can be attributed to between-group differences. Thus in 1976, 6.1 per cent of the variance in the number of club memberships could be attributed to the mean differences between directors positioned in the core, inner margin, and outer margin.
20. For instance, in 1996 former Ontario premier William G. Davis, former Alberta premier Peter Loughheed, and Ronald Southern, CEO of Atco Ltd, were all in the core of the network of directorships. Yet none belonged to any of the seven key clubs. Contemporaneously, some individuals on the outer margin of the network of corporate directorships were central in the network of club co-memberships. J. Michael G. Scott (a consultant and director of two top firms) belonged to the York, Toronto, Mt Royal, and Vancouver clubs, while André Bisson (a consultant, Chancellor of the Université de Montréal, and director of three top firms) belonged to the Toronto, Mt Royal, and St James clubs.
21. Both Taylor and Ritchie were retired bankers, formerly with the Bank of Nova Scotia and Royal Bank respectively. Turner was also a retired capitalist, having served within Paul Desmarais's corporate empire as CEO of papermaker Consolidated Bathurst.
22. The eta^2 statistic for variance attributable to ethnic-group differences fell after 1976 from 0.039 to 0.021.
23. In June 1996 University of Western Ontario's Richard Ivey School of Business commenced a six-day course on corporate governance, in conjunction with the Toronto Stock Exchange and the ICD. Taught by university faculty and private-sector personnel to 30 corporate directors at a time, the course is offered at the school's Mississauga campus in three two-day segments (Hard target: The new wave of directors taking over Canada's boardrooms is finding that the work is harder than it used to be, 1996). For information on Toronto-based ICD, go to http://www.icd.ca/, where the strategic concern underlying much of the group's ethical initiatives is acknowledged: 'One of our main focuses is director liability. We advocate the need to protect investors and other stakeholders, without exposing directors to unnecessary risk. The ICD represents director concerns in discussions with government and regulating bodies about director liability.'
24. The emergence and circulation of a risk-management discourse has been part and parcel of the corporate governance movement, as the accumulation process becomes more 'reflexive' (Lash, 1994). Dey himself, reflecting two and a half years after his 1994 report, considered that the report had had a two-fold impact: (1) driving home directors' responsibility for managing risk that a company takes on 'when it invests in a particular pool of assets'; (2) driving home to the same directors their responsibility for 'managing risk whether environmental, currency, commodity or asset risk' (quoted in Cohen 1997:105). For a thoughtful discussion of crisis theories see O'Connor (1987).

25. As one journalist observed in 1997, 'There's no need now for membership in the right clubs; the modern businessman or woman would rather network beyond the encrusted crowd that's already ensconced.... Increasingly, business success can occur anywhere a good idea combusts. The very notion of an all-powerful Establishment with arcane rules and inbred bloodlines is being called into question' (McQueen, 1997:8).

26. In July 2000, a task force was convened by the Toronto and Calgary stock exchanges to investigate a financial scandal at the Royal Bank's pension arm, which 're-ignited fears that confidence in Canadian markets could be undermined' (Marr, 2000:C1). Task force Chair Guylaine Saucier, chair of the Canadian Broadcasting Corporation and former chair of the Canadian Institute of Chartered Accountants, noted that 'The world has not stayed still—governance process has improved all around the world. We have to ensure we are at the forefront of good governance in Canada' (Marr, 2000:C9).

27. As Arthur Felts (1992:511) suggests in his discussion of organizational communication, 'developing more symmetrical relations is a means by which communications will not be hindered or constrained by facets of the communicative situation per se. At base and from an organizational perspective, the creation of more symmetrical relationships involves the ability to communicate more freely without the fears or one-sided privileges that inevitably arise in settings that emphasize hierarchical status. In an important sense, it creates conditions under which communication is understood as a learning-based exchange.'

28. See the discussion of this and other issues in the final report of the Saucier Committee, *Beyond Compliance: Building a Corporate Governance Culture* (2001). The Committee was a joint endeavor by the TSE, the Canadian Venture Exchange, and the Canadian Institute of Chartered Accountants.

29. As if to anticipate possible objections to this alignment, the discourse of corporate governance includes as a minor theme the idea of 'stakeholders', a broader and more diffuse group than shareholders, whose presence potentially subverts the entire moral baggage of the reform project. The reunited Dey Commission, for instance, emphasized that while directors must endeavour to create shareholder value, they also 'must act in an enlightened manner in addressing the interests of all stakeholders. Directors must be increasingly conscious of social and environmental issues and be alert to ways that responses to these issues can also enhance shareholder value' (2000:3). Within this formula, shareholder value, and with it the interests of corporate investors, are privileged, but other interests are to be integrated into strategic calculations, as subordinate 'issues', in a way that ultimately enhances shareholder value.

30. The connection between this development and neoliberal policy bears mention. Just as free trade has intensified the competition that ultimately drives 'shareholder value', deregulation is implicated in the rise of activist institutional investors. Consider the Ontario Teachers Pension Plan, a fund that by the close of the twentieth century owned 1.5 per cent of all TSE shares, with more than $500 million in shares of each of BCE, the Royal Bank, CIBC, and Bank of Montreal. In 1990, the Plan was still legally limited to holding non-marketable debentures. But that year, Ontario freed it to invest in stocks and bonds. Within a few years the Plan's equity positions were so big it could not dump a stock without disrupting the market. With its exit option blocked, in the face of a non-performing investment the Plan could either do nothing or confront management (Rubin, 1998:8). Similarly, the Canada Pension Fund, which pools deferred earnings of most Canadian workers, was as of 1 March 1999 empowered to direct funds into the stock market. According to one estimate, in eight years it could have $80 billion in equities (McQueen, 1999:D4).

31. The increasingly directive role of institutional investors in corporate-governance reform was underlined with the founding in April 2003 of the Canadian Coalition for Good Governance, a Toronto-based group composed of 19 institutional investors with $350

Notes to pp. 38–46   237

billion in total assets. Chaired by former federal finance minister Michael Wilson, the coalition lobbies individual companies to adopt the TSE governance norms, with particular emphasis on 'the importance of fully independent directors on boards' (McFarland, 2003).

32. The quotation is from as Arden Haynes, chair of the Bank's corporate governance committee (in 'Banking more on directors', 1997:13). The notion of aligning the interests of directors with those of shareholders builds naturally upon Michael Jensen's finance-based theory of corporate governance, which gained currency in the 1980s. Jensen and Mackling (1976) argued that stock options should be employed to align the interests of executives with those of shareholders. In both cases the goal is to ensure that the interests of shareholders predominate in corporate decision-making. See the discussion in Henwood (1997:265–85).

33. By 1997, one observer noted that compared to the mid-1970s 'today's bank board is half the size it was then and is more concerned with corporate governance and return on shareholder's equity than attracting candidates with connections' (McQueen, 1997:9).

34. See the illuminating list of major American-based corporations mired in scandal as of the summer of 2002, published as 'The Corporate Crime Scorecard', in *Multinational Monitor* (July/Aug 2002, no. 7/8), available online at http://multinationalmonitor.org/mm2002/02july-aug/july-aug02corp7.html.

CHAPTER 3

1. Linda McQuaig's (1995:72–121) analysis of the dramatic shift in the 1980s by the Bank of Canada to an investor-friendly 'war on inflation', in which the weapon was a high interest-rate policy and the major casualty the jobs and livelihood of many middle- to low-income Canadians, is instructive on this point.

2. The seventh company, the Provincial Bank of Canada, was minority-controlled by the Caisse Populaire Desjardins—the Quebec-based ensemble of credit unions. A number of Canada's major life insurers were converted to mutuals in the 1950s as protection against possible foreign takeover (Babad and Mulroney, 1993:28).

3. For instance, in my earlier study (1986:124) I reported that in 1976 Sun Life shared five directors with the Royal Bank, five with the Bank of Montreal, and four with the CIBC while Canada Life shared three directors with the Bank of Nova Scotia, three with the CIBC and two with the Royal Bank. Although we group these life insurance mutuals along with other non-proprietary companies, in some ways the life insurers, which in any case moved in the late 1990s to de-mutualize as a way of securing greater capital for expansion, lie much closer to our 'control by a constellation of interests' category—as the corporate interlocking examples just given make clear.

4. The five included companies that have long been central to the Canadian corporate network—Manulife, Sun Life, Mutual Life and Canada Life—plus Industrial-Alliance Life, a Quebec City-based company that became a mutual in 1969, aggressively expanded through mergers and takeovers in the 1980s and 1990s, and demutualized in February 2000 to become a capital stock company traded on the Toronto Stock Exchange.

5. There is a striking regional distribution of these companies. The life-insurance mutuals, key centres of allocative financial power, are located predominantly in corporate capital's Canadian metropole, Toronto. In contrast, companies representing a democratic alternative to corporate business tend to be based where more collectivist and communitarian values have had resonance, with the agricultural cooperatives headquartered on the prairies (six) and in Quebec (two) and the credit-union and similar financial institutions headquartered mainly in Quebec (four) and BC (two).

6. For simplicity's sake, all Canadian firms controlled by foreign-based corporations are grouped in a single category, regardless of whether they were ultimately controlled by persons or by constellations of interests. One company (Lafarge Cement) was found to be under the control of a foreign state (namely, France). It is grouped under the rubric of state control. All other state-controlled companies were controlled by the Canadian state, whether federal or provincial.

7. The issue of foreign control will be explored in the next chapter as part of a wider discussion of the transnationalization of corporate capital.

8. Our definition of control by institutional investors is fairly narrow. We consider as institutional investors only companies that exist as pools of financial capital (e.g., pension or mutual funds) and that invest in a wide range of instruments, including corporate shares. These companies do not generally seek active strategic control over other corporations, which is how they differ from *bona fide* investment companies.

9. Niosi's observations on the case of Abitibi Paper, circa 1974, provide a useful reference point, and an excellent example of control by a constellation of interests. At that time, 11 institutional shareholders—including three banks and two trusts—held a total of 34 per cent of Abitibi's voting stock, but no one institution owned a block of 10 per cent or more. By 1996 Abitibi was controlled by Julian H. Robertson, Jr, through two private investment companies.

10. For instance, the Ontario Teachers' Pension Plan held 13 per cent of Domtext while the Caisse held nearly nine. A check of three companies in our 1996 sample that manage vast pension and mutual funds revealed the following. Trimark Investment Management shared no directors with any of the eight Top 250 firms in which it held 10 per cent or more of shares. MacKenzie Financial Corporation had no interlocks with two of the three firms in which it held 10 per cent or more of share capital, but its president and one other MacKenzie director sat on the board of Midland Walwyn Ltd, in which MacKenzie held a 22 per cent interest. The Caisse de dépôt et placement du Québec had investments of 10 per cent or more in nine Top 250 firms, but only in the case of Provigo did its interest exceed 21 per cent. Two Caisse directors, one a vice-president and the other the Caisse's vice-chair, sat on the Provigo board, overseeing the Caisse' 37 per cent dominant interest. Neither Midland Walwyn nor Provigo had any shareholder owning larger blocks than MacKenzie and the Caisse. On the basis of the multiple-director interlocks and strong investment positions, we classified Midland Walwyn and Provigo as under direct, minority corporate control by MacKenzie and the Caisse, respectively. There was only one other case in which significant share ownership by one of these institutional investors coincided with board interlocks. In 1996 the Caisse held 13 per cent of Westburne Inc. and its vice president sat on the Westburne board. However, three other institutional investors also held significant positions in Westburne, the largest being Trimark's 18.5 per cent interest. In the circumstances, Westburne was categorized as controlled by institutional investors. In general, the incidence of institutional investors gaining direct representation on the boards of corporations in which they invest remained rare in early 1997.

11. The exceptions were Semi-Tech Corporation, majority controlled by J.H. Ting of Hong Kong, and Husky Oil, wholly owned by Li Ka-shing, also of Hong Kong. In 1995 Li Ka-shing was also the largest single shareholder of a Canadian chartered bank, with just under 10 per cent of the shares of the CIBC. See Huang and Jeffery, 1995.

12. See McNish, Marotte, and Seguin (2002). In 1996 the Caisse held secondary blocks of shares in several companies controlled by French-Canadian capitalists, including Quebecor Printing (controlled by the Peladeau family) and Groupe Vidéotron (controlled by André Chagnon).

13. For interlocking as a whole, this 'levelling' of differences was mainly due to the decreased structural prominence of companies controlled by complex constellations or by non-pro-

prietary interests. For primary interlocks the decline in the prominence of these firms combined with an increased relative prominence of companies controlled by persons and the state.

14. Montreal-based SNC-Lavalin was interlocked with 22 Top 250 companies. Sault-Sainte Marie-based Algoma Steel was interlocked with 11.
15. Legislation to privatize Petro-Canada was enacted in 1991. In 1995 the federal government sold what amounted to 50 per cent of Petro-Canada's shares in a partial privatization, retaining the biggest block of share capital (20 per cent). Although in 1997 the Government of Canada continued to own the largest block of Petro-Canada (at 18 per cent) and James Stanford (appointed in 1993) continued to serve as president, the 11-member board resembled the kind of board one encounters in companies controlled by constellations of interests. Stanford himself had no other Top 250 directorships, but eight directors were members of our corporate elite, deeply ensconced in the corporate network. They carried interlocks to the boards of seven major financial institutions (including three chartered banks) and 15 leading industrial corporations.
16. Partly because of the integrative impact of the Caisse, Quebec-based companies in and around the state-capitalist sector tended to be densely interlocked with each other. With the exception of Avenor Inc., which was heavily interlocked to Ontario-based companies but detached from the Quebec segment, the density of interlocking among 10 Montreal-based corporations in Figure 2.3 (four of them ultimately controlled by the government of Quebec) was 0.40.
17. For methodological details please consult Appendix 2.
18. For instance, in 1976 the Hudson Bay Company owned 21 per cent of Hudson's Bay Oil and Gas (a minority interest compared to the 53 per cent block held by Continental Oil), and Bell Canada held 69 per cent of Northern Telecom. In 1996 Jim Pattison Inc. owned a 28 per cent controlling interest in B.C. Sugar.
19. Besides Hudson's Bay Oil and Gas, in 1976 two dyads and one triad were structures of partial or complete foreign control (Japanese-controlled Mitsui Canada owned 53 per cent of Canadian Motor Sales. Canadian-controlled Simpsons owned half of US-controlled Simpson-Sears. US-controlled Gulf Canada and Imperial Oil each held minority positions in Interprovincial Pipe Line). In 1996 US-controlled Anglo-Canadian Telephone owned 51 per cent of BC Telecom, and British-controlled Imasco owned 98 per cent of CT Financial Services.
20. In 1976, besides the triad mentioned in note 19, Canadian Tire, National Trust and GSW formed a triad. In 1996 there were four ownership triads: Donohue Inc., Quebecor Inc. and Quebecor Printing Inc.; Power Corporation of Canada, Power Financial Corp. and Great-West Lifeco; Canadian Pacific, Laidlaw Inc. and PanCanadian Petroleum Ltd; and United Grain Growers Ltd, Alberta Wheat Pool and Manitoba Pool Elevators.
21. The fate of companies once controlled by Canadian Pacific provides a sense of the massive restructuring of corporate capital that has occurred since the 1980s. In 1997 CP sold its controlling interest in Laidlaw (which declared bankruptcy in 2001). Control of Cominco, long a CP subsidiary, was sold to Teck Corp. in 1986, which fully amalgamated with Cominco to form Teckcominco in 2001. Years after CP sold off its minority stake in MacMillan Bloedel the latter was purchased by American-based Weyerhaeuser in 1999. Control of Algoma Steel, once part of the CP empire, was acquired by Dofasco in 1988, after which the firm's employees, led by the United Steelworkers union, purchased majority control in 1992. By 2002, in the wake of declaring bankruptcy, Algoma was restructured with Mackay Shields (a mutual fund owned by New York Life Insurance Co.) holding 32 percent of shares. Mackay sold its block later in the year, leaving Algoma apparently without a single dominant shareholder. Finally, CP sold off its 45 percent stake in Dominion Bridge (renamed as United Dominion Industries)

between 1993 and 1995. In 2001 United Dominion, which had moved its executive offices to Charlotte, NC, was acquired by SPX Corporation.

22. Along the way, Massey Ferguson, once a leading Canadian-based TNC, declared bankruptcy, was reorganized as Varity Corp. and moved in 1991 to the USA. Dominion Stores disappeared into a retooled Hollinger Inc., Black's lead corporation, in 1984–85. Domtar entered the Caisse stable in 1982, and control of Noranda (which absorbed Fraser Companies in 1985) was gained by Brascan in 1981. BC Forest Products was merged with Crown Forest to form New Zealand-controlled Fletcher Challenge in 1987. It was renamed as NorskeCanada in 2001, after Norway-based Norske Skog gained control of Fletcher Challenge's worldwide pulp and paper assets.

23. For simplicity's sake, we have trimmed these two-mode networks by removing corporations on which only one of the central directors sat (38 firms in 1976 and 35 in 1996).

24. The boundary criterion we have used to create these sociograms—selecting only the 27 or 28 most central individuals—omits individuals who may belong to an enterprise group but not be sufficiently central in the network of thick interpersonal ties. For instance, in 1976 Albert A. Thornbrough was the salaried president of Massey-Ferguson (an Argus firm) and William I.M. Turner Jr was the salaried president of Consolidated Bathurst (a Power firm). However, the seven thick ties that each had to members of the corporate elite was two less than required for inclusion in the group of 28 central individuals on which Figure 3.6 is based.

25. Also, George Hart, CEO of the Bank of Montreal from 1959 to 1974, continued in his retirement to sit on the boards of the Bank and some of its closely affiliated firms, but he also directed a Power Corporation affiliate (Consolidated Bathurst) as well as US-controlled Pratt-Whitney, which Bélanger also directed. John A. Tory was in 1976 making the transition from corporate lawyer (a partner with Tory, Tory, Deslauriers and Binnington) to corporate executive that would see him play a major role within Ken Thomson's corporate empire. In addition to his directorships with Sun Life and the Royal Bank, Tory sat with Bélanger on the board of Abitibi Paper, which in 1976 was in the process of acquiring the Price Company. J. Douglas Gibson, chair of Consumers Gas and retired vice-president of the Bank of Nova Scotia, sat on the board of Imperial Life, part of the Power Corp. group but also directed Stelco and both firms in the Bell Canada group.

26. In 1996 Lougheed combined his two Brascan-group directorships (Noranda and Norcen) with directorships in leading corporations ultimately controlled by constellations (CP, Nortel and the Royal Bank) as well as directorships in two family controlled comapanies (Atco, controlled by the Southerns and Bombardier, controlled by the Bombardier-Beaudoins). This set of affiliations made Lougheed a kind of mediator between various controlling interests, most importantly the Power and Brascan groups. He sat with André Desmarais on the Bombardier board while also collaborating with Trevor Eyton, Jack Cockwell, and other Brascan principals in directing Noranda and Norcen. For his part, Mazankowski, well ensconced as a leading advisor in the Power group (along with retired Privy Council Clerk Senator Michael Pitfield and investment consultant Guy St.-Germain), also served as an outside director of Ronald Southern's Canadian Utilities. The integrative role that retirees from state service have come to play as other sources of elite integration have weakened is striking. In this regard David Peterson, former Premier of Ontario, deserves mention. Although in Figure 3.7 he appears only as an outside director of the two companies controlled by Edward and Loretta Rogers, the reader will recall that our diagrams have been trimmed, resulting in the removal of 35 companies that in 1996 had only one central director on their boards. Peterson was an outside director of five such companies, and in this he followed the career path of William G. Davis, also a former Ontario Premier, who although not tightly linked into the network of thick interpersonal ties was in 1996 an outside director of seven leading corporations including Power Corporation, Seagram, and the

Canadian Imperial Bank of Commerce. Continuing the tradition, former NDP leader and Ontario Premier (1990–5) Bob Rae became a partner in Goodman, Phillips and Vineberg in 1996 and by 1999 directed Atlas Steels, Canadian Airlines, Credit Lyonnais Canada and two other companies.

CHAPTER 4

1. For full discussions of organized capitalism as an economic, political, and social form developing out of the liberal capitalism of the nineteenth century see Kocka (1974) and Lash and Urry (1987), who draw upon Kocka, extending the analysis to an emergent phase of disorganized capitalism in the late twentieth century. Among the features emphasized by Lash and Urry (1987:4–5) are the concentration and centralization of industrial, banking, and commercial capital and the increased interconnection of banks and industry; the concentration of industrial capitalist relations within relatively few industrial sectors and nation-states; and the growth and increased importance of very large industrial cities that dominate particular regions through the provision of centralized services.
2. Such a loosening of ties could be amplified by an increase in foreign control of large corporations, if the directorates of foreign-controlled subsidiaries were linked to their parents and not to the local corporate elite (Fennema and Schijf, 1985), which would create a structural hole in the national network. However, our finding of decreased levels of foreign control over the largest Canadian corporations (in Chapter 3) suggests that no such general trend exists in Canada.
3. There is no series of data on total investment reaching back to 1970, with which to compare foreign direct investment. Thus in the last column of Table 4.1 I compare the accumulated stock of foreign investment (or Canadian investment abroad) to the annual GDP. See Burgess (2002:179ff) for a discussion of this issue and a more extensive analysis.
4. Note, however, that deregulation of national markets has been accompanied by the development of more transparent and harmonized rules, developed and overseen by such international agencies as the WTO, to provide a more predictable and stable international business environment (Whitley, 2001). The disorganization of national capitalism does not do away with the issue of regulation. It transposes it to the field of 'global business regulation' (Braithwaite and Drahos, 2000).
5. As Coleman (1994:265) observes, 'removal of capital and credit controls and the evolution of international financial markets increase greatly the free movement of capital across national borders. The degrees of freedom for any given state in the use of financial policy instruments have declined proportionately....'
6. *Corporate Governance Trends: 2000* (Paris: Organization for Economic Cooperation and Development); abstract available at http://www.oecd.org/linklist/0,2678,en_2649_37439_2735046_1_1_1_37439,00.html#3178330.
7. Although pension funds and mutual funds ostensibly represent 'patient money', intense competition over profit margins has meant that institutions now employ 'hired guns' to administer vast portfolios that are regularly scrutinized for profitability. Shareholder power in great part expresses this relentless push for immediate profit, which 'exerts pressure on executives to keep stock prices cooking—whatever the human cost' (McMurdy, 1996:33).
8. In all, only 17 of the 257 companies had such ownership interests: four Dutch, four French, four Japanese, one German, two South African, and two other European. With the exception of the four Japanese trading companies (without production facilities in Canada), most of the non-Anglo-American interests were centred in the resource and manufacturing sectors.

9. The cross-tabulation in Table 4.2 gives an overall sense of the changes at work, but its categories do not take into account the relative size of different firms. The apparent resurgence of Canadian control at the top of the corporate hierarchy could be illusory if companies controlled domestically were smaller in comparison with those controlled by foreign interests. This does not appear to be the case: in 1976 the median Canadian-controlled manufacturer had assets 16 per cent larger than those of the median US-controlled manufacturer. In 1996 the corresponding indigenous firm was 29 per cent larger than the median for US-controlled manufacturers. The difference is more dramatic for financial institutions. In 1976 the median Canadian-controlled financial had assets 114 per cent larger than those of the median US-controlled financial. In 1996 the corresponding indigenous firm was 171 per cent larger than the median for US-controlled financials and 407 per cent larger than the median for the eight financials controlled outside of North America. Only in the resource sector does the 1996 asset median for US-controlled firms exceed (by 30 per cent) the median for Canadian-controlled firms, but in this case the US median is based on only two companies compared to 24 indigenously-controlled resource concerns, six of which had assets larger than the largest US-controlled resource firm.

10. For the purposes of this research, 'multinational' and 'transnational' are interchangeable terms. The meaning of transnational corporation is rather indeterminate. TNCs are sometimes distinguished as more decentred from particular national bases than MNCs. However, Dicken (1992:47–8) regards as a TNC any firm with direct investments beyond its home base, including non-multinationals that operate in two countries.

11. The source for these data (see Appendix 2) provided 89.9 per cent coverage of the 1976 sample and 84.1 per cent coverage of the 1996 sample. A limitation of this method is its insensitivity to how large the subsidiaries are, and to how the magnitude of foreign operations compares to that of domestic operations, firm by firm. Such information is, however, not systematically available.

12. This is not to say that many financial institutions do not participate in international circuits of capital, through portfolio investments of various kinds, currency speculation, and so on.

13. Each of these had subsidiaries in 17 or more foreign countries in 1996. The six long-standing TNCs, listed with the number of foreign countries in which they had subsidiaries respectively in 1976 and 1996, are the manufacturers Seagram Co. Ltd (23, 33), Moore Corp. (28, 28) and Alcan Aluminum (34, 26), the utility BCE Inc. (9, 22), and the mining companies Falconbridge Ltd (14, 19) and Inco Ltd (18, 19). Note that Seagram was acquired by the French media conglomerate Vivendi in 2000. See Niosi (1985) for case histories of these firms.

14. The five include Nortel Networks (telecommunications, subsidiaries in 33 countries), SNC-Lavalin Group (engineering, subsidiaries in 24 countries), The Thomson Corp. (electronic and print media, subsidiaries in 18 countries), BCE Mobile Communications (telecommunications, subsidiaries in 17 countries) and Newbridge Networks (information technology, subsidiaries in 17 countries). Note that Newbridge was acquired by the French telecommunications company Alcatel in 2000.

15. See Carroll (1986:123–4), where the dense interlocks between banks and life insurers as of 1976 are depicted, along with ties between life insurers and trust-mortgage companies.

16. In fact, many of these weaker ties occur as by-products in the creation of primary interlocks. For example, if the CEO of Nortel Networks sits on the board of both the Bank of Montreal and Canadian Pacific, (s)he creates two primary interlocks (Nortel-Bank of Montreal, Nortel-Canadian Pacific) but also one secondary interlock between the bank and Canadian Pacific.

17. Indeed, much of the difference in mean board size for the entire Top 250 has to do with changes in the size of bank boards, which is why the median board size in 1976 (11.02) was not much smaller than the median for 1976 (11.85).
18. In 1996 three Quebec-based credit unions were interlocked with each other via officers but isolated from the larger corporate network.
19. Three banks, however, ranked among the twelve most central companies in degree of primary ties. In 1976 the big five banks ranked 1, 2, 3, 4, and 7.
20. In fact, the declining presence of foreign-controlled industrials, evident in Table 4.2 above, meant that the 1996 density value of .026 between domestic finance and foreign industry represented only 52 ties, compared to the 223 secondary interlocks that in 1976 contributed to a density of .045 between domestic finance and foreign industry.
21. By the same token, the flagging participation of non-transnational financial institutions meant that by 1996 these companies—which include most of the country's largest financial institutions—accounted for only 16.6 per cent of all secondary interlocks, compared with 32.5 per cent in 1976.
22. Seven of the 51 TNCs had no board-level ties to other TNCs in the sample. Two of these isolates from the dominant component were foreign-controlled.
23. The criterion for this distinction was that every company included in the centre be interlocked with at least six other members of the centre—forming a so-called 6-core (Seidman, 1983).
24. Namely, BCE and its affiliates Nortel Networks and BCE Mobility, Teleglobe Canada, and Thomson Corp.
25. Namely, NOVA, TransCanada PipeLine, Alberta Energy, and TransAlberta Utilities.
26. Namely, Seagram (liquor and entertainment), Bombarbier (transportation equipment), Moore Corp. (business forms), Domtex (textiles), and MacMillan Bloedel (wood products).
27. Respectively, Rio Algom, Barrick, Falconbridge, CAE, Teck Corp., Inmet and Cominco; and Amoco Canada, Talisman, and Westcoast Transmission.
28. Similarly, most of the primary interlocks (shown in bold in Figure 4.3) either joined industrial TNCs and financial institutions or followed lines of intercorporate ownership. For instance, in the mining sector, Noranda held 46 per cent controlling interest in Falconbridge. In the IT/telecommunications field, BCE held controlling interest in both Nortel (52 per cent) and BCE Mobility (65 per cent), and the largest single block of shares in Teleglobe (22 per cent). Thus several primary interlocks among Canadian TNCs seemed built around capital relations of ownership and credit.
29. For instance, banks' holdings of foreign currency assets expanded from about 10 per cent of total assets in the mid-1950s to over 30 per cent in the mid-1990s (Armstrong, 1997:12).
30. As non-financial corporations have come to rely more on issuance of commercial paper, bonds and equities, bank's share of the business credit market in Canada has dropped from a high of 52 per cent in 1982–83 to about 33 per cent as of the mid-1990s. At the same time, however, with securitization of loans, banks' holdings of securities have increased, as has their fee income from setting up securitization transactions through their investment-bank subsidiaries. Indeed, one-tenth of big six banks' total income in 1996 derived from investment banking and other securities fees (calculated from Armstrong, 1997:30).
31. 'Bought deals' were pioneered in North America in the 1980s and involve purchase of an entire issue of securities by a financial institution. The relationship between 'creditor' and 'debtor' lasts only as long as it take to complete the transaction. Stanford (1999:58) reports that for the five biggest Canadian banks, between 1990 and 1998 the proportion

of assets held in the form of traditional loans fell from nearly three-quarters to barely one-half, and that in 1998 'for the first time, the non-lending business activities of the five largest banks exceeded their net interest income.'

32. Relatedly, British Petroleum's director of money transactions is reported to have stated that 'our currency dealing is at least as important as our oil trading' (Dillon, 1997:26).

Chapter 5

1. See, however, the recent work of O'Hagan and Green (2002), which interprets inter-urban interlocks as 'tacit knowledge transfers', within a resource-dependence perspective on intercorporate relations.
2. In one significant case we did not exclude state-controlled companies. The Montreal-based Caisse de Dépôt et Placement, established in 1965 to manage the Quebec pension fund and other assets, has through its extensive strategic investments in various Quebec-based companies given support to French-Canadian capitalists (Niosi, 1981:45–6). No other state-controlled investment company has played such a major role in regional accumulation strategies, and in view of our interest in the emergent politics of Quebec nationalism, the Caisse was included as an investment company in the 1976 and 1996 samples. See Appendix 2 for methodological details.
3. The Bay's head office remained in London, England, until its transfer to Winnipeg in 1970. In 1987 its head office was moved to Toronto. The other extra-Canadian head office was that of Minnesota and Ontario Paper Company, headquartered in Minneapolis in 1946.
4. Since nearly all the Alberta-based corporations in this study were headquartered in Calgary in any given year, for brevity's sake we have combined the few Edmonton-based firms with those based in Calgary. Edmonton was the home of one leading corporation in 1976 (Canadian Utilities) and two in 1996 (Canadian Utilities and Telus Corp.).
5. It is well to remember the constraints imposed on our analysis by our comparison of multiple cross-sections. The various categories in the analysis contain different corporations at different times. For instance, while in 1946 the four industrial firms based in Atlantic Canada were all forestry companies, the one industrial corporation based there in 1996, McCains, was a transnational corporation in the agribusiness sector.
6. Throughout the half-century, the very largest financial institutions remained under indigenous control: in 1946 all 23 were; by 1996 20 were, with two controlled in the US. Hence the inroads made by foreign investors between 1976 and 1996, which we observed in Chapter 4, mostly involved the second tier of the Top 50 financials.
7. The foreign-controlled firms based in Vancouver in 1996 were BC Tel and its parent investment company Anglo-Canadian Telephone (controlled in the US), Fletcher-Challenge (controlled in New Zealand), and Hong Kong Bank of Canada (controlled in Britain).
8. The firms were, consecutively, Shell Canada, Husky Oil, and AMOCO Canada Petroleum.
9. To simplify the table, one interlock—linking Saskatoon-based Potash Corporation of Saskatchewan to Calgary-based Renaissance Energy Ltd in 1996—is not shown.
10. These results correspond closely to those of Rice and Semple (1993), who studied the 'Canadian spatial interlocking network' between 1971 and 1989—a set of inter- and intra-urban flows from directors' cities of residence to the cities in which their corporate head offices were situated.
11. The 181 interlocks make up a 'bipartite' network in that by focusing exclusively on them we partition the network into two metropolitan regions and consider only the ties that

Notes to pp. 99–107   245

cut across the regions. Interlocks between companies based in the same region are not included in this part of the analysis.

12. Norcen's interlocks were underlain by capital relations to dominant Toronto-based shareholders Conrad Black (Hollinger) and the Brascan group (including Brascan affiliates Trilon Financial and Noranda).

13. For instance, in 1996 the Royal Bank had directors of Nova, TransAlberta, TransCanada PipeLine, and Norcen on its board, and the Toronto-based Bank of Nova Scotia was interlocked with Nova, TransAlberta, TransCanada PipeLine, and PetroCanada.

14. As a point of comparison, the somewhat denser 1946 network was carried by only 208 directors who averaged 4.0 directorships, indicating that in the early post-war period the corporate elite was more tightly organized as a relatively small, centralized group—a veritable old boys' network .

15. In fact, only one of the 16 carried more than a single interlock in 1996. Robert Wyman, Chair of Suncor and a BC resident, served on four western-based boards (including BC Tel, Fletcher Challenge, and Westcoast Transmission), carrying a total of six interlocks. Perhaps one of the clearest indications that the rise of the west has not meant a deep fractioning of the corporate elite is given in the trajectory of Peter Lougheed, from an architect of Alberta's regional economic growth strategy in the 1970s, when he served as provincial premier, to a central member of the corporate elite in 1996, sitting on the boards of western-based Norcen and eastern-based Bombardier, Canadian Pacific, Royal Bank, Noranda, and Nortel, among the Top 103 corporations we consider in this chapter.

16. In all, the 60 finance capitalists whose directorships span east and west account for 347 of the 719 interlocking directorships of 1996.

17. Recent realignments in Canada's securities exchanges underline the continuing dominance of Toronto and Montreal, with the former hosting the bourse designated for senior issues and the latter hosting the bourse designated for trading derivatives. The third bourse, reserved for trading junior securities, became based in Calgary in 1999, with the merger of the Vancouver and Calgary exchanges. In May 2000 the Quebec government announced an agreement to establish a branch of the New York-based Nasdaq in Montreal, dedicated to trading high-tech securities (Edur, 2000).

18. The noteworthy exception is BCT.Telus (formed in 1999 with the merger of Edmonton-based Telus and Vancouver-based BC Tel), whose ongoing struggle with Montreal-based BCE Inc. for control of the national telecommunications market demonstrates that inter-capitalist competition can have a 'regional' dimension even in the absence of sharply defined fractions.

19. Recent figures show that the volume of Canadian exports to the US has increased by more than 50 per cent in the past decade and now accounts for more than 30 per cent of Canada's GDP. In the same period, cross-border investments between Canada and the USA doubled, as reported in *Policy Research Initiatives Horizon* 3, 2 (August 2000), 24.

CHAPTER 6

1. For 1976, US data come from Bearden and Mintz's (1985) study, graciously supplied by Beth Mintz. They include 202 nonfinancials and 50 financial institutions. Some additional verification of the interlock data was carried out upon discovering inaccuracies in the file. For 1996, data were collected for this study. The sample includes 204 nonfinancials and 50 financial institutions. Four of the non-financials are investment companies that held blocs of shares in major US corporations in 1996. Because investment companies have played a much smaller role in the organization of American corporate capital, our US Top 250s include only two investment companies in 1976 and four in 1996.

2. As Mintz and Schwartz (1985) found, in the 1960s financial–industrial coalescence in the US brought industrial clients onto the boards of commercial banks, not vice versa, in a system of 'financial hegemony'. Since the TSE reforms of 1995, the Canadian network has come to resemble the American pattern in this regard, as bankers have backed away from directing industrial corporations.
3. For instance, five inside directors participated on the boards of US retailer Kresge and its Canadian subsidiary: three executives of the parent sat on the board of the subsidiary and two executives with the subsidiary sat on the parent board. US retailer Woolworth also shared five inside directors with its subsidiary. John Deere shared four insiders with its Canadian branch plant. Phillip Morris, Sears, and American Motors shared three insiders with their respective Canadian subsidiaries; and a number of other US parents shared one or two.
4. Both Kresge and Woolworth had two executives from the Canadian subsidiary sitting on the US parent board.
5. Five bankers played such an advisory role (e.g., William Mulholland of the Bank of Montreal directed Kimberly-Clark; W. Earle McLaughlin of Royal Bank directed GM, Metropolitan Life, and Standard Brands; James Leitch of CIBC directed American Airlines). However, five of these 20 lines were carried by executives in foreign-controlled firms. For instance, W. Wearly, an executive with Ingersoll-Rand's Canadian subsidiary, directed American Cynamide, Babcox-Wilcox, and the Bank of New York. Semon E. Knudsen, an executive with White Motor Corp. (Canadian subsidiary of White Motor Corp. of Ohio), directed United Airlines. H. Fraser, an executive with South-African-controlled Hudson Bay Mining and Smelting, directed US-based Engelhard Minerals and Chemicals Corp.
6. On the concept of go-between relations in foreign direct investment see Clement (1977:115). European TNC Nestlé had a primary tie to its Canadian subsidiary, through its American subsidiary. Japanese TNCs Itochu, Marubini and Mitsubishi had similar arrangements through their American subsidiaries, and in Mitsubishi's case the continental connection was carried by two inside directors.
7. Of the 26 primary lines remaining in 1996, eight led from a Canadian executive to an outside position on a US directorate, and two of these (Nestlé and Mitsubishi) followed intercorporate ownership lines reaching into Canada. Thirteen had the opposite directionality, and 11 of these involved strategic control of firms headquartered in Canada. (Compaq, Goodyear, Great A&P Inc. (two shared directors), McDonald's, Occidental Petroleum (two shared directors), Mitsubishi and Marubeni, Sears, and Weyerhaeuser account for these lines.) The remaining five primary lines involved officers in both the Canadian and American firms, in most cases connections between US-based parents and Canadian subsidiaries. The 26 primary lines continued a longstanding asymmetry of continental intercorporate ownership and control, whereby American capitalists controlled Canadian corporations using board-level interlocks as a means of oversight. Yet in comparison to 1976 the 1996 formation furnished a rather scant continental network of strategic control—in part an expression of the reduced American control over large Canadian firms.
8. Actually, only 35 of the 111 fitted the parent–subsidiary motif. The others were more diffuse, as occurs with interlocks created by outside directors.
9. The prime examples were Dutch/British-controlled Shell Oil and British-controlled Standard Oil of Ohio. In other cases, secondary continental interlocks involving Canadian firms controlled outside North America seemed more diffuse. For instance, three of the four lines linking Genstar into the US network were carried by Royal Bank Chair McLaughlin as a presumably unintended consequence of his many other corporate affiliations.

10. US-based McDonald's, GTE, Costco, Textron, and Shell maintained secondary interlocks with their Canadian subsidiaries. Shell's ultimate parent is of course the Dutch/British giant Royal Dutch Shell.
11. In 1996 two companies, US-based Costco and its Canadian subsidiary Price Costco Canada, formed a dyad that was detached from the dominant component.
12. Namely, in 1976 Mercantile Bank, Pratt & Whitney, Iron Ore Company of Canada, Simpson-Sears, and Celanese Canada; in 1996 Weyerhaeuser Canada and Sears Canada.
13. General Electric is the sole industrial firm appearing on both lists. Prudential, Chase Manhattan, and Bank of New York are the financial institutions.
14. Another facet of the same contrast is the fact that there were no Canadian parents of major American firms, a situation that Clement noted in the 1970s and that continued in the 1990s. At the level of strategic control, there were only two partial exceptions in 1996. The Bronfmans' 20.4 per cent interest, through Seagram, in US-based Dupont was the largest block of shares, but was not matched by any interlocking directorships between Seagram and Dupont. Similarly, Nova's 33.7 per cent interest in US-based NGC Corp (matched by an investment of equal size by British Gas) was unaccompanied by any interlocks between Nova and NGC.
15. The mean rush for 51 wholly owned American subsidiaries in 1976 was 0.00137. The mean for 37 wholly owned American subsidiaries in 1996 was 0.00183.
16. The mean degree of interlocking among the 30 Canadian companies drops from a remarkable 11.40 to 7.13. The mean degree among American companies drops from a more modest 5.93 to 3.07. The mean inter-sectoral degree between the 30 Canadian and 30 American firms drops from 2.27 to 1.47.
17. For instance, in 1976 Canadian Pacific's rush score of 0.0379 reflected its extensive ties to other central companies in the continental network—most of them Canadian but some American. CP's immediate social circle included 26 of the 60 companies in Figure 6.1. Among the 21 Canadian firms with which CP shared directors were financial institutions like the Bank of Montreal (five shared directors), the Royal Bank (five), Sun Life (four) and CIBC (three), and industrial corporations like its subsidiary Cominco (four shared directors), Bell Canada (two) and Inco (two), as well as investment company Power Corporation (two). In comparison to the extensive and thick interlocks that embedded CP within the Canadian network, all of its continental connections (to Metropolitan Life, General Motors, Union Carbide, Uniroyal, and Standard Brands) were carried by single directors, and only one of these involved a corporate executive (CP president Ian Sinclair's directorship with Union Carbide). In 1996 CP's social circle included 18 of the 60 corporations in Figure 6.2, 17 of them domiciled in Canada. Among the latter were thick ties to three leading financial institutions—Sun Life (four shared directors), the Royal Bank (three), and the Bank of Montreal (two)—and to three industrials: affiliate Laidlaw Inc. (two shared directors), Inco (two) and United Dominion Industries (two). CP's sole cross-border tie in 1996 was a shared outside directorship with Pharmacia & Upjohn.
18. IU International's interlocks with six Canadian firms (including its subsidiary, Canadian Utilities) accounted for the mean degree of three for the two US-based investment companies.
19. The five individuals composing this category in 1976 could lay claim to being members of *both the Canadian and American corporate elites*. Howard B. Keck was the major shareholder in Superior Oil of Nevada, which held majority control of Canadian Superior Oil and (through the latter) Falconbridge Nickel. Keck was an outside director of two major American corporations—Armco and First City Bancorp of Texas—and also sat on the Falconbridge and Canadian Superior Oil boards. G.W. Humphrey was an outside director of US-based General Electric and National Steel as well as Canadian-based Massey-Ferguson and Sun Life. Robert Scrivener was not only CEO of Nortel and a director of

Bell Canada, the CIBC, Hiram Walker, and Power Corporation. He also directed US-based Caterpillar and US Steel. W. Earle McLaughlin was not only Chair of the Royal Bank and director of Canadian Pacific, Algoma Steel, Genstar, Power Corporation, Allied Chemical, and Ralston Purina (the latter two US-controlled branch plants). He also sat on the boards of three major US companies: General Motors, Metropolitan Life, and Standard Brands. Consultant John H. Coleman, a retired Royal Bank vice-president and an outside director of nine Canadian corporations (including the Royal Bank, Great West Life, Westburne International Industries, Calgary Power, TransCanada PipeLine, and Thomson Newspapers, as well as foreign-controlled companies like Imasco, Hawker Siddeley [both British-controlled], Xerox Canada, and Chrysler Canada), also directed US-based Chrysler Corporation and Beatrice Foods. McLaughlin and Coleman can be recognized as paragons of continental corporate power. In 1976 they directed major Canadian financial and industrial firms, some of them controlled by Canadian capitalists, others by American TNCs, and they also sat on the boards of major American corporations with substantial investments in Canada. Except for the fact that McLaughlin's Canadian directorships show him to have been more a finance capitalist than a commercial capitalist uninterested in domestic Canadian industry, McLaughlin and Coleman would seem to personify Clement's notion of a continental corporate elite. The problem for Clement's thesis lies in the lack of cases, beyond these two, that appear to support it. In fact, by 1996 there were no corporate directors whose portfolios included multiple firms on both sides of the boarder.

20. These categorizations were made on the basis of the principal occupation given in biographical listings in various sources.
21. For instance, in 1996 John R. Hall, chair and CEO of Ashland Oil, also directed Bank One, CSX, Humana, and Reynolds Metals—all US-based—but his outside directorship with Canada Life created five interlocks between the American and Canadian networks. Frank C. Carlucci III, a merchant banker and former US Secretary of Defense, also directed Ashland Oil as well as Bell Atlantic, Massachusetts Mutual, and Westinghouse, but his seat on the Nortel board is what created four ties between the respective national networks. Sears CEO Arthur C. Martinez's directorship with Sears Canada reflected a continental relation of strategic control, but because Martinez was well-connected within the American elite (with seats on the boards of Amoco and Amtech) his directorship with Sears Canada created three continental linkages, one of which was a relation of direct strategic control. Finally, the case of Donald J. Schuenke is instructive on the changing form of continental connections. Formerly CEO of US-based Northwestern Mutual Life and long a member of the American corporate elite, Schuenke was recruited as the non-executive chair of Nortel in 1994. In 1996 he also directed Northwestern Mutual and Federal Home Loan Mortgage Co., thus carrying two cross-border interlocks.
22. Namely, Arthur Martinez, CEO of Sears (USA); John W. Creighton, Jr, president of Weyerhaueser US and director of Weyerhaueser Canada; James F. Hardymon, president and chair of Textron, both US and Canada; Eckhard Pfeiffer, president of Compaq, both US and Canada; and Michael R. Quinlan, president of McDonald's, both US and Canada.
23. In 1976 among the key members of the Canadian elite with a seat on a major US board were Allen Lambert (chair and president of TD Bank), Alastair Campbell (chair of Sun Life) and J. Daniel Leitch (vice-president of the CIBC); by 1996, however, Richard M. Thompson, president of the TD Bank, was the only Canadian-based financial executive with multiple directorships domestically as well as a directorship with a US-based firm.
24. Marie-Josée Kravitz, senior policy analyst at the Hudson Institute in Indianapolis, was an outside director of Molson, Seagram, CIBC, and Ford Motor Company (the latter being the US-based parent), and spouse to US-based corporate buyout specialist Henry Kravis (Banks and North, 1996).

25. By the early 1990s, as business use of email and the internet mushroomed, TNCs could begin connecting their different parts easily, cheaply, and across all levels of organization, in some cases eliminating the need for interlocking directorates as primary vehicles of communication and oversight. As my colleague Prof. A.R. Elangovan of the University of Victoria Faculty of Business has suggested in a personal communication (July 2002), 'a multi-level, multi-layered, inexpensive virtual interlocking' may well have rendered interlocking directorates less critical in TNC's exercise of strategic and operational control.
26. Our findings in this respect are at odds with Arthurs's (2000:40) comparison of the boards of the 115 largest foreign-controlled Canadian corporations of 1985 and 1995, which showed a modest increase in non-resident directors, particularly for firms taken 'private'.

Chapter 7

1. In assembling the 1996 data we have followed the selection procedure used by Fennema (1982), which meant for each stratum selecting the largest financial institutions by assets and the largest non-financials by revenue, and excluding wholly owned subsidiaries such as General Motors of Canada, whose 1996 revenue ranked second in Canada. We include Power Corporation among the seven Canadian-based non-financial institutions for that year even though its 1996 revenue placed it 18th among major Canadian firms. This is in recognition of the fact that as a holding company Power Corporation's revenue, which consists in great part of profits from its various affiliates and subsidiaries, gives only a very conservative estimate of the capital actually under its control. Not surprisingly, Power ranked seventh in assets among the 208 Canadian non-financial institutions of 1996. In fact, by this measure Power was slightly larger than Seagram, twice the size of Nortel, Alcan, and TransCanada PipeLine and five times the size of Weston—all members of our select Canadian 11, shown in Figure 7.2.
2. In 1976 corporations that had long been at the centre of the Canadian network shared as many as five directors (e.g., the Bank of Montreal and Canadian Pacific). By 1996 only one pair shared as many as four directors (Alcan and the Royal Bank), while four pairs each shared three directors. Concomitantly, the density of interlocking among the eleven Canada-based firms dropped from 0.382 to 0.327.
3. Recall that in Fennema's (1982) original study, wholly owned subsidiaries were excluded from consideration. For consistency's sake we have applied this selection criterion in defining the peak Canadian firms of 1996.
4. This is not to say that Canada's two most continentalized industrials were in the process of shedding ties to Canadian banks. In 1996, as the sociogram shows, Bank of Montreal CEO Matthew Barrett, despite his vocal commitment to the new corporate governance regime, remained on the Seagram board, and Nortel CEO Jean Monty sat on the Bank of Montreal Board.
5. Although with the purchase of Universal in 1996 Seagram embarked on a continental business strategy of diversification into the entertainment industry under the direction of Edgar Bronfman Sr's son, Edgar Jr, it is interesting in view of the 1999 merger between Paris-based Vivendi and Seagram, that Charles Sr's directorship with Power in 1996 already put the Bronfmans into close contact with several key players within French corporate capitalism.
6. Namely, Price-Costco Canada and Compaq Canada, both subsidiaries of US-based companies.
7. In a bipartite network, all the lines connect actors from two distinct sets, in this case Canadian-based and foreign-based corporations.

8. The dyads were for the most part board-level versions of parent-subsidiary relations. Four involved Japanese-based Mitsubishi, Honda, Bank of Tokyo Mitsui, and Itochu, and their Canadian subsidiaries, and in each of these the interlock was carried by an executive (in the case of Honda and Honda Canada, two executives), signalling a close blending of strategic control and hands-on, operational management. The two dyads tracing the power of US-based Compaq and Costco over their Canadian subsidiaries were carried by outside directors, as were the interlocks in the other three dyads, which did not entail strategic control but did involve financial institutions and the potential exercise of allocative power. McDonalds Canada was interlocked with UK-based Lloyd's TSB Group. Canada Life was interlocked with US-based Banc One Corp. United Dominion Industries was interlocked with US-based First Union Corp.
9. Paul Desmarais Sr is joined by Paul Jr on the Power and Fina boards and by Desmarais's lieutenant Michel François-Poncet on the Paribas and AXA boards.
10. For example, not shown in the sociogram are Price Costco Canada, Compaq Canada, and Honda Canada. With its foreign-based parent, each formed a dyad detached from the network.
11. In addition to his seats on the Barrick and Fina boards, Mulroney also directed Archer Daniels Midland Company, a Top 250 US-based manufacturer that was too small to be included in our Global 350.
12. Financial institutions figured heavily in these ties. The two Euro–Japan interlocks were effected by Yasuyuki Wakahara's outside directorships with the Dutch-based financial institution Fortis and the Japanese industrial Fujitsu and by Itochu president Minoru Murofushi's outside directorship with the British-based bank HSBC Holdings. The sole US–Japan interlock resulted from Masataka Shimasaki's outside directorships with Lehman Brothers Holdings and Nippon Life.
13. This level of transatlantic network integration is all the more remarkable when we observe that five of the 20 European corporations formed a separate component. These companies—Spanish-based Banco Santander S.A. and Italian-based Instituto Banca san Paolo di Torino, Banca di Roma, Societa Finanziaria Telefonica (STET), and IRI—scored high in rush because they brought otherwise disconnected southern European companies indirectly into the Canada–Europe formation, through Banco Santander's interlocks with two US-based companies: First Union Corp. (itself interlocked with Canada's United Dominion Industries) and Rockwell International (linked indirectly to various Canadian firms via its interlocks with Amoco Corporation and Prudential Life).
14. Specifically, 24 of 32 German firms, 20 of 34 British, 18 of 25 French, eight of nine Dutch, four of seven Swiss, all four Belgian, and all three Swedish corporations.
15. On average, the 34 British firms were interlocked with 2.882 British and 0.529 north western continental European firms; the 81 northwestern continental firms were interlocked with 7.605 north-western continental firms but with only 0.222 British firms.
16. Eight of the 34 British companies in our Global 338 had 16 interlocks with the 90 US-based companies. Eight German companies also interlocked with the Top 90 American corporations, but the number of interlocks between them was only 10. Four Dutch, two French, two Swiss, and one Spanish company had ties to American corporations. In all, 25 European-based companies interlocked with a total of 30 American corporations.
17. From Switzerland and France northward and from Germany westward.
18. Japanese corporate capital is primarily integrated through extensive cross-shareholding within *keiretsu*, which are highly organized enterprise groups that include banks and industrial firms. Within a *keiretsu*, personnel exchanges among members tend to occur not as simultaneous cross-appointments but as *flows* between companies, with the director or executive maintaining contact after being delegated, to return to the sending firm some time later (Westney, 1996).

19. The global network we have examined includes all 258 top Canadian corporation but only the top 73 Japanese, the top 32 German, the top 25 French companies, etc. It is not out of the question that a Canadian-based TNC might control, say, the 100th largest Italian industrial, and that the two boards might be interlocked. Our data do not afford such an observation. Moreover, in composing each sample (Canadian Top 258 and Global Top 350) we enforced a rule that excluded any firms wholly owned by other companies large enough to qualify for the sample. This rule carried different implications for the two samples and for our mapping of interlocks between Canada and the rest of the world. In selecting the Canadian Top 258 we excluded firms that were wholly owned by other Canadian firms but included companies that were wholly owned by foreign corporations, since some of these number among the largest and most important Canadian companies. The Global 350 was selected in a way that excluded all companies that were wholly owned by other companies large enough to qualify for the global sample. Thus, in our database a non-Canadian firm's 100 per cent ownership of a leading Canadian corporation might generate an interlocking directorate, but a Canadian firm's 100 per cent ownership of a non-Canadian company would not.
20. Paul Desmarais and son Paul Jr, Mitsui (Japan) principal Susumu Myamoto, Toronto-Dominion CEO Richard M. Thompson, *éminence grise* Marshall Cohen, and corporate advisor Marie-Josée Kravis each directed two or more large Canadian corporations.
21. In autumn of 1996 the North American membership of the TC numbered 92. The European membership was somewhat larger (136) and the Japanese membership somewhat smaller (68). In the same year, the ICC Executive Committee had 27 members, the Foundation Board and Members Council of the WEF had 45 members (combined), and the WBCSD had 121 members, 13 of whom belonged to the Council's Executive Committee. The 1997 Bilderberg meeting attracted 114 attendees.
22. The criterion Colin Carson and I used in designating affiliations with the Bilderberg Conference (a group that has no permanent membership other than its organizing committee, which Conrad Black chaired as host of the meetings in 1996) was that an individual have attended both the 1996 meeting in Toronto and the 1997 meeting near Atlanta. While Black's heavy involvement with Bilderberg is well established, that of his Canadian cohorts seems more casual. Indeed, Black's influence may well have been a factor in Allan Gotlieb's participation at the 1996 Conference and in Fredrik Eaton's and Maureen Sabia's participation in 1997. Gotlieb, Eaton, and Sabia were all directors of Black's Hollinger in 1996. Sabia did attend the 1998 Bilderberg Conference, so her involvement appears to be more ongoing.
23. Note that as in other aspects of our analysis, our exclusive focus on corporate interlockers means that we do not consider certain corporate directors who play important roles in the power structure. For instance, in 1996 Maurice Strong, a director of Ontario Hydro and founder of one of the predecessors to the WBCSD, was one of 12 members of the Foundation Board, the World Economic Forum's top decision-making body.
24. R.E. Kadlec, president of BC Gas, private investor David A. Lewis, former Bank of Montreal CEO William Muholland, and former US Ambassador to Canada Edward Ney are members of Canada's corporate elite who belonged to the Council on Foreign Relations in 1996. Ney (a principal in public-relations giant Burson-Marsteller and a director of Peter Munk's Barrick Gold and Trizec Hahn) and Kravis are based primarily in the US and have been keen advocates of continental 'free trade', Ney from a position of some political power during his diplomatic stint (1989–92), Kravis as a policy analyst and newspaper columnist. They are two members of the Canadian corporate elite with American professional affiliations and an abiding commitment to full-scale continentalism.

Chapter 8

1. For discussions of neoliberalism in a Canadian context see Burke, Mooers, and Shields (2000).
2. A hegemonic project 'involves the mobilization of support behind a concrete, national-popular program of action which asserts a general interest in the pursuit of objectives that explicitly or implicitly advance the long-term interests of the hegemonic class (fraction) and which also privileges particular "economic-corporate" interests compatible with this program' (Jessop, 1983:100).
3. Recall from Chapter 1 (note 9) that Gramsci did not view the bourgeoisie and its organic intellectuals as mutually exclusive categories but recognized a considerable confluence. The present chapter's investigation of overlaps between the governance of large corporations and neoliberal policy groups directly addresses the extent to which corporate capitalists play a direct role as organic intellectuals in neoliberal policy formation.
4. Analysis of two CDHI reports on social policy, from 1975 (Maxwell, 1975) and 1994 (Watson, Richards, and Brown, 1994), reveals the shift that took place. While the 1975 report explored the complex structural factors underlying such problems as unemployment and high inflation rates, the 1994 report portrayed social programs and government spending as root causes of Canada's economic problems; as economist William Watson put it, 'is there anyone in this country who is not on the dole?' (1994:15). Many of the structural conditions and market forces that in the 1975 report were considered susceptible to regulation were treated in the 1994 report as beyond control of any national government. As CDHI policy analyst David Brown stated in the 1994 report: 'the structural changes Canada is undergoing are so fundamental as to require that the social contract be rewritten.... the old social contract has been rendered obsolete by global events beyond the control of any national government' (Watson, Richards, and Brown, 1994:116, 122).
5. Since their introduction in 1988, Fraser Institute Student programs have expanded to include Student Seminars on Public Policy Issues, Student Leaders' Colloquia, the *Canadian Student Review* quarterly newsletter, an internship program, and the provision of student bursaries. Particular attention is paid to 'the development of the student program as the Institute and its supporters recognize the importance of encouraging the study of competitive markets among students and young people' (Fraser Institute, 1998).
6. In the early 1980s, the Social Credit government of BC not only 'approached' the Fraser Institute for ideas, but inserted some of these ideas directly into government policy (Havemann, 1986:19–22). FI recommendations to the BC government lent focus and intensity to a right market agenda in Canada that until that point had 'seemed unclear, divided, and less populist than its British or American counterparts and, therefore, unlikely to capture the overt platform of any major political party' (Havemann, 1986:13).
7. The Council was constituted from the start in an exclusivist, not corporatist, mode—it was to be a vehicle for achieving consensus *within the corporate capitalist community*, and its members were hand-picked from the leading CEOs of Canadian business. Moreover, although the Council may have lacked some of the Fraser Institute's ardour in its formative years, its project was framed explicitly as a reaction *against* the perceived problems in the Keynesian paradigm of national regulation and the welfare state.
8. As elsewhere in this volume, this analysis does not consider people's directorships with non-Top 250 firms, which can be extensive. Thus our estimate of the extent of business ties to the policy boards is conservative.
9. Line multiplicity (i.e., two or more shared directors between a pair of boards) is taken into account in these calculations. Only paths of length three or less (i.e., situations in which a pair of organizations are linked at no more than two removes) are included in

the analysis. See Stokman, Ziegler, and Scott (1985:31–2) for a description of the rush index.

10. The concept of an inner circle of the corporate elite was developed extensively in the 1980s by Michael Useem (1984), who argued that the embeddedness of such corporate capitalists—their common participation on multiple corporate and policy directorates—leads them to embrace a 'class-wide rationality' (Dreiling, 2000:29). Dreiling's (2000) own study of American corporate political action in support of NAFTA illustrates the facilitative role played by the 'policy formation network' of large corporations and policy groups.

11. In 1996, a total of six policy-group linkers directed these two banks, while two other members of the group of 22 directed foreign-controlled banks that had established a presence in Canada—the Dutch-controlled ABN and the British-controlled Hong Kong Savings Bank. By 1996 key bankers played less of a role in the network. For instance, while in 1976 the Chair of the Royal Bank, W. Earle McLaughlin, was affiliated with the Conference Board, the BCNI, and seven leading corporations, in 1996 the Chair of the Royal Bank, J. Cleghorn, was affiliated with the same two policy groups but directed only two corporations.

12. The interlocks are carried by Brian Levitt, president of Imasco Ltd, Roger Phillips, president of IPSCO Inc., and P.J. Hill, chair of Crown Life.

13. Namely Paul Gagné, president of Avenor Inc., William Dalton, president of the Hong Kong Bank of Canada, Diane McGarry, president of Xerox Canada, and Robert Peterson, president of Imperial Oil Ltd.

14. It is well to remember that our diagrams map only a small part of the entire network: the 22 individuals who make up the inner circle are a subset of a group of 262 people who in 1996 served on any one of the policy groups, most of whom were also directors of one or more of the Top 250 corporations. As an example of one of the 240 policy-group directors not shown in Fig. 8.2, consider the integrative role played by Purdy Crawford. Chair in 1996 of Imasco and CT Financial and director of Avenor, Dominion Textile, Inco, Maple Leaf Foods, the CNR, and Petro-Canada, Crawford was in the same year chair of AIMS (a position he had held since AIMS's founding) as well as chair of a major policy group affiliated with the Conference Board (the National Council on Education) and a governor of McGill University.

15. Our mapping of the policy bloc has focused on the key sites for neoliberal policy formation. Left unprobed is the important issue of how more 'moderate' groups—the Canadian Policy Research Network, the Institute for Research on Public Policy, etc.—whose perspectives have been reshaped by neoliberalism, might be articulated discursively and organizationally with the neoliberal bloc.

16. For a study of left-oriented policy groups that addresses their counter-hegemonic prospects see Mulvale (2001).

17. Methodological details are given in Appendix 2.

18. In 1979, 54 per cent of foreign-controlled dominant companies made no political contributions whatsoever, 10 per cent of them made contributions under $5000 (1997 dollars) and 10 per cent (12 firms) made contributions that totalled over $50,000. For comparison, 15 per cent of dominant companies controlled by Canadian capitalist interests made no contributions, 28 per cent made contributions under $5000, and 23.4 per cent (26 firms) contributed $50,000 or more in total. Fully 72.3 per cent of all political donations from dominant corporations came from firms controlled in Canada. In 1997, four in ten foreign-controlled dominant corporations did not contribute to any Canadian federal party, three in ten made total contributions under $5000, and only five firms (6.5 per cent) contributed $50,000 or more in total. In the same year, three in ten dominant companies controlled by Canadian capitalist interests made no contributions, one in ten

made contributions under $5000, and 30 firms (22.4 per cent) contributed $50,000 or more in total. Fully 87.4 per cent of all political donations from dominant corporations came from firms controlled in Canada.

19. At another crucial political conjuncture, in September 1997, one month before the referendum on Quebec independence, members of Quebec's business elite, including Power Corp. chair Paul Desmarais Sr and Bombardier chair Laurent Beaudoin, formed the Conseil des gens d'affaires du Québec pour le Canada, a political action committee with an initial $400,000 budget to voice corporate Quebec's opposition to the proposal for negotiating Quebec independence (Came and Janigan, 1995).

20. The National Bank of Canada gave a whopping (and intriguing) $25,000 to Reform and a token $250 to the Liberals. Algoma Steel Inc.—a worker co-op at the time—gave $2000 to Reform and $872 to the Liberals. Seven additional companies gave to Reform but favoured one of the old-line bourgeois parties, among them Conrad Black's Hollinger Inc. (which gave $1520 to Reform and $4054 to the Tories) and the Bank of Nova Scotia (which gave $39,520 to Reform and $73,126 to the Tories). The fact that in 1997 two of Canada's six major banks gave substantial amounts to Reform, and nothing (or nearly nothing) to the Liberals, suggests some emerging differences within the corporate elite on the question of which political parties can best serve the interests of corporate capital.

21. Fully 72 per cent of the 50 most central corporations in the Canadian corporate network gave to both the Liberals and Tories in the 1997 election year. This compares with only 31.3 per cent of the 208 less central firms.

22. As Royal Bank senior vice-president Bryan Davies observed, 'there was an anomaly created in the 1993 to 1997 period, in that we [i.e., the RBC] essentially made a policy decision that until the next election we would give treatment to the Progressive Conservative Party as though it was still in an Official Opposition capacity' (quoted in McFarland, 2000).

CHAPTER 9

1. It is useful at the outset of this analysis to consider the role and purposes of the Board of Governors in Canadian universities. A.D. Gregor, in 'The Universities of Canada', *Commonwealth Universities Yearbook 1997* (London: Association of Commonwealth Universities, 1998), describes the Canadian university board as a body that normally 'attends to management of the university, to its relationship with government and the general community, and to the planning of its resources and programs'. Ernst B. Benjamin, Ken McGovern, and Guy Bourgeault, in *Governance and Accountability: The Report of the Independent Study Group on University Governance* (Ottawa: Canadian Association of University Teachers, 1993), point out that while the principal statutory obligation of the board is to ensure the university's fiscal well-being, 'it is obvious that this can occur only in circumstances in which the board understands that, in setting the budget, they are establishing the academic priorities of the university as well' (p. 31). While university boards typically include representatives of stakeholders within the institution, there is also provision for appointments from 'the community', usually by provincial governments (p. 34). The corporate–university interlocks we map out here stem from the latter appointments, as the 'business community' often stands in for the community, 'a state of affairs that is to some extent explained by the requirement that there be present on the board individuals capable of circumnavigating through the various minefields involved in university financing' (p. 36).

2. As Janice Newson (1994) observes, this has serious implications for future decision making. The market-led transformation has the potential for narrowing the knowledge

base and limiting the range of choices that will be available for deciding on political, economic and social alternatives.
3. Drakich et al. (2002:255) summarize the main internal transformations well: 'university presidents have become chief executive officers and universities increasingly mimic large-scale corporations. A specialization of administrative functions has occurred, the number of administrative officers has increased, and more of these officers are drawn from outside of the academy. Decision making is increasingly centralized, affecting the budget allocation process, as well as the policies and practices and various aspects of academic life. In many universities, budget and finance have been divorced from academic functions. Formerly organic relations have become more bureaucratic and driven by concerns about greater efficiency.'
4. Even though most university funding in Canada comes from the state and tuition fees, there are many recent examples of corporate donations that skew university resources in a business-oriented direction; see Giberson (1997); Cole (1998).
5. Since our analysis includes only those individuals holding directorships in more than one Top 250 corporation, we capture *only the top layer* of corporate–university ties. Ties carried by directors of only one dominant corporation or by directors of non-dominant corporations are excluded from this analysis. As estimates of the extent of corporate–university networking, our results are conservative.
6. There is another sense in which our findings, particularly for 1996, are conservative indications of corporate–university interlocking. While for 1976 we were able to examine membership lists of university boards and to code each member of the corporate elite on that basis, for 1996 we relied primarily on biographical sources such as *Who's Who in Canada* and *The Canadian Who's Who*. Only 11 of 426 corporate-elite members were not listed in these sources. However, there is no guarantee that each entry was complete in its listing of university-board affiliations in 1996.
7. For instance, in 1996 former federal cabinet members Barbara McDougall and Donald Mazankowski were outside directors of four and six dominant corporations respectively, and also university governors, bridging the worlds of capital and academe in an advisory capacity on both sides.
8. Elizabeth Parr-Johnston (UNB) was on the board of the Bank of Nova Scotia and the Empire Company. J. Robert Prichard (University of Toronto) was on the board of Imasco, Moore Corp., and Onex Corp. D.W. Strangway (UNB) was a director of BC Gas and MacMillan Bloedel.
9. In this bipartite network, only ties between universities and corporations are considered; interlocks among the corporations are examined in Chapters 3–7 of this book.
10. As usual, we are referring only to ties carried by directors who held positions in multiple Top 250 corporations, i.e., the corporate elite proper. Other directors of some of these firms, not in the elite, may well have sat on university boards, but these relations are not considered here.
11. In 1976 the mean number of university contacts per firm was .93 for Canadian-controlled companies, .34 for US-controlled companies, and .50 for British-controlled companies. The corresponding means in 1996 were .79, .22, and .80.
12. See, respectively, the *Globe and Mail's Report on Business Magazine*, July 1997, p. 100; Thomas Hatzichronoglou 'Revision of the High-Technology Sector and Product Classification', STI Working Paper 1997/2 (Paris: Organization for Economic Co-operation and Development, 1997).
13. Also, although these foreign-owned companies engage in some research and development in Canada, a good deal of that activity tends to be centralized in the head office of the parent firm. Hence it may be that the foreign-held high-tech firms have less of an

instrumental interest in Canadian universities than do the domestically controlled high-tech companies.

14. By definition, every member of a block must be tied to at least two other members of the same block. Organizations linked to only one other member of the dominant component are excluded.

15. University of Manitoba's ties to Canadian Airlines and United Grain Growers—two structurally marginal firms in the corporate-university network—did not integrate it into the biggest block.

16. D.A. Chisholm was executive vice president of Northern Telecom. B.G. Coté was CEO of Celanese Canada. J.V.R. Cyr was executive vice president of Bell Canada. A.J. O'Connor was general manager of New Brunswick Power. J.A. Pollock was president of Electrohome Ltd.

17. Finance Minister Paul Martin, in establishing the CFI, stated that in the 'new economy' of the twenty-first century 'it is only through knowledge, information and ideas that new products and new services will be created' (Martin, 1997).

18. Notes for an address by J. Keith Brimacombe, President and CEO of the Canada Foundation for Innovation, to the third annual University–Industry Synergy Symposium organized by NSERC and The Conference Board of Canada, 24 Oct. 1997, Richmond, BC, http://www.innovation.ca/english/new/notes.html.

19. NCE's mandate includes all levels of education, from primary through post-secondary. Its board brings members of the corporate elite together not only with academics but with members of various school boards, etc. While 15 of its members were corporate directors or executives and 12 were academic and educational administrators, five were federal or provincial state functionaries, two were professional employees of the sponsoring Conference Board, and three represented, respectively, Decima Research, YMCA Canada, and the Canadian Federation of Labour. As for the CFI, its 30 directors and members included seven representatives of the 'non-profit private sector', comprising groups such as the Canadian Cancer Society. Both the CFI and NCE can be described as corporatist organizations that tilt compositionally towards big business.

20. Namely Angus Bruneau, an executive with Fortis Inc.

21. Its goals as stated in one of its reports are to promote mutual understanding through the exchange of ideas and points of view; to develop policy statements of mutual interest and concern; to provide a vehicle for corporate and university leadership to reflect upon questions of national significance; and to support programs consistent with the philosophy of the organization. Judith Maxwell, Judith and Stephanie Currie, 'Partnership for Growth. The Corporate Higher Education Forum' (unpublished, Montreal, 1984), 101.

22. Namely David Strangway, who in 1996 was Director of the Corporate Higher Education Forum and President of UBC; see Figure 9.3. After his retirement from UBC Strangway spearheaded the 'Sea to Sky University' (the first private, secular liberal arts university in Canada, accredited in May 2002) and became president of CFI.

23. For information on this international assembly of corporate–university fora, see http://www.work.org/assemblies/1998/.

24. The relatively small size of Mount Allison prevented us from including it in our sample and thus in Figure 9.3. The Atlantic Institute for Market Studies (AIMS) is discussed in Chapter 8.

25. In addition to the three mentioned earlier, it is worth noting that a fourth university president—Lorna Marsden of Wilfrid Laurier University (now president of York University)—belonged to the corporate elite in 1996. However, Wilfrid Laurier was judged too small to qualify for our sample, pointing up again the conservative character of our methodology. Also, as we have seen, former University of Toronto President John

Evans has moved smoothly into the upper echelons of corporate capital while also chairing the CFI.

26. In a revealing sidelight to the campaign, in 1999 then-president Robert Prichard was obliged to apologize to the University of Toronto's Governing Board for lobbying the federal government on behalf of Apotex Inc., a firm that had promised the University an 'investment' of $55 million (Toronto *Globe and Mail*, 16 Sept. 1999, p. A5).

CHAPTER 10

1. The chimera of the 'soulful corporation' has a long history in American management science. See for instance Berle (1959).
2. Relatedly, in February 2003 the Ontario Teachers Pension Fund and the Canada Pension Plan Investment Board joined forces with a few other institutional investors in launching Mid-Ocean Partners LP, an investment company that bought the private equity unit of Deutsche Bank AG, with portfolio stakes in 80-odd companies (Stewart, 2003).
3. For further details see note 10, Chapter 3.
4. Harry Arthurs (2000) speculates further that changes in the regime of transnational corporate governance may be 'hollowing out' Canada's business community. However, his study focused exclusively on foreign-controlled corporations in Canada, and did not distinguish between American, European, and Japanese control centres. By ignoring domestically controlled corporate capital, which we have shown to be quite resilient— and the leading segment of the Canadian corporate elite—Arthurs mistakes the decline of the comprador corporate elite for a hollowing-out of the business community.
5. As an example worth noting parenthetically, there is evidence that Canada–US free trade has begun to weaken the controlling positions of wealthy families in Canada by ratcheting up competitive pressures and 'thereby raising the price that families must pay to maintain corporate control' (Morck, Strangeland, and Yeung, 2000:361–2). In Morck et al.'s analysis, 10 of 100 leading Canadian corporations controlled by families or individuals in 1988 had by 1994 become widely held (i.e., controlled by a constellation of interests), and three of the 100 had fallen under the control of investment funds (i.e., institutional investors) (2000:361).
6. Li Ka-shing's Canadian holdings include control of Husky Oil, Concord Pacific (owner of much of the former Expo site in Vancouver) and a 10 per cent equity stake in the CIBC (with joint CIBC ventures in Hong Kong). The latter holding is the largest block of shares in any of the big six chartered banks. The Cheung Kong Group, Li's lead investment company, accounts for 15 per cent of the total capitalization of the Hong Kong stock exchange (Warren, 2000).
7. The Péladeau family, whose Canadian investments include major media and cable companies, also controls Europe's largest commercial printer ('Pressing his case', 2002).
8. Yanarella and Reid's analysis of 'humanware' is helpful here: 'despite the pseudoegalitarianism evident in lean production factories and the absence of symbols of organization hierarchy between management and labor, the language of the post-Fordist text marginalizes the human dimension to the point of obliteration, absorbing the laboring subject as humanware completely into the corporate circuitry of the post-Fordist organization and production system' (1996: 203).
9. In 1999 94 per cent of all stocks held outside RRSPs (which are vehicles of passive investment) was owned by the richest 20 per cent of Canadian family units. The poorest 60 per cent claimed a total of only 1 per cent. Even within the richest quintile, share ownership was highly concentrated. Only 27 per cent owned stocks outside RRSPs—that is,

approximately five percent of family units owned 94 per cent of stocks outside RRSPs (Kerstetter, 2002).

10. As public pension schemes atrophy for lack of funding, upper-stratum workers have ploughed deferred wages into RRSPs that often include portfolios of shares. The survey cited earlier (Market Trend Canada, 2002) found that of the 46 per cent of adult Canadians who owned any corporate shares in 2002, most were passive shareholders by virtue of mutual funds, and more than three-quarters had total portfolios of less than $100,000. Still, the 46 per cent figure represents an enormous net gain. In 1983 only 13 per cent of adult Canadians owned any corporate shares, directly or through funds. By 2002, approximately one-tenth of adult Canadians owned $100,000 or more in corporate shares. Although excluded from the control of corporate capital, small shareholders may view their economic interests as closely aligned with the profitability of corporations in which they hold stock.

11. As Shorris notes, neoliberal democracy conflates two quite different organizational principles—those of the market and democracy: 'Political democracy is a relation among human beings who control themselves. Market democracy is a competition in which people try to control each other ... this one is a misnomer, for the control of one human being by another, no matter how subtle the means, is no democracy' (1994:137).

12. This refers not only to policies of 'sound money,' deregulation, and privatization—the most obvious elements of neoliberalism—but to public administration and the provision of social services. As they assume a commodity form, services such as health, education, and public broadcasting become transformed under the pressures of competition. 'What begins as the provision of a service to fulfil collectively determined socio-political purposes ends up as a drive to find mass-produced goods that can be sold profitably. The collective needs and values that the service was originally created to serve are gradually marginalised and finally abandoned' (Leys, 2001:4).

13. The results of Gallup International's Millennium Survey of more than 50,000 people in 60 countries, summarized in the UN Report (p. 63), are instructive. When asked, 'Does government respond to the will of the people?' only 10 per cent answered affirmatively.

14. See, for instance, Drainville (2001), Klein (2001), Welton and Wolf (2001), Carroll (2003), McNally (2002).

15. Within Canada, the last quarter of the twentieth century witnessed a stunning rise in income disparities. While in 1973 the richest 10 per cent of families with dependent children received 21 times the income of the poorest decile of Canadian families, by 1996 the richest decile received 314 times more than the poorest decile. In the same period Canada's middle-income category (earning between $24,500 and $65,000) shrank from 60 per cent to 44 per cent of families with dependent children (Centre for Social Justice, 1998).

16. See Lee (2002). In just five years, between 1988 and 1993, nearly 4 per cent of world income was redistributed upward into the top income decile, so that by 1993 this stratum claimed 50.8 per cent in comparison to the 22.3 per cent claimed by the poorest 75 per cent (ibid).

17. Although our study has not examined the relation between corporate power and ecological crisis, the evidence supporting a deep connection is clear enough. See especially Kovel (2002), who emphasizes the contradiction between on the one hand capitalism's dynamic of endless self-expansion through the production and consumption of commodities (exchange values) and on the other hand the homeostatic processes that govern the natural world: 'Capital cannot recuperate the ecological crisis because its essential being, manifest in the "grow or die" syndrome, is to produce such a crisis, and the only thing it really knows how to do, which is to produce according to exchange-value, is exactly the source of the crisis' (Kovel, 2002:82).

18. In reference to its name change, the Council explained that 'as Canada entered the 21st century, it became clear that "national issues" increasingly had global dimensions. Addressing the key challenges facing the country therefore required a much greater degree of global engagement on the part of Canadian chief executives.' See the group's website at www.ceocouncil.ca.

APPENDIX 2

1. The logic and approach taken here closely match my previous study of Canadian corporate power in the period 1946 through 1976, and the reader is directed to the methodological appendix of that volume for a fuller discussion (Carroll, 1986).
2. Namely, Hans Bahlow, *Deutsches Namenlexikon* (Munchen: Keyser, 1967); Charles W.E. Bardsley, *A Dictionary of English and Welsh Surnames* (Baltimore: Genealogical Publishing Co., 1967); F. Bogdan, *Dictionary of Ukrainian Surnames in Canada* (Winnipeg: Onomastic Commission of UVAN, 1974); Albert Dauzat, *Dictionnaire étymologique des noms de famille et prénoms de France* (Paris: Larousse, 1951); Patrick Hanks and Flavia Hodges, *A Dictionary of Surnames* (New York: Oxford University Press, 1989); Benzion C. Kaganoff, *A Dictionary of Jewish Names and Their History* (New York: Schocken Books, 1977); Percy H. Reaney, *A Dictionary of British Surnames* (London: Routledge and Kegan Paul, 1976); Elsdon C. Smith, *American Surnames* (Philadelphia: Chilton, 1969), and Smith, *New Dictionary of American Family Names* (New York: Harper & Row, 1973); Patrick Woulfe, *Irish Names and Surnames* (Baltimore: Genealogical Publishing Co., 1967).
3. Executive positions were considered to be full-time, salaried positions internal to the company, such as CEO, president, vice-president, treasurer, and secretary. Board chairs and vice-chairs were not considered executives. For further clarification, see note 11 of Chapter 2.
4. Second-generation in the sense of coming after the initial wave of network-analytic software designed for mainframe computers, but before the adoption of third-generation graphic interfaces with programs such as UCINET version 5 and KRACKPLOT. GRADAP was released initially as a first-generation program in 1981, in close association with an extensive research program into the structure of corporate power, in the Netherlands and globally. See Fennema (1982).
5. UCINET was developed by Steve Borgatti, Martin Everitt, and Lin Freeman; version 5.0 was released in 1999. Full documentation is available at www.analytictech.com/, where KrackPlot is also available. For further information on KrackPlot see David Krackhardt, Jim Blythe, and Cathleen McGrath, 'KrackPlot 3.0: An improved network drawing program,' *Connections* 17 (2): 53-5 (December 1994).

References

Abelson, Donald E., and Christine M. Carberry. 1998. 'Following Suit or Falling Behind? A Comparative Analysis of Think Tanks in Canada and the United States'. *Canadian Journal of Political Science* 31(3):524–55.
Adams, Paul. 2002. '"Peace Has a Cost," Bronfman Says'. *Globe and Mail* (Toronto), 30 May: A11.
Alderson, Arthur S., and Jason Beckfield. 2002. 'Globalization and the Centralization of Power in the World City System: A Neural Network Approach'. XV World Congress of Sociology. 7–13 July.
Amin, Samir. 1974. *Accumulation on a World Scale*. New York: Monthly Review Press.
Amoore, Louise, and Richard Dodgson. 1997. 'Overturning "Globalization": Resisting the Teleology, Reclaiming the "Political"'. *New Political Economy* 2(1):179–95.
Andreff, W. 1984. 'The Internationalization of Capital and the Reordering of World Capitalism'. *Capital & Class* 25:58–80.
Andrews, Charles. 2000. *From Capitalism to Equality*. Oakland, CA: Needle Press.
Antoniou, A., and R. Rowley. 1989. 'Canadian Corporate Structure: The Importance of Shadow Groups'. *South African Journal of Economics* 57:380.
Armstrong, J. 1997. 'The Changing Business Activities of Banks in Canada'. *Bank of Canada Review* (Spring):10-38.
Arthurs, Harry W. 2000. 'The Hollowing out of Corporate Canada?' Pp. 29–51 in *Globalizing Institutions*, ed. Jane Jenson and Bonaventura de Sousa Santos. Burlington, VT: Ashgate.
Ashley, C.A. 1957. 'Concentration of Economic Power'. *Canadian Journal of Economics and Political Science* 23:105–8.
Atkins, Fiona. 1986. 'Thatcherism, Populist Authoritarianism and the Search for a New Left Political Strategy'. *Capital and Class* 238(29):25–48.
Atlantic Institute for Market Studies. 1997/98. *Annual Report*. Halifax: Atlantic Institute for Market Studies.
Axelrod, Paul. 1982. *Scholars and Dollars: Politics, Economics, and the Universities of Ontario 1945–1980*. Toronto: University of Toronto Press.
———. 1986. 'Service or Captivity? Business University Relations in the Twentieth Century'. In *Universities in Crisis: A Mediaeval Institution in the Twenty-First Century*, ed. William A.W. Neilson and Chad Gaffield. Toronto: Institute for Research on Public Policy.
Babad, Michael, and Catherine Mulroney. 1993. *Pillars: The Coming Crisis in Canada's Financial Industry*. Toronto: Stoddart.
Bachrach, Peter, and Morton S. Baratz. 1970. *Power and Poverty*. New York: Oxford University Press.
Baltzell, E. Digby. 1964. *The Protestant Establishment*. New York: Vintage Books.

'Banking More on Directors'. 1997. *Financial Post*, 18 February:13.
Banks, Brian, and David North. 1996. 'Madam Chairman, I Presume?' *Canadian Business* 69(8):13.
Bannerji, Himani. 2000. *The Dark Side of the Nation: Essays on Multiculturalism, Nationalism and Gender*. Toronto: Canadian Scholars' Press.
Barnes, Roy C., and Emily R. Ritter. 2001. 'Networks of Corporate Interlocking: 1962–1995'. *Critical Sociology* 27(2):192–220.
——— and Steven Ward. 2002. 'The Role of Policy Planning Organizations and Social Clubs for the Small World of the Corporate Elite' Paper presented at the 22nd International Sunbelt Social Networks Conference, New Orleans, Louisiana, USA. 13–17 February.
Barnet, Richard J., and John Cavanagh. 1994. *Global Dreams: Imperial Corporations and the New World Order*. Toronto: Simon and Schuster.
Barnet, Richard J., and Ronald E. Muller. 1974. *Global Reach: The Power of the Multinational Corporations*. New York: Simon and Schuster.
Barrett, Matthew. 1999. 'How Bank of Montreal Got a Leaner, Meaner Board of Directors'. *Financial Post*, 15 May:D5.
Barrow, Clyde W. 1990. *Universities and the Capitalist State: Corporate Liberalism and the Reconstruction of American Higher Education, 1894–1928*. Madison: University of Wisconsin Press.
Baxter, James, and Tim Naumetz. 2001. 'Big Banks, Business Boost Party Coffers'. *Calgary Herald*, 5 July:A5.
Bearden, James, and Beth Mintz. 1985. 'Regionality and Integration in the American Interlock Network'. Pp. 234–49 in *Networks of Corporate Power*, ed. Frans N. Stokman, Rolf Ziegler, and John Scott. Cambridge: Polity Press.
———. 1987. 'The Structure of Class Cohesion:The Corporate Network and Its Dual'. Pp. 187-207 in *Intercorporate Relations*, ed. Mark S. Mizruchi and Michael Schwartz. Cambridge, MA: Cambridge University Press.
Beauchemin, Jacques. 1997. 'Transformations du discours éthique au sein des sociétés engagées dans le passage au néo-libéralisme'. *Canadian Review of Sociology and Anthropology* 33(4):369–83.
Beaverstock, Jonathan V., and Joanne Smith. 1996. 'Lending Jobs to Global Cities: Skilled International Labour Migration, Investment Banking and the City of London'. *Urban Studies* 33(8):1377–94.
Bell, Daniel. 1961. *The End of Ideology*. New York: Collier-Macmillan.
Berkowitz, S.D. 1980. 'Structural and Non-Structural Models of Elites: A Critique'. *Canadian Journal of Sociology* 5(1):13–30.
——— and William Fitzgerald. 1995. 'Corporate Control and Enterprise Structure in the Canadian Economy: 1972-1987'. *Social Networks* 17:111–27.
Berle, Adolf. 1959. *Power Without Property*. New York: Harcourt, Brace.
——— and G.C. Means. 1932. *The Modern Corporation and Private Property*. New York: Macmillan.
Bettis, Richard A., and Michael A. Hitt. 1995. 'The New Competitive Landscape'. *Strategic Management Journal* 16:7-19.
Beyond Compliance: Building a Corporate Governance Culture. 2001. Final Report of the Joint Committee on Corporate Governance. Toronto: Toronto Stock Exchange, Canadian Venture Exchange, and Canadian Institute of Chartered Accountants. Available at www.jointcomgov.com.
Blank, Stephen, and Jerry Haar. 1998. *Making NAFTA Work*. Miami: North-South Center Press.
Blau, Peter. 1964. *Exchange and Power in Social Life*. New York: John Wiley.
Block, Fred. 1977. 'The Ruling Class Does Not Rule: Notes on the Marxist Theory of the State'. *Socialist Revolution* 7 (3):6–28.
Bodkin, Jill. 1990. 'Deregulation of Canada's Financial Sector'. Pp. 153–73 in *Privatisation and Deregulation in Canada and Britain*, ed. J.J. Richardson. Aldershot, UK: Dartmouth.

Bottomore, Tom. 1981. 'Introduction to the Translation'. Pp. 1–17 in Rudolph Hilferding, *Finance Capital*, ed. Tom Bottomore. London: Routledge.
Bowles, Samuel, and Herbert Gintis. 1986. *Democracy and Capitalism*. New York: Basic Books.
Bradford, Neil. 2000. 'The Policy Influence of Economic Ideas: Interests, Institutions and Innovation in Canada'. Pp. 50–79 in *Restructuring and Resistance: Canadian Public Policy in an Age of Global Capitalism*, ed. Mike Burke, Colin Mooers and John Shields. Halifax: Fernwood.
Braithwaite, John, and Peter Drahos. 2000. *Global Business Regulation*. New York: Cambridge University Press.
Brenner, Neil. 1998. 'Global Cities, Glocal States: Global City Formation and State Territorial Restructuring in Contemporary Europe'. *Review of International Political Economy* 5(1):1–37.
Bridge, Gary. 1997. 'Mapping the Terrain of Time-Space Compression: Power Networks in Everyday Life'. *Environment and Planning D: Society and Space* 15: 611–26.
Brieger, R.L. 1974. 'The Duality of Persons and Groups'. *Social Forces* 53:181–9.
Brodie, Janine. 1997. 'The New Political Economy of Regions'. Pp. 240–61 in *Understanding Canada*, ed. Wallace Clement. Montreal: McGill-Queen's University Press.
Brooks, Stephen, and Andrew Stritch. 1991. *Business and Government in Canada*. Scarborough, Ontario: Prentice-Hall.
Brown, Robert D. 1994. 'Corporate Governance: The Director as Watchdog, Juggler or Fall-Guy?' *Canadian Business Review* 21(1):39–41.
Brunet, R. 1999. 'Mind Over Media'. *Vancouver Courier* 90(57):1, 4–5, 57.
Bryan, Dick. 1995. *The Chase Across the Globe - International Accumulation and the Contradictions for Nation States*. Boulder: Westview Press.
Brym, Robert J. 1985. 'Introduction'. In *The Structure of the Canadian Capitalist Class*, ed. Robert J. Brym. Toronto: Garamond Press.
———. 1989. *From Culture to Power: The Sociology of English Canada*. Toronto: Oxford University Press.
Buckley, F.H. 1997. 'The Canadian Keiretsu'. *Journal of Applied Corporate Finance* 9(4):46–56.
Bukharin, Nikolai. 1973. *Imperialism and World Economy*. New York: Monthly Review Press.
Burbach, Roger, and William I. Robinson. 1999. 'The Fin de Siècle Debate: Globalization as Epochal Shift'. *Science and Society* 63(1):10–39.
Burgess, Bill. 2002. 'Canada's Location in the World System: Reworking the Debate in Canadian Political Economy'. Ph.D. diss. University of British Columbia.
Burke, Mike, Colin Mooers, and John Shields. 2000. *Restructuring and Resistance: Canadian Public Policy in an Age of Global Capitalism*. Halifax: Fernwood.
Burris, Val. 1992. 'Elite Policy-Planning Networks in the United States'. *Research in Politics and Society* 4:111–34.
Business Council on National Issues. 2000. 'Global Champion or Falling Star: The Choice Canada Must Make'. BCNI CEI Summit 2000. Toronto, 5 April.
Came, Barry, and Mary Janigan. 1995. 'Quebec Inc. Stirs'. *Maclean's* 108(40):40.
Cameron, Duncan. 1997. 'Selling the House to Pay the Mortgage: What is Behind Privatization?' *Studies in Political Economy* 53:11–36.
Canadian Democracy and Corporate Accountability Commission. 2002. *The New Balance Sheet: Corporate Profits and Responsibilities in the 21st Century*. Final Report. Toronto: Thistle Printing.
Carchedi, Guglielmo. 1977. *On the Economic Identification of Social Classes*. London: Routledge.
———. 1983. *Problems in Class Analysis*. London: Routledge.
Carroll, William K. 1982. 'The Canadian Corporate Elite: Financiers or Finance Capitalists?' *Studies in Political Economy* 8:89-114.
———. 1984. 'The Individual, Class, and Corporate Power in Canada'. *Canadian Journal of Sociology* 9:245–68.

———. 1985. 'Dependency, Imperialism and the Capitalist Class in Canada'. Pp. 21–52 in *The Structure of the Canadian Capitalist Class*, ed. Robert J. Brym. Toronto: Garamond Press.
———. 1986. *Corporate Power and Canadian Capitalism*. Vancouver: University of British Columbia Press.
———. 1989. 'Neoliberalism and the Recomposition of Finance Capital in Canada'. *Capital and Class* 38:81–112.
———. 1990. 'Restructuring Capital, Reorganizing Consent: Gramsci, Political Economy, and Canada'. *Canadian Review of Sociology and Anthropology* 27(3):390–416.
———. 2003. 'Undoing the End of History: Canada-Centred Reflections on the Challenge of Globalization'. Pp. 33–55 in *Global Shaping and Its Alternatives*, ed. Yildiz Atasoy and William K. Carroll. Toronto: Garamond Press.
——— and Malcolm Alexander. 1999. 'Finance Capital and Capitalist Class Integration in the 1990s: Networks of Interlocking Directorships in Canada and Australia'. *Canadian Review of Sociology and Anthropology* 36(3):331–54.
——— and Colin Carson. 2003. 'The Network of Global Corporations and Elite Policy Groups: A Structure for Transnational Capitalist Class Formation?' *Global Networks* 3(1):29–57.
——— and Meindert Fennema. 2002. 'Is There a Transnational Business Community?' *International Sociology* 17(2):393–419.
——— John Fox, and Michael D. Ornstein. 1982. 'The Network of Directorate Interlocks Among the Largest Canadian Firms'. *Canadian Review of Sociology and Anthropology* 9:245–68.
——— and Scott Lewis. 1991. 'Restructuring Finance Capital: Changes in the Canadian Corporate Network 1976-1986'. *Sociology* 25(3):491–510.
Cassin, A. Marguerite, and J. Graham Morgan. 1992. 'The Professorate and the Market-Driven University: Transforming the Control of Work in the Academy'. Pp. 247–60 in *Fragile Truths: 25 Years of Sociology and Anthropology in Canada*, ed. William K. Carroll, et al. Ottawa: Carleton University Press.
C.D. Howe Institute. 1995. *Annual Report*. Toronto: C.D. Howe Institute.
Centre for Social Justice. 1998. *The Growing Gap*. Toronto: Centre for Social Justice.
Chandler, A.D. 1962. *Strategy and Structure*. Cambridge, MA: MIT Press.
Chossudovsky, Michel. 1975. 'The Neo-Liberal Model and the Mechanisms of Economic Repression—The Chilean Case'. *Co-Existence* 12(1):34–57.
Clarke, Jesse, and Sarah Schmidt. 1998. 'York Prez Flees Campus in Cop Car'. *University of Toronto Varsity Online* 118 (42) 5 March. <www.varsity.utoronto.ca/archives/118/mar05/news/york.html>.
Clarke, Tony. 1997. *Silent Coup: Confronting the Big Business Takeover of Canada*. Toronto: Lorimer.
Clement, Wallace. 1975. *The Canadian Corporate Elite*. Toronto: McClelland and Stewart.
———. 1977a. *Continental Corporate Power*. Toronto: McClelland and Stewart.
———. 1977b. 'The Corporate Elite, the Capitalist Class, and the Canadian State'. Pp. 225–48 in *The Canadian State: Political Economy and Political Power*, ed. Leo Panitch. Toronto: University of Toronto Press.
——— and John Myles. 1994. *Relations of Ruling*. Montreal: McGill-Queen's University Press.
Coffey, W., and A. Bailly. 1992. 'Producer Services and Systems of Flexible Production'. *Urban Studies* 29:857–68.
Cohen, Dian. 1997. 'Death of a Giant: The Ramifications from the Collapse of Confederation Life'. *Benefits Canada* 21(6):105–6.
Cohen, Joshua, and Joel Rogers. 1983. *On Democracy*. New York: Penguin Books.
Cole, Trevor. 1998. 'Ivy-League Hustle'. *Report on Business Magazine* 14(12):34–44.
Coleman, William D. 1994. 'Keeping the Shotgun Behind the Door: Governing the Securities Industry in Canada, the United Kingdom, and the United States'. Pp. 244–69

in *Governing Capitalist Economies*, ed. J. Roger Hollingsworth, Phillippe C. Schmitter, and Wolfgang Streeck. New York: Oxford University Press.
Conference Board of Canada. 1998. *Corporate Restructuring: Workforce Adjustment Strategies.* Task Force on the Future of the Canadian Financial Services Sector. Ottawa: Conference Board of Canada.
———. 1999a. *Performance and Potential.* Annual Report Supplement: Member's Briefing. Ottawa: Conference Board of Canada.
———. 1999b. 'Without Change, the Canadian Way is Unsustainable'. In News Advisory. <http://www.conferenceboard.ca/press/1999/pp99.htm>.
Corporate-Higher Education Forum. 1998. 'Getting the Story Right. Expert Learners in the Knowledge Economy: Issues and Opportunities'. <www.work.org/assemblies/1998/98media/wb98.pdf>.
Cox, Robert W. 1987. *Production, Power and World Order.* New York: Columbia University Press.
Creighton, Donald. 1956. *The Empire of the St. Lawrence.* Toronto: Macmillan.
Critchley, Barry. 2002. 'Altamira Costs National Bank Less'. *Financial Post*, 13 August:8.
Curran, James, and Michael Gurevitch. 2000. *Mass Media and Society.* New York: Oxford University Press.
Curran, John. 1997. 'GE Capital: Jack Welch's Secret Weapon'. *Fortune*, 10 November: 116–34.
Dahl, Robert A. 1961. *Who Governs?* New Haven: Yale University Press.
Dahrendorf, R. 1959. *Class and Class Conflict in an Industrial Society.* London: Routledge and Kegan Paul.
Daniels, Ronald J. and Randall Morck, eds. 1995.*Corporate Decision-Making in Canada*. Calgary: University of Calgary Press.
D'Aquino, Thomas Paul and David Stewart-Patterson. 2001. *Northern Edge: How Canadians Can Triumph in the Global Economy.* Toronto: Stoddart.
D'Aquino, Thomas. 1991. 'An Anatomy of the Business Council on National Issues'. Pp. 193–7 in *Essays on Canadian Public Policy*, ed. Thomas Courchene and Arthur Stewart. Kingston: Queen's University.
Dauphinais, G. William, and Colin Price. 1998. 'CEOs Demand the ABCs—Awareness, Belief, and Conduct'. Pp. 15–22 in *Straight from the CEO: The World's Top Business Leaders Reveal Ideas That Every Manager Can Use*, ed. G. William Dauphinais and Colin Price. New York: Simon and Schuster.
Davis, Angela Y. 1996. 'Gender, Class and Multiculturalism: Rethinking "Race" Politics'. Pp. 40–8 in *Mapping Multiculturalism*, ed. Avery Gordon and Christopher Newfield. Minnesota: University of Minnesota Press.
Davis, Arthur K. 1971. 'Canadian Society and History as Hinterland Versus Metropolis'. Pp. 6–32 in *Canadian Society: Pluralism, Change, and Conflict*, ed. Richard J. Ossenberg. Scarborough, Ontario: Prentice-Hall of Canada.
Davis, G.F., and M.S. Mizruchi. 1999. 'The Money Center Cannot Hold: Commercial Banks in the U.S. System of Corporate Governance'. *Administrative Science Quarterly* 44(2):215–39.
Davis, Wade. 2002. 'The Ticking Bomb'. *Globe and Mail* (Toronto), 6 July.
Day, Richard J.F. 2000. *Multiculturalism and the History of Canadian Diversity.* Toronto: University of Toronto Press.
De Grass, Richard P. 1977. 'Development of Monopolies in Canada from 1907–1913'. Masters Thesis. Waterloo, Ontario: University of Waterloo.
De la Mothe, John. 1992. 'A Dollar Short and a Day Late: A Note on the Demise of the Science Council of Canada'. *Queen's Quarterly* 99(4):873–86.
De Smidt, Marc. 1991. 'Management Centers and Internationalization of Firms in the Netherlands'. *Tijdschrijt Voor Economishe en Sociale Geografie* 82(2):148–54.
Dhinga, Harbins L. 1983. 'Patterns of Ownership in Canadian Industry'. *Canadian Journal of Sociology* 8:21–44.

Dicken, Peter. 1992. *Global Shift: The Internationalization of Economic Activity*. New York: Guilford Press.
———. 1998. *Global Shift. Third Edition*. New York: Guilford Press.
Dillon, John. 1997. *Turning the Tide: Confronting the Money Traders*. Ottawa: Canadian Centre for Policy Alternatives.
Dobbin, Murray. 1998. *The Myth of the Good Corporate Citizen: Democracy Under the Rule of Big Business*. Toronto: Stoddart.
Dobson, Wendy. 2002. 'Shaping the Future of the North American Economic Space: A Framework for Action'. Toronto: C.D. Howe Institute.
Dobson, W., R. Lipsey, and M. Smith. 1983. *Flexibility as the Best Protection*. Commentary No. 5. Toronto: C.D. Howe Institute.
Domhoff, G. William. 1998. *Who Rules America?: Power and Politics in the Year 2000*. Mountain View, Calif.: Mayfield Publishing Co.
Drainville, André C. 2001. 'Quebec City 2001 and the Making of Transnational Subjects'. Pp. 15–42 in *Socialist Register 2002*, ed. Leo Panitch and Colin Leys. London: Merlin Press.
Drakich, Janice, Karen R. Grant, and Penni Stewart. 2002. 'The Academy in the 21st Century: Editors' Introduction'. *Canadian Review of Sociology and Anthropology* 39(3):249–60.
Dreiling, Michael C. 2000. 'The Class-Embeddedness of Corporate Political Action: Leadership in Defense of the NAFTA'. *Social Problems* 47:21–48.
Du Boff, Richard B. 2001. 'NAFTA and Economic Integration in North America'. Pp. 35–63 in *Continental Order? Integrating North America for Cybercapitalism*, ed. Vincent Mosco and Dan Schiller. New York: Rowman and Littlefield.
Easterbrook, W.T., and H.G.J. Aitkin. 1956. *Canadian Economic History*. Toronto: Macmillan.
Edur, Olev. 2000. 'Shakeup Revives Competition: Canadian Exchanges'. *Financial Post*, 19 June:C15.
Ernst, A. 1992. 'From Liberal Continentalism to Neoconservatism: North American Free Trade and the Politics of the C.D. Howe Institute'. *Studies in Political Economy* 39:109–40.
Evans, B. Mitchell, Stephen McBride, and John Shields. 2000. 'Globalization and the Challenge to Canadian Democracy'. In *Restructuring and Resistance: Canadian Public Policy in an Age of Global Capitalism*, ed. Mike Burke, Colin Mooers and John Shields. Halifax: Fernwood Publishing.
Feder, Barnaby J., and Seth Schiesel. 2002. 'Worldcom Finds $3.3 Billion More in Irregularities'. *New York Times*, 9 August:A1.
Felts, Arthur A. 1992. 'Organizational Communication'. *Administration and Society* 23(4):495–516.
Fennema, Meindert. 1982. *International Networks of Banks and Industry*. Boston: Martinus Nijhoff.
———, and Huibert Schijf. 1979. 'Analysing Interlocking Directorates: Theory and Methods'. *Social Networks* 1:297–332.
———. 1985. 'The Transnational Network'. Pp. 250–66 in *Networks of Corporate Power*, ed. Frans N. Stokman, Rolf Ziegler, and John Scott. Cambridge: Polity Press.
Ferguson, Thomas. 1995. *Golden Rule: The Investment Theory of Party Competition and the Logic of Market Political Systems*. Chicago: University of Chicago Press.
Fillmore, Nick. 1989. 'The Big Oink: How Business Won the Free Trade Battle'. *This Magazine* 22(8):13–20.
Fleming, James. 1991. *Circles of Power: The Most Influential People in Canada*. Toronto: Doubleday Canada.
Fox, Bonnie J. 1989. 'The Feminist Challenge: A Reconsideration of Social Inequality and Economic Development'. Pp. 120–67 in *From Culture to Power: The Sociology of English Canada*, ed. Robert J. Brym. Toronto: Oxford University Press.
Fox, John, and Michael D. Ornstein. 1986. 'The Canadian State and Corporate Elites in the Post-War Period'. *Canadian Review of Sociology and Anthropology* 23:481–506.

Francis, Diane. 1986. *Controlling Interest*. Toronto: Macmillan.
Fraser, Nancy. 1997. *Justice Interruptus: Critical Reflections on the 'Postsocialist' Condition*. New York: Routledge.
Fraser Institute. 1983. *Annual Report*. Vancouver: Fraser Institute.
———. 1997. *Annual Report*. Vancouver: Fraser Institute.
———. 1998. 'Annual Report'. <www.fraserinstitute.ca/about_us/annual_reports/1998/index.html>.
Freeman, Aaron. 2002. 'Lobby Firms Increasingly Giving More to Political Parties'. *The Hill Times* 8 July. <www.thehilltimes.ca/hilltimes/freeman.html>.
———. 2003. 'Canadians Come Clean'. *Multinational Monitor* 24, 3 (March):6–7.
Fukuyama, Francis. 1992. *The End of History and the Last Man*. New York: Free Press.
Gamson, William A. and Gadi Wolfsfeld. 1993. 'Movements and Media as Interacting Systems'. *Annals of the American Political Science Society* 528:114–27.
Germain, Randall D. 1997. *The International Organization of Credit*. Cambridge: Cambridge University Press.
Giberson, Mark. 1997. 'Giving Big'. *University Affairs*, June–July:8–9.
Gill, Stephen. 1990. *American Hegemony and the Trilateral Commission*. Cambridge: Cambridge University Press.
———. 1995. 'Theorizing the Interregnum: The Double Movement and Global Politics in the 1990s'. Pp. 65–99 in *International Political Economy*, ed. Bijorn Hettne. Halifax: Fernwood Books.
Gillies, James. 1997. 'Nowhere to Hide: Corporate Directors Face Growing Pressure to Do Their Jobs Well'. *Financial Post*, 22–24 November, P8, P12.
Gitlin, Todd. 1980. *The Whole World is Watching: Mass Media and the Making and Unmaking of the New Left*. Berkeley: University of California Press.
Glasberg, Davita Silfen. 1987. 'The Ties That Bind? Case Studies in the Signficance of Corporate Board Interlocks with Financial Institutions'. *Sociological Perspectives* 30(1):19–48.
———. 1989. 'The Importance of Financial Institutions in the Political Economy'. Pp. 1–24 in *The Power of Collective Purse Strings*. Los Angeles: University of California Press.
Godsoe, Peter. 1996. 'Canadian Universities: Competing to Win'. Address to the Canadian Club. Toronto, 4 March.
Gramsci, Antonio. 1971. *Selections from the Prison Notebooks of Antonio Gramsci*. New York: International Publishers.
Green, Milford, and R. Keith Semple. 1981. 'The Corporate Interlocking Directorate as an Urban Spatial Information Network'. *Urban Geography* 2(2):148–60.
Grubel, Herbert, and Michael Walker. 1978. 'Moral Hazard, Unemployment Insurance and the Rate of Unemployment'. In *Unemployment Insurance: Global Evidence of Its Effects on Unemployment*, ed. Herbert Grubel and Michael Walker. Vancouver: Fraser Institute.
Hackett, Robert, and Yuezhi Zhao. 1998. *Sustaining Democracy? Journalism and the Politics of Objectivity*. Toronto: Garamond Press.
Hamilton, Roberta. 1996. *Gendering the Vertical Mosaic*. Toronto: Copp Clark.
Hardt, Michael, and Antonio Negri. 2000. *Empire*. Cambridge, Mass.: Harvard University Press.
'Hard Target: The New Wave of Directors Taking Over Canada's Boardrooms is Finding That the Work is Harder Than It Used to Be'. 1996. *Financial Post*, 11–13 May:6.
Harmes, Adam. 1998. 'Institutional Investors and the Reproduction of Neoliberalism'. *Review of International Political Economy* 5(1):92–121.
Harvey, David. 1982. *The Limits to Capital*. Chicago: University of Chicago Press.
Havemann, Paul. 1986. 'Marketing the New Establishment Ideology in Canada'. *Crime and Social Justice* 26:11–37.
Heenan, David A., and Howard V. Perlmutter. 1979. *Multinational Organizational Development*. Reading, Mass.: Addison-Wesley.
Held, David, et al. 1999. *Global Transformations*. Cambridge: Polity Press.

Henwood, Doug. 1997. *Wall Street*. London: Verso.
Hilferding, Rudolf. 1981 [1910]. *Finance Capital*. London: Routledge.
Hill, Charles W.L. 2000. *International Business*. Boston: McGraw-Hill.
Hill, Stephen. 1995. 'The Social Organization of Boards of Directors'. *British Journal of Sociology* 46(2):245–78.
Hirst, P., and G. Thompson. 1996. *Globalization in Question*. Cambridge: Polity Press.
Hobson, J.A. 1965. *Imperialism*. Ann Arbor, Mich.: University of Michigan Press.
Huang, Evelyn, and Lawrence Jeffery. 1995. 'One in a Billion: Li Ka-Shing Has a New Mission'. *Canadian Business* 68(11):78–83.
Hughes, Karen D. 2000. *Women and Corporate Directorships in Canada: Trends and Issues*. CPRN Discussion Paper No. CPRN|01. Ottawa: Canadian Policy Research Networks. 39 pp.
Hunt, Courtney Shelton, and Howard E. Aldrich. 1998. 'The Second Ecology: Creation and Evolution of Organizational Communities'. *Research in Organizational Behavior* 20:267–301.
Hymer, Stephen. 1979. *The Multinational Corporation: A Radical Approach*. Cambridge, England: Cambridge University Press.
Innis, Harold A. 1956. *The Fur Trade in Canada*. Revised Edition. Toronto: University of Toronto Press.
Jackson, Andrew. 1999. 'Free Trade, a Decade Later'. *Studies in Political Economy* 58:141–60.
Jensen, Michael C., and William H. Mackling. 1976. 'The Theory of the Firm: Managerial Behavior, Agency Costs and Ownership Structure'. *Journal of Financial Economics* 3: 305–60.
Jenson, Jane. 1989. '"Different" but not "exceptional": Canada's Permeable Fordism'. *Canadian Review of Sociology and Anthropology* 26:69–94.
Jessop, Bob. 1983. 'Accumulation Strategies, State Forms, and Hegemonic Projects'. *Kapitalistate* 10/11:89–112.
———. 1993. 'Towards a Schumpetarian Workfare State? Remarks on Post-Fordist Political Economy'. *Studies in Political Economy* 40: 7–39.
Jog, Vijay M., and Werner Hofstatter. 1998. 'Wealth and Value Creation in Canada'. *Canadian Investment Review* 11(3):24–7.
Johnston, William, and Michael D. Ornstein. 1982. 'Class, Work and Politics'. *Canadian Review of Sociology and Anthropology* 19:196–214.
Kates, Josef. 1977. *Technological Sovereignty: A Strategy for Canada*. Annual Statement of the Chairman. Ottawa: Science Council of Canada.
———. 1978. *Toward International Technological Interdependence*. Annual Statement of the Chairman. Ottawa: Science Council of Canada.
Kauffman, George G., ed. 1992. *Banking Structures in Major Countries*. Boston: Kluwer Academic Publishers.
Kerstetter, Steve. 2002. *Rags and Riches: Wealth and Inequality in Canada*. Ottawa: Canadian Centre for Policy Alternatives.
Klein, Naomi. 2000. *No Logo: Taking Aim at the Brand Bullies*. Toronto: Alfred A. Knopf.
———. 2001. 'Farewell to "The End of History": Organization and Vision in Anti-Corporate Movements'. Pp. 1–14 in *Socialist Register* 2002, ed. Leo Panitch and Colin Leys. London: Merlin Press.
Kocka, Jurgen. 1974. 'Organisierter Kapitalismus oder Staatsmonopolistischer Kapitalismus? Begriffliche Vorbemerkungen'. Pp. 19–35 in *Organisierter Kapitalismus*, ed. H. Winckler. Gottingen: Vanderhoeck and Ruprecht.
Kono, Clifford, et al. 1998. 'Lost in Space: The Geography of Corporate Interlocking Directorates'. *American Journal of Sociology* 103(4):863–911.
Korten, David. 1995. *When Corporations Rule the World*. West Hartford, Conn.: Kumarian Press.
Kovel, Joel. 2002. *The Enemy of Nature*. Halifax: Fernwood Publishing Ltd.
Kravis, Marie-Josée. 1999. 'Europe Will Reform, Despite Itself'. *Financial Post*, 23 April:C7.

Kurasawa, Fuyuki. 2002. 'Which Barbarians at the Gates? From the Culture Wars to Market Orthodoxy in the North American Academy'. *Canadian Review of Sociology and Anthropology* 39(3):323–47.

Kurtzman, Joel. 1993. *The Death of Money*. New York: Simon and Schuster.

La Porta, Rafael, Florencio Lopez-De-Silanes, and Andrei Shleifer. 1999. 'Corporate Ownership Around the World'. *Journal of Finance* LIV(2):471–517.

Langille, David. 1987. 'The Business Council on National Issues and the Canadian state'. *Studies in Political Economy* 24:41–85.

Lash, Scott, and John Urry. 1994. *Economies of Signs and Space*. London: Sage.

———. 1987. *The End of Organized Capitalism*. Cambridge: Polity Press.

Laxer, James. 1998. *The Undeclared War: Class Conflict in the Age of Cyber Capitalism*. Toronto: Penguin Books.

Lazonick, William, and Mary O'Sullivan. 2000. 'Maximizing Shareholder Value: A New Ideology for Corporate Governance'. *Economy and Society* 29(1):13–35.

Lee, Marc. 2002. 'The Global Divide: Inequality in the World Economy'. *Behind the Numbers* 4 (2) 18 April. <http://www.policyalternatives.ca/>.

Leger, Kathryn. 1997. 'Power in Europe'. *Financial Post*, 12–14 July:6, 7.

Levitt, Kari. 1970. *Silent Surrender*. Toronto: Macmillan of Canada.

Leys, Colin. 2001. *Market-Driven Politics: Neo-Liberal Democracy and the Public Interest*. London: Verso.

Li, Peter S. 2003. 'Visible Minorities in Canadian Society: Challenges of Racial Diversity'. In *Social Differentiation: Patterns and Processes*, ed. Danielle Juteau. Toronto: University of Toronto Press.

Lindquist, Evert. 1990. 'The Third Community, Policy Inquiry, and Social Scientists'. In *Social Scientists, Policy, and the State*, ed. S. Brooks and A. Gagnon. New York: Praeger.

———. 1998. 'A Quarter Century of Canadian Think Tanks: Evolving Institutions, Conditions and Strategies'. Pp. 127–44 in *Think Tanks Across Nations: A Comparative Approach*, ed. Diane Stone, Andrew Denham, and Mark Garnett. Manchester: Manchester University Press.

Lipsey, Richard, and Murray Smith. 1985. *Taking the Initiative: Canada's Trade Options in a Turbulent World*. Toronto: C.D. Howe Institute.

Litvak, Isaiah A. 2001. 'The Marginalization of Corporate Canada'. *Behind the Headlines* 58(2).

Lorinc, John. 1994. 'Hold the Fries and the Social Programmes'. *Saturday Night*, March: 11–12, 15–16, 61.

Lukes, Steven. 1974. *Power: A Radical View*. London: Macmillan.

McBride, Stephen. 2001. *Paradigm Shift: Globalization and the Canadian State*. Halifax: Fernwood.

McCarthy, Shawn. 2000. 'Business Sounds Alarm on Vulnerability'. *Globe and Mail* (Toronto), 8 May: B1, B3.

MacDermid, R. 2001. 'Toward an Investment Theory of Canadian Electoral Politics'. Paper presented at the Annual General Meeting of the Canadian Political Science Association, Quebec, 27–29 May.

McFarland, Janet. 2000. 'Corporate Funds Fuel Election Campaigns'. *Globe and Mail*, 4 November.

———. 2003. 'Good Governance Group Set'. *Globe and Mail*, 12 April:B3.

McKie, Craig. 1976. 'Review of Wallace Clement's The Canadian Corporate Elite'. *Canadian Journal of Sociology* 1(4):547–9.

Maclem, Katherine. 2001. 'Can Bay Street Survive?' *Maclean's*, 14 May:46.

McMurdy, D. 1996. 'Cozying up to the CEO'. *Maclean's* 109(23):32–4, 23.

McNally, David. 2002. *Another World Is Possible: Globalization and Anti-Capitalism*. Winnipeg: Arbeiter Ring Publishing.

McNish, Jacquie. 2000. 'Resource Sector Ripe for Fresh Takeover Wave'. *Globe and Mail*, 17 Feb.:B6.

———, Bertrand Marotte, and Rhéal Séguin. 2002. 'New CEO Rousseau Pledges to Recast the Caisse'. *Globe and Mail*, 20 May:B1, B9.

MacPherson, C.B. 1962. *The Political Theory of Possessive Individualism*. Oxford: Clarendon Press.
———. 1977. *The Life and Times of Liberal Democrcy*. New York: Oxford University Press.
McQuaig, Linda. 1995. *Shooting the Hippo: Death by Deficit and Other Canadian Myths*. Toronto: Penguin Books.
McQueen, Rod. 1997. 'The Second Coming of Jack Cockwell'. *Financial Post* 91(23):8–9, 23.
———. 1999. 'The Rise of the Savvy Shareholder'. *Financial Post*, 20 February:D4.
——— and Peter Kuitenbrouwer. 1999. 'Canadian Boards Behind in Adopting TSE Guidelines: Independence from Management is TSE Mantra'. *Financial Post*, 18 June:C5.
Mander, Jerry. 1996. 'Facing the Rising Tide'. In *The Case Against the Global Economy: And for a Turn Toward the Local*, ed. Jerry Mander and Edward Goldsmith. San Francisco: Sierra Club Books.
Market Trend Canada. 2002. *Canadian Shareowners Study July 2002*. Toronto: Toronto Stock Exchange.
Marr, Garry. 2000. 'New Guidelines Being Drafted by Exchanges: Old Boys Under Fire'. *Financial Post*, 11 July:C1, C9.
Marshall, J. Neill, and Simon Raybould. 1993. 'New Corporate Structures and the Evolving Geography of White Collar Work'. *Tijdschrijt Voor Economishe en Sociale Geografie* 84(5):362–77.
Martin, Paul. 1997. *Budget Speech 1997*. Ottawa: Ministry of Finance.
Marx, Karl. 1967. *Capital, Volume 3*. New York: International Publishers.
Maxwell, Judith. 1975. *Policy Review and Outlook, 1975: Restructuring the Incentive System*. Toronto: C.D. Howe Institute.
Micklethwait, John, and Adrian Wooldridge. 2000. *A Future Perfect: The Challenge and Hidden Promise of Globalization*. London: Heinemann.
Mills, C. Wright. 1956. *The Power Elite*. New York: Oxford University Press.
Mintz, Beth, and Michael Schwartz. 1985. *The Power Structure of American Business*. Chicago: University of Chicago Press.
Mizruchi, Mark S. 1996. 'What Do Interlocks Do? An Analysis, Critique, and Assessment of Research on Interlocking Directorates'. *Annual Review of Sociology* 22:271–99.
Mokken, Robert J., and Frans N. Stokman. 1978. 'Traces of Power IV: The 1972 Intercorporate Network in the Netherlands'. Joint Sessions of Workshops of the European Consortium for Political Research. Grenoble, April 6–12.
Moore, Steve, and Debi Wells. 1975. *Imperialism and the National Question in Canada*. Toronto: Privately published.
Morck, Randall, and Masao Nakamura. 1995. 'Banks and Corporate Governance in Canada'. Pp. 481–502 in *Corporate Decision-Making in Canada*, ed. Ronald J. Daniels and Randall Morck. Calgary: University of Calgary Press.
Morck, Randall, David A. Strangeland, and Bernard Yeung. 1998. *Inherited Wealth, Corporate Control and Economic Growth: The Canadian Disease?* Working Paper No. 6814. Cambridge: National Bureau of Economic Research.
———. 2000. 'Inherited Wealth, Corporate Control, and Economic Growth: The Canadian Disease?' Pp. 319–72 in *Concentrated Corporate Ownership*, ed. Randall K. Morck. Chicago: University of Chicago Press.
Mulvale, Jim. 2001. *Beyond the Keynesian Welfare State*. Toronto: Garamond Press.
Myers, G. 1972. *A History of Canadian Wealth*. Toronto: James Lewis and Samuel.
Naylor, R.T. 1972. 'The Rise and Fall of the Third Commercial Empire of the St Lawrence'. Pp. 1–41 in *Capitalism and the National Question in Canada*, ed. Gary Teeple. Toronto: University of Toronto Press.
———. 1975. *The History of Canadian Business 1867–1914*. Toronto: James Lorimer.
Neufeld, E.P. 1972. *The Financial System of Canada*. New York: St. Martin's Press.
Newman, Peter C. 1975. *The Canadian Establishment*, Vol. 1. Toronto: McClelland and Stewart.

———. 1982. *The Establishment Man*. Toronto: McClelland and Stewart.
———. 1998. *Titans: How the New Canadian Establishment Seized Power*. Toronto: Viking.
———. 1999. 'Year of Living Dangerously'. *Maclean's*, 20 December:50–4, 56.
Newson, Janice. 1992. 'The Decline of Faculty Influence: Confronting the Effects of the Corporate Agenda'. Pp. 227–46 in *Fragile Truths: 25 Years of Sociology and Anthropology in Canada*, ed. William K. Carroll, et al. Ottawa: Carleton University Press.
———. 1994. 'Subordinating Democracy: The Effects of Fiscal Retrenchment and University-Business Partnerships on Knowledge Creation and Knowledge Dissemination in Universities'. *Higher Education* 27:141–61.
——— and Howard Buchbinder. 1990. 'Corporate-University Linkages in Canada: Transforming a Public Institution'. *Higher Education* 20:355–79.
Niosi, Jorge. 1978. *The Economy of Canada: Who Controls It?* Montreal: Black Rose Books.
———. 1981. *Canadian Capitalism*. Toronto: Lorimer.
———. 1985. *Canadian Multinationals*. Toronto: Garamond Press.
Noakes, Susan. 1997. 'Relating to Boards: The Senate Committee on Corporate Governance Has Recommended That the CEO's Job Be Different from That of the Chairman of the Board'. *Financial Post Daily* 10(40):20, 40.
Noble, David F. 1977. *America by Design: Science, Technology, and the Rise of Corporate Capitalism*. New York: Alfred A. Knopf Inc.
———. 2001. *Digital Diploma Mills: The Automation of Higher Education*. New York: Monthly Review Press.
Nock, David A. 1976. 'The Intimate Connection: Links Between the Political and Economic System in Canadian Federal Politics'. Ph.D. Diss. Edmonton: University of Alberta.
Nooteboom, Bart. 1999. 'Voice- and Exit-Based Forms of Corporate Control: Anglo-American, European, and Japanese'. *Journal of Economic Issues* 33(4):845–60.
Nottingham, Lucy. 1996. 'Integrated Risk Management'. *Canadian Business Review* 23(2):26–8.
O'Connor, James. 1974. 'The Theory of Surplus Value'. Pp. 16–42 in *The Corporations and the State*, ed. James O'Connor. New York: Harper and Row.
———. 1987. *The Meaning of Crisis*. New York: Blackwell.
Offe, Claus, and Helmut Weisenthal. 1980. 'Two Logics of Collective Action: Theoretical Notes on Social Class and Organizational Form'. *Political Power and Social Theory* 1:67–115.
Ogmundson, Richard, and James McLaughlin. 1992. 'Trends in the Ethnic Origins of Elites: The Decline of the Brits?' *Canadian Review of Sociology and Anthropology* 29(2).
O'Hagan, Sean, and Milford B. Green. 2002. 'Interlocking Directorates: An Example of Tacit Knowledge Transfer'. *Urban Geography* 23 (2):154–79.
Olsen, Dennis. 1980. *The State Elite*. Toronto: McClelland and Stewart.
Ornstein, Michael D. 1984. 'Interlocking Directorates in Canada: Intercorporate or Class Alliance?' *Administrative Science Quarterly* 29:210–31.
———. 1988. 'Corporate Involvement in Canadian Hospital and University Boards, 1946–1977'. *Canadian Review of Sociology and Anthropology* 25(3):365–88.
———. 1989. 'The Social Organization of the Canadian Capitalist Class in Comparative Perspective'. *Canadian Review of Sociology and Anthropology* 26:151–77.
———. 1998. 'Three Decades of Elite Research in Canada: John Porter's Unfulfilled Legacy'. Pp. 145–79 in *The Vertical Mosaic Revisited*, ed. R. Helmes-Hayes and J. Curtis. Toronto: University of Toronto Press.
Ornstein, Michael D., and H. Michael Stevenson. 1984. 'Ideology and Public Policy in Canada'. *British Journal of Political Science* 13:313–34.
O'Sullivan, Mary. 2000. 'Corporate Governance and Globalization'. *Annals of the American Academy of Political and Social Science* 570:153–72.
Overbeek, Henk. 1980. 'Finance Capital and the Crisis in Britain'. *Capital and Class* 2:99–120.
———, and Kees van der Pijl. 1993. 'Restructuring Capital and Restructuring Hegemony: Neo Liberalism and the Unmaking of the Post War Order'. Pp. 1–27 in *Restructuring Hegemony in the Global Political Economy*. New York: Routledge.

Palmer, Bryan. 1994. *Capitalism Comes to the Backcountry*. Toronto: Between the Lines.
Park, Libbie, and Frank Park. 1973. *The Anatomy of Big Business*. Toronto: James Lewis and Samuel.
Parkin, Frank. 1979. *Marxism and Class Theory: A Bourgeois Critique*. London: Tavistock Publications.
Partridge, John. 1998. 'The Weakening of the Old Boys' Network'. *Globe and Mail*, 4 July: B1, B6.
Perlo, Victor. 1958. '"People's Capitalism" and Stock Ownership'. *The American Economic Review* 48:333–47.
Perry, Robert. 1971. *Galt, U.S.A.: The 'American Presence' in a Canadian City*. Toronto: Maclean-Hunter.
Petras, James, and Henry Veltmeyer. 2001. *Globalization Unmasked: Imperialism in the 21st Century*. Halifax: Fernwood Publishing.
Pettigrew, Andrew, and Terry McNulty. 1995. 'Power and Influence in and Around the Boardroom'. *Human Relations* 48(8):845–73.
Piedalue, Gilles. 1976. 'Les Groupes financiers au Canada'. *Revue d'Histoire de l'Amérique Française* 30(1):3–34.
Polster, Claire. 2002. 'A Break from the Past: Impacts and Implications of the Canada Foundation for Innovation and the Canada Research Chairs Initiatives'. *Canadian Review of Sociology and Anthropology* 39(3):275–99.
Porter, John. 1965. *The Vertical Mosaic*. Toronto: University of Toronto Press.
Poulantzas, Nicos. 1975. *Political Power and Social Classes*. London: New Left Books.
———. 1976. 'The Capitalist State: A Reply to Miliband and Laclau'. *New Left Review* 95.
Pred, A. 1977. *City Systems in Advanced Economies*. London: Hutchinson.
'Pressing his Case: Pierre Karl Péladeau at the Helm of Printing Giant Quebecor'. 2002. *Globe and Mail*, 30 November:B4.
Ratner, R.S. 1994. 'Canada in the 1990s: A Case of Neo-Colonization of the Semi-Periphery'. Pp. 275–98 in *Culture and Development in a New Era and in a Transforming World*, ed. M. Lee, et al. Kyungnam, South Korea: Institute for Far Eastern Studies, Kyungnam University.
Resnick, Philip. 1989. 'From Semiperiphery to Perimeter of the Core: Canada's Place in the Capitalist World-Economy'. *Review, A Journal of the Fernand Braudel Center* 12(2):263–97.
Rice, Murray D., and R. Keith Semple. 1993. 'Spatial Interlocking Directorates in the Canadian Urban System, 1971–1989'. *Urban Geography* 14(4):375–96.
Richards, John, and Larry Pratt. 1979. *Prairie Capitalism*. Toronto: McClelland and Stewart.
Richardson, R. Jack. 1987. 'Directorship Interlocks and Corporate Profitability'. *Administrative Science Quarterly* 32:367–86.
Richardson, R.J. 1982. 'Merchants Against Industry: An Empirical Study'. *Canadian Journal of Sociology* 7:279–96.
———. 1988. '"A Sacred Trust": The Trust Industry and Canadian Economic Structure'. *Canadian Review of Sociology and Anthropology* 25:1–22.
Robinson, William I., and Jerry Harris. 2000. 'Towards a Global Ruling Class? Globalization and the Transnational Capitalist Class'. *Science and Society* 64(1):11–54.
Robock, Stefan H., and Kenneth Simmonds. 1989. *International Business and Multinational Enterprises*. Boston: Irwin.
Ross, Robert J.S., and Kent C. Trachte. 1990. *Global Capitalism: The New Leviathan*. Albany, New York: SUNY Press.
Rubin, Sandra. 1998. 'Walk Softly, Carry a Big Stick'. *Financial Post*, 21–3 March:8.
Rupert, Mark. 2000. *Ideologies of Globalization*. New York: Routledge.
Rusterholz, Peter. 1985. 'The Banks in the Centre: Integration in Decentralized Switzerland'. Pp. 131–47 in *Networks of Corporate Power*, ed. Frans N. Stokman, Rolf Ziegler, and John Scott. Cambridge: Polity Press.
Rytina, Steve, and David L. Morgan. 1982. 'The Arithmetic of Social Relations: The Interplay of Category and Network'. *American Journal of Sociology* 88(1):88–113.

Sassen, Saskia. 1991. *The Global City*. Princeton: Princeton University Press.
———. 1999. 'Making the Global Economy Run: The Role of National States and Private Agents'. *International Social Science Journal* 51(3):409–15.
Schiller, Dan, and Vincent Mosco. 2001. 'Introduction: Integrating a Continent for a Transnational World'. Pp. 1–34 in *Continental Order? Integrating North America for Cybercapitalism*, ed. Vincent Mosco and Dan Schiller. New York: Rowman and Littlefield.
Schwartz, Michael, ed. 1987. *The Structure of Power in America: The Corporate Elite as Ruling Class*. New York: Holmes and Meier.
Scoffield, Heather. 1998. 'Canada Adjusts to Free Trade Realities'. *Globe and Mail* (Toronto), 31 December, B1, B4.
Scott, Beverley. 1994. 'Against Social Programs: The Campaigns of the Fraser Institute'. In *Directions for Social Welfare in Canada: The Public's View*, ed. John Crane. Vancouver: UBC Press.
Scott, John. 1986. *Capitalist Property and Financial Power*. Hassocks: Wheatsheaf.
———. 1991 *Social Networks: A Handbook*. London: Sage.
———. 1997. *Corporate Business and Capitalist Classes*. New York: Oxford University Press.
———, ed. 2002. *Social Networks: Critical Concepts in Sociology*. London: Routledge.
———, and Michael Hughes. 1980. 'Capital and Communication in Scottish Business'. *Sociology* 14:29–47.
Seidman, S. 1983. 'Network Structure and Minimum Degree'. *Social Networks* 5:269–87.
'Shareholder Values'. 1996. *Financial Post*, 18–20 May: 6-7.
Shields, John, and B. Mitchell Evans. 1998. *Shrinking the State*. Halifax: Fernwood.
Shorris, Earl. 1994. *A Nation of Salesmen: The Tyranny of the Market and the Subversion of Culture*. New York: W.W. Norton.
Simpson, Jeffrey. 1999. 'Lowly Loonie Still Stirs U.S.'. *Globe and Mail* (Toronto), 27 Oct.:A13.
Sklair, Leslie. 1995. *Sociology of the Global System*. Baltimore: Johns Hopkins University Press.
———. 2001. *The Transnational Capitalist Class*. Oxford: Blackwell.
Slaughter, Sheila, and Larry L. Leslie. 1997. *Academic Capitalism: Politics, Policies and the Entrepreneurial University*. Baltimore: Johns Hopkins University Press.
Sonquist, J.A., and T. Koenig. 1975. 'Interlocking Directorates in the Top U.S. Corporations: A Graph Theory Approach'. *Insurgent Sociologist* 5(3):196–229.
Sprenger, C.J.A., and F.N. Stokman 1989 *GRADAP: Graph Definition and Analysis Program*. Groningen, The Netherlands: iec ProGAMMA.
Stanford, Jim. 1999. *Paper Boom*. Toronto: Lorimer.
State of Governance in Canada, The. 2000. An account of deliberations and recommendations from the reunion of the Dey Committee. Toronto: Institute of Corporate Directors and Toronto Stock Exchange.
Statistics Canada. 2001. *Canada's International Investment Position, 2000*. Cat. No. 67-202. Ottawa: Minister of Industry.
Steven, Rob. 1994. 'New World Order: A New Imperialism'. *Journal of Contemporary Asia* 24(3):271–96.
Stewart, Sinclair. 2003. 'Teachers, CPP funds put $1-Billion in deal for Deutsche Unit'. *Globe and Mail* (Toronto), 22 February:B1, B4.
Stokman, Frans N., Rolf Ziegler, and John Scott. 1985. *Networks of Corporate Power: A Comparative Analysis of Ten Countries*. Cambridge: Polity Press.
Sweezy, Paul. 1972. 'Power Elite or Ruling Class?' Pp. 92–109 in *Modern Capitalism and Other Essays*, ed. Paul Sweezy. New York: Monthly Review Press.
Teeple, Gary. 2000. *Globalization and the Decline of Social Reform: Into the Twenty-First Century*. Amherst, New York: Humanity Books.
Thain, Donald H. 1995. 'The TSE Corporate Governance Report: Disappointing'. *Business Quarterly* 59(1):76–86.
Thompson, Graham. 1977. 'The Relationship Between the Financial and Industrial Sector in the United Kingdom Economy'. *Economy and Society* 6:235–83.

Toronto Stock Exchange. 2001. *Toronto Stock Exchange Company Handbook*. Toronto: CCH.
'Under the Gun: Growing Responsibilities and Perils of the Toughest Spot in Corporate Governance, the Director's Chair'. 1996. *Financial Post* 90(18):6–7, 18.
United Nations Development Programme. 2002. *Human Development Report*. New York: Oxford University Press.
Useem, Michael. 1981. 'Business Segments and Corporate Relations with U.S. Universities'. *Social Problems* 29(2):129–41.
———. 1982. 'Class-Wide Rationality in the Politics of Managers and Directors of Large Corporations in the United States and Great Britain'. *Administrative Science Quarterly* 27:199–226.
———. 1984. *The Inner Circle*. New York: Oxford University Press.
Vacca, Giuseppe. 1982. 'Intellectuals and the Marxist Theory of the State'. Pp. 37–69 in *Approaches to Gramsci*, ed. Anne Showstack Sassoon. London: Writers and Readers.
Van Apeldoorn, Bastien. 2002. *Transnational Capitalism and the Struggle Over European Integration*. London: Routledge.
van der Pijl, Kees. 1984. *The Making of an Atlantic Ruling Class*. London: Verso.
———. 1998. *Transnational Classes and International Relations*. New York: Routledge.
Veblen, Thorstein. 1954. *Higher Learning in America: A Memorandum on the Conduct of Universities by Business Men*. Califormia: Academic Reprints.
Wallerstein, Immanuel. 2000. 'Globalization or the Age of Transition? A Long-Term View of the Trajectory of the World-System'. *International Sociology* 15(2):249–65.
Warren, Robert. 2000. 'An Interview with Dr. Li Ka-Shing'. *Manitoba Business* 22(9):10–13.
Watson, William, John Richards, and David Brown. 1994. *The Case For Change: Reinventing the Welfare State*. Toronto: C.D. Howe Institute.
Wearing, Joseph. 1987. 'Political Bucks and Government Billings: A Preliminary Enquiry Into the Question of Linkage Between Party Donations by Business and Government Contracts'. *Journal of Canadian Studies* 22(2):135–49.
——— and Peter Wearing. 1990. 'Mother's Milk Revisited: The Effect of Foreign Ownership on Political Contributions'. *Canadian Journal of Political Science* 23(1):115–23.
Weber, Max. 1947. *The Theory of Social and Economic Organization*. New York: Oxford University Press.
Welton, Neva, and Linda Wolf. 2001. *Global Uprising: Confronting the Tyrannies of the 21st Century*. Gabriola Island, BC: New Society Publishers.
Westney, D.E. 1996. 'The Japanese Business System: Key Features and Prospects for Change'. *Journal of Asian Business* 12(1):21–50.
Whitley, Richard. 2001. 'Changing Regulatory Regimes and the Management of International Business Transactions'. Conference on Corporate Governance in a Globalizing World. Netherlands Institute for Advanced Study in the Humanities and Social Sciences, Wassenaar, 24 April.
Williams, Raymond. 1977. *Marxism and Literature*. New York: Oxford University Press.
Wilson, Maureen G., and Elizabeth Whitmore. 1998. 'The Transnationalization of Popular Movements: Social Policy Making from Below'. *Canadian Journal of Development Studies* 19(1):7–36.
Windolf, Paul. 2002. *Corporate Networks in Europe and the United States*. New York: Oxford University Press.
Wolfe, David A. 1984. 'The Rise and Demise of the Keynesian Era in Canada: Economic Policy, 1930–1982'. In *Modern Canada 1930- 1980's*, ed. Michael S. Cross and Gregory S. Kealey. Toronto: McClelland and Stewart.
Wood, Ellen Meiksins. 1995. *Democracy Against Capitalism*. Cambridge: Cambridge University Press.
Workman, Thom. 1996. *Banking on Deception: The Discourse of Fiscal Crisis*. Halifax: Fernwood.
Wright, Erik Olin. 1978. *Class, Crisis, and the State*. London: New Left Books.
Yanarella, Ernest J., and Herbert G. Reid. 1996. 'From "Trained Gorilla" to "Humanware": Repoliticizing the Body-Machine Complex Between Fordism and Post-Fordism'.

Pp. 181–219 in *The Social and Political Body*, ed. Theodore R. Schatzki and Wolfgang Natter. New York: Guilford Press.

Zeitlin, Maurice. 1989. *The Large Corporation and Contemporary Classes*. New Brunswick, NJ: Rutgers University Press.

Zweigenhaft, Richard L., and G. William Domhoff. 1998. *Diversity in the Power Elite: Have Women and Minorities Reached the Top?* New Haven: Yale University Press.

Index

NOTE: Entries in italic type refer to illustrations.

abbreviations, corporate, 226–30
accumulation base: changes in, 43–55; domestic, 84
activism, business, 154–6, 163, 170, 172, 210–12
advisors, corporate, 20
Air Canada, 52
Alberta, 91
Alcan Aluminum, 84, 132, 167
Alexander, Malcolm, 48, 53
Altamira Investment Services, 204
American Enterprise Institute, 160
Andreff, W., 68
Anthonisse's 'rush', 110–11, 139, 165–7
Argus Corp., 56, 58, 59, 60–1, 64
Asia-Pacific, 73
Atlantic Institute for Market Studies (AIMS), 160, 162
Australia, 48–9
'authoritarianism, new', 217
Axelrod, Paul, 184

banks, 67–8, 75–6, 77–9, 85–6, 205; and centrality, 25–6, 27–8, 39; and continentalism, 108; foreign, 75; and network, 214; and policy groups, 168; and political contributions, 178
Bank of Canada, 45, 52
Bank of Montreal, 36, 90, 114, 132, 141, 168, 174, 204
Bank of Nova Scotia, 132, 174
Bank of Tokyo–Mitsubishi, 139–40
Bannerji, Himani, 215
Barber, Lloyd, 195, 196

Barnes, Roy C., 108
Barnet, Richard, 127
Barran, D., 130
Barrett, Matthew, 36, 37, 39, 95
Barrick Gold, 135
BC Tel, 135
BCE, 48, 57, 100, 132
Bélanger, Marcel, 62
Bell Canada, 42, 61, 62
Berkowitz, Stephen, 23
Bertelsmann AG, 132
Bettis, Richard A., 124
Bilderberg Conference, 145–50
Black, Conrad, 58, 147, 149
Black, James, 167
Blau, Peter, 2
Bloc Québécois, 173
Block, Fred, 201
Bombardier, 84
Bourke, W.O., 130
Boyle, T. Patrick, 160
Brascan Ltd, 24, 45, 57, 58, 62, 63–4, 79, 99, 149, 203; Brascan-Edper group, 135
Brimacombe, J. Keith, 193
Britain, 41–2, 69, 73; links with, 142
British charter group, 16, 17, 22, 28
British Columbia Packers, 44
Bronfman, Charles R., 132, 209
Bronfman, Peter and Edward, 42, 45, 57, 63
Brooks, Stephen, 173
Brown, Robert, 34–5
Bruneau, Angus, 195
Bryan, Dick, 9
Brym, Robert J., 88

Buchbinder, Howard, 182, 183, 197
Burbidge, Frederick, 61
Burgess, Bill, 55, 207
Burris, Val, 163
'business community', 210–12
Business Council on National Issues (BCNI), 156, 159–60, 162–72, 176, 211, 218

C.D. Howe Institute (CDHI), 157–9, 208
Cadillac Fairview, 204
Caisse de Dépôt et Placement du Québec, 46, 48, 52, 56, 57, 58, 103, 135
Calgary, 91, 92, 94, 95, 96, 97, 100, 103, 205–6
Canada Development Corp., 48
Canada Global Leadership Initiative, 160
Canada Post, 45, 46
Canadian Alliance for Trade and Job Opportunities, 160, 176
Canadian Centre for Policy Alternatives, 162, 172
Canadian Council of Chief Executive Officers, 159, 218; *see also* Business Council on National Issues
Canadian Foundation for Innovation (CFI), 192–4, 195, 196
Canadian Imperial Bank of Commerce (CIBC), 25, 60–1, 62, 90, 168, 174, 204; and globalization, 129, 130, 132, 135, 137, 139, 140, 149
Canadian National Railway (CNR), 52
Canadian Pacific Ltd, 24, 56, 58, 61, 62, 84, 99, 130, 201
Canadian Reform Conservative Alliance, 178; *see also* Reform party
Canadian Taxpayers Foundation, 156
capital: accumulation of, 4–7; concentrations of, 2–3; finance, 62, 66–8, 100–2; integration of, 6, 67; and nationality, 207; recomposition of, 96–9, 102; reorganization of, 66
capitalism: 'academic', 181; analysis of, 2; corporate, 1; disorganized, 66–86; family, 54, 202–3; organized, 66–7; 'prairie', 91
Carchedi, Guglielmo, 19
Carson, Colin, 133, 145, 147, 151
Carson, John, 39
Celestica Inc., 204
Centres of Excellence, 182

'charter groups': British, 16, 17, 22, 28; French, 16, 22, 28
Chrétien, Jean, 149
Clarke, Tony, 10
Clarkson, Stephen, 206
class, 19–23; and board membership, 21–2; and marginality, 27–8; and power, 2–4; ruling, 3–4; 'transnational capitalist', 85, 127, 145, 211
Clement, Wallace, 7, 16, 17, 43, 73, 74, 90, 106, 109, 111, 114, 116, 117, 172–3, 184
closure, social, 14–16; reduction in, 17–19, 213
clubs, elite, 18, 19, 29–32, 210
Cockwell, Jack, 63, 192
Cohen, Dian, 196
cohesiveness, elite, 7, 14–16
Collomb, Bertrand, 132, 148, 149
Cominco, 61
committees, governance/executive, 36
competition: heightened, 35, 36, 38; international, 156–7, 171
compradorization, 43, 92, 95, 104
concentration, geographic, 201–2
Confederation Life, 33, 35
Conference Board of Canada, 156–7, 158, 162–72, 194
continentalism, 125, 206–7; sectoral patterns in, 117–19; *see also* North America
continentalization, 106, 117
contributions, political, 172–9
control: agencies of, 202–4; corporate, 20–1, 41–8; direct/personal, 44–5; foreign, 43, 46, 54, 55, 79–84, 92, 94, 95; state, 45, 54; strategic, 48–51; transnational, 71–5
core: continental, 110–17; network, 99; –periphery, 26–8
Corporate–Higher Education Forum (C–HEF), 182, 194–7
corporate–policy group network, 145–50, 151–2, 154–6, 163–72
corporate–university network, 180–1, 182–98; and class hegemony, 183; and instrumental domination, 183
corporations: financial, 59–60, 67, 95, 96; industrial, 95; names and abbreviations, 226–30; 'peak', 128–33; relations between, 6
corporatism, 158

corporatization, 197–8
Cox, Robert, 171
Crawford, Purdy, 162, 195
credentialism, 15, 215
credit unions, 46, 74–5, 79, 203
Creighton, Donald, 90
cronyism, 35
culture, corporate, 33–8
Culver, David, 176
Curry, Peter, 60
cybercapitalism, 206

D'Aquino, Thomas, 171, 176, 180, 211–12
Dalhousie University, 186, 192
Davis, Arthur K., 88
Davis, G.F., 107–8
Davis, William, 132
de Grandpré, Jean, 61, 62
De Smidt, Marc, 88
democracy: and corporate elite, 213–15; liberal, 217; neoliberal, 200–18; post-industrial, 1
democratization, 36, 40, 215–18
density, 26–7; global network, 134; network, 24, 108; sectoral, 79–81
'dependence, unilateral', 2
deregulation: financial, 85; and network, 75–6; and transnationalization, 70
Desmarais, André, 147
Desmarais, Paul, 42, 59–60, 64–5, 131, 132, 144, 147
Desmarais-Frère group, 135, 137, 143, 208
Dey, Peter, 33; Dey task force, 35, 37, 213
Dicken, Peter, 69, 202, 209
Dimma, William, 192
directorates: corporate, 3; interlocking, 6; and power, 5–6; reform of, 33–8; size of, 23–4, 34, 76
directorships: categories of, 20–1; inside/outside, 76–7; multiple, 17
discourses, political, 155
disorganization, capitalist, 66–86
disparities, global, 218
distance, network, 24, 25
Dobbin, Murray, 160, 161
Domhoff, G. William, 163
Domtext, 48
Dreiling, Michael C., 163

Edmonton, 94
Edper Group, 45, 57–8; Edper-Brascan, 147, 192
education: and corporate power, 180; and elite, 18, 19; see also universities
election, federal (1988; 'Free Trade'), 160, 176–7
Elections Expense Act, 172
elite, corporate, 1, 17; class structure of, 19–23; composition of, 17–19, 40; continental, 136–7; diversification of, 213–15; as 'dominant stratum', 17; and political bipartisanship, 176; 'reach', 7–8; as ruling class, 3–4
Emerson, H.G., 62
'éminences grises', 20
empires, corporate, 42–3
enterprise groups, 203; and globalization, 63–5; and intercorporate ownership, 55–8; and interpersonal ties, 58–63
eta^2, 29, 50–1
ethics, corporate, 34
ethnicity, 214–15; and board membership, 16, 17–18, 22–3; and marginality, 27
Europe: and corporate control, 73; corporations in, 128; links with, 129, 132, 135–6, 137, 139, 141–5, 151, 206–9
Evans, John, 195, 196
Eyton, Trevor, 24, 64, 149, 192

Falconbridge, 58, 63
families, capitalist, 54, 202–3
Fennema, Meindert, 128, 141
Ferguson, Thomas, 173
Fillmore, Nick, 176
Fina, 129, 139
'finance capital', 62, 66–8, 100–2; 'pillarization' of financial services, 67
financial-industrial axis, 67, 68, 81, 82, 86, 100, 205
Financial Post, 36
financiers, 42
Ford Canada, 129–30, 131, 141, 167
fordism, 'permeable', 115, 158
foreign direct investment (FDI), 202
Foreign Investment Review Agency, 92, 95
Fortier, Yves, 147
Fox, Bonnie, 17
Francois-Poncet, Michel, 132

Fraser Institute (FI), 158, 160–3, 162–72, 211
fraud, 40
Freeman, Aaron, 178
free trade: agreements, 70, 95, 106, 156, 158, 176–7, 207–8; election (1988), 160, 176–7
French charter group, 16, 22, 28
Frère, Albert, 64–5
Friedman, Milton, 161
Fukuyama, Francis, 215, 217

Gagné, Paul, 149
Gaz Metropolitain, 52
gender, 214–15; and board membership, 16–19, 21–2; and marginality, 28
General Motors Canada, 100
'geography of corporate power', 88–105; shift in, 93–6
George Weston Ltd, 44
Gillies, James, 38
globalization, 8–11, 35, 38, 66, 125, 127–8,154; as Americanization, 127; and Canada, 137–41; of capital, 10–11; and enterprise groups, 63–5; and policy groups, 157, 170–1; structural forms of, 209–10
Globe and Mail, 58
Godsoe, Peter, 182, 183, 195
Gotlieb, Alan, 147, 149
governance: corporate, 33–9, 76–7, 85, 204–5; international, 208; reform, 33–8, 213–14; and transnationalization, 70–1; university, 180–1, 182–92, 197–8
government: and policy groups, 160; and political donations, 172–3; 'shadow', 159
Gramsci, Antonio, 4, 213
Great-West Life, 60, 137
Groupe Bruxelles Lambert, 64–5
Grubel, Herbert, 161
Gulf Canada, 130, 167

Hackett, Robert, 161–2
Hara, Art, 140
Harding, Robert, 63
Harris, Jerry, 85, 127, 145, 211
Harris, Mike, 149
Harvey, David, 205
Hayek, Friedrich, 156, 161

head offices, 88–91, 93–6, 102–5, 135, 201–2
Heenan, David A., 125
hegemony: class, 183; elite, 7–8; neoliberal, 154–79; neoliberalism as 'hegemonic project', 154
Herkstroter, Cornelius, 147, 149
Hilferding, Rudolph, 66–7
Hill, Charles W.L., 54
Hirst, P., 9
Hitt, Michael A., 124
Hofstatter, Werner, 37
Hollinger Inc., 149
Hong Kong Bank of Canada, 95, 135
Hudson's Bay Company, 62
Hymer, Steve, 127

Imasco, 114
imperialism, 9; collective, 136, 218
Inco Ltd., 48, 84, 100, 115, 132, 153
individuals: as continental linkers, 119–24; and control, 54
Innis, Harold, 88
Institute of Corporate Directors, 33
integration: capital, 6; elite, 7–8, 23–6; social, 142; transnational elite, 142–5
intellectuals: 'organic', 4, 7, 8, 19–20, 62, 115, 212; 'traditional', 213
interests, 'constellations' of, 42, 46, 47, 55
interlocks: and banks, 78–9; in Canada-global network, 134–7; continental, 107–26; corporate–policy group, 145–50, 163–72; corporate–university, degree of, 49, 142; between directorates, 6, 23; and governance reform, 76–7; inter-regional, 143; introverted/extroverted, 114; primary, 49–50; and state capital, 51–2; transnational, 128–33; volume of, 96–9; *see also* linkages
International Chamber of Commerce (ICC), 128, 145–50
'international competitiveness', 10
investment: Canadian abroad, 81–2; foreign, in and from Canada, 69–70
Investment Canada, 95
investors: institutional, 38, 46, 47, 203–4, 205; 'investor aristocracy', 216
Itochu Canada, 135

Japan: corporations in, 128–9; links with, 135, 136, 137, 139, 140, 141–5, 151
Jenson, Jane, 115
Jessop, Bob, 154, 181
Jog, Vijay M., 37
John Labatt, 62

'k-core', 26, 27
Kerr, David, 63, 149, 163
Keynesianism, 154, 157
Kravis, Marie-Josée, 131–2, 143, 149

labour, organized, 158, 159, 171–2
Lash, Scott, 66, 68, 84, 86
leadership: business, 7–8, 200–1; cultural, 183
Levitt, Kari, 43, 104, 127
Lewis, Scott, 68
Leys, Colin, 10
Liberal party, 174–8
Li Ka-Shing, 208
Lindquist, Evert, 161
linkages: continental, 106–26; *see also* interlocks; linkers; networks
linkers: 'big', 24–5, 77, 143, 147, 165; 'continental', 107–10, 119–24; intercorporate, 17; university, 185–8
Litvak, Isaiah, 207
lobbying: and policy groups, 159, 176
Lodge, L., 167
London Life, 58, 64
Lougheed, Peter, 25, 59, 62
Lukes, Steven, 2

M. Loeb Ltd., 46
McBride, Stephen, 45
McCain, Wallace, 204
Macdonald Royal Commission on the Economic Union and Development Prospects for Canada, 158
McDougald, John A., 60, 61
McGill University, 184, 186, 188, 192, 195
MacIntosh, Alexander, 62
Mackenzie Financial, 57, 58
MacMillan Bloedel, 160
McLaughlin, W. Earle, 61
MacPherson, C.B., 12
McQueen, Rod, 44
managers: and strategic power, 42

Manulife, 52, 79, 84, 135
Maple Leaf Foods, 204
markets: and social life, 154; *see also* neoliberalism
Marsden, Lorna, 195
Martin, Paul, 149
Marx, Karl, 2, 4
Matschullat, Robert W., 132
Mazankowski, Donald, 62
media: and policy groups, 161–2
Meighen, Max, 60
Memorial University of Newfoundland, 184
meritocracy, 35–6, 39, 213–15
Metropolitan Life, 114
Midland Walran, 58
Miliband, Ralph, 172
Mintz, Beth, 5
Mitsubishi Canada, 135
Miyamoto, Susumu, 135
Mizruchi, M.S., 107–8
Molson Companies, 140–1, 167
monetarism, 154
Montreal, 90–1, 93, 94–5, 97, 99–102, 103, 206
Moore, John H., 24, 25, 61–2
Morgan, David L., 27
Morgan Stanley, 132, 137
Mosco, Vincent, 206, 208
Müller, Ronald, 127
Mulroney, Brian, 139
multiculturalism, 16, 214–15; 'Eurocentric', 17–18

names, corporate, 226–30
nation states, and globalization, 9, 10; *see also* state
National Bank, 204
National Citizens Coalition, 156
National Council on Education (NCE), 194–7
National Post, 58
nationality: and corporate capital, 207
neoliberalism, 10–11, 45, 46, 48, 145; consolidation of, 154–79; and democracy, 200–18; and education, 181–2, 194–7, 197–8; and 'new authoritarianism', 217; and social programs, 157, 158
networks: analysis of, 23–33, 40; and cities, 99–100; corporate, 67–8; corporate-

policy, 145–50, 151–2, 154–6, 163–72; and enterprise groups, 58–63; global, 127–52, 208–10; national, 66, 85, 202, 209, 218; national and continental, 107–10, 117–19, 123–6; old boys', 14, 23–33, 212; spatial distribution, 88–105
New Democratic Party, 173–4
Newman, Peter C., 14, 127, 147, 149
Newson, Janice, 182, 183, 197
Nininger, James, 157
Niosi, Jorge, 20–1, 73, 75, 90, 91, 103
Noble, David F., 181
'non-proprietary' organizations, 45, 46, 203
Noranda, 58, 63, 84, 99, 114, 167
Norcen Energy, 46, 58, 63, 99, 100, 167
Nortel Networks, 111, 114–15, 132, 135, 174, 214
North America: corporate elite in, 106–26; links with, 136, 137; *see also* continentalism
North America Free Trade Agreement (NAFTA), 208; *see also* free trade
Northern Telecom, 61, 62
Nova, 99, 100

O'Brien, David, 195–6
Ontario Hydro, 52
Ontario Municipal Employees Retirement Board, 204
Ontario Teachers' Pension Fund Board, 204
Oreffice, Paul, 132
Organization for Economic Co-operation and Development (OECD), 70–1
organizations: 'non-proprietary', 45, 46, 203; 'peak', 128, 156; 'third-party', 192–4; 'organizational effectiveness', 156–7, 158–9
Ornstein, Michael D., 184
Osborne, Ronald, 196
ownership: corporate, 41–8; and enterprise groups, 55–8; intercorporate, 42–3, 44; and network marginality, 53–5; personal and impersonal, 42, 203
Oxford Properties, 204

parent–subsidiary relations, 108–9, 111, 113–17, 123, 124–5
Pargessa, 64
Paribas, 64, 132, 137
Parke, James A., 123
Parkin, Frank, 14–15

Parti Québécois, 92, 94–5
parties, political, 172–9, 211; corporate contributions to, 176–7
pension funds, 204
Perlmutter, Howard V., 125
Peterson, David, 62
Petras, James, 217
Petro-Canada, 51, 52, 99, 100
Peyrelevade, Jean, 132
Piedalue, Gilles, 90
Plourde, Gérard, 62
policy groups, 145–50, 151–2, 154–72, 211; 'left', 172; and lobbying, 159, 176; ties among, 167–9; and universities, 194–7
political financing bill (2003), 178
Polster, Claire, 193
Porter, John, 7, 16, 17, 42, 212, 215
Poulantzas, Nicos, 172
power: allocative, 5, 41, 172–3, 194; class, 2–4; concentration of, 201–2; corporate, 2–4; cultural and political, 7–8, 200; and democracy, 200–18; forms, agents, and sites of, 4; and exit option or voice, 38; in global network, 133–4; operational, 5; strategic, 5, 41–3; terrains of, 11; in transition, 8–11; vectors of, 205–10
Power Corp., 56, 58, 59–60, 61, 64, 114, 132, 135, 137, 147, 174, 203
Powis, Alfred, 159, 167
prestige, social, 15
Price, Timothy, 63, 192
Prichard, J. Robert, 195, 198
Private Planning Association of Canada (PPAC), 157–8
privatization, 45, 52, 70, 203
productivity, 156–7
Progressive Conservative party, 174–8
Protestant Establishment, 14
Provigo, 46, 52, 58
Prudential, 137, 139–40

Quebec, 92, 95, 103; industrial strategy in, 203; and state capital, 52
Queen's University, 184, 188, 192

Reform Party, 156, 161, 162, 173, 174, 177–8
reform, moral, 33–8, 213
research: and development (R&D), 189;

funding, 192–4; Internet resources, 219–21; methodology, 222–5; neoliberal, 156–63; university, 181
'Rio Algom model', 35
Ritter, Emily R., 108
Robertson, H. Rocke, 193
Robinson, William I., 85, 127, 145, 211
Rogers, Edward, 59, 62
Rogers Cantel, 62–3
Royal Bank of Canada, 39, 61, 78, 83, 90, 111, 114, 132, 166, 167, 168, 174, 204; and universities, 188, 192, 195
Royal Commission: on Bilingualism and Biculturalism, 215; on the Economic Union and Development Prospects for Canada, 158
'rush', Anthonisse's, 110–11, 139, 165–7
Rytina, Steve, 27

Saint-Pierre, Guy, 196
Sassen, Saskia, 71
Savage, G., 62
scandals, financial, 33, 40, 213, 214
Schiller, Dan, 206, 208
Schwartz, Gerry, 204
Schwartz, Michael, 5
Science Council of Canada, 192–3, 195
science, funding for, 192–4; *see also* research
Scott, John, 5, 41–2, 66, 84, 203
Scrivener, Robert, 61
Seagram, 15, 129, 132, 135, 137
Seidman, S., 26
shareholders: as directors, 20, 21; major, 202–3; and strategic power, 42; 'shareholder value', 36–7, 204, 214
shares, dispersal of, 44–5
Shell Canada, 135, 147
Shepard, C.D., 130
Sinclair, Helen, 19
Sinclair, Ian, 24, 25, 61, 62, 130
Sklair, Leslie, 126, 145
SNC-Lavalin, 84
social: programs, 157, 158; structure, 23–33
Social Union framework, 157
sociograms, *59, 60, 61*, 83, 129–33, 167–9, 190–1, 195–6
state: and globalized capitalism, 9, 10, 66; in neoliberal democracy, 203, 216; and organized capitalism, 67; 'state capital',

51–2, 53
Stelco, 48
Stewart-Patterson, David, 180
Stoik, J.L., 130
Strangway, David, 195
Stritch, Andrew, 173
Suncor, 173
Sun Life, 79, 84, 94, 167
surplus, economic, 2–3

Taylor, Allan, 19, 195
Taylor, E.P., 42
terrains: hegemonic, 11, 154–98; organizational, 11, 13–86; spatial, 11, 88–152
Thatcher, Margaret, 3
think-tanks, 155, 156–7; *see also* policy groups
Thompson, G., 9
Thomson, Peter N., 60, 61
Thomson, Richard M., 140
Thomson Corp. 135
Toronto Stock Exchange Company Manual, 33–4, 39, 71
Toronto, 90–104, 206
Toronto-Dominion Bank, 62, 135, 137, 140, 168, 174
Toronto–Montreal axis, 90–1, 96, 99, 206
TransAlberta Utilities, 100
TransCanada PipeLine, 99, 100, 132
transnational corporations (TNCs), 2, 9, 68, 71–5, 124–5
transnationalization, 65, 71–9, 83–4; and corporate power, 69–71, 84–6; meanings of, 202; and network, 68, 71–9; structural impact of, 79–84; university–corporate, 180–1, 182–92, 197–8
Trilateral Commission (TC), 145–50, 151, 211
Trilon Financial, 58, 63
Trimark Investment Management, 57, 58
trust companies, 79
Turner, William Jr, 149
Twaits, W.O., 159, 167

Unemployment Insurance, 158, 161
United Nations Human Development Report, 217
United States: corporations in, 41–2, 128–9; and corporate control, 67, 73, 92, 95; and

globalization, 9; hegemony, 103–4; and investment, 69; links with, 106–26, 137, 139, 141, 151; relations with, 157–8, 206–9

Université de Montréal, 187, 188, 190

universities, 212, 213; corporate links with, 180–98; as 'profit centres', 181; and economic sectors, 186, 188–9; and 'third-party' organizations, 192–4; *see also* education

University of British Columbia (UBC), 187, 188, 195

University of New Brunswick (UNB), 187, 188, 192

University of Toronto, 184, 186, 188, 192, 195, 197–8

Urry, John, 66, 68, 84, 86

Useem, Michael, 17, 183, 210

Van der Pijl, Kees, 151

Vancouver, 94, 95, 97, 99, 206

Veltmeyer, Henry, 217

'Vertical Mosaic', 14, 16–19

Walker, Michael, 160, 161, 211, 212

Wallerstein, Immanuel, 1

Wearing, Peter and Joseph, 173

Weber, Max, 2, 15

Winnipeg, 94

women, 214, 215; as continental linkers, 123; exclusion of, 16–17

Wood, Ellen, 217

workers, 3; *see also* labour

World Business Council for Sustainable Development (WBCSD), 145–50

World Economic Forum (WEF), 128, 145–50, 211

World Trade Organization (WTO), 66, 208

York University, 182, 186, 188, 192

Zeitlin, Maurice, 102

Zhao Yuezhi, 161–2